COURTS AND SOCIAL TRANSFORMATION IN NEW DEMOCRACIES

To address the dramatic inequalities in wealth and power new democracies suffer from, we often bet on entrepreneurs and markets, or trust in presidents and bureaucracies. As this volume argues forcefully, we might be well advised to turn to judges and courts. Judicial institutions, this innovative and provocative volume contends, may act as effective agents of social transformation that help establish the social bases of democratic citizenship. Rich in theoretical reflection, empirical analysis, and policy implications, the book represents a highly commendable contribution to the comparative study of democratization, judicial politics, and democratic citizenship. Both scholars and practitioners will benefit greatly from this multi-faceted study.

Dr Andreas Schedler, University of Vienna, Austria

A very interesting volume, which brings together the latest scholarship on the constitutional protection of welfare rights. A must-read for legal and political theorists interested in this issue, as well as anti-poverty activists and lawyers.

Dr Cecile Fabre, London School of Economics, UK

A just society seeks to safeguard the fundamental interests of individuals even against the majority will. This is often done through basic legal rights adjudicated and enforced through the courts. Many have claimed that this method is unsuitable for protecting basic social and economic interests – in food, safe water, essential drugs, and non-discrimination, for example. The present authors dispute this claim through detailed analyses of recent experience in countries where this method has taken root. Studying this experience is important for anyone concerned with protecting the fundamental interests of the least advantaged.

Thomas Pogge, Professorial Research Fellow, Centre for Applied Philosophy and Public Ethics, Australia, The Australian National University, Australia, Charles Sturt University, Australia, and University of Melbourne, Australia

Much has been written about the growing "judicialisation" of politics around the world. But can social rights be effectively promoted through the courts of fragile new democracies? This important volume focuses on trends in a wide range of key countries where social rights litigation has indeed recently developed some real momentum. It explores the factors behind these developments, tracing their origins and institutional trajectories, and also considers the broader political dynamics involved, recognising the limitations as well as the potential of this approach to social incorporation of the poor.

Laurence Whitehead, Fellow at Nuffield College, University of Oxford, UK

Courts and Social Transformation in New Democracies

An Institutional Voice for the Poor?

Edited by
ROBERTO GARGARELLA
Torcuato di Tella University and UBA Argentina, and the Christian Michelson Institute, Norway
PILAR DOMINGO
University of Salamanca, Spain
THEUNIS ROUX
South African Institute for Advanced Constitutional, Public, Human Rights and International Law, South Africa

Routledge
Taylor & Francis Group
LONDON AND NEW YORK

First published 2006 by Ashgate Publishing

2 Park Square, Milton Park, Abingdon, Oxon OX14 4RN
711 Third Avenue, New York, NY 10017, USA

Routledge is an imprint of the Taylor & Francis Group, an informa business

First issued in paperback 2016

British Library Cataloguing in Publication Data
Courts and social transformation in new democracies : an
Institutional voice for the poor?
1.Social rights 2. Distributive justice 3.Sociological
jurisprudence 4.Social rights - Case studies 5. Distributive
justice - Case studies 6.Sociological jurisprudence - Case
studies 7.New democracies 8.New democracies - Case studies
I.Gargarella, Roberto, 1964- II.Domingo, Pilar III.Roux,
Theunis
340.1'15

Library of Congress Control Number: 2006925026

ISBN 13: 978-0-7546-4783-6 (hbk)
ISBN 13: 978-1-138-26454-0 (pbk)

Contents

List of Contributors

Christian Courtis teaches law at the University of Buenos Aires Law School, and at the Law Department of ITAM (Instituto Tecnológico Autónomo de México). He was a Visiting Scholar and Professor at University of Toulouse-Le Mirail (France), Valencia, Castilla-La Mancha, Pablo de Olavide and Carlos III (Spain), California-Berkeley (USA), Diego Portales (Chile), and Nacional Autónoma de Honduras. His published work includes *Los Derechos Sociales como Derechos Exigibles* (Madrid: 2002), *Derechos Sociales: Instrucciones de Uso* (Mexico: Fon Tamara, 2003), *Protección Internacional de los Derechos Humanos: Nuevos Desafíos* (Mexico: Porrea, 2005) and publishes extensively on human rights, constitutional law, disability law and jurisprudence.

Javier A. Couso is Associate Professor of Law and Sociology at the Universidad Diego Portales, in Santiago, Chile. He holds a J.D. (Catholic University of Chile) and a Ph.D. in Jurisprudence and Social Policy (University of California at Berkeley). His current research, and recent publications; focus on the politics of law and courts in Latin America.

Pilar Domingo is Researcher at the Instituto de Estudios de Iberoamérica at the University of Salamanca in Spain. She has held teaching and research positions in the Politics Division at CIDE (Centro de Investigación y Docencia Económica) in Mexico, and the Politics Department at Queen Mary, University of London. Her research and recent publications focus on rule-of-law construction, judicial reform and human rights in weak democratic states, with particular focus on Latin America.

Jackie Dugard is Senior Researcher and Head of the Basic Services & Housing Project at the Centre for Applied Legal Studies (CALS), University of the Witwatersrand, Johannesburg. Her fields of specialisation embrace local government accountability and delivery, housing and water rights, and access to justice by the poor. Prior to joining CALS she worked in the Political Affairs Division at the Commonwealth Secretariat in London. Her current projects include research into access to South Africa's Constitutional Court, social housing options for the poor and public interest litigation on the right of access to sufficient water.

Roberto Gargarella has a S.J.D. from the University of Chicago, a doctorate in law from the University of Buenos Aires, and undertook post-doctoral studies at Balliol College in Oxford. He is currently Professor of Law and Constitutional Theory at the University of Torcuato Di Tella, Buenos Aires, and holds a research position at the Chr. Michelsen Institute in Bergen. He has been awarded a John Simon Guggenheim grant (2000) and the Harry Frank Guggenheim grant (2002–2003). He has published on issues of legal and political philosophy, as well as on US and Latin American constitutionalism and legal theory.

Siri Gloppen heads the 'Courts in Transition' research programme at the Chr. Michelsen Institute in Bergen and is Associate Professor at the Department of Comparative Politics, University of Bergen, Norway. Currently (2005–2006 academic year) she is Visiting Fellow at Harvard Law School, Human Rights Programme. Her research focus is on the political role of African courts. Recent publications include: 'Social Rights Litigation as Transformation: South African Perspectives', (in Jones and Stokke (eds) *Democratising Development* (Leiden: Martinius Nijhoff, 2005); and, with Roberto Gargarella and Elin Skaar (eds), *Democratization and the Judiciary* (London: Frank Cass, 2004).

José Reinaldo de Lima Lopes is Professor of Law at the University of São Paulo, where he previously received his Doctor's degree in Law (1991), and his degree of Livre-Docente (habilitation) (2003). He also teaches law at the Law School of the Fundação Getúlio Vargas in São Paulo. His recent research interests include working in areas of the history of legal ideas and doctrines, legal philosophy, legal sociology and social rights.

Theunis Roux has a Ph.D. in law from the University of Cambridge. He is the Director of the South African Institute for Advanced Constitutional, Public, Human Rights and International Law and an Honorary Reader in Law at the University of the Witwatersrand, Johannesburg. His main areas of research are constitutional property law and land reform and, more recently, the politics of constitutional law in South Africa. Recent publications include: 'Legitimating Transformation: Political Resource Allocation in the South African Constitutional Court', in Siri Glippen, Roberto Gargarella and Elin Skaar (eds), *Democratization and the Judiciary* (London: Frank Cass, 2004); and 'Pro-poor Court, Anti-poor Outcomes: Explaining the Performance of the South African Land Claims Court', *South African Journal on Human Rights*, 20 (2004): 511–43.

András Sajó is University Professor at Central European University Budapest and New York University Law School, Global Faculty. Professor Sajó was the founding dean of Legal Studies at the Central European University. He has been deeply involved in legal drafting throughout Eastern Europe. In addition, he has participated or advised in drafting the Ukrainian, Georgian and South African constitutions.

José Octávio Serra Van-Dúnem holds a Ph.D. in Sociology from the Instituto Universitário de Pesquisas do Rio de Janeiro (IUPERJ). He is Associate Professor and Researcher at the Law Faculty of the University of Agostinho Neto and the Catholic University in Angola. He is Senior Researcher of the Angola Institute of Economic and Social Research (AIP). His research interests are in the fields of political sociology, legal sociology and philosophy, and human rights.

Elin Skaar, holds a Ph.D. in Political Science from the University of California, Los Angeles. She is a Senior Researcher at the Chr. Michelsen Institute, Bergen, Norway, where she is part of the research programme on 'Courts in Transition' and former head of the Human Rights Programme. She has worked with the UNDP in Namibia on poverty reduction issues. She has worked extensively on human rights, reconciliation, and judicial reform in Latin America. Recent books include: with Siri Gloppen and Roberto Gargarella (eds), *Democracy and the Judiciary: The Accountability Function of Courts in New Democracies* (London: Frank Cass, 2004); and, with Siri Gloppen and Astri Suhrke (eds), *Roads to Reconciliation* (Lanham, Maryland: Lexington Books, 2005).

R. Sudarshan is the policy advisor for legal reforms and justice at the UNDP Regional Centre in Bangkok. In that capacity, he is involved in developing programmes to improve access to justice for the poor and disadvantaged groups in several Asian countries, using a variety of strategies, informed by a human rights-based approach. He was also the Justice Advisor for three years at the UNDP Oslo Governance Centre, where he contributed to the evolution of UNDP policies in the area of justice and human rights. He has over 20 years of experience working on governance issues in India and Indonesia, as the assistant representative in the Ford Foundation, New Delhi, and in UNDP offices in India and Jakarta. He has edited a number of books connecting law to poverty concerns. His current research interests include constitution-making processes for democratisation in the Asia region.

Rodrigo Uprimny Yepes is a Colombian lawyer with a doctorate in economics. He was deputy justice at the Colombian Constitutional Court from 1994 to 2004. He currently directs the Centre of Studies on Law, Justice and Society in Colombia and is Law Professor at the National University of Colombia. His current research focuses on human rights, constitutional law, transitional justice and sociology of law. Recent works include: co-authored with César Rodríguez and Mauricio García, 'Justice and Society in Colombia: A Sociological Analysis of Colombian Courts', in Lawrence Friedman and Rogelio Pérez-Perdomo (eds), *Legal Culture in the Age of Globalization* (Stanford: Stanford University Press, 2003); and 'The Constitutional Court and Control of Presidential Extraordinary Powers in Colombia', in Siri Glippen, Roberto Gargarella and Elin Skaar (eds), *Democratization and the Judiciary* (London, Frank Cass, 2004).

Foreword

The history of this book begins in May 1954 when the Supreme Court of the United States announced its decision in *Brown v. Board of Education*. That decision not only declared unconstitutional racial segregation in public schools, but in so doing brought into being a new understanding of the purpose of law. Many view the maintenance of order as the primary function of government, with the constitution serving merely to establish the structures of government that will rule society. The *Brown* decision, however, saw within the US Constitution an even grander purpose – the articulation of the ideals of the nation.

The Supreme Court's decision in *Brown* was based on the provision of the Fourteenth Amendment guaranteeing the equal protection of the laws. The Court read this provision as a broad national commitment to racial equality and used this standard to measure the system of racial segregation that stood before it. Over the next two decades, the Court extended its judgment to a broad array of social practices, most state fostered, that were responsible for the racial caste structure that had scarred America from the very beginning. In so doing, the Court did not see itself as merely policing a set of limits on the state, but – as the authors of this book envision – also as giving concrete meaning to the ideals of the Constitution and crafting the rights needed to implement that meaning. The Court's approach to the Fourteenth and other Civil War Amendments was later adopted in its construction of the Bill of Rights and was reflected in the decisions of the 1960s regarding freedom of speech, religious liberty, privacy, due process, and the operation of the criminal justice system.

Brown not only revised our understanding of constitutionalism but also confounded our expectations of the judiciary, which had long been thought to be nothing more than an instrument of the ruling elite and, as such, thoroughly unsympathetic to the claims that lie at the heart of this book. Of course, the Court did not operate in a vacuum. The Justices were subject to the pressures for change that were afoot in America and in the world in general. Still, the fact remained that *Brown* was rendered by a group of nine white lawyers who were accountable to no one other than Justitia. Even more remarkably, the Supreme Court placed itself and the lower federal courts at the helm of the reconstructive endeavour it decreed.

Throughout the 1960s, the executive and legislative branches also played a vital role in the project of social transformation that has become known as the Second Reconstruction. At crucial junctures, the President used the military forces at his disposal to enforce federal court orders requiring school desegregation. Through the Attorney General, the President also launched lawsuits to protect civil rights and proposed bold new legislation to extend the reach of *Brown*. Congress, for its part, passed a number of statutes between 1957 and 1968 that created new enforcement mechanisms. It also added to the list of rights enunciated by the judiciary. The hallmark of the civil rights era in the United States was a co-ordination and not a separation of powers; each of the three branches exercised its distinctive powers in pursuit of the same end – equality.

The social transformation decreed by *Brown* also depended on a robust civil society. Organisations were needed, for example, to initiate lawsuits, to present facts and legal arguments, and to ensure that judicial decrees were obeyed. The United States had long been blessed with organisations that could perform these functions such as the National Association for the Advancement of Colored People, and *Brown* itself was spearheaded by the legal wing of that organisation. Citizens were mobilised as well, and in countless demonstrations and protests insisted upon all that the Constitution promised. The judiciary was greatly influenced by such social action, and many achievements of that period were dependent upon it, as they were dependent upon the initiatives of the legislative and executive branches. Nevertheless, it was the judiciary that directed the Second Reconstruction. The Court issued the initial edict, protected civil rights activists, transformed social action into claims of justice, encouraged and facilitated the participation of the legislative and executive branches, and without exception sustained whatever action those branches had taken to further equality.

This book is not just concerned with the social and economic rights of a racial minority but speaks more generally to all disadvantaged groups, especially those whose disadvantage is defined in purely economic terms – the poor. Those whose rights were vindicated in *Brown* were blacks, but in 1954 virtually all blacks were poor. Given this tie between race and class, it was not at all surprising that in the mid 1960s, during the halcyon days of the struggle for civil rights, the President of the United States announced a 'War on Poverty'. To some extent this war could be seen as a supplement to the civil rights movement linked to *Brown* since a disproportionate number of blacks were poor. But the President must have had a grander ambition in mind because a larger proportion of the poor were white. Economic status – poverty – was to be treated as an independent and sufficient basis for corrective action.

As part of the 'War on Poverty', Congress enacted numerous measures to provide special assistance to the poor. The Economic Opportunity Act provided for job training, adult education, and loans to small businesses. Medicaid was established to provide health-care assistance to the poor. Two education acts were passed that gave federal money to the states based on the number of their children from low-income families. The Legal Services Corporation was created to provide for the legal needs of the poor. During this same period, the Supreme Court insisted upon several reforms of the welfare system then in place. For example, it denied the states the power to condition the receipt of welfare on lengthy residence requirements. In 1970, it required the states to provide evidentiary hearings before independent decision makers prior to the termination of welfare benefits. By the mid 1970s, however, the 'War on Poverty' was abandoned, not just in the political domain, but in the courts as well. In 1973, the Supreme Court decided that poverty was not to be treated the same as race and that the transformation of American society envisioned by *Brown* was not to extend to removing the structural impediments faced by the poor.

This decision of the Supreme Court was announced at a moment in United States history marked by the resurgence of a belief in orthodox capitalism and a growing faith in the market as the primary ordering mechanism of society. At such a time, reform measures such as those embodied in the Economic Opportunity Act, or a litigation program aimed at eradicating poverty or alleviating its hardships must have seemed anomalous. Capitalism envisions wide disparities in incentives and thus easily accommodates extensive economic stratification. It also privileges bilateral exchanges between individuals, rendering suspect any government intervention beyond enforcing contracts and protecting property rights. More than a resurgent capitalism must have been involved, however, for the Court not only turned its back on the poor but at the same time also expressed second thoughts about *Brown*. In fact, the Court tried to bring the Second Reconstruction to a close. As a purely formal matter, *Brown* remained on the books, but it was limited by the Court in countless ways and deprived of its generative power. The Court now repudiated the vision of constitutionalism upon which that decision rested.

From the vantage point of the United States in the mid-1970s, this book could not have been. Yet over the next twenty-five years, the essential background of this book, changes occurred in the world that created new possibilities, and a remarkable thing happened – *Brown* went global. Countries throughout the world began to view *Brown* as an inspiration not as an aberration. The protection of rights came to be seen as the highest function of a constitution. It was also understood that only an independent judiciary, fully committed to public reason, could safely be entrusted with giving practical reality to the ideals of the constitution.

America's insistence upon the primacy of the market has not abated over the last twenty-five years. To the contrary, it has been transformed into a model for economic development throughout the world. Where this model – now known as neo-liberalism – has been adopted, often with a push by the World Bank and the International Monetary Fund, strong exercises of the judicial power to protect the poor remain untenable. Yet it would be a mistake to see the closing decades of the twentieth century as nothing more than a triumph of neo-liberalism. During this same period, we have also witnessed the transition from dictatorship to democracy in Latin America, the collapse of the Soviet Empire in eastern and central Europe, the dissolution of the Soviet Union, and the transformation of South Africa into a multiracial democratic society. These developments have made this book possible. They led to the adoption of constitutions that emphasised rights over structure, that saw these rights as the embodiment of the highest aspirations of the nation, and that empowered the judiciary to turn these aspirations into a living reality. These developments changed the course of world history, and enabled us, once again, to imagine courts as an engine of social transformation and as an institutional voice for the disadvantaged.

Owen Fiss
Sterling Professor of Law
Yale University

Acknowledgements

The book brings together research presented at the Workshop on 'Courts and Social Transformation in New Democracies. An Institutional Voice for the Poor?' held at the Torcuato di Tella University in Buenos Aires in December 2004.

The editors want to express their gratitude to the Ford Foundation, the Christian Michelsen Institute in Bergen and the Research Council for their contribution towards funding the Workshop, and to the Torcuato di Tella University for hosting the event. We also extend our thanks to the University of Bergen.

Special thanks are due to those colleagues who participated in the workshop, and whose comments have proved invaluable to the intellectual effort behind the final papers, namely, Cathi Albertyn, Maja Brix, Morten Kinander, Rachel Sieder, Catalina Smulovitz, Luis Pásara and Stuart Wilson. We would also like to extend our special gratitude to Maja Brix for her substantive contribution during the editorial stage of the book. Last, but not least, we thank Marcela Villarrazo and Lucas Arrimada Antón, Sara Niedzwiecki and Vicky Ricciardi, without whom the smooth running of the workshop would not have been possible.

The Editors

Introduction

Pilar Domingo

Recent developments in social rights litigation signal new trends in contemporary understandings of democratic citizenship. As the frontiers of *what* constitutes minimum entitlements for the realisation of basic human dignity are shifting, so are our perceptions of *how* best to protect and promote socially inclusive notions of rights-based citizenship. We are witness to the unfolding of an era of human rights which involves pushing forward novel versions of the 'rights revolution', new patterns in legal mobilisation and growing recourse to the courts by different social groups in pursuit of emancipatory forms of social transformation. And courts in some cases are taking up the challenge.

It is these phenomena that this book seeks to analyse. In particular, our study examines the changing role of courts as a channel for social redress for disadvantaged sectors of society. Can judges lead, or at least contribute in meaningful ways to, processes of social and economic transformation and the reduction of inequalities in society?

Rights-based development and judicial politics generally have become prominent issues on the public agenda of young or fragile democracies, and are increasingly the subject of scholarly analysis. As yet, though, few studies engage in observing the *social transformation* potential of courts, and less so from an inter-disciplinary perspective.[1] This volume addresses some of the gaps in the literature, drawing on expertise in the fields of law, legal and political theory, and political science.

The book offers novel insights both at the descriptive and normative levels. At the descriptive level, it watches 'courts in action' in order to assess the real impact of progressive judicial activism and legal mobilisation on processes of social transformation. The case studies presented in the book shed light on the conditions that enable legal mobilisation strategies, and the factors that encourage or obstruct pro-poor judicial activism in the courts. On the one hand, the different cases allow us to get a better understanding of what the anatomy of social rights litigation is. In other words, they allow us to recognise what the different factors (social, institutional, juridical, cultural and political) that came into play in the process of social rights litigation are. On the other hand, these cases illustrate what strategies, legal procedures, and judicial decisions have been more favourable for this litigation to become successful.

Thus, the book illustrates the powerful movement in search of new remedial mechanisms that is emerging in Latin America, in some cases through the creative participation of courts; the self-restrained social-rights revolution that has been taking place in South Africa; the way in which sub-altern discourses are increasingly being framed in terms of rights, even in largely underdeveloped legal communities; the sudden and unexpected explosion of social-rights litigation that took place in India; and the peculiar role assumed by judges in Eastern Europe, where the invocation of social rights came to prevent, rather than support or encourage, economic reform measures.

At the same time, the book shows how these practical developments belong to a historic trend (Couso). More importantly, the book seeks to demonstrate that these developments can be normatively justified, even in the face of the many criticisms that have been directed at 'judicial activism' regarding social rights. In part, many of the cases presented here allow us to test the theoretical issues about the 'different' character of social and economic rights, in contrast to the civil and political liberties of traditional liberal-democratic thought. More significantly, many of the contributors advance arguments in support of the view that this type of judicial activism promotes, rather than offends, democratic values. This line of argument is particularly important, given that the 'democratic objection' may reasonably be considered to be the main objection against both the decision of activists to engage in social rights litigation, and the initiatives adopted by judges in trying to give effect to these rights.

Social transformation, throughout the volume, is taken to mean 'the altering of structured inequalities and power relations in society that reduce the weight of morally irrelevant circumstances, such as socio-economic status/class, gender, race, religion or social orientation' (developed by Gargarella, and cited in Gloppen's chapter). While the emphasis is on new or fragile democratic settings, the theoretical and empirical findings are of relevance to more general debates on the political and social role of courts, and on the normative underpinnings of modern democracies regarding issues of social justice.

Theoretical Issues

Gargarella's chapter explores the theoretical question as to whether judges should decide on social and economic rights issues as a matter of democratic probity. In an endeavour to set the bounds for what judges may or may not do, he challenges two concepts of democracy which have been explicitly or implicitly used by judges in order not to enforce social and economic rights. On the one hand, Gargarella reviews *elitist* versions of democracy, in which judges act as gatekeepers against passionate majoritarian impulses. In this case, the Constitution is seen as the real and only embodiment of 'We the people,' and it is read as valuing the right of 'freedom of contract' over 'the power of the State to legislate' (*Lochner v. New York* 198 U.S. 45 (1905)). As a result of this, the (democratic) role of judges here is to take on a protective role in favour of the right to property and liberty. On the other hand, Gargarella objects to a specific and also very common understanding of *participatory* conceptions of democracy, according to which judges should not enforce social and economic rights in order to give due respect to the will of the people *here and now*. In this case, it is assumed that the will of the people is primarily manifested in the legislature and, given that legislators are not taking decisive action regarding these rights, judges – it is here maintained – should not replace them and enforce social and economic rights. From a critique of both positions, Gargarella develops a third view based on a conception of *deliberative* democracy which he maintains would actually require judges to play the role of supportive engine of public debate, prompting the political branches to act on the decisions reached through democratic deliberation. Gargarella's chapter thus establishes the possibility of an active role for judges, in which there is an ongoing and constructive dialogue between the political and judicial branches as a way of enriching and reinforcing the deliberative process. In terms of this view, judges can and should be encouraged to contribute to pro-poor social action, through providing voice to disadvantaged groups, whilst at the same time not adopting the role of supreme constitutional interpreter.

If Gargarella's chapter is about a normative justification for active judges (within reason), Gloppen develops an analytical framework by which to observe courts in action on social and economic rights, and litigation processes in support of disadvantaged groups more generally. Her framework situates the process of adjudication within a broader context of structural, institutional and attitudinal factors. Through unpacking the anatomy of the litigation process, Gloppen allows us to identify different conditions which facilitate or obstruct pro-poor court action at different stages. Gloppen accepts that courts can contribute to social transformation by providing a channel for legal redress in a number of ways. Court action can impact on the law and policy or administrative action, for instance, through either the promotion of social rights, encouraging corrective measures by the political branches when the state fails to meet its obligations, the protection of established services against possible erosion of existing pro-poor arrangements (typically in post-communist, but also social-democratic welfare-state settings), and the protection of rights against the attack of other social interests. Courts can also act as an alternative arena for social struggles through the activation of legal mobilisation strategies. Gloppen's analytical framework distinguishes four dimensions of the litigation process: *voice*, as the ability or choice of disadvantaged groups to articulate their demands through legal action; court *responsiveness*, as the degree to which judges are receptive and willing to protect social rights, or proceed with legal measures which benefit disadvantaged groups; *capability*, understood as judges' capacity to give effect to pro-poor legal action; and *compliance*, as the range of (post-litigation) factors, in large measure determined by the broader political, social and economic context, that either ensure or obstruct the implementation of judicial decisions. Gloppen's chapter therefore establishes an analytical map by which to observe the prospects and impact of court action on processes of social transformation.

Clearly the broader social, political and economic context is relevant, although not in itself indicative of how court tendencies will develop. Couso engages with the complex intersection between legal and political trends of growing acceptance of social and economic rights, and the imperatives of neo-liberal economic development in a post-Cold War era, with a particular focus on the ideological and economic trends in Latin America. Couso's chapter speaks to the need for greater dialogue between these opposing trends: namely the re-emergence of a new form of social democratic discourse centred on rights – including social and economic rights – increasingly embraced by the left, and supported by a growing web of international human rights treaties, on the one hand, and, on the other, a still dominant neo-liberal model of economic development which has on the whole not contributed to reducing poverty, and in many cases has led to deteriorating socio-economic conditions. How these conflicting trends are playing out in new or fragile democratic or post-authoritarian settings varies enormously, subject to the complex interaction between institution and state-building endeavours towards democratic consolidation, new forms of social struggle built upon inclusive notions of rights-based citizenship, and the configuration of economic policy options which more often than not, especially in younger democracies, are dictated by global trends and less by the 'deliberative' dimension of democracy defended in Gargarella's chapter.

The question, then, is whether courts can provide an appropriate arena for the confrontation of these trends. Can they effectively channel pro-poor legal action or progressive social rights litigation? Moreover, how effective or, indeed, significant is this as a path to social transformation? And what kind of social groups are most likely to benefit from successful social and economic rights litigation?

Empirical Case Studies

The selection of empirical cases is weighted towards examples of creative and overall pro-poor court action in recent times. Contrary to received wisdom on the conservative nature of courts, or their 'reactive' as opposed to 'pro-active' nature by definition, a number of countries reveal innovative experiences in unprecedented levels of court activism in favour of disadvantaged groups. Of particular note is that this 'rights revolution' of sorts, supported by progressive judges, is taking place in countries with conditions of scarcity, exclusion and widespread poverty. Our spectrum of cases also includes at the weaker end countries where pro-poor court action is practically absent, but even there, the discourse of development revolves around inclusive rights-based citizenship, and courts are given privileged attention in institution-building and state reform processes.

The chapter on Hungary by Sajó presents a case of courts acting 'conservatively', but in protection of existing levels of services against economic measures which threaten to dismantle the socialist welfare state. Sajó makes the conceptual distinction between more minimalist court action based on status quo protection argued in terms of a classical liberal concept of dignity, as opposed to a welfarist concept of dignity premised on a more explicit acceptance of the justiciability of social and economic rights. In the Hungarian case, the Court does not act to enforce rights to non-existent social or welfare benefits, but rather acts in protection of existing levels of services, the reduction of which would deprive citizens of services already provided. Sajó goes so far as to suggest that this court action is not necessarily in favour of the neediest groups, and indeed may act to prevent a more beneficial reallocation of resources to the more disadvantaged, and less mobilised sectors of society. Nonetheless, this is a noteworthy example of court action being resorted to by social groups to challenge the premises of economic liberalisation which in the case of post-communist countries includes attempts to reduce state welfare obligations.

The South African case provides an example of a court that has consciously decided to act in support of political and social endeavours to redress the apartheid legacy, and in favour of that country's historically disadvantaged black majority. Following the transition to democracy, the political branches and the Constitutional Court appear to share a common view of the general direction that processes of social transformation should take. Nevertheless, as Dugard and Roux argue in their chapter, even under these very favourable conditions, there are limitations on the Court's capacity to act as an institutional voice for the poor. On the one hand, given its comparatively low caseload, the Court's doctrinally well-justified strategy of 'judicious avoidance' has limited its capacity to initiate pro-poor norm changes, especially in the area of access to justice. On the other, the Court's social rights jurisprudence illustrates that the arguments once made against the judicialisation of these rights remain relevant to understanding courts' capacity to enforce them. In particular, limits on the Court's democratic credentials and dispute-resolution methods mean that its social rights orders have rarely conferred direct benefits on poor litigants. Rather, the role of the Court has been to intervene in the policy arena, by forcing re-assessment of the reasonableness of legislative and executive action. Still, the South African experience indicates that social rights can be successfully enforced by a judicious court, and that they may play an important role in defending progressive social and economic reforms against constitutional attack by elite groups.

The Colombian Constitutional Court, established in the 1991 constituent process, has been both creative and forceful in advancing pro-poor court action, albeit in an unfavourable political and social setting of unabating political violence and human rights violations. Even here, though, as Uprimny indicates, the justiciability of social and economic rights has been qualified in the legal reasoning of the Court. In particular, it has resorted to the legal doctrine of 'connection', in terms of which social rights are defended to the extent that they are a necessary condition for the protection of other fundamental rights and human dignity. Nonetheless, as in the South African case, there has been an important normative shift in the boundaries of social and economic rights litigation in Colombia. Uprimny also engages with the question of how appropriate it is for courts to dictate decisions that have political consequences and can involve a re-allocation of public resources. Here there is an important distinction to be made between negative and positive forms of remedial activism, that is, court rulings that enforce prohibitions versus court rulings that require the state to act positively in the provision of a service. Both can be pro-poor, but the latter is perhaps more vulnerable to obstruction or resistance by the political branches.

Sudarshan's chapter reviews the record of the Indian Supreme Court, which began handing down a series of pro-democracy and pro-poor rulings in the late 1970s. The chapter stresses the hugely important role of the Court in acting as an effective guardian of democratic principles, and in defence of the rights of the poor and other disadvantaged groups. The Court came into its own in the context of a state of emergency, almost as a question of survival. Since then, it has engaged in judicial activism and pro-poor legal decisions. It has overcome limitations in the rules of standing by deliberately initiating a paradigmatic shift in judicial procedures in 1977, thus opening up direct access to the court for the poor, with the aim of building a more enabling framework for legal mobilisation strategies from below. Through the evolution of progressive judicial activism, the Supreme Court has built a generous pool of institutional legitimacy. The Court also seeks to maintain a cooperative relationship with the other branches, but has no qualms about dictating remedies that can alter policy and administrative decisions. Nonetheless, the dramatic social reality of poverty and marginality in India means that pro-poor court activism cannot be the solution to structural social transformation. At best it can contribute modestly to poverty alleviation. Moreover, access to the court system is inevitably unsatisfactory, as huge sections of the population live at a geographical and cultural distance from formal courts. Voice is further hampered by a lack of knowledge of rights, and widespread (and well-founded) distrust of lower courts, which are overall perceived as ineffective channels for dispute settlement. As Sudarshan thus duly reminds us, whilst recognising the merits of a pro-poor Supreme Court, there are substantial limits to what can be obtained in terms of social transformation through court action.

Courtis's chapter offers a panorama of obstacles and challenges for the judicial enforceability of socio-economic rights in Latin American countries, with examples of the contrasting reactions of different national courts in the region. In his view, the controversy starts with debates about the conceptual definition of socio-economic rights as rights. Even when this point has been overcome, some practical issues have also posed difficulties and created challenges which need concrete answers. These include: the need to define the content of rights and correlative obligations in order to make socio-economic rights operative before courts, the position adopted by courts vis-à-vis their own powers to control the activity and omissions of the political branches of government, the fact that some procedural arrangements presently available are not completely fit to cope with typical socio-economic rights problems – such as the need for collective remedies, or the enforcement of judicial orders requiring positive obligations by the administration – and the lack of a tradition among victims of resorting to the judiciary as a forum to discuss socio-economic rights. Despite these obstacles, courts in different countries of the region – among them Argentina, Brazil and Colombia – have confronted them and gradually started to devise a set of standards and criteria to overcome them. The experience is still too young, and not generalised in the region, but seems at this stage to be promising.

Lopes presents a study of the Brazilian judiciary based on a survey of cases from 1989–2003, focusing on class-action cases in the health and education sector at the federal and state level, and examining patterns in court rulings in the High Court of Justice and in the São Paulo State Court. Social rights litigation represents a relatively small proportion of all cases. The 1988 Constitution, however, does provide room for judicial activism. Social movements, though, have been slow to engage in legal mobilisation strategies. Moreover, in the 1990s, class action was mostly a matter for the middle classes, less as a question of social and economic rights, and more as a matter of resolving contractual conflicts. It was only in the late 1990s that health and education issues affecting the poor began to reach the courts and with some positive results. Nonetheless, there are obstacles which have to do with legal traditions and resources. Lopes makes the relevant point that the matter of 'capacity' outlined in Gloppen's framework should also be extended to lawyers and the legal profession more generally.

The final two case studies in this volume deal with processes of political and social change where in fact courts have not been active in pro-poor social and economic rights litigation, for various reasons. Nonetheless, democratic advancement is premised on rule-of-law construction and inclusive rights-based notions of citizenship, contained moreover in constitutional texts. The study of Angola by Skaar and Van-Dúnem paints a particularly dramatic portrait of weak judicial institutions specifically, but also a fragile democratic process generally. Here the structural obstacles to rights-based citizenship are still formidable. Courts are not engaging in social and economic rights litigation; but moreover, they are at pains to provide the most basic of legal services generally. At the same time, this is a rapidly changing situation in terms of new legislation and institutional reform, including judicial reforms. The constitutional text is favourable to social rights provision, but subsequent (and existing) legislation has proved ambivalent and in some cases contradictory to the social transformation process in a dramatic context of poverty and exclusion. Voice channelled through legal mobilisation strategies through the courts is deterred both by these structural obstacles as well as by long-standing distrust of formal legal procedures and the existence of a network of traditional forms of conflict resolution in the form of de facto legal pluralism.

In Bolivia, there is a more long-standing legal tradition, and socially inclusive constitutionalism has been around since the 1930s, achieving its maximum political expression in the 1952 National Revolution, with some important gains for social transformation. Subsequent military rule and democratisation, eventually structured around a neo-liberal model of economic development, altered the ideological references of the population, and political struggle is now channelled through new forms of social movements which have in some respects taken up the banner of innovative forms of inclusive citizenship based on a combination of social and economic rights, and legal pluralism, in recognition of Bolivia's ethnic diversity. A parallel top-down process of state reform has included important innovations, first in the judicial branch, and secondly in the creation of a human rights ombudsman. Domingo's chapter suggests that, while the courts have not actively taken up pro-poor judicial activism, and in some cases continue to reflect subordination to the executive branch and to powerful economic interests, the human rights ombudsman has become an important institution which channels rights-based complaints, and the new constitutional tribunal, more modestly, is quietly responding in interesting ways to some rights claims. Although social movements by no means give priority to legal mobilisation strategies, there has been an important shift in the language of social struggles in partial recognition of the emancipatory potential of the law, the maximum expression of which possibly lies in the current wager on the forthcoming constituent assembly process.

An Interdisciplinary Approach to the Study of Social Rights Litigation

The case studies provide important empirically grounded lessons for considering changing patterns in court activism and social rights litigation. Our concluding chapter returns to the questions asked in the theoretical chapters, and on the basis of the lessons learned through the empirical studies ventures some tentative conclusions on the judicial enforcement of social rights, the place of judges in democratic processes, and the prospects for effective pro-poor litigation. Overall, we conclude that legal mobilisation and litigation in favour of disadvantaged groups, in the form of social rights litigation or otherwise, is positive and can contribute to processes of emancipatory social transformation. Moreover, this can be justified within the confines of a deliberative conception of democracy. Traditional arguments against social rights enjoy less acceptance today, both within the theoretical debate, but also as a consequence of *real court action* in which judges have in some cases developed creative legal reasons to justify social rights or pro-poor rulings. We also return to the anatomy of social rights litigation, retracing Gloppen's steps in highlighting the various factors in the different stages of the litigation process to map both the prospects of pro-poor court action happening in the first place, and the subsequent impact of court decisions on social transformation. The concluding chapter also situates these discussions within broader political and developmental trends and debates regarding social rights and the evolving definition of citizenship contained in contemporary models of democratic development. Finally, but crucially, we consider two important caveats to the argument of this volume. First, social rights litigation and pro-poor court action is only *one* possible, and by no means the most important, path to social transformation. Indeed, social transformation is inevitably the consequence of broader processes of social conflict and political struggle. But the courts may have, under certain conditions, a role to play here. Secondly, there is a great deal still to learn about how transformative court processes really can be, and what social groups are most likely to benefit from court action.

In summary, the volume constitutes an inter-disciplinary endeavour to engage in an analysis of changing patterns of legal action, with a focus on social and economic rights litigation and the consequences for processes of social transformation.

Note

1 Our concluding chapter engages with the theoretical debates and findings on the social and political role of courts across various disciplines.

PART 1
Theory

Chapter 1

Theories of Democracy, the Judiciary and Social Rights

Roberto Gargarella

Introduction

The most important arguments against the judicial enforcement of social rights emanate from democratic theory. The conclusion most commonly reached is that due respect for democracy requires judges not to enforce social rights. This conclusion implies treating social rights differently from civil and political rights, which judges are unequivocally bound to enforce.

In this chapter I will challenge the two main views that connect democracy with a limited role for judges in relation to social rights. The first, more conservative view, which I will associate with democratic theorists such as Alexander Hamilton and Justice Marshall, maintains that, if judges want to respect democracy, they have to recognise the primacy of the constitution they are enforcing. Where a constitution is hostile to social rights, this means that judges should refuse to enforce these rights, even where they are incorporated into ordinary legislation. The second, more progressive view, which I will associate with theorists such as Michael Walzer, maintains that, if judges want to respect democracy, they should not pre-empt democratic deliberation on crucial issues. Where the legislature chooses not to enact social rights, judges should accordingly resist the temptation to legislate on their behalf.

In conclusion, I will suggest a third approach to social rights, one that is more favourable to judicial enforcement, based on a deliberative conception of democracy.[1] The main aim of the chapter, however, is not to assert the superiority of the deliberative model. Rather, my interest is to show that – contrary to what is usually suggested – the argument from democratic theory does not come down obviously in support of the idea that judges have no role to play in the enforcement of social rights.

Pluralist Democracies

The first argument from democratic theory that I wish to challenge asserts that neither judges nor government should enforce social rights. Democracy, it is here assumed, should leave as much room as possible for individual initiative. The view I have in mind is something like a *pluralist conception of democracy*.[2] It may be described as one that is mainly directed at ensuring political stability and which is hostile to popular intervention in politics. It is also particularly concerned with the protection of certain individual rights, mainly those related to personal security and private property, through a system of checks and balances.

Pluralist views of democracy are characterised by a profound distrust of the people. The main assumption behind them is that people tend to behave irrationally when they get together in large groups. In the US, and during the Founding Period, this assumption was translated into the idea that, in collective assemblies, 'passion' always tends to take the place of 'reason'.[3] This is what James Madison presented as an inevitable principle of politics, when he affirmed that 'in all very numerous assemblies, of whatever character composed, passion never fails to wrest the scepter of reason'.[4] Alexander Hamilton defended the same view in *The Federalist Papers*, asking: 'Are not popular assemblies frequently subject to the impulses of rage, resentment, jealousy, avarice, and of other irregular and violent propensities? Is it not well known that their determinations are often governed by a few individuals, in whom they place confidence, and are of course liable to be tinctured by the passions and views of those individuals?'[5] In both cases, the idea was that, in collective assemblies, people find it difficult to engage in 'proper and sedate reflection', and that, consequently, they tend to become prey to demagogues. These testimonies reveal a profound individualist/anti-collectivist bias, so common during that time.

In line with these assumptions, the Framers of the US Constitution declared that the main problem to be solved by the Constitution was the problem of *factions*. For them, the presence of factions justified the establishment of multiple controls capable of preventing transient majorities from imposing their selfish economic plans. James Madison explained why they associated the concept of factions with (transient) majorities in the following way:

> [If] a faction consists of less than a majority, relief is supplied by the republican principle, which enables the majority to defeat its sinister views by regular vote. It may clog the administration, it may convulse society; but it will be unable to execute and mask its violence under the forms of the Constitution. When a majority is included in a faction, the form of popular government, in fact, enables it to sacrifice to its ruling passion or interest both the public good and the rights of other citizens. To ensure the public good and private rights against the danger of such a faction, and at the same time to preserve the spirit and the form of popular government, is then the great object to which our inquiries are directed.

Notably, the American Founding Fathers believed that the main threat posed by majority factions resided in the socio-economic sphere, through the adoption of measures that directly or indirectly affected individual rights (mainly property rights). This danger was conclusively established for them by early American history, which included several examples in which unchecked majorities had issued paper money as a temporary debt-relief measure. In order, therefore, 'to ensure the public good and private rights against the danger [of faction]', the Founding Fathers crafted a Constitution that would prevent – or so they believed – the passing of such economic laws.[6]

In Latin America, during the drafting of the first post-colonial constitutions, many legal theorists shared these individualist assumptions and suggested quite similar solutions, based on a profound distrust of collective action. The Colombian intellectual José María Samper, one of the most influential legal thinkers in Latin America during the nineteenth century, summarised this view as follows: '[if] what we want is to have stability, liberty and progress … what we need is that public officers adopt the practice of regulating as little as possible, trusting in the good sense of the people and the logic of freedom; they should make efforts to simplify situations, suppressing all artificial questions whose only purpose is our mutual embarrassment.'[7] Like many intellectuals of his time, Samper defended an invisible-hand argument, or what he defined as an 'individualist, anti-collectivist and anti-state' position.[8]

Similarly, in Argentina, the intellectual leaders of the so-called '1837 generation' dedicated a great deal of their energies to justifying the shift from the sovereignty of the people to the sovereignty of reason, as Natalio Botana described it.[9] In other words, these public figures argued that the idealistic aspirations of the first revolutionaries should be abandoned in favour of 'more mature' ideas, namely, ideas that recognised that the new nations were completely unprepared for majoritarian democracy. As President Domingo Sarmiento famously argued, the will of the nation 'is only expressed through the reason of educated men, and this is what is called national reason … We are democrats with regard to the establishment of liberty in favour of national reason [but we oppose the] national will.'[10]

These assumptions about majority groups and the way in which they tend to act were accompanied by other assumptions regarding the main interests to be protected from the excesses of majoritarianism, and the way in which they should be protected. The answers that the Founding Fathers advanced in both Latin America and North America are well known. Most of them defended what, in modern times, Isaiah Berlin identified as a *negative* concept of liberty, meaning the existence of an area within which individuals can act unobstructed by others, free of direct coercion.[11] John Stuart Mill also believed that there should be areas of people's lives free from state regulation, in respect of which even a democratically elected government could not legislate.[12]

This view of liberty differs from a *positive* notion of liberty, which is associated with moral autonomy or free will. Here, a person is free when she is her own master, namely when she is a 'thinking, willing, active being, bearing responsibility for [her] own choices and able to explain them by references to [her] own ideas and purposes'.[13]

The distinction between negative and positive liberty is problematic and debatable, and yet it helps us recognise something important for the pluralist view, namely that greater freedom requires less interference by other human agents in a person's life. Note that, according to the alternative, positive notion, to increase freedom may require not only the absence of interference by others but also, and most importantly, the provision of means, say goods and opportunities, to enable people to become the master of their own destiny.

It is also worth noting that the defenders of the negative view of freedom usually consider the state to be the main or only agent of coercion. This is the reason why, as we saw in the above examples, they associate individual freedom with the existence of a limited or 'minimal' state. This association between freedom and a 'minimal' state seems *prima facie* reasonable, given that the state is usually characterised as having a monopoly on the means of coercion, and also the historical fact that the worst violations of individual rights have usually occurred at the hands of a tyrannical state. It is no surprise, then, that the defenders of this view tend to support what Sandel called a 'proceduralist' form of liberalism as a way of maximising individuals' ability to pursue their own ends.[14]

A bill of rights is usually proposed as a way of defending (negative) freedom by defining the limits beyond which 'others' are not allowed to trespass, and thereby ensuring that everyone is able to pursue their own life plan. The content of this list of rights has varied from context to context depending, among other things, on particular political and philosophical assumptions. Those who adopted more extremist or pluralist views tended to identify as fundamental only those freedoms associated with the protection of property and personal security, even at the expense of political freedoms. This was, for example, what Juan Bautista Alberdi proposed for Argentina, when he suggested expanding *economic freedoms*, such as the freedom 'to buy, sell, work, navigate, trade, travel and undertake any industry,' even at the cost of reducing *political freedoms* that, as he asserted, in the hands of the 'locals' could only became 'the instrument of ambition and unrest'.[15] Most commonly, the list of rights includes references to both economic and political freedoms, which are usually referred to as civil and political rights, setting apart all references to social rights, which are seemingly reserved for those who defend a more robust, or positive idea of freedom.

In each case, the selected liberties define the area within which individuals can act unobstructed by others – in Berlin's terms – and thus, also, a private or personal sphere, exempt from public intrusion. This area, also protected by Mill's liberty principle, is contrasted with the public sphere, where certain interferences by the state are, in principle, permissible.

In addition, a system of checks and balances is normally proposed as the best way of enforcing limits upon state authorities. This system includes a division of power, typically between three branches (the executive, the judiciary and a bicameral legislature) and the establishment of multiple controlling mechanisms between them. Commonly, each of the branches is provided with the means to restrain the others. Usually, the executive is given veto powers, each legislative house is allowed to control the decisions of the other, both houses are able to override the presidential veto, and judges are given the power to control the validity of all enacted norms.

In sum, a system of internal controls, rather than external or popular controls is suggested here. This is not surprising given the distrust of collective decision-making and majoritarianism that characterises pluralist views. Pluralists also suggest that *political apathy* is not only a foreseeable product of modern democracies (given the lack of time or will on the part of most citizens to participate in politics), but also a desirable result of the system, on the assumption that widespread political participation would endanger both political stability and individual rights.[16]

Pluralist Democracies, the Judiciary and Social Rights

Having defined the main contours of the pluralist view, it is necessary now to focus on the role that it reserves for judges. Of course, in principle, the institutional model defended here seems equally open to a diversity of outcomes. However, there are also significant caveats to be mentioned. First, as we have seen, pluralist democracies tend not to provide for social rights in their constitutions. Obviously, this fact establishes an initial limitation on what judges can do in enforcing the constitution. Secondly, the lack of incentives for, and the obstacles in the way of, popular participation make it, if not impossible, then at least very difficult for certain demands to reach political and judicial institutions. This seems so, at least, if we assume that popular demands have a greater chance of being heard when people have an opportunity to associate with each other, create collective rules, exert pressure on their representatives, and hold their representatives to account when they do not satisfy their demands. Thirdly, pluralism and other similar theories recommend that judges should not enforce social rights for a variety of reasons. For pluralists, an 'activated' citizenry represents a threat of the most serious kind for political stability. In addition, they maintain that the state should not impose significant limits on individual initiatives, which means for instance that judges should be prepared to invalidate norms that interfere with (their broad interpretation of) freedom of contract. This way of proceeding is necessary, they assume, for the sake of freedom, and also for economic development.

For a long time, and in different parts of the world, judges have interpreted constitutions roughly along these lines. In the US, for example, the Supreme Court used the 'commerce clause' of the Constitution to restrict the powers of Congress, invoked the right to 'liberty of contract' to restrict any public attempt to regulate the relationship between employers and employees, and set limits on Congress's initiatives to delegate powers to the President and federal agencies. In addition, from the beginning of the twentieth century, it invalidated hundreds of regulatory norms through the use of the Fourteenth Amendment, which provides that 'no State can deprive any person of life, liberty or property without due process of law'. Alexander Hamilton inaugurated this reading of the Constitution in the

Federalist Papers,[17] in which he maintained that the sedate, deliberative, genuine will of the people resided in the Constitution, and not in the transient decisions of the legislature. For that reason, it was totally justified for judges, in certain circumstances, 'to pronounce legislative acts void'. In his opinion, this 'conclusion [does not] by any means suppose a superiority of the judicial to the legislative power. It only supposes that the power of the people is superior to both; and that where the will of the legislature, declared in its statutes, stands in opposition to that of the people, declared in the Constitution, the judges ought to be governed by the latter rather than the former.' In this way, Hamilton inaugurated a new way of thinking about the relationship between the constitution, democracy, and the judiciary. According to this view, to protect democracy meant to guard the Constitution against the irrational impulses of the representatives of the people. Later on, Justice Marshall transformed this opinion into a judicial dictum that made history. In the well-known decision of *Marbury v. Madison* he justified both judicial review and judicial supremacy as ways of protecting the real will of the people. In his opinion, 'the people have an original right to establish, for their future government, such principles as, in their opinion, shall most conduce to their own happiness'. And, he added, 'as the authority, from which they proceed, is supreme, and can seldom act, they are designed to be permanent'.[18] If committed to protecting democracy, judges had no alternative but to invalidate all those norms that defied the authority of the constitution. Many of the most respected legal authorities of the time, including Justice Story and Thomas Cooley, supported this view, arguing for the need to protect private property against the 'absolutism' and caprices of legislative majorities. Thus, in his famous 1868 treatise, Cooley affirmed that a 'legislative enactment is not necessarily the law of the land', particularly if it affected the people's 'liberty of contract'.[19]

In line with these developments, in the (in)famous case of *Lochner v. New York*,[20] the US Supreme Court directly confronted this problem by asking itself 'which of two powers or rights shall prevail – the power of the State to legislate or the right of the individual to liberty of person and freedom of contract'. Again, for the judges, the question was whether collective or individual choices should prevail, and their answer was clearly the latter. In their own words: 'It is impossible for us to shut our eyes to the fact that many of the laws of this character, while passed under what is claimed to be the police power for the purpose of protecting the public health or welfare, are, in reality, passed from other motives ... It seems to us that the real object and purpose were simply to regulate the hours of labor between the master and his employees ... in a private business.'[21]

The strong individualist and anti-collectivist bias defended by the Court in *Lochner* persisted within the tribunal for at least 25 years. During this time, the Supreme Court invalidated numerous economic laws, typically by invoking the due process clause of the Constitution. One of the most remarkable demonstrations of this bias came in *Coppage v. Kansas*[22] – one of many similar cases where the Court invalidated public attempts to redress workers' unequal bargaining power.

According to the Court's opinion in *Coppage*, 'although a worker has a right 'to join the union, he has no inherent right to do this and still remain in the employ of one who is unwilling to employ a union man, any more than the same individual has a right to join the union without the consent of that organization'. Similarly, in *Adkins v. Children's Hospital*,[23] the Court invalidated a statute establishing minimum wages for women stating: 'We cannot accept the doctrine that women of mature age, *sui juris*, require or may be subjected to restrictions upon their liberty of contract which could not lawfully be imposed in the case of men under similar circumstances.' In other American countries, the courts followed a similar anti-collectivist path, beginning with the Argentinean Supreme Court's decision in *Hilleret v. Provincia de Tucuman,* decided in 1903. According to the Court in this case:

> If the regulation imposed on sugar production were acceptable, it could be rendered extensive to all industrial activities; then the economic life of the Nation, along with the liberties grounding it, would be placed in the hands of legislators or congresses who would usurp, by ingenious means, all individual rights. Governments would be empowered to set the quantity of grape the vine grower can lawfully produce; the quantity of grains the farmer can produce; the quantity of livestock the rancher can raise, and so on, until we sink into State communism, in which governments would rule industry and trade and manage capital and private property.[24]

Against Pluralism, Against Lochner

Pluralist conceptions of democracy have been subjected to multiple critiques, from different perspectives. These critiques came to undermine both the plausibility of this theory and the plausibility of the judicial view that is associated with it. Many argued, for example, that this view upholds an impoverished, purely negative, conception of democracy.[25] For pluralists, in fact, the avoidance of conflicts and the achievement of political stability appear as paramount goals, rather than other significant goals such as collective self-government and/or individuals' self-realisation. Similarly, David Held has criticised pluralism, maintaining that this view 'put[s] aside' or answers 'merely by reference to current practice' questions, such as the scope of citizen participation, that 'have been part of democratic theory from Athens to nineteenth-century England'.[26] It has also been maintained that pluralists improperly translate their description of modern democracies into prescriptions about how democracies should be organised. For example, pluralists may properly say that the absence of political participation is a common feature of many modern democracies, but this claim is quickly and incorrectly translated into the claim that a democratic regime that wants to become stable needs to ensure low levels of political participation. In addition, the distinction between negative and positive liberty has also been subjected to serious criticism,[27] in the same way that the private/public distinction has been repeatedly challenged.[28]

More importantly for our purposes, some of the main arguments that pluralists have advanced regarding the judiciary and social rights do not necessarily take them where they believe they do. For example, the idea that, in order to protect democracy, judges have to invalidate all those norms that defy the authority of the constitution is very problematic. Bruce Ackerman has perceptively challenged this view, showing it to be vulnerable to an *inter-temporal* objection. According to him, many laws (for example, the laws enacted during the years of the 'New Deal') may reasonably claim to have as much support and be the outcome of as much discussion as the US Constitution itself. What then would be the democratic reason for privileging the Constitution over these new democratic laws? Other authors have challenged the Hamilton-Marshall view, showing its multiple weaknesses, among them its lack of discussion of crucial interpretative problems. Alexander Bickel, for example, challenged this view by stating that 'a statute's repugnancy to the Constitution is in most instances not self-evident; it is, rather, an issue of policy that someone must decide. The problem is who: the courts, the legislature itself, the President, perhaps juries for purposes of criminal trials, or ultimately and finally the people through the electoral process?'[29]

Pluralists' overwhelming concern with property rights is also problematic. Constitutions include many other rights that may come into conflict with property rights but which may still demand urgent attention. Most tribunals in the world have conceded this point, and by the 1940s pluralist views began to lose force both within and outside legal circles. Accordingly, the state began to increase its intervention in public (and sometimes 'private') affairs, particularly through the regulation of private property. At the same time, judges began to accept these interventions as a necessary part of modern public life. In the United States, these changes put an end to the *Lochner* era. In *West Coast Hotel Co. v. Parrish*, the Court clearly marked the end of that epoch by a rather abrupt change of language and the adoption of novel arguments, which included a recognition that certain inequalities were constitutionally problematic, and that the adoption of certain collective decisions to resolve them were appropriate. The majority of the Court thus asserted: 'The exploitation of a class of workers who are in an unequal position with respect to bargaining power and are thus relatively defenseless against the denial of a living wage is not only detrimental to their health and well being, but casts a direct burden for their support upon the community. What these workers lose in wages the taxpayers are called upon to pay.'[30] In Latin America, similar changes have taken place, both at a political and judicial level. In Argentina, one of the leading decisions marking this transformation was *Ercolano v. Lanteri de Renshaw*,[31] in which the Court accepted the validity of economic regulation, affirming that 'the regulation or limitation of rights constitutes a necessity derived from living in the same society … There are restrictions to property and individual activities that cannot be discussed in principle, but only in their scope, namely those that come to guarantee the public order, health and collective morality.'

The purpose of summarising these critiques of pluralist democracy – and its view of the proper role of the judiciary in relation to social rights – is not to suggest that this approach should be abandoned. Rather, my point is that it is far from clear that the pluralist view's claims about social rights are correct. In particular, this view's concern for political stability and fidelity to the text of the constitution do not necessarily lead to the conclusion that judges have to assume a passive role regarding social rights.

Participatory Democracy

The second view of democracy examined here, the *participatory conception,* is quite the opposite of the pluralist view in most of its assumptions and conclusions. Notably, however, these differences seem to fade away in relation to social rights. It seems that a commitment to a strong version of democracy also requires judges to adopt a passive rather than active role in relation to such rights.

The participatory view of democracy has gradually come to challenge more traditional (pluralist) conceptions of democracy and the limited role they reserve for political participation. This view disapproves of the levels of apathy found in many contemporary Western democracies, and also rejects the ideas of privacy and neutrality defended by its rivals, asserting the need to 'cultivate' those values that are indispensable for the existence of a vibrant democracy. According to (at least some versions of) the participatory conception, democracy requires a self-governing community, based on active and virtuous citizens. In its ideal form, this self-governing society is composed of citizens who are identified with their community and who have strong solidarity bonds with their peers. Here we have an active state that makes an effort to ensure self-government.

Defenders of participatory democracy may look to the ancient Greeks in search of a historical antecedent to their project. In addition, the participatory conception of democracy finds theoretical support in the work of Jean-Jacques Rousseau, who defended a view of freedom according to which to be free meant to be self-governing. For the French philosopher, freedom consists in obeying laws that a person has a role in drawing up. By actively participating in the making of laws, he said, we remain free, in the sense that we are not subject to the commands of others but only to the rules that we have collectively created. These norms, which come to serve the people's common interests, are an expression of the 'general will', which differs from the 'will of all' that is no more than a sum of 'particular wills'.[32]

Rousseau gave impetus to a new way of thinking about democracy that is still influential in our time. Although many of the defenders of this basic approach have tried to resist the authoritarian features of Rousseau's theory, they always tend to preserve two aspects of it that are highly relevant for our purposes. First of all, they affirm with Rousseau that, in order for the citizenry to be able to participate properly in politics, certain social and economic preconditions need to be met. Usually, these preconditions include the organisation of the community in small units and the 'cultivation' of civic virtue. More interestingly for our purposes, they require the existence of an egalitarian society, composed of individuals situated in similar social positions. For Rousseau, the existence of disparate or opposing interests – in other words, the fragmentation of society into factions – makes it impossible for people to recognise their common interests. On the contrary, in these cases, each individual tends to identify with and defend the interests of his group, wrongly considering that this partial interest represents the interest of the whole. In sum, the formation of the 'general will' – in the end, self-government – requires equality. That is why a society committed to the value of self-government should be primarily concerned with the distribution of resources.[33] Clearly, these types of concern differ radically from what pluralists suggest. Pluralists, as we have seen, attempt to remove all these socio-economic questions from the political agenda, believing that the final distribution of resources should be the outcome of spontaneous interaction between the different members of society.

In addition, adherents of the participatory view defend an institutional framework that pays more attention to popular intervention in politics than to the establishment of controls and limits upon the people's will. Indeed, some proponents of this view object to the idea of representative democracy, suggesting a connection between the delegation of power and tyranny. They claim that, 'as soon as the delegated power gets too far out of the hands of the constituent power, a tyranny is in some degree established'.[34] The most radical, Rousseauist version of the participatory tradition objects to the imposition of checks and balances in favour of a 'strict separation of powers'.[35] In France, after the Revolution, both the Constitution of 1791 and the Jacobin Constitution of 1793 explicitly refused to accept any possibility of dividing the 'will of the people' in two or more branches of power: the will of the people, the drafters of these two documents claimed, was indivisible. Moreover, they rejected the idea that each branch of power should have the power to interfere in the affairs of the other branches. Most of all, by defending a system of strict separation of powers, they wished to preserve the integrity of the legislature, which they perceived as the 'core' of democracy. They did not want the most popular branch of government to be under the supervision of, say, the judicial elite, the aristocratic senate, or a single person in the executive.

In Latin America, this Rousseauist trend nourished the radicals' critique of the old authoritarian regimes, and their boldest statements in favour of majority will. For example, the Argentinean Bernardo de Monteagudo, an extreme radical at the beginning of the revolutionary process, argued in 1812, that 'any constitution that lacks the seal of the general will is arbitrary, there is no reason, no pretext, no circumstance that could authorise it. The people are free and they will never err if they are not corrupted or forced by violence.'[36] A similarly strong statement about the infallibility of the majority also appears in the demands of the first Mexican revolutionaries. In the well-known document, 'Elementos circulados por el señor [Ignacio] Rayón', a pamphlet that constitutes one of the most important antecedents of the radical Mexican Constitution of 1814, the author made clear references to the 'infallible' [*inerrante*] character of the will of the legislature.

Similar considerations appear in the writings of Mariano Moreno in Argentina, in the proclamations of the radical Chilean priest Camilo Enríquez, in the papers of the Mexican thinker Fernández de Lizardi, in the writings of the patriots Vidaurre and Laso in Peru, and in the work of the Venezuelan Juan Germán Roscío.[37]

In this period, defenders of participatory democracy proposed the establishment of a variety of institutional mechanisms, capable of ensuring a much stricter connection between the representatives and the people. They proposed direct elections for most public positions, and rotation in office in order to promote wider popular participation and reduce the risks of tyranny. They also favoured the people's right to instruct their representatives, accompanied by the right to recall them in case of violation of their mandates. These tools came to ensure that certain popular demands were respected and bolstered representatives' accountability. Some others proposed augmenting the number of representatives, in order for the legislature to 'mirror' society, or the holding of annual elections, on the assumption that long mandates favoured abuses of power. Given their belief that '[power] often converts a good man in private life to a tyrant in office', they did not want to delegate the 'power for making laws ... to any man for a longer time than one year'.[38]

It is important to note how much this view differs from the one advanced by pluralists. While the latter group fears popular assemblies and town meetings, the radicals show a total confidence in open, mass meetings. That was why for them an increase in the number of representatives increased the chances of passing good legislation. An interesting illustration of this contrast appears, for example, in a letter by the 'Federal Farmer', where he argued that, while his opponents considered popular meetings as 'tumultuous and a mere mob', he believed that 'the most respectable assemblies we have any knowledge of and the wisest, have been those, each of which consisted of several hundred members'.[39] Actually, the 'Federal Farmer', like many other radicals, seemed to defend a more general principle according to which '[the] more numerous state assemblies and conventions have universally discovered more wisdom, and as much order, as the less numerous ones'.[40]

Participatory Democracy, the Judiciary and Social Rights

The participatory view of democracy has arguably influenced the longstanding tradition of including social rights in constitutions and international legal documents.[41] My concern in this chapter, however, is to explore the role that this conception of democracy reserves for judges in relation to social rights.

In this respect one thing seems true, namely that the participatory conception of democracy does not fit in very well with a system of judicial review or, more generally, with a system where judges, rather than the people, have the last say in relation to the most fundamental constitutional questions. Historically, this tension appeared both after the French and American revolutions, when radical republicans confronted the authority of the judiciary. In France, this confrontation moved the revolutionaries to defend the idea of the judiciary as the mere 'mouthpiece' of the law, who lacked the authority to interpret (and thus distort) the content of the law. In 1789, Deputy Bergasse, who was in charge of writing a report on 'the organisation of the judicial power', concluded his report by stating that it would be improper for judges to enjoy the 'dangerous privilege' of interpreting the law. In the United States, this confrontation between radical democrats and judges resulted in several popular rebellions against judicial authority, including the famous rebellion of Shays.[42] For many years, this radical view was accompanied by the certainty that judicial authority was not – and should not be – the same as judicial supremacy. In other words, radicals did not want judges to become the last interpreters of the law.[43]

This view of the relationship between democracy and the judiciary, which is so radically opposed to judges having final authority over the constitution, has begun to re-emerge in recent years, after many decades in which it was largely absent. Why? There are several reasons, but one is particularly interesting for our purposes, since it relates to the period of intense judicial activism in the mid-twentieth century in the United States. During this period, the Supreme Court under Chief Justice Earl Warren handed down a number of progressive decisions impacting on important areas of social policy, including race and gender relations, electoral and political rights, due process, prisoners' rights, and even – in a very exploratory way – welfare rights. Paradoxically, the 'democratic' counter-attack to which this period of intense judicial activism gave rise came to defend a status quo of inequality and injustice.

The proponents of the democratic counter-argument openly acknowledged that the Warren Court was promoting the interests of the disadvantaged. However, in their opinion, the Court was pursuing this goal at the expense of the Constitution. Judges, they maintained, were not supposed to 'transcend' the Constitution, by 'creating' new laws or 'looking' for values beyond the 'four corners' of the Constitution. Their duty was simply to apply the Constitution that the Framers had made. Those who were dissatisfied with the Constitution – for example, because they found it too conservative – should promote constitutional reform rather than require judges to do violence to the plain meaning of the text. In this way, respect for the Constitution and for democracy were seen as requiring judges to be passive rather than active, conservative rather than progressive.

Remarkably, this view of the Constitution has not only been adopted by conservatives and judges, but also by some of the most progressive scholars of our time. Michael Walzer thus gave strong impetus to this view in his book, *Philosophy and Democracy*, in which he attacked the idea of judges as philosopher kings.[44] Walzer's work persuaded Frank Michelman,[45] who had been one of the leading proponents of interpreting the US Constitution in favour of social rights, to change his views, at least in part. In line with his commitment to a broad (republican) view of democracy, Michelman maintains that social rights can only become operative when a governmental body decides to provide welfare benefits to particular individuals.[46]

A few comments are in order – first, a note about hypocrisy. At the beginning of the twentieth century, conservative judges invalidated progressive legislation by invoking the democratic 'will of the people' that they claimed to find in the Constitution. At the end of the last century, conservative judges invoked the principle of judicial restraint to uphold conservative legislation. As Cass Sunstein puts it:

> The early twenty-first century has witnessed a remarkable shift in conservative legal thought. In the 1980s, conservative legal scholars reacted against the liberal decisions of the Warren Court by urging a principle of judicial restraint. They wanted courts to back off – to allow restrictions on abortion, aggressive practices by the police, and a degree of public assistance to religious organizations. These criticisms of the Warren Court were founded on an understandable desire to let the people rule themselves, with limited judicial oversight. But there is no question that among contemporary Republicans, the New Deal has now become a principal target.[47]

In other words, there is an interesting democratic argument in favour of dismantling the welfare state, but we should also be warned against a mere hypocritical use of the Constitution.

Secondly, I would like to add a short comment on interpretative theory. Originalism is the interpretative theory that seems most closely connected to the views of democracy analysed in this chapter. This theory maintains that the Constitution needs to be interpreted in line with its original meaning. According to proponents of this view, any other alternative would transform judges into legislators. And then, as conservative Judge Robert Bork astutely asked: 'Why should the Court, a committee of nine lawyers, be the sole agent for overriding democratic outcomes?'[48] Another conservative judge, Frank Easterbrook, comes to the same conclusion, asserting the need to interpret the Constitution according to what the people wrote into that document.[49]

In countries with old constitutions, which are exclusively committed to negative liberties, this combination of the argument from democracy and originalism militates against the enforcement of social rights. Thus, for the influential Justice Richard Posner, 'the [US] Constitution is a charter of negative liberty; it tells the state to let people alone; it does not require the federal government or the state to provide services, even so elementary a service as maintaining law and order'. Similarly, Justice Scalia believes that 'our constitutional traditions [do not] mandate the legal imposition of even so basic a precept of distributive justice as providing food to the destitute'.[50] Justice Bork also believes in 'the impossibility of finding welfare rights in the Constitution' (the title of one of his articles on the topic). For him, 'the consequence of [a philosophical approach that recognised those rights] almost certainly would be the destruction of the idea of law … Once freed of text, history, and structure, this mode of argument can reach any result.'[51]

Remarkably, this argument has been used not only in relation to constitutions, like the US Constitution, which are silent about social rights, but also in relation to constitutions that contain social rights, like most Latin American constitutions. In Latin America, judicial abstinence in relation to social rights has been justified by the argument that references to social rights in the constitution are directed at the political branches, which control the national budget and have the necessary democratic legitimacy to distribute resources among different social groups. This was, for example, what Argentina's Supreme Court maintained in the case of *Ramos, Marta v. Provincia de Buenos Aires*,[52] in which the Court refused to act in the face of what it recognised to be a 'dramatic social situation'. In its opinion, the Court was neither invited to participate in this kind of case nor capable of 'distributing the available budgetary resources', because 'the Constitution did not require the judiciary [but the political branches] to guarantee the general welfare'.[53]

This conclusion is not exactly the same as the one reached by pluralist theories of democracy. Whereas participatory theories require judges to respect whatever legislators do in relation to social rights, pluralist theories encourage them to invalidate any state action that violates a (very broad) conception of property rights. However, in spite of this difference, both conservative (pluralist) and progressive (participatory) theories of democracy coincide in their conclusion that judges are allowed and required to enforce civil and political, but not social rights. This is perplexing. First of all, it is not obvious that a defence of a Rousseauist conception of democracy should lead us to defend judicial passivity, particularly judicial passivity with regard to social rights. If we wish to honour the ideal of self-government, and we acknowledge – as Rousseau acknowledged – the close connection between self-government and a certain degree of individual economic independence, why not guarantee the latter by all possible public means, including judicial activism?

In addition, there are important objections to be made against the interpretative theory used by the US Supreme Court, and the way it has developed that theory. In fact, originalist theories are probably the most controversial interpretative proposals we know in legal theory. At first glance, originalist theories look attractive because of their promise of certainty and their alleged capacity to preclude the need for judicial discretion. However, once we accept originalism, the doors of judicial discretion become wide open again because we do not know exactly how to honour originalist goals. Do we have to take into account the original intention of the framers or only their written words? Do we have to take into account the documents (for example, letters and articles in newspapers) that they wrote outside the constitutional convention? Do we have to interpret each article of the constitution taking into account the arguments advanced during the discussion of that specific article, or can we go beyond those discussions? How should we weigh, in any case, the opinions of the dissidents and those of minority groups? Should we concentrate our attention on the participants in the constitutional convention or on the dominant social ideas of the time? In sum, these problems only illustrate the difficulties originalism faces in order to satisfy its promise of certainty. The conclusion is that our commitment to democracy cannot demand us simply to stick to what the framers said. In addition, and probably more importantly, it is not at all obvious why participatory theories should demand judicial passivity rather than judicial activism in reference to social rights, because they conceive of such rights as preconditions for participatory democracy. Why should judges be required to wait for the decisions of a democratic process that may be fundamentally vitiated? In fact, if participatory theories are right in their assumptions, we should not expect an imperfect democracy to make decisions in the interests of the whole. In the next section, I will explore these issues a little further.

Deliberative Democracy, the Judiciary and Social Rights

Contrary to what judges have been claiming both in the United States and in (at least some countries of) Latin America, a commitment to democracy does not require them to refrain from enforcing social rights. I believe that the proposal for judicial abstinence rather derives from some specific – and, I would add, not particularly appealing – theories of democracy (that is, pluralist theories), or from at least questionable readings of what democracy demands. In this section I will suggest that other equally or even more attractive theories of democracy require judges to deal with social rights in a completely different manner.

Imagine, for example, that we adopt the perspective of deliberative democracy.[54] Although it is possible to distinguish many different versions of this view, I will here propose a version characterised by the following two features. First, I will suppose that this view of democracy requires public decisions to be adopted after an ample process of *collective discussion*. Second, I will suppose that that the deliberative view requires, in principle, the participation of *all those potentially affected* by the decision.[55]

On the one hand, this means that deliberative democracy differs significantly from pluralist democracy, particularly because of its second distinctive feature. In effect, deliberative democracy requires public decisions to be grounded on an ample consensual base, shaped by the participation of different sections of society. For this view, the less the scope and intensity of civic participation, the weaker the reasons for considering the final outcome of the deliberative process impartial.[56] Ample collective intervention is an essential precondition for that impartiality. Of course, popular intervention does not guarantee impartiality by itself. However, the absence of popular participation, which would be welcomed by pluralist views, would threaten the entire value of the deliberative process.

On the other hand, the deliberative model shares some similarities with Rousseauist versions of democracy in the emphasis that both place on political participation. However, it differs from some important versions of the participatory view as a consequence of its defence of public debate. According to Rousseau's *Social Contract*, public deliberation was not only unnecessary for the sake of creating impartial decisions, but something that made impartiality impossible. In effect, for Rousseau, public deliberation threatened to divide society into factions. It worked against social unity and helped citizens to think more about their own interests, and less about what they had in common with the rest. In other words, deliberation undermined the very ideal of creating a 'general will'.[57]

What are the implications of adopting a deliberative view of democracy for understanding the proper role of the judiciary?[58] First of all, I believe that a deliberative view would reject the conventional wisdom that judges should have the 'final say' about the meaning of the Constitution.[59] In particular, a deliberative conception of democracy would reject *judicial supremacy* (as opposed to judicial review), since it assumes that all important constitutional matters should be open to *ongoing discussion* among all affected parties. This principle conflicts with the idea of courts having a privileged role in these discussions.[60] Democratic deliberation requires that, in principle, all participants take part in collective debates about basic constitutional matters, and that the people as a whole retain the 'final say' in all these matters. As Jeremy Waldron puts it:

> Those who value popular participation in politics should not value it in a spirit that stops short at the threshold of disagreements about rights ... [those who fought for] the franchise [did not do so] because they believed that controversies about the fundamental ordering of their society – factory and hours legislation, property rights, free speech, police powers, temperance, campaign reform – were controversies for them to sort out, respectfully and on a basis of equality, because *they* were the people who would be affected by the outcome.[61]

Once we accept this version of the deliberative conception of democracy, and reject judicial supremacy, what role should be reserved for judges, if any? In my opinion, when we accept that judges are subordinate to – indeed, servants of – public debate, then we may begin to see the judiciary as a crucial engine of public debate.[62] In effect, judges are exceptionally well situated for fulfilling this task, because their principal function is to receive complaints from all those who are marginalised or severely affected by the decisions of the political branches. Institutionally speaking, the judiciary represents the main channel that disadvantaged groups have for becoming heard, when the political branches refuse to hear or unduly dismiss their claims. Judges are exceptionally well placed to require a better justification of their decisions from the people and their representatives.

In this way judges may play a very important role in relation to rights, including social rights, which are normally claimed by groups that consider themselves marginalised by the dominant political forces. Judges could decisively contribute to 'activate' and enrich these discussions, thus favouring the making of more impartial public decisions. The need to strengthen the impartiality of the decision-making process would suffice to justify this type of judicial activism. However, judicial intervention in these matters would be additionally supported by reasons like the following: the relationship between certain basic rights (for example, each person's right to question the government) and the preservation of the democratic process; the intimate connection that exists between social rights and political participation;[63] and the need to respect the constitution, particularly when constitutions expressly include social rights, as is the case in most Latin American countries.

Confronted with cases that involve social rights, and contrary to the passivity that they tend to show in these cases, judges could adopt a variety of responses: they could require the political branches to give more explicit reasons as to why they have excluded or disregarded certain demands, they could ask them to rethink or re-elaborate their reasoning, or they could order them to provide solutions to certain unresolved problems. Judges could define guidelines that authorities should follow, rather than direct orders dictating particular solutions. They could even propose the adoption of certain particular outcomes, without imposing them on the legislature, who could then adopt these suggestions or try different alternatives. In sum, through this dialogue between the different branches, and between them and the people, the deliberative process would be enriched and the quest for impartiality improved.[64] In the end, the search for impartiality is a collective enterprise where we are all involved, from our different public or private positions.

Of course, one may object that this view neither guarantees impartiality nor full respect for individual rights. Clearly, when judicial supremacy is rejected, we may open the door to majoritarian abuses. The answer to this challenge, however, should be obvious. Unfortunately, we still do not know which institutional system can guarantee complete respect for rights. And unless we assume that a particular elite, say the judicial elite, has complete certainty concerning what rights we have and how we have to interpret these rights in every particular circumstance, then we have to accept that we can all make mistakes and abuse our portion of power. The question is how to minimise these mistakes, how to improve our discussions, how to force each other to think twice before making a decision, and how to do all this and yet honour the idea that we are all equal. Theories of deliberative democracy have a lot to tell us in this regard. In particular, these theories suggest that judges should be more active in enforcing social rights, but in ways that are not only compatible with, but also necessary for, a more robust and just democracy.

Notes

1 I will be discussing here what I assume to be the three 'more familiar traditions of democratic discourse', namely 'democratic elitism', 'participatory democracy' and 'deliberative democracy'. In this respect, I follow, for example, the work of Robert E. Goodin, *Reflective Democracy* (Oxford: Oxford University Press, 2003), pp. 2–3.

2 See, for example, David Held, *Models of Democracy* 2nd edn (Stanford: Stanford University Press, 1996).

3 Many of the comments that follow will be focused on the United States and its Constitution. The main reason for this is the enormous influence exerted by US constitutional history on the rest of world and, more specifically, on the development of Latin American constitutionalism.

4 Alexander Hamilton, James Madison, and John Jay, *The Federalist Papers*, ed. G. Wills (New York: Bantam Books, 1988), no. 55.

5 Ibid., no. 6.

6 Michael Sandel has described this view as a proceduralist philosophical conception, and described it by stating that, '[s]ince people disagree about the best way to live, government should not affirm in law any particular vision of the good life. Instead, it should provide a framework of rights that respects persons as free and independent selves, capable of choosing their own values and ends. Since this liberalism asserts the priority of fair procedures over particular ends, the public life it informs might be called the procedural republic.' Michael J. Sandel, *Democracy's Discontent: America in Search of a Public Philosophy* (Cambridge, MA: Harvard University Press, 1996), p. 4.

7 J.M. Samper, *Historia de una Alma. Memorias Intimas y de Historia Contemporánea*, (Bogotá: Imprenta de Zalamea hnos, 1881), pp. 486–8.

8 See Jaramillo Uribe, *El Pensamiento Colombiano en el Siglo xix*, (Bogotá: Editorial Temis, 1964), p. 50. Juan Bautista Alberdi, probably the most important constitutional thinker in the Southern Cone during the nineteenth century, ratified this view. For him: 'The state intervenes everywhere, everything is done because of its initiatives ... The state becomes the producer, the constructor, the entrepreneur, the banker, the merchant, the editor and, therefore, is distracted from its essential and only mission, which is that of protecting the individuals against all internal and external aggressions.' J.B. Alberdi, *Obras Selectas*, ed. and revised by J.V.González (Buenos Aires: Librería La Facultad, 1920), p. 157. And he added: 'individual liberty ... is the main and most immediate basis of all [the] progress, all [the] improvements and all the conquests of civilization ... But the most terrible rival of ... civilized countries is the omnipotent and all-powerful fatherland, personified in omnipotent and all-powerful Governments, that do not [want that freedom] because it is the most sacred limit to its omnipotence.' Ibid., pp. 170–71. In similar terms, the Peruvian Tejada objected to the public authority that 'pretended to know it all and, for that reason, pretended to decide it all: it prescribed the selection of raw materials, prohibited certain procedures, fixed the quality of our products, its form ... its colour ... The state was the merchant who traded tobacco, salt, coffee, sugar, snow, cards, explosives, paper ... the exclusive manager of banks, channels, bridges, routes, mines and everything else. Its regulations ... defined the laws of offer and supply while economic law was silent.' J. Tejeda, *Libertad de la Industria* (Lima, 1947).

9 N. Botana, 'La transformación del credo constitucional', in *Estudios Sociales* (Univ. Nacional del Litoral, 1996), pp. 23–48.

10 D. Pérez Guilhou, *El Pensamiento Conservador de Alberdi y la Constitución de 1853*, (Buenos Aires: Depalma, 1984), p. 158. We find exactly the same opinions in the influential work of Esteban Echeverría, *Dogma Socialista de la Asociación de Mayo, Precedido de una Ojeada Retrospectiva sobre el Movimiento Intelectual en el Plata desde el Año 37* (Buenos Aires: Librería La Facultad, 1915), pp. 185–6. There, he maintained that 'the sovereignty of the people is absolute when it has reason as its norm. Only collective reason is sovereign, and not the collective will. The will is blind, capricious, irrational.' Democracy, he said, was not 'the absolute despotism of the masses or the majorities, but the regime of reason'. Similarly, Alberdi maintained that

'liberty does not simply reside in the will but also in the intelligence ... that is why sovereignty belongs to the intelligence. The people are sovereign when they are intelligent.' Alberdi believed that 'to elect is to discern and to deliberate [but the ignorant] cannot discern. Misery cannot deliberate, it sells itself. To take away suffrage from the hands of ignorance and indigence is to ensure its purity and [its success]' (J. Alberdi, 'Elementos del Derecho Público Provincial Argentino', in J. Alberdi *Obras Completas*, (8 vols, Buenos Aires, 1886), vol. 5, p. 66. Inspired, as many other Latin Americans, by Benjamin Constant's ideas, the Mexican José María Mora achieved equally anti-Rousseauist conclusions. 'National sovereignty is', he argued, 'the sum of individual sovereignties'. In his opposition to majoritarian politics he argued that popular passions tended to turn collective bodies into 'passive bodies' subject to 'the will of a small number of factious charlatans and adventurers'. See Charles A. Hale, *Mexican Liberalism in the Age of Mora, 1821-1853* (New Haven: Yale University Press, 1968), pp. 86–7. Also, the influential group of the so-called *gólgotas*, in New Granada, shared both these views and its anti-collectivist assumptions.

11 Isaiah Berlin, 'Two Concepts of Liberty', in Isaiah Berlin, *Four Essays on Liberty* (Oxford: Oxford University Press, 1969), p. 118.

12 According to Mill's 'liberty or harm principle', the only purpose for which power can be rightfully exercised over any member of a civilised community, against his will, was to prevent harm to others. See John Stuart Mill, *On Liberty and Other Essays* (Oxford: Oxford University Press, 1991).

13 Berlin, *Four Essays on Liberty*, p. 31.

14 Sandel, *Democracy's Discontent*, p. 4.

15 Alberdi, *Obras Completas*, vol. 14, pp. 64–5.

16 Robert A. Dahl, *A Preface to Democratic Theory* (Chicago: University of Chicago Press, 1963); Joseph Schumpeter, *Capitalism, Socialism and Democracy* (London: George Allen, 1943).

17 Hamilton, Madison and Jay, *The Federalist Papers*, no. 78

18 *Marbury v. Madison* 5 US 137, 176 (1803).

19 Thomas M. Cooley, *A Treatise on the Constitutional Limitations Which Rest Upon the Legislative Power of the States of the American Union* (Boston: Little, Brown, and Co., 1868).

20 198 US 45, 57 (1905).

21 Ibid., 64.

22 236 US 1 (1915).

23 261 US 525 (1923).

24 CSJN 98 Fallos 20 (1903). I take this translation from S. Berensztein and H. Spector, 'Business, government and law', in G. della Paolera and A. Taylor, *A New Economic History of Argentina* (Cambridge: Cambridge University Press, 2003), p. 340.

25 Carlos Santiago Nino, *The Constitution of Deliberative Democracy* (New Haven: Yale University Press, 1996).

26 Held, *Models of Democracy*, p. 209.

27 Charles Taylor, for example, has suggested that the absence of numerous traffic lights in former communist Albania does not mean Albanians were freer there than people in England – where traffic lights abounded – because in the former case people were more 'unobstructed' than in England. See Charles Taylor, 'What's Wrong with Negative Liberty', in *Philosophical Papers* (2 vols, Cambridge: Cambridge University Press, 1986), vol 2, pp. 211-29. The idea is simply that the discussion of freedom needs to

evolve around different issues, that is, the significance of the restrictions imposed on individuals, or the significance of the goods there involved (being able to drive quickly, being able to engage in politics).

28 Jean Hampton, for example, wonders whether 'it is because liberalism has persisted in thinking of large areas of public life as immune from political intervention that various forms of abuse and subordination have persisted'. Jean Hampton, *Political Philosophy,* (Westview Press: Colorado, 1997), p. 202.

29 Alexander Bickel, *The Least Dangerous Branch: The Supreme Court at the Bar of Politics* (New Haven: Yale University Press, 1986), p. 3.

30 300 US 379, 399 (1937).

31 CS, 1922/04/28.

32 Jean-Jacques Rousseau, *The Social Contract* trans. Maurice Cranston (London: Penguin Books, 1968).

33 There are many good illustrations of this view, including Thomas Jefferson's agrarian writings; Thomas Paine's proposals for a 'basic income'; José Artigas's 'Reglamento Provisorio' for an egalitarian distribution of resources in Uruguay (1815); and Ponciano Arriaga's initiatives (in Mexico's 1857 Constitutional Convention) in favour of a constitutional solution to the problem of unequal land distribution.

34 Thomas Young, from Vermont. Included in Michael Sherman, *A More Perfect Union: Vermont Becomes a State, 1777-1816* (Vermont: Vermont Historical Society, 1991), p. 190.

35 Maurice J.C. Vile, *Constitutionalism and the Separation of Powers* (Oxford: Oxford University Press, 1967).

36 J.L. Romero, *Las Ideas Políticas en la Argentina* (México: Fondo de Cultura Económica, 1969), p. 78.

37 B. Lewin, *Rousseau en la Independencia de Latinoamérica* (Buenos Aires: Depalma, 1980).

38 Demophilus, *The Genuine Principles of the Ancient Anglo Saxon* (Philadelphia, 1776), p. 5.

39 H. Storing, *The Complete Anti-Federalist* (7 vols, Chicago: University of Chicago Press, 1981), vol. 2, p. 369.

40 Ibid., p. 284.

41 The demand for social rights can be traced to the work of early egalitarians like Francois Babeuf, who advocated a universal right to education in 1796; Robespierre's defence of the right to work; Thomas Paine's numerous proposals for guaranteeing the rights of the most disadvantaged; and the work of early socialists such as Louis Blanc and Pierre Proudhon. These proposals were practically realised at the end of the nineteenth century in Chancellor Bismarck's initiatives to establish new social insurance schemes in Germany and, later on, through the emergence of the International Association for the Legal Protection of Workers in 1900, the Russian Revolution, and the creation of the International Labour Organization (ILO) in 1919. See A. Eide, C. Krause, A. Rosas (eds), *Economic, Social and Cultural Rights: A Textbook* (The Hague: Kluwer, 1994). Franklin Roosevelt's defence of an 'economic bill of rights' in his 1944 State of the Union Address represented another crucial step in the recognition of social rights. At the international level, this tendency became apparent in the United Nations decision to adopt the International Covenant on Economic, Social and Cultural Rights (ICESCR) by General Assembly resolution in December 1966. At the national level, the Mexican Constitution of 1917 was the first to incorporate a long list of norms relating to labour

and social security issues. Many Latin American countries followed suit, either by amending their existing constitutions or by writing new ones. Chile's Constitution of 1925 included differing 'Constitutional Guarantees' and Peru's Constitution of 1933 had a specific chapter on 'Social and National Guarantees'. Uruguay changed its constitution in the same direction in 1932; Brazil did the same in 1934; Colombia in 1945; Nicaragua in 1939; Paraguay, Cuba and Panama in 1940; Bolivia and Guatemala in 1945; Ecuador in 1947; Haiti in 1946; Venezuela in 1947; and Argentina in 1949. In the late twentieth century, there was another wave of constitutional reforms in the whole region, which reinforced the sections on social rights. Most of the new Latin American constitutions incorporated participatory rights into their texts. Some went so far as to include the right to carry out 'popular legal initiatives'. In addition, many of them adopted rights for indigenous peoples, recognising the 'ethnical and cultural preexistence of the indigenous people' (Argentina, 1994; Paraguay, 1992); the 'multiethnic and multicultural' character of the state (Bolivia, 1994; Colombia, 1991; Ecuador, 1998; Mexico, 1992; Peru, 1994); indigenous people's rights to develop their own identity and culture (Nicaragua, 1995); or the need to recognise and respect the existence of indigenous people (Panama, 1994). Many European countries – France, Spain and Italy, for example – have also included provisions guaranteeing social rights in their constitutions.

42 Gordon S. Wood, *The Creation of the American Republic, 1776-87* (Chapel Hill: University of North Carolina Press, 1969).

43 Larry D. Kramer, *The People Themselves: Popular Constitutionalism and Judicial Review* (Oxford: Oxford University Press, 2004).

44 Michael Walzer, 'Philosophy and Democracy', *Political Theory*, 9 (1981): 379–99.

45 Michelman partially accepts, and partially rejects Walzer's proposal. See a discussion of this topic in Frank Michelman, 'Possession vs. Distribution in the Constitutional Idea of Property', *Iowa Law Review*, 72 (1987): 1319–50.

46 Michelman's view concerns what judges should do in the United States, and is based on the assumption that US democratic authorities are hostile to social rights. However, he does support the judicial enforcement of social rights in other countries, such as South Africa, where these rights are expressly included in the constitution. See, for example, Frank Michelman, 'The Constitution, Social Rights and Reason: A Tribute to Etienne Mureinik', *South African Journal on Human Rights*, 14 (1998): 499–507.

47 Cass Sunstein, *The Second Bill of Rights*, 57.

48 Robert H. Bork, *The Tempting of America: The Political Seduction of the Law* (New York: The Free Press, 1989), p. 201 and R. Bork, 'The Impossibility of Finding Welfare Rights in the Constitution', *Washington University Law Quarterly* (Summer 1979): 695–701.

49 Frank Easterbrook, 'Abstraction and Authority', *University of Chicago Law Review*, 59 (1992): 349–80.

50 Quoted in P. Edelman, 'The Next Century of Our Constitution: Rethinking Our Duty to the Poor', *Hastings Law Journal*, 39 (1987–88): 1–31, 23–4.

51 Bork, 'The Impossibility of Finding Welfare Rights', 696.

52 12/3/2002; JA 2002-IV-466.

53 Ibid.

54 Jon Elster (ed.), *Deliberative Democracy* (Cambridge: Cambridge University Press, 1998); James Bohman and William Rehg (eds), *Deliberative Democracy: Essays on Reason and Politics* (Cambridge, MA: The MIT Press, 1997); J. Cohen, 'The Economic Basis of a Deliberative Democracy', *Social Philosophy and Policy*, 6/2 (1989): 25–50.

55 This definition is connected to the one advanced by Jon Elster. For him, 'the notion includes collective decision making with the participation of all who will be affected by the decision or their representatives: this is the democratic part. Also, all agree that it includes decision making by means of arguments offered *by* and *to* participants who are committed to the values of rationality and impartiality: this is the deliberative part' (Elster, *Deliberative Democracy*, p. 8).

56 Carlas Santiago Nino, *The Ethics of Human Rights* (Oxford: Clarendon Press, 1991).

57 B. Manin, 'On Legitimacy and Political Deliberation', *Political Theory*, 15/3 (1987): 338–68.

58 For an important discussion in this respect, see Jürgen Habermas, *Between Facts and Norms: Contributions to a Discourse Theory of Law and Democracy* trans. William Rehg (Cambridge: Polity Press, 1996), chap. 6.

59 I will not address here another important discussion, which has to do with what types of constitutions, if any, deliberative democrats should accept or propose.

60 In many modern democracies (for example, the United States or Argentina), judges have themselves proclaimed or simply assumed that they have this 'final say', even though the text of the constitution they were enforcing did not expressly grant them this power.

61 Jeremy Waldron, *Law and Disagreement* (Oxford: Clarendon Press, 1999).

62 To state this contradicts the common assumption according to which deliberative democracy should propose a more passive role for judges, given the need to foster open, public, popular participation. In Cass Sunstein's words: 'A judicial effort to protect social and economic rights might seem to preempt democratic deliberation on crucial issues. It would undermine the capacity of citizens to choose, in accordance with their own judgments, the kinds of welfare and employment programs that they favor.' Cass Sunstein, *The Second Bill of Rights: The Last Great Speech of Franklin Delano Roosevelt and America's Unfinished Pursuit of Freedom* (New York: Basic Books, 2004), p. 57.

63 See in this respect, for example, Cohen, 'The Economic Basis of a Deliberative Democracy'. More generally, see John Rawls's discussion of the 'fair value' of political liberties in *Political Liberalism* (New York: Columbia University Press, 1993). I thank Pablo Gilabert for his comments on this issue.

64 In this sense, the very existence of constitutionally enforceable social rights may be seen as a way to 'promote democratic deliberation, not preempt it, by directing political attention to interests that would otherwise be disregarded in ordinary political life' (Sunstein, *The Second Bill of Rights*, p. 228).

Chapter 2

Courts and Social Transformation: An Analytical Framework

Siri Gloppen

Introduction and Overview[1]

This investigation is motivated by a simple question, namely: *When are courts relevant to poor and marginalised people's struggle to better their life prospects?* Poverty reduction and promotion of social rights are usually seen as matters of policy and not legal adjudication. The conventional wisdom is that the law and the courts favour the powerful and vested interests in society, and it is not difficult to find examples to substantiate this. Yet, in recent years, poor groups in different parts of the world have chosen to fight for their social rights in court, and have in some cases won important legal victories – as illustrated by the oft-cited cases from the Indian Supreme Court and the South African Constitutional Court.[2] We know that legal systems respond very differently to the concerns of poor people – *but what accounts for the difference?* Why do some courts, at certain times, function as agents of social transformation and inclusion of marginalised groups? Why do poor groups in some cases turn to the legal system rather than opting for other forms of political mobilisation? What are the explanatory factors? Current knowledge in this field is too thin and fragmented to provide reliable answers. Systematic comparative investigations may help us to understand which factors – and constellations of factors – are most crucial for whether courts are socially conservative or serve as agents and arenas of social change. The conceptual framework outlined here aims to facilitate such analyses by identifying various categories of explanatory variables and clarifying the relationship between them. Some of these variables are aspects of the legal systems, some relate to the socio-political contexts in which the courts operate, while others have regard to the ability and resources of poor and marginalised groups themselves.

Improving our understanding of courts' 'social transformation performance' is particularly significant at a time when many of the world's poorer counties are undergoing extensive legal and judicial reform as part of a democratisation process, reflecting an unprecedented emphasis on law and rights as driving forces of social change.[3] The past two decades have seen massive investments in judicial reform.[4] A strong, more transparent and independent judiciary is seen as a key factor in securing the rule of law, improving rights protection and encouraging investment, thereby facilitating democratic consolidation and development.[5] Economic and social rights are generously incorporated in the legal frameworks of most of these countries – yet little progress has been made in accommodating these rights to the needs of the poor. On the contrary, the establishment of democratic regimes has generally not been followed by significant changes in the social and economic structure of society, and the twin processes of political and economic liberalisation have, in many cases, exacerbated poverty, and led to the retraction of social services.

Despite the political focus on judicial reform and rights protection for vulnerable groups, there is little systematic research on how the changing role of judiciaries has affected marginalised groups in poorer societies, and the conditions under which courts are likely to function as an institutional voice for the poor.[6] The framework outlined here aims to contribute to a better understanding of these dynamics by providing the basis for broad comparative studies of the courts' transformation performance in different legal-political systems – or, as in the present volume – by serving as an overarching conceptual tool linking together in a coherent manner more narrowly framed studies. The latter approach enables cross-fertilisation between different academic disciplines and close integration of different types of studies (in-depth case studies of particular cases and institutions; comparative studies of sub-themes, specific types of litigation, legal strategies of particular groups, factors impacting on access to justice, social composition of courts, jurisprudential developments in particular areas of law, and so on). Thus it contributes to a more nuanced understanding of the complex processes shaping the role of courts in social transformation.

The framework is in principle applicable to any society, although the problems addressed here are more acute in poorer countries, where the consequences of poverty and social marginalisation tend to be particularly devastating, inequalities particularly stark, and the social distance between judges and ordinary people particularly wide. The framework may be used to investigate all aspects of courts' relationship to poor and marginalised groups. In the following presentation the focus is on social rights litigation. This is clearly not the only relevant aspect when assessing the court's transformative role – and arguably not even the most significant in social terms – but it is where the judges' role as agents of social change takes the most direct and spectacular form. And as a controversial area for adjudication, and a field where legal reasoning and jurisprudence is rapidly evolving, it merits particular attention.

The first part of the chapter sets out the theoretical reasoning underpinning the analytical framework and discusses the dependent variable, the concept of social transformation and the courts' *transformation performance*. Besides demarcating the concept theoretically, this section discusses the methodology for identifying social transformation performance, and possible indicators.

The second part deconstructs the litigation process into four stages. For each stage, a 'nexus' or cluster of factors is identified that impact on the judiciary's role in social inclusion and transformation. The stages are labelled 'voice', 'responsiveness', 'capability', and 'compliance'. *Voice* concerns the ability of marginalised groups effectively to voice their claims or have them voiced on their behalf. Court *responsiveness* refers to the willingness of the courts to respond to the concerns of marginalised groups. *Capability* refers to judges' ability to give legal effect to social (and other) rights in ways that significantly affect the situation of marginalised groups, while *compliance* concerns the extent to which these judgments are politically authoritative, and whether the political branches comply with them and implement and reflect them in legislation and policies.

The four stages serve as intermediary variables in the theoretical framework. For each stage, this chapter seeks to identify the most relevant factors, or independent variables, that combine to determine the overall 'score' (factors enabling/hampering marginalised groups' voice; factors influencing courts' responsiveness to social rights cases; factors determining judges' choice of jurisprudential strategies to give effect to (or block) social rights claims; and factors influencing compliance with judgments where the courts make rulings that are significant from the perspective of social transformation.

Indicators are suggested for each of the variables. To function as a basis for cross-national comparison, these must be specific and 'constraining' enough to guide the analysis in ways that produce truly comparative data, yet they must be general enough to be applicable to different legal systems and socio-political contexts, and to allow for a rich contextual analysis that brings out the significance of each case and the dynamics at play. Here indicators are suggested for each stage of the framework. These should, however, be regarded as tentative and open to revision.

Why present such a detailed theoretical framework when the present volume does not aim to 'test' it through a broad cross-national statistical analysis of courts' transformation performance? The short answer is that specification is sobering and facilitates a common understanding of the phenomena under investigation. In order for the framework to link together diverse studies in a way that produces genuinely comparative insights, it is crucial that we agree, not only on common variables, but also what they imply in concrete terms – what we should look for 'on the ground'. By specifying them into operational indicators, we 'put our head on the block' as it were, diverging understandings become evident and clarifications can be reached.

Social Transformation and Courts' Performance: Tracing the Dependent Variable

Before going into the details of the theoretical framework, some normative and methodological issues need to be discussed in relation to the dependent variable: the court's impact on social transformation and inclusion of marginalised groups (*transformation performance*). Social transformation can be defined as the altering of structured inequalities and power relations in society in ways that reduce the weight of morally irrelevant circumstances, such as socio-economic status/class, gender, race, religion or sexual orientation.[7] Courts' transformation performance is their contribution to the altering of such structured inequalities and power relations, or in other words, whether they serve as an institutional voce for the poor and contribute to the social inclusion of disadvantaged and marginalised groups. Which groups are the most vulnerable and marginalised varies between societies, depending on the structure and depth of social inequalities.

Courts may contribute to social transformation directly:

- By providing an arena in which concerns of marginalised groups can be raised as legal claims – with social rights litigation as the paradigmatic case – and by giving legal redress in ways that have implications for law, policy and/or administrative action.
- By serving as a bulwark against erosion of existing pro-poor institutional arrangements. This is particularly relevant in countries formerly pursuing some form of socialism, where state subsidies for social priorities (pensions, welfare benefits, education, health, basic foods) have been discontinued or reduced, due to ideological change and/or financial strain resulting in the introduction of structural adjustment policies and liberalisation of the economy.[8]
- By bolstering pro-poor state policies in the face of attacks from other social interests.[9]

Courts may also contribute to social inclusion in more indirect ways:

- By enabling marginalised groups to more effectively fight for social transformation in other arenas – through securing their effective rights of political participation, rights to information, collective action, and so on. And, more fundamentally, by securing the integrity of the democratic political system as such.
- By 'passively' serving as a public platform where claims can be articulated. As a focal point for mobilisation and publicity this may have important political effects even in the absence of a judgment acknowledging the claim.

So, while social rights litigation is the focus here, it should be kept in mind that courts may serve a pro-poor function in many other ways.

The conception of the courts' social transformation performance raises several fundamental questions. As it is understood here, it is value laden, that is, social transformation is assumed to be a desirable social goal to which the courts should contribute. This is controversial at different levels. Ideological positions differ on what constitutes morally irrelevant differences and whether a particular change in the legal and social status of particular groups in itself is positive or negative.[10] And even in the absence of such differences, views are likely to diverge regarding what the wider implications of 'social transformation decisions' are – socially, economically, and morally – and whether or not they are conducive to the long-term development of society.

The idea that courts should be geared towards the social transformation of society also opens fundamental controversies regarding the proper role of courts and the demarcation between law and politics. What is the legitimate role of courts in processes of social transformation? Should the institutional conditions be reformed to encourage social rights litigation – or does an active role for the courts on social rights issues turn them into purely political bodies, and undermine their legally grounded legitimacy? I will only consider the main arguments here as the questions are discussed in more depth elsewhere in this volume.[11]

An active role for courts in social transformation poses questions regarding the separation of powers and the proper relationship between courts and the political branches. This is part of a long-standing debate on judicial review and the legitimate right of unelected judges to overrule decisions of the representatives of the people. Social rights litigation raises these issues in a particularly stark manner, since they involve questions of social policy and tend to affect budgetary allocation in a direct and significant way – matters that are often seen to belong to the 'core of politics', outside the area of judges' competence.[12] Giving rights claims legal force typically releases resources unconditionally (or with priority), trumping other concerns and other forms of expenditure, which, if implemented, has profound resource allocation implications.[13] And the more goods are recognised as legal entitlements, the less room there is for politically based priority setting, for example, with a view to economic development. Rights enforced by the courts are thus potentially costly, economically and in terms of 'democratic space'. Resource scarcity adds to the trade-off problems – but also strengthens the need to proritise the most vital concerns, which is what rights are there to protect.

A related argument is that social rights raise issues in which the room for rational disagreement is particularly wide, and that this makes them inherently political matters not suitable for courts.[14] It is feared that to use the courts as an arena to fight such battles will politicise the judiciary, undermine their ability to generate trust as an independent and impartial arbiter – and tempt those in power to interfere with the independence of the judiciary. The courts should rather limit themselves to what has been referred to above as an indirect transformative role – that of securing the 'rules of the political game', keeping open other channels in which such matters can be fought.

A counter-argument is that social rights are needed to secure the equal value of political rights, enabling marginalised groups to effectively fight for social transformation in other arenas. The proper role of the courts should be seen in the context of the broader political system, what other channels there are to address such concerns, how effective they are, and the opportunities available to vulnerable groups to have their concerns addressed. In a democratic system, judges are obliged to protect all citizens' rights and to ensure that 'collective decisions be made by political institutions whose structure, composition, and practices treat all members of the community, as individuals, with equal concern and respect'.[15] Courts should repair the malfunctioning of the democratic process when the latter systematically impairs the interests of marginalised groups.[16] But this does not preclude a role for the other branches of power: ensuring social equality is mainly a task for elected politicians.

The problem of costs and room for reasonable disagreement is not peculiar to social rights. Other rights are also costly and complex, and require courts to exercise political judgement. And, of course, courts can enforce social rights in a range of ways, some more politically interventionist than others. It is important, on normative as well as prudential grounds, to preserve political space for democratic decision-making by elected political bodies, but the (fluid) demarcation line between legal and political judgement – between the constitutional domain and the domain of the political – cuts across the different categories of rights, and boundaries for legitimate judicial action must be sought within the domain of social rights jurisprudence.

An additional normative argument for adjudicating economic and social rights is that such rights are incorporated into the legal frameworks of most countries, either in the national constitutions, or in the form of human rights provisions in customary international law and legally binding treaties. In this perspective, social rights litigation and judicial activism in defence of the poor and marginalised may be seen as mandated by the will of the people as enshrined in the basic norms defining the terms of their community.

Moving to the practical level, the concept of courts' *transformation potential* is difficult to delineate and measure. It is not easy to systematically single out actions that have consequences (positive and negative, direct and indirect) for social transformation – court decisions (and non-decisions) that alter structured inequalities and power relations in society in ways that reduce the weight of morally irrelevant circumstances. Operational definitions that are broad enough to cover the entire set of possibilities are likely to be too loose to be of much practical use. And by narrowing down, the flexibility of the theoretical framework is lost. The best strategy thus seems to be to stay with the broad, theoretical definition for the general formulation of the framework, and develop different operational definitions of the dependent variable for the purpose of specific analyses.

To indicate how this can be done, the framework is specified for the purpose of analysing differences in courts' responses to social rights litigation. (Social rights cases may be defined broadly, for example in terms of the rights included in the UN Convention on Economic, Social and Cultural Rights; or as a more narrowly defined set of rights that are of importance to poor and marginalised groups (housing rights, women's rights, and land rights).) Transformation performance is in this context the *jurisprudence* developed in response to social rights claims raised in the courts, and the *political effects* of such judgments. The frequency and significance of social rights judgments are here the main indicators of courts' transformation performance, and we need to find criteria and methodologies that are suitable for establishing significance and frequency.

Regarding *frequency* of social rights judgments, we may look at the share of judgments relative to the number of social rights cases lodged (and within this set, at the share of 'transformative'/pro-poor judgments). Taken alone this could, however, distort the picture. A court faced with very few (carefully selected and argued) social rights cases, and responding positively to them, will receive a better transformation score than a court faced with a multitude of such claims (of different quality and substance) where a substantial proportion is turned down – even if the total number of 'transformative' judgments is much higher in the latter case. This is particularly problematic since the number of social rights cases lodged will be in part a response to how the courts have previously responded to such challenges. Courts with a good 'transformation performance' may thus, by stimulating litigation of varying quality, drive down their own performance score. This frequency indicator should thus be combined with a measure taking account of the absolute number of social rights cases (although this may unduly favour large and/or very litigious societies), or that looks at the share social rights cases make up relative to the courts' total caseload. Alternatively, a procedure could be included for distinguishing cases lodged according to merit/significance.

Assessment of *significance* is relevant both with regard to the nature of the case (legal merit, social importance); with regard to the judgement itself (social/political implications and extensiveness of legal remedies); and with regard to actual political effect/implementation.

Criteria for political effect are difficult to establish in the abstract as these need to be evaluated against the specific legal-political context. Furthermore, effects of court decisions on social change can rarely be measured directly. Structural inequalities and power relations in a particular area are the combined outcomes of a host of different factors, and the impact of a court decision is normally impossible to isolate. (In other words, if a court decision on housing or health rights is followed by fluctuations in levels of homelessness or morbidity, this cannot automatically be ascribed to the decision as such, as these indicators are also affected by a range of other factors, such as economic fluctuations, climatic changes and pandemics.) While correlation with macro-level changes in relevant social indicators clearly may be useful to consider, this is not sufficient. A complementary and often more realistic methodology for assessing the extent of particular judgments' transformative effect is to look qualitatively at their 'ripple effects', that is, to carefully investigate the steps taken to comply with and implement the judgment, and to examine whether it has led to changes in laws, regulations and policies, or has changed the pattern of administrative/lower court decisions, and the norms applied by other institutions (for example in the monitoring standards of human rights commissions).

Another approach is, for each country, to compose a panel of knowledgeable representatives from the national legal community (academics, practitioners, politicians and people from civil society/media, with diverse political views) and ask them to scale the judgments on a continuum from insignificant to highly significant.[17] This methodology is suitable for the assessment of significance at all levels (merit and social relevance of cases lodged/accepted and significance of judgments, in addition to political significance/implementation). It could also play a useful role in case selection, as we shall see.

So far, the focus has been on how to conceive social transformation and establish differences in courts' transformation performance (the dependent variable). Now we move to what explains these differences in outcome, which brings us to the theoretical framework itself.

Explaining Courts' Social Transformation Performance: Mapping the Litigation Process

When does social rights litigation succeed? Which factors are decisive? In order to understand how various factors interact to determine the outcome, we start by dissecting the litigation process to bring out its main structural components.

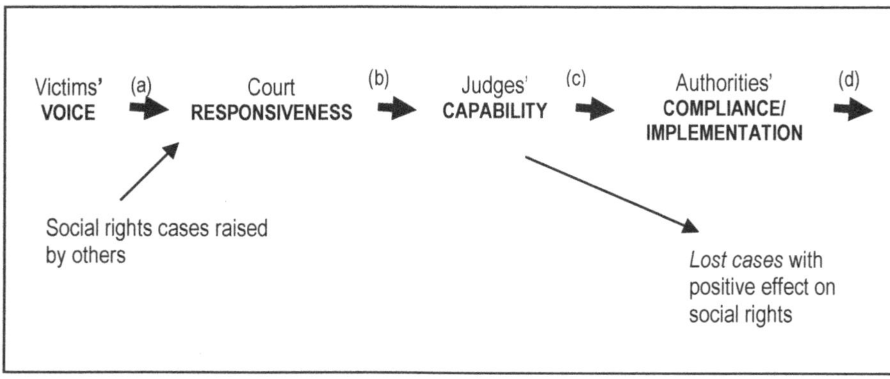

Figure 2.1: The Main Components of the Litigation Process
(a) Social rights cases brought to court; (b) cases accepted by the courts; (c) judgements giving effect to social rights; (d) transformation effect (impact on social rights/inclusion of marginalised groups).

At the most basic level, there are four main stages or variables in the litigation process that interact to determine the success or failure of social rights litigation: first, the extent to which people whose social rights are violated *voice* their claims in the courts; secondly, the courts' *responsiveness* to these claims; thirdly, the judges' *capability* to give legal effect to the social rights claims that are voiced; and fourthly, the authority of the courts' social rights decisions, seen in terms of *compliance* with the terms of the judgment, directly and in terms of subsequent legislation and policies.

Even if the case is not decided in favour of the claimants, litigation may have a transformative impact. Authorities threatened with court action may settle out of court, and when courts provide a platform for voicing social rights concerns, this may generate or intensify popular debate and create political momentum. This indirect, political effect is represented in the figure by the downwards-sloping arrow.

The argument underlying the theoretical framework is that differences in courts' transformation performance can be explained in terms of variations at the four stages: the voicing of claims; the responsiveness of the courts, the capability of judges and the compliance of political authorities. But this is not the whole story. Each of these variables or stages of the litigation process is itself the outcome of a range of other factors. They should in other words be seen as nexuses, or intermediate variables linking together the complex web of institutions and practices impacting on the litigation process and conditioning the social transformation role of the courts. For each nexus there is a sub-web of conditioning factors. The logic is illustrated in Figure 2.2 below.

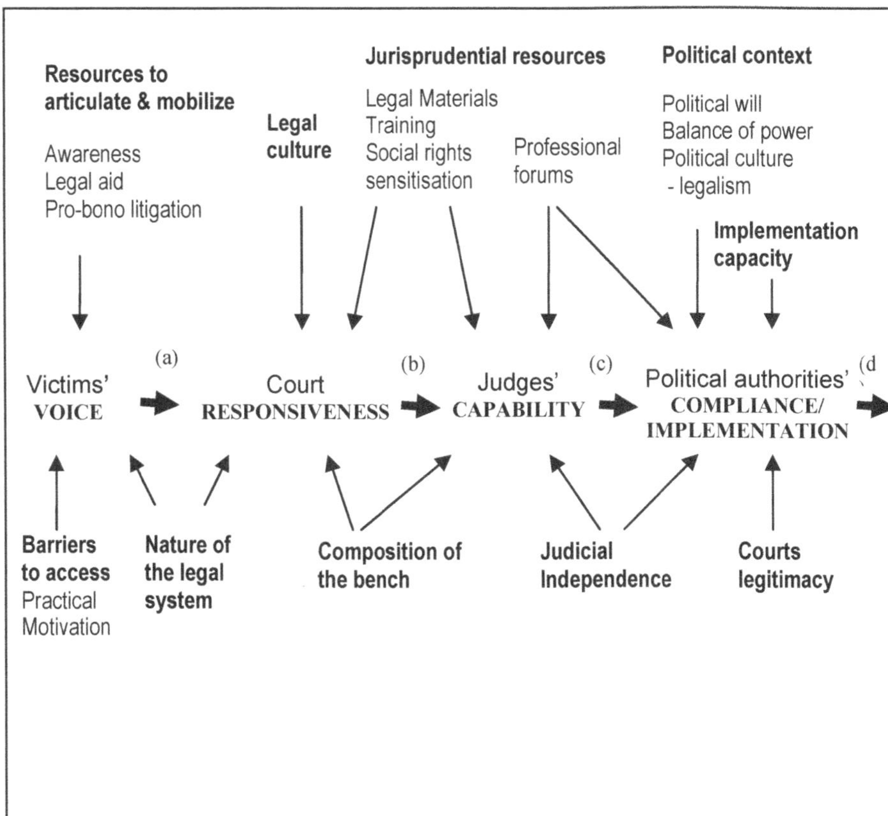

Figure 2.2: The Anatomy of the Social Rights Litigation Process

(a) social rights cases brought to court; (b) cases accepted by the courts; (c) judgements giving effect to social rights; (d) transformation effect (impact on social rights/inclusion of marginalised groups).

In what follows, the assumptions regarding the relationship between the independent variables and the outcome for each nexus (the intermediary variables) are spelled out, and indicators are suggested. Thus, two types of indicators are required: indicators to evaluate the output from each of the nexuses in the framework in terms of their contribution to social transformation (the bold arrows in the framework); and indicators to capture the factors and processes that combine to produce each output (the slim arrows).

On the basis of the output indicators it should be possible to assess the social transformation performance of courts across legal systems, and gain a better understanding of where the main impediments are in a particular case – whether failure by the courts to fill a social transformation role stems from lack of voice (few social rights/transformation cases lodged, poor framing of the cases); from failure on the part of the courts to respond to such claims and recognise the cases as within their proper domain; from inability to give legal effect to the claims; or from failure to have the judgments implemented and translated into social action.

The output or performance indicators do not, however, in themselves explain why one indicator is or is not translated into another; why social rights claims are voiced in some cases and not in others; why the responsiveness and capabilities of courts differ; and why judgments are implemented and have effects on social transformation in some cases, but not in others. To understand these relationships, it is necessary to look at the factors that combine to enable or prevent each of these outcomes, and this is what the process indicators seek to capture. The variables range from institutional characteristics of the courts that are assumed to be significant for their accessibility, responsiveness and capability with regard to social transformation, and for the authority of the rulings, to aspects of agency within these processes, and the resources enabling action. They also aim to capture important contextual factors, outside of the courts' control, which impact on voice and compliance. Below, the process and outcome indicators are specified in relation to each nexus.

For a stringent cross-national study of the transformative role of courts, it is also of the utmost importance that a reliable methodology be developed for purposes of consistent *case selection.* There are many possibilities, both with regard to what type of litigation to include, which level(s) in the court structure to focus on, and which stage in the litigation process to take as the baseline for inclusion. To start with the latter: should we select on the basis of outcome ('successful' social rights litigation; all social rights litigation), or take the lodging of cases as the point of departure, or cases accepted by the courts? Or should we also try to include cases that never make it to the litigation stage? The easiest option will usually be to select on the basis of (successful) outcome. This means that we would choose cases that resulted in a transformative outcome and 'work backwards'. This does, however, give limited opportunities to understand what distinguishes cases that make it at the various stages from those that do not. If we want to understand these dynamics at every stage we need to select at the stage of pre-litigation mobilisation, or the lodging of cases. But this is a much more demanding research process, and trade-offs will in practice have to be made between scope and depth. Also, with regard to the level of analysis, there is a trade-off between depth and scope – whether to focus only on cases decided by the highest court in the land, consider all cases on social rights in the higher courts, or also include cases in the lower courts. If the case selection criteria are broad and include a high number of cases, the initial case selection could be complemented by a procedure to select the most significant cases within the set for closer analysis (for example through using an expert panel, as discussed earlier).

Voice

The first stage of the litigation process is the articulation of rights claims by, or on behalf of, victims of social rights violations, and the voicing of the claims into the legal system. The factors influencing whether, and how forcefully, social rights claims are voiced differ in nature – some are related to the institutional structure of the legal system, others concern the social and political context, while yet others concern the resources available to poor people. Figure 2.3 shows the different factors in some detail, and tentative indicators for each.

Figure 2.3: Factors Affecting Litigants' Voice

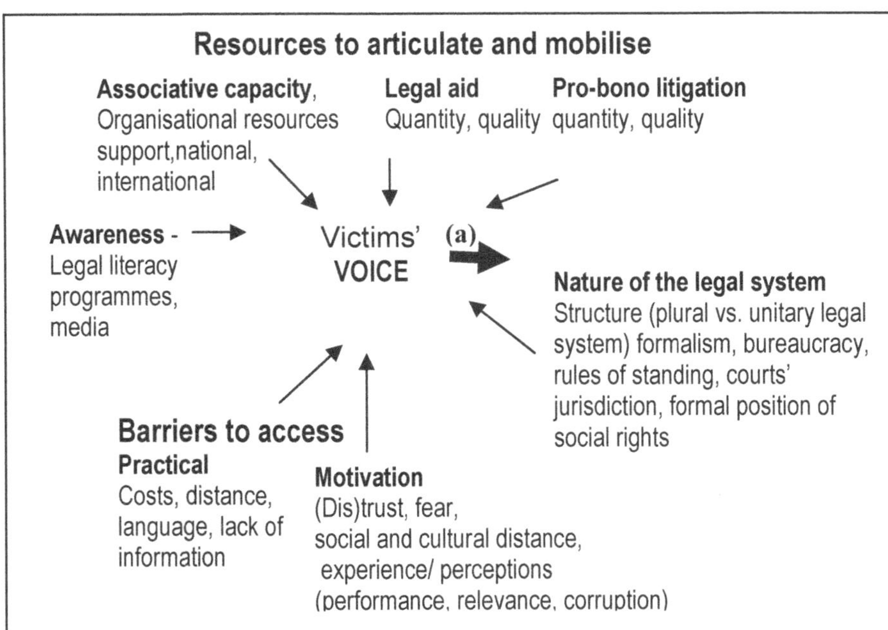

Figure 2.3: Factors Affecting Litigants' Voice
(a) Social rights cases brought.

For social rights litigation to succeed, those whose social rights are violated must be able to articulate their concerns and effectively voice them in court as legal claims, or have someone else do so on their behalf.

This requires, firstly, that potential litigants should be *aware* of their rights, the right-violation and the possibility for redress through the courts. Often, those whose social rights are most severely violated lack this knowledge. The extent of civil society and community mobilisation around social rights issues and the existence of legal literacy and rights awareness programmes, human rights education in schools, and a focus on social rights issues in the media, are important factors influencing the level of rights awareness and legal literacy and thus the likelihood of social rights claims being voiced.

For courts to play a transformative role, the claims of the poor and marginalised must be channelled into the legal system. A crucial parameter of the poor's ability to defend rights or seek redress through the legal system is their opportunity situation, which defines the poor as litigants in the legal process.[18] Their opportunity situation is defined by the formal or 'systemic' and informal *barriers* to seeking justice or redress through the judicial system.[19] Some of the barriers preventing people from accessing the justice system are *practical*. These include the costs of litigating, rules of standing, geographical distance, language barriers, and lack of information.

Other barriers keeping people from pursuing a legal strategy are motivational and psychological. Fear and distrust of the courts is often widespread among poor and socially marginalised groups due to cultural and social distance. Lack of legitimacy for the legal norms of the formal legal system in marginalised communities may discourage litigation – as may negative prior experience with the legal system (or negative perceptions) of poor performance, delays and backlogs, corruption and bias – or a general belief that court decisions are irrelevant.

Another important factor that impacts on the poor and marginalised's motivation for pursuing legal action is the state and availability of alternative channels and strategies for mobilising on social right issues or addressing individual grievances, such as electoral mobilisation, lobbying of political bodies, strikes and demonstrations or media campaigns – or through alternative court-like institutions such as ombudsman institutions, human rights commissions or traditional courts and tribunals. If other strategies (are perceived to) offer better chances of success, are seen as more cost-effective, or more appropriate, this might discourage litigation. Litigation may, however, also be part of a broader social/political mobilisation strategy.

Access to the justice system for various groups in society also depends on the nature of the legal system itself. Issues of *substantive law* are assumed to be important for whether litigation is chosen as a strategy to advance social rights – in particular whether or not there is a clear legal basis for social rights litigation in the country's constitutional and legal framework. The *structure of the court system* and the extent to which outreach mechanisms (such as circuit courts) and access to justice programmes are in place are important for whether the poor are able to voice their claims in court. So is the degree of *formalism* and bureaucracy (for example, whether there are possibilities of direct access to the higher courts and how lenient their criteria are, and whether the legal system is based on parties compiling their own case or has inquisitorial judges). A very important barrier concerns who is qualified to take a case to court (the criteria for *locus standi*), in particular whether an organisation or individual can litigate on behalf of others, and whether it is possible to claim a right on behalf of a larger category of people similarly situated (in a class action). A related issue regards the standards for judicial review – whether the courts review legislation (only) in the abstract or (only) in response to concrete cases.

As a rule, new democracies are characterised by legal pluralism, which often includes a strong *informal judicial system* based on 'traditional' or 'customary law'.[20] In many cases the lower costs, easy access to, as well as, in some cases, high local legitimacy of informal judicial systems may provide poor people with a disincentive to seek redress through the formal judicial system.[21] Whether this is the case or not needs to be established empirically as part of the assessment of the opportunity situation facing poor litigants. Customary systems may be integrated with the formal judicial apparatus (fulfilling functions within the lower courts) or function as an independent judicial system operating in parallel to the formal one.

These are the factors that affect the likelihood that grievances and claims will be pursued through the judiciary. In a number of cases, such obstacles prevent poor people from initiating a legal claim and mute their collective 'voice'.[22]

Nonetheless, we know that poor groups occasionally are able to overcome these barriers, and it is important to examine the resources, strategies and personal initiative they have used to launch a court case even when faced with formal and informal barriers.[23] To overcome the barriers against litigation, groups or individuals whose social rights are violated must also have (access to) *resources* enabling them to effectively articulate their rights claims.

'Associative capacity' – the ability to join forces, form associations with the capacity to mobilise around social rights issues, generate expertise and financial resources locally and internationally, and sustain collective action, is a central variable in this regard.[24] 'Capacity' here also includes immaterial resources (ethnic identity, group solidarity) that people can draw on to mobilise group members and launch collective action through the judiciary. Furthermore, it refers to the strategies used – the ways in which claims and grievances are publicised (for example though protest-marches and public rallies) and eventually turned into a mainstream legal process. This, in turn, leads to a focus on personal agency as a means in which members of poor and marginal groups (or their associates) are able to articulate their concerns so as to pave the way for a judicial process or inquiry.

Another central resource is legal aid and other legal assistance. Social rights cases are typically complex legal matters and the ability of lay people to effectively argue their own case – in a form that the legal system recognises – is limited (depending on the standards of proof, and whether the litigants are assumed to provide all information). For poor people (whose social rights are most at risk) this means that their ability to voice social rights claims is strongly related to the availability of free/affordable legal assistance. Public legal aid schemes, pro-bono arrangements organised by the legal community and non-governmental organisations providing legal advice and litigating cases in court, are thus central, and the availability of such resources is a key variable impacting on victims' *voice*. However, it is important not only to look at whether such services are available to the poor, but also to assess their quality. Legal aid work is often low status and poorly paid, and may not attract good, experienced lawyers. The availability of such lawyers to take social rights cases will in turn affect the quality of the claims that are voiced. It is thus important to consider the role of third-party intervention on behalf of the poor, such as the role of local and international NGOs, individuals/professionals and the media in aiding poor groups in advancing their claims in a court of law.

All these factors affecting the likelihood and form of legal mobilisation 'from below' are relevant for whether social rights claims are voiced into the legal system, and how frequent and forceful such claims are. In order to capture them adequately the process indicators relating to 'voice' should include:

- barriers preventing access to justice for marginalised groups:
  - practical (costs, geographical and linguistic barriers, lack of information);
  - motivational (cultural, social distance; fear and distrust; experience/perceptions of poor performance, irrelevance, corruption, bias);
- structure of the legal system (pluralism, formalism, bureaucracy, outreach);
- awareness and legal literacy among disadvantaged sections of the population; and
- resources available to articulate and mobilise on legal issues:
  - associative capacity; and
  - access to quality legal services.

When comparing the strength of voice over time or across legal systems, indicators of socially marginalised groups' voice are the:

- frequency of cases brought to court concerning social rights issues (by marginalised groups/transformation cases brought by others); and
- significance of the cases voiced (politically and in terms of legal substance).

Again, the question arises of how to measure significance, and how to determine the frequency of social rights cases (in absolute terms or as a share of all cases). These challenges were discussed in relation to the dependent variable, and I will not repeat them, except to say that different methodologies are suitable for different purposes. If there are few instances of social rights litigation, or if only a narrow sub-set of cases is selected, the most suitable approach might be to qualitatively assess all the variables in the analysis, using the indicators as a guideline. If the number of cases is higher, the panel approach discussed above may be more adequate, which means that that key informants are asked to evaluate the status of the process variables on a scale, and similarly for the significance of the social transformation cases constituting the content of the 'voice'. Both the in-depth qualitative approach and the panel approach create opportunities for investigating 'negative cases' where claims have been 'in the pipeline' but dropped, or mobilised in other forums.

Courts' Responsiveness

For social rights litigation to succeed, the legal system must also be responsive to the claims that are voiced. They must be recognized as a legitimate matter for the court to decide. As Figure 2.4 indicates, responsiveness is in part a function of 'voice' – it depends on the manner in which the claims are articulated, the legal strategies employed by the litigants and the skill with which the case is framed (and of course also on the merit of the case itself). But the responsiveness of the legal system to social rights claims also depends on other factors.

Figure 2.4: Factors Conditioning Courts' Responsiveness

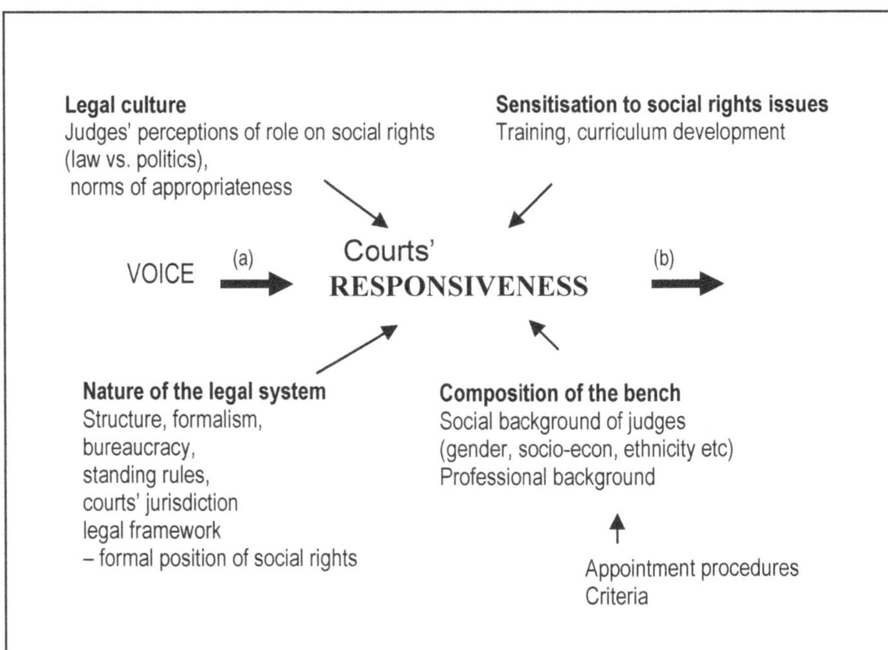

Figure 2.4: Factors Conditioning Courts' Responsiveness
(a) Social rights cases brought; (b) cases accepted.

Again, the nature of the legal system is crucial. The factors discussed above as relevant for prospective litigants' decisions concerning whether to spend their resources on legal strategies rather than alternative forms of mobilisation – substantive law, rules of standing and legal formalities – are also relevant for courts' responsiveness. The legal basis for social rights is particularly important, including the status of international social rights conventions. And where social rights are formally recognised it is important whether they are justiciable rights or merely 'directive principles' outside the scope of the courts' jurisdiction.

How judges interpret the law is equally important to the courts' responsiveness to social rights claims. This depends in part on the nature of the legal culture – theories of legal interpretation and the prevailing understanding of the relationship between law and politics. The legal culture (in combination with judges' personal ideological and professional values) influences the judges' perception of their own role – their norms of appropriateness concerning how they should deal with social rights, and to what extent social rights are seen to be within the proper domain of the courts.

Lastly, the courts' responsiveness to social rights issues depends on the judges' sensitivity – individually and collectively – to the concerns voiced. This is influenced by the composition of the bench, the judges' social and ideological background, their legal education, and so on. Institutionally, the composition of the bench is a function of the system and criteria for appointment of judges, but judges may also be sensitised to social rights issues and the concerns of marginalised groups more generally, through ongoing training.

To sum up, the process indicators should include:

- the strength of 'voice' (output of the first stage) – how effectively the legal claims are articulated;
- the legal system (particularly the legal basis for social rights, and the courts' jurisdiction and competence on social rights, but also rules of standing and procedure);
- legal culture and norms of appropriateness in the judiciary (are social rights regarded as being within the proper domain of the courts?); and
- judges' sensitivity to social transformation concerns:
    - composition of the bench (social, ideological background, legal education);
    - appointment procedures, criteria; and
    - sensitivity training.

The *output indicators* for the courts' responsiveness should assess the extent to which courts are sensitive to the social rights/transformation claims voiced and accept them as matters belonging within their competence. This can be seen in terms of:

- frequency of social rights /transformation cases accepted by the courts, relative to the number of such cases that are lodged;
- the nature of the cases that are accepted (substantive content in relation to the law); and
- their significance from a social transformation perspective.

It may also be interesting to look at patterns of 'opting out' – that is, to investigate to what extent social rights/transformation claims by, or on behalf of, marginalised groups are channelled into other arenas: for example, arbitration, traditional tribunals, or political bodies. The use of informal mechanisms and social networks is likely to substitute for law where the use of formal law becomes impossible. Where such mechanisms are developed, the poor may choose to exit rather than exercise voice through the judicial system.[25] While 'opting out' may indicate a relative lack of responsiveness on the part of the courts, it is not necessarily bad. If there are other channels where marginalised groups can address their concerns, this may be preferable.

Again, the indicators identified here are applicable either as a checklist in an in-depth qualitative analysis or as the basis for a more formalised evaluation by a panel.

Judges' Capability

The third stage of the litigation process concerns judges' capacity to handle social rights issues. That judges are willing to consider and respond to social rights claims is not sufficient for litigation to succeed, they must also be able to find adequate legal remedies to repair the violation. As indicated in Figure 2.55, court performance depends on the skill and capacity of the judges, and on the jurisprudential resources at their disposal.

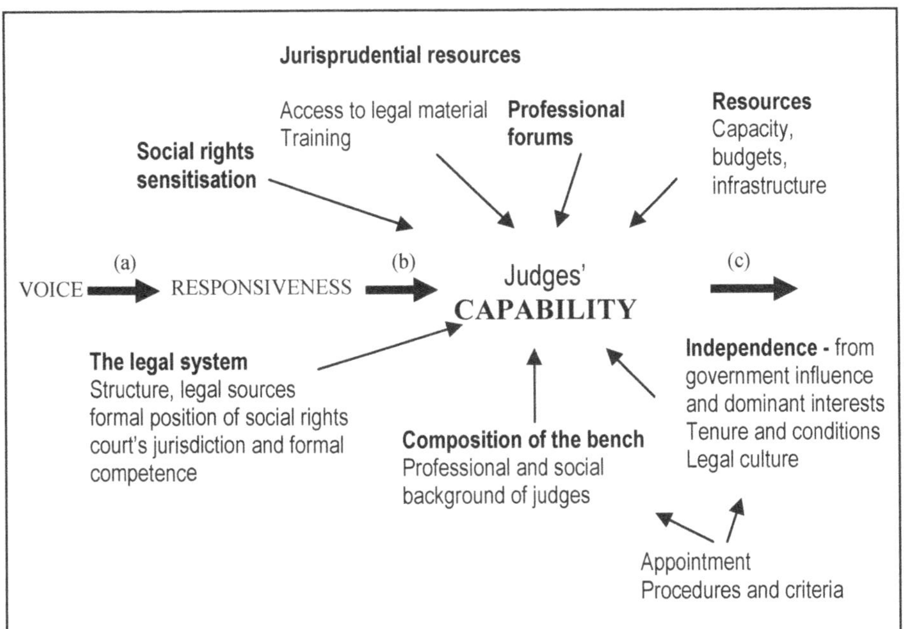

Figure 2.5: Factors Affecting Judges'Capability
(a) Social rights cases brought; (b) cases accepted; (c) social rights judgements.

Judges' ability to find adequate legal remedies depends on a range of factors. The options include 'minimal affirmation', merely requiring the state to respect a social right in the negative sense of non-interference, or the courts may rule that the state has a duty to protect social rights against encroachment by others, order the state to actively promote particular social rights by developing policies to this effect, or make concrete orders for state agencies to fulfil the individual claimants' social rights. Furthermore, court orders may be declaratory (stating that laws or actions are in breach of a social rights obligation, but leaving it to the state to devise a remedy), mandatory (requiring specific actions to be taken) or supervisory (requiring the relevant agency to report back within a set time-frame).[26] As indicated in Figure 2.5, court performance depends on the skill and capacity of the judges, and on the jurisprudential resources at their disposal. The choice of legal remedy depends in part on matters of substantive law (what the law says regarding the relevant rights and the courts' jurisdiction). It also depends on their ability – individually and as a professional community – to find and develop remedies in order to repair a violation of rights.[27] While most legal orders restrict themselves to a short list of judicial remedies, some are introducing non-orthodox remedies to ensure the protection of rights. The ability of judges to collect the necessary evidence is also important (for example, whether they have the capacity to create research commissions or appoint experts).

The development of a sophisticated social rights jurisprudence requires highly skilled judges, research capacity and access to a range of legal materials (and often also considerable capacity on the part of those litigating the cases – the quality of voice has an independent impact here). Infrastructure and financial resources are also obviously of importance.

Legal culture is also important at this level, and in particular, the prevailing theories of judicial interpretation. (Are 'originalist' approaches dominant, or do they try to 'adapt' existing norms to new circumstances and social needs?) Professional forums to exchange ideas and knowledge may contribute positively to the courts' transformative potential, and strengthen judges' professionalism and independence.

Courts' capacity to deliver social rights judgments depends on their independence from the state and dominant social interests. Judicial decisions may be influenced by political pressures, the authority exercised by higher judicial officers, or the influence of extra-institutional actors (the economic elite, pressure groups, lobbies, demonstrations).[28] It is thus important to explore interactions between the different branches of power to see whether there is a dynamic of 'mutual interference', 'dialogue' or 'confrontation' between them, as well as between higher and inferior courts.[29] Judicial decisions in cases concerning the poor can also be biased due to the composition of the bench. Assuming that judges' responsiveness to the concerns of the poor depend on their social, ideological and professional background, it is important to consider the politics and practice of judicial appointments.

To capture the factors impacting on the courts' ability to give legal effect to social rights/transformation concerns in their judgments, the *process indicators* at the capability stage should include:

- substantive law (legal basis for adjudicating the rights);
- legal culture (dominant theories of legal/constitutional interpretation);
- the professional quality of the judges (whether they have the skills required to make legally sound and authoritative judgements); and
- access to jurisprudential resources:
  - relevant legal materials, 'jurisprudential tools' developed in other cases;
  - research capacity; and
  - training (knowledge of and sensitivity to transformation concerns).

In addition to these indicators that seek to capture the ability of judges to make sound 'transformative' legal judgments, it is necessary to capture factors impacting on their willingness to act on this capability, that is, indicators relating to:

- judicial independence (security of tenure, procedures for appointment and dismissal); and
- professional forums (making professional reputations matter and constituting a protective community).

The *output indicators* at the capability level should assess the extent to which the social rights cases taken on by the courts result in 'transformation rulings'. The following indicators are suggested to establish the capability score:

- frequency of rulings giving legal effect to rights (against cases accepted);
- the legal significance of rulings affirming social rights; and
- jurisprudential strategies used to give effect to rights (extensive, effective).

Compliance

The fourth stage of the litigation process, and the last step in the theoretical framework, is compliance. For litigation to improve the rights situation on the ground the relevant authorities must comply with the judgment and political action must be taken to implement the ruling. Compliance is again the outcome of a range of factors, as shown in Figure 2.6.

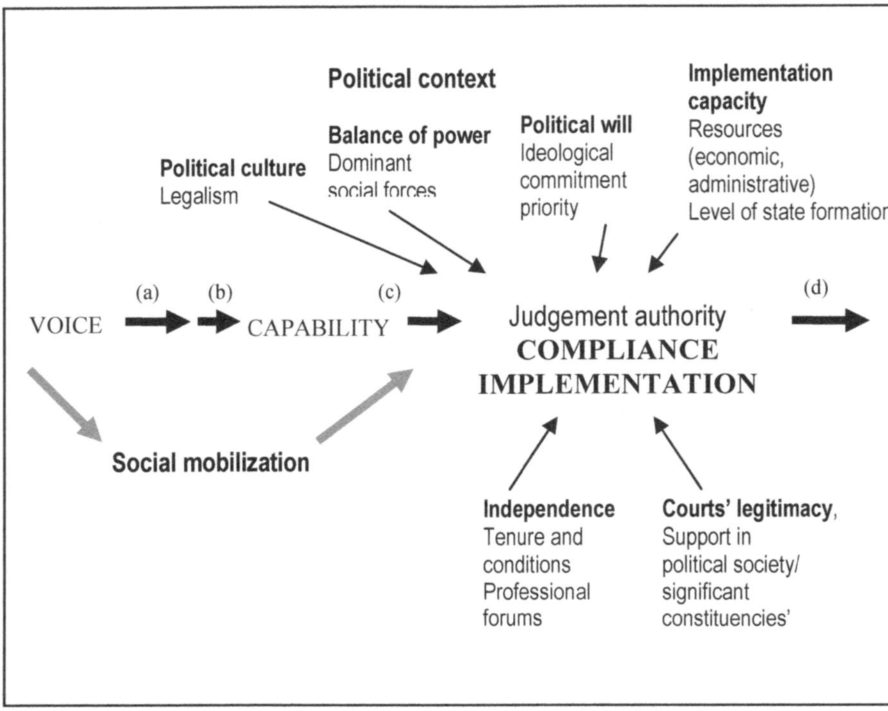

Figure2. 6: Factors Affecting Compliance with Social Rights Judgments
(a) Social rights cases brought; (b) cases accepted; (c) social rights judgements; (d) transformative performance.

Compliance is influenced by the other factors in the legal chain, as laid out in the framework. Of most immediate importance is the authority of the judgment itself – the judges' professionalism and capacity to devise acceptable legal remedies (the score on the capability variable), and in particular whether they include enforcement mechanisms in social rights judgments – such as the use of mandatory/supervisory orders – or issue contempt of court orders in cases of non-compliance.[30] Compliance thus to some extent depends on the courts themselves – the extent to which they are able to make their rulings authoritative, their independence and legitimacy in various sections of society, and their skilfulness in balancing political forces.

However, compliance also depends on factors outside of the legal system, and by and large outside of judges' control. It is important to note that even where the courts make pro-transformation judgments, factors beyond their control may undermine their decisions. These are related to the fundamentals of the political and economic context, the level of state formation and the government's capacity to implement rulings.

The nature of the political context is always important to consider. This includes, most importantly, the balance of power between the competing political forces (whether there is a dominant party that can afford to ignore court decisions, or a more balanced political situation where overruling or ignoring court decisions many be politically costly); the prevailing political culture (whether there is a strong tradition of legalism; and whether the social rights decisions of the courts are at cross-purposes with the government's ideology and broader policy goals); and, perhaps most important, compliance depends on the extent to which there is the political will to follow up and give priority to social rights issues. Lastly, implementation of court rulings depends on the state's capacity – financial, institutional and administrative.

To understand how court decisions affect the poor, we also need to assess the extent to which judgments are implemented on the ground. Furthermore, we need to understand how this is related to aspects of the political context (political will, power-structures) and to the financial and institutional capacity to implement the decisions.

The compliance *process indicators* suggested here seek to capture the various factors impacting on the authoritativeness of the courts' decisions vis-à-vis the political bodies, compliance with orders made and the broader political impact of the rulings:

- political context:
  - the balance of power;
  - political will (and whether social rights rulings are at cross-purposes with the governments' broader policy goals);
  - political culture, legalism; and
  - judicial independence;
- courts' legitimacy in various sectors of society (trust, perceived social relevance, significant protective 'constituencies'); and
- the capacity of the government/relevant authorities to implement decisions (level of state formation and rule of law, economic capacity, administrative capacity).

The ultimate proof of successful compliance with social rights rulings is of course whether or not the situation changes for people on the ground with regard to the relevant right. When this is not included in the framework, it is – as was noted earlier in the discussion of courts' 'transformation performance' – because it is notoriously difficult to establish a causal link between particular legal actions and the overall social development in a field. The *outcome indicators* for the compliance nexus are therefore more modest, and are constructed to identify direct and immediate compliance as well as ripple effects of the judgments. To assess this it is useful to look at whether the judgment is acknowledged and accepted as authoritative by the losing party and the relevant authorities' compliance with the terms of the court order as set out in the judgment. Furthermore, it is useful to scrutinise the actions taken to implement the ruling and, to the extent possible, assess the implications of court's rulings for legislation, policies and regulations and for executive and administrative action. The suggested outcome indicators are thus:

- acceptance of the judgment as authoritative;
- compliance with the terms of the court order as set out in the judgment;
- actions taken to implement the ruling;
- implications for legislation, policies and administrative action;
- how other public bodies relate to the judgments; and
- effect on social mobilisation.

If this sounds familiar, it should, because we are now back to the dependent variable in the analysis of courts' transformation performance. As indicated in the first part of this chapter, courts' transformation performance considers both the quality of the courts' judgments, and their political and social significance, and thus takes into account both the capability of the courts in crafting sound and authoritative social rights judgments, and compliance.

Concluding Remarks

This investigation was sparked by an interest in *how* and *why* the performance of courts differs – between legal systems, between various institutions within the same legal system, as well as over time. This has raised theoretical questions regarding the conditions under which courts effectively protect and advance social rights: What motivates and enables groups deprived of social rights to voice their claims through the legal system? What influences the judicial system's responsiveness to such claims? Which jurisprudential tools and strategies are most suitable for dealing with social rights in ways that make them politically authoritative? What affects the political system's compliance with the courts' social rights decisions? And what are the wider political implications of social rights jurisprudence under different levels of resource scarcity?

These are not only interesting as research questions, but also highly significant from a policy perspective. Particularly if we assume – or have as a goal – that courts should advance social rights and that the legal system should function as an arena where groups deprived of social rights can effectively voice their concerns, a key question is what enables the courts to fill such a role, and what can be done to facilitate social rights litigation.

Taken as a whole, the framework as presented here could serve as the basis for a comprehensive investigation into the social transformation role of courts in different legal systems. This is, however, arguably more useful as an overarching theoretical frame linking individual case studies in a way that aids systematic collection of data and facilitates genuine comparison. And this is the purpose of the framework for the current volume.

The common framework allows us to focus on interesting questions regarding the role of courts in social transformation at different levels of generalisation. Empirically, we are interested not only in the overall social rights performance of courts. We are equally interested in comparative knowledge about how social groups and individuals use the courts to claim social rights, in the strategies they use, how the courts treat their claims, how court decisions on social rights are received and implemented, as well as the wider political and financial implications of social rights litigation. The chapters in this volume each contribute in different ways to such insights.

Notes

1 The framework builds on collaboration within the 'Courts in Transition' research group. Thanks are due to Roberto Gargarella, Elin Skaar, Morten Kinander, Are Knutsen, Pilar Domingo and Theunis Roux, as well as participants at workshops where earlier drafts were presented: 'Courts and Social Transformation in New Democracies: An Institutional Voice for the Poor?' (Di Tella University, Buenos Aires, December 2004); 'Human Rights, Democracy and Social Transformation: When do Rights Work?' (University of the Witwatersrand, Johannesburg, November 2003); 'Making Socio-Economic Rights Justiciable: The South African Experience' (NCHR, Oslo, October 2003); 'The Politics of Socio-economic Rights in South Africa – Ten Years after Apartheid' (University of Oslo, June 2004).

2 Ajay Verma, 'The Experience in India', in Roger Blanpain (ed.), *Law in Motion* (The Hague: Kluwer Law International, 1997); Maja K. Brix, 'The Impact of Judicial Activism in India', unpublished Masters thesis, University of Bergen (June 2004); Peris Jones and Kristian Stokke (eds), *Democratising Development: The Politics of Socio-Economic Rights in South Africa* (Leiden: Martinus Nijhoff, 2005).

3 See Bruce Ackerman, 'The Rise of World Constitutionalism', *Virginia Law Review*, 83 (1997): 771–97; C. Neil Tate and Torbjörn Vallinder (eds), *The Global Expansion of Judicial Power* (New York: New York University Press, 1995); Martin Shapiro and Alec Stone Sweet, *On Law, Politics, and Judicialization* (Oxford: Oxford University Press, 2002); Charles R. Epp, *The Rights Revolution: Lawyers, Activists, and Supreme Courts in Comparative Perspective* (Chicago: University of Chicago Press, 1998); Herbert Jacob et al., *Courts, Law, and Politics in Comparative Perspective* (New Haven: Yale University Press, 1996).

4 Pilar Domingo and Rachel Sieder (eds), *Rule of Law in Latin America: The International Promotion of Judicial Reform* (London: Institute for Latin American Studies, 2001); Thomas C. Heller and Erik G. Jensen (eds), *Beyond Common Knowledge: Empirical Approaches to the Rule of Law* (Stanford: Stanford University Press, 2003).

5 See Maria Dakolias, *Court Performance Around the World: A Comparative Perspective*, World Bank Technical Paper 430 (Washington, DC: The World Bank, 1999); Irwin Stotzky (ed.), *Transition to Democracy in Latin America: The Role of the Judiciary* (Boulder: Westview Press, 1993); Linn Hammergren, *The Politics of Justice and Justice Reform in Latin America* (Boulder: Westview Press, 1998).

6 See Juan E. Méndez, Guillermo O'Donnell, and Paulo Sérgio Pinheiro (eds), *The (Un)Rule of Law and the Underprivileged in Latin America* (Notre Dame: University of Notre Dame Press, 1999); Rudolf Van Puymbroeck, *Comprehensive Legal and Judicial*

Development: Toward an Agenda for a Just and Equitable Society in the 21st Century (Washington, DC: World Bank, 2001).

7 This is Roberto Gargarella's formulation.

8 See András Sajó's chapter in this volume, arguing that in Eastern Europe this phenomenon has benefited the middle class rather than the poor.

9 See Theunis Roux's analysis of the South African Constitutional Court in 'Legitimating Transformation: Political Resource Allocation in the South African Constitutional Court', in Siri Gloppen, Roberto Gargarella and Elin Skaar (eds), *Democratization and the Judiciary: The Accountability Function of Courts in New Democracies* (London: Frank Cass, 2004), p. 92.

10 A court decision aiming to change structured inequalities in South African society, which is prone to ideological controversy over what constitutes morally relevant differences, is the *Khosa* case, in which the Constitutional Court held that permanent residents (with foreign citizenship) are entitled to social assistance on a par with citizens (*Khosa v. Minister of Social Development* 2004 (6) BCLR 569 (CC)). See Julia Sloth-Nielsen, 'Extending Access to Social Assistance to Permanent Residents', *ESR Review* 5/3 (2004), available at <http://communitylawcentre.org.za/ser/esr_review.php>.

11 See Gargarella's chapter in this volume.

12 See Roux, 'Legitimating Transformation'; Shapiro and Stone, *Law, Politics and Judicialization*; Cass R. Sunstein, *Legal Reasoning and Political Conflict* (New York: Oxford University Press, 1996).

13 For the notion of rights as trumps see Ronald Dworkin, *Taking Rights Seriously* (Cambridge, MA: Harvard University Press, 1977).

14 On reasonable disagreement see John Rawls, 'The Idea of Public Reason', in James Bohman and Willam Rehg (eds), *Deliberative Democracy: Essays on Reason and Politics* (Cambridge, MA: The MIT Press, 1997), pp. 93–141.

15 Ronald Dworkin, *Freedom's Law: The Moral Reading of the American Constitution* (Oxford: Oxford University Press, 1996), p. 24.

16 See John Hart Ely, *Democracy and Distrust: A Theory of Judicial Review* (Cambridge, MA: Harvard University Press, 1980).

17 For similar approaches to evaluate the political significance of judgments see Peter von Doepp, 'Comparing the Political Role of the Courts in Zambia and Malawi', paper presented at the ASA annual meeting in New Orleans, 11–14 November 2004, and Gretchen Helmke, *Courts under Constraints: Judges, Generals, and Presidents in Argentina* (Cambridge: Cambridge University Press, 2005).

18 Sally Falk Moore, *Law As Process: An Anthropological Approach* (Oxford: Oxford University Press for the International African Institute, 1978). See also Roberto Gargarella et al., 'The Poor and the Judiciary', application to the Norwegian Research Council (Bergen: Chr. Michelsen Institute, 2004).

19 See Roberto Gargarella, '"Too far removed from the people": Access to Justice for the Poor: The Case of Latin America', UNDP Issue Paper (Bergen: Chr. Michelsen Institute, 2002).

20 Laura Nader, 'Certainties Undone: Fifty Turbulent Years of Legal Anthropology, 1949-1999', *Journal of the Royal Anthropological Institute*, 7 (2001): 95–116.

21 See Gargarella et al., 'Poor and the Judiciary' and Nader, 'Certainties Undone'.

22 Olivia Harris (ed.), *Inside and Outside the Law: Anthropological Studies of Authority and Ambiguity* (London: Routledge & Kegan Paul, 1996).

23 Laura Nader, *No Access to Law: Alternatives to the American Judicial System* (New York: Academic Press, 1980).

24 For the importance of mobilisation from below, see Epp, *The Rights Revolution.*

25 See Hernando de Soto, *The Mystery of Capital: Why Capitalism Triumphs in the West and Fails Everywhere Else* (New York: Basic Books, 2000).

26 See Roux, 'Legitimating Transformation'.

27 Epp, *The Rights Revolution*; Herbert et al., *Courts, Law, and Politics.*

28 Helmke, *Courts under Constraints.*

29 Maurice J.C. Vile, *Constitutionalism and the Separation of Powers* (Oxford: Oxford University Press, 1967); Bruce Ackerman, *We the People: Volume 2: Transformations* (Cambridge, MA: Harvard University Press, 1998).

30 R. Dhavan, R. Sudarshan, and S. Khurshid, *Judges and the Judicial Power* (London: Sweet & Maxwell, 1985).

Chapter 3

The Changing Role of Law and Courts in Latin America: From an Obstacle to Social Change to a Tool of Social Equity

Javier A. Couso

Social Change and Judicial Power

Some time after social scientists became interested in the role that courts can play in strengthening democracy in transitional regimes,[1] the question of whether the judiciary may also contribute to processes of social transformation captured the imagination of those frustrated with the new Latin American democracies' failure to deliver socio-economic progress.[2] Prompted by the widespread poverty, social exclusion, and huge income inequalities that characterise the region,[3] and encouraged by the many international human rights law instruments that concern themselves with so-called 'second generation rights' (that is, rights of a socio-economic nature, such as the right to social security, employment, education, housing and health care),[4] those concerned with social justice are increasingly looking to the courts as potential bearers of reform.[5]

Given the hegemonic status in policy-making circles achieved by neo-classical economic thinking over the last decade and a half,[6] progressive social movements and non-governmental organisations have started to develop rights-based litigation strategies aimed at getting from the courts what the traditional channels of representation – political parties, unions, and the government – seem unable to provide. This trend toward courts, which was inspired by the example of rights-based litigation in developed countries, particularly the United States, takes on different forms and goals, depending on the political and economic background of the region concerned. Thus, while in Eastern Europe litigation has been used to prevent or minimise privatisation processes and the dismantling of the social security schemes inherited from the socialist era,[7] in Latin America (where most states had not developed comprehensive welfare systems before the neo-classical economic trend became dominant), litigation strategies typically aim at getting support from the courts in forcing governments to fulfil their international obligations.

In the case of Latin America, the trend just sketched has overshadowed the remarkable shift towards law and legality among the region's progressive groups over the last generation, which only thirty years ago regarded law and the courts not as an instrument, but as an obstacle to social change. In this chapter, my aim is to show how it was that in Latin America law came to be seen as a tool for social transformation by the very same groups that previously considered it an instrument of social domination. I will then analyse what I take to be the most important challenges and risks stemming from this new approach to social transformation.

The Troubled Role of Law in Latin America's History

Ever since its colonial origins, law has played an important role in Latin America. The main function of law, however, has not been the protection of individual rights against government action, but instead to serve the rulers, first, the Spanish and Portuguese empires, and then, the oligarchic regimes which replaced them after independence.[8]

During the colonial era, imperial law was a fundamental element of governance in what were then remote possessions of two vast empires. As was the norm in continental Europe, law and the courts represented just another expression of royal power. Later, after most of the colonies gained independence, law – specifically constitutional law – was used as a legitimating device by the elites that replaced the colonial administration. In particular, the new rulers used the republican language of the 1787 US Constitution[9] and the French Declaration of the Rights of Man to mark the rejection of their countries' monarchical past. This development did not, however, translate into equal rights for all the population, most of whom remained as excluded from citizenship as before.[10] In the following decades, the hollow rhetoric of liberal-republicanism continued to characterise the legal systems of most Latin American states, which remained in the service of the rulers and the powerful.[11]

This state of affairs only started to improve towards the beginning of the twentieth century, when a handful of countries in the region began to implement at least some of the constitutional rights that had been dormant for most of the previous century. This shift towards the actual implementation of fundamental rights proved, however, to be a painfully incomplete and gradual process, which is indeed still underway a full century later. Analysing the rare instances of actual implementation of constitutional rights in that period, it appears that they were the result, rather than the cause, of political mobilisation and the expansion of electoral democracy.[12] Only when the previously disenfranchised majority managed to accumulate sufficient political power did some of the promises of constitutionalism reach them. This suggests that – at least in Latin America – the actual realisation of the fundamental rights established in constitutional charters and legislation requires that the marginalised are first able to gain a minimum amount of political power.

This necessarily brief sketch gives an idea of how removed from the ideal of social justice law has been in Latin America, and explains the traditional scepticism exhibited in progressive circles about the potential role of law in providing relief to the socially excluded. It was thus not surprising that, when the poor began to organise in unions and left-wing parties, the last arena they looked to in order to advance their aspirations was the legal system. Instead, they turned to unions, progressive political parties, and even the Catholic Church.[13] In hindsight, this appears to have been a realistic approach since in most countries of the region the judiciary was government-dependent, and applied laws whose content by and large reflected the social, economic, and political interests of the privileged.[14] The indifference of early Latin American law toward social justice is illustrated by the paradigmatic example of law in the countries of the region: the various civil codes adopted during the nineteenth century, which were almost exclusively concerned with the legal problems of the propertied classes.[15]

This general description of the social and political context surrounding law and courts in Latin America's history is, of course, a compressed account of a much more complicated story, which includes the occasional social revolution and the rise of populist leaders who sometimes passed social legislation,[16] but even such events did little to fundamentally transform a legal system skewed towards the rich and the powerful. From this state of affairs emerged the traditional perception within progressive circles of law and courts as mostly irrelevant – if not hostile – to social transformation.

If the failure of law and the courts to fulfil the promise of equal treatment contained in constitutional charters and social legislation led Latin American progressives to dismiss liberal legalism as an agent of social transformation, the penetration of Marxist thought during the second half of the century transformed this indifference into outright hostility. Although Marxist thought had always had a presence in the region,[17] its influence in mainstream politics remained marginal until the huge intellectual and political impact of the Cuban Revolution of 1959, which captured the imagination of the left and other progressive circles, completely altering the political landscape of many Latin American countries.[18]

The relevance of Marxist thought eventually led progressive lawyers and jurists to reach the conclusion that law, instead of providing a path for social transformation, was in fact an obstacle to it. This understanding is well represented in Eduardo Novoa Monreal's book *Law as an Obstacle to Social Change* (1975), in which this noted jurist – and key legal adviser to Chile's socialist president Salvador Allende – argued that the problem with the legal system then prevalent in Latin America was that it belonged to an ideological milieu hostile to social reform. In his words:

> It is important to note that all those grand legislative monuments – such as that of the Code Civil – belong to that political ideology of the French Revolution, and are the expression of the triumph of the bourgeoisie over feudal privileges … The Code Civil – and many others – are thus clearly dominated by liberal-individualist conceptions, in tune with the then prevalent bourgeois worldview.[19]

As we can see from this passage, Novoa Monreal thought that the incompatibility of socialism and the law derived from the historical pedigree of the legal systems prevalent in Latin America, that is, nineteenth-century political liberalism. This legal heritage, brought to the twentieth century thanks to the codification process (which had somehow 'frozen' the political and economic ideas of a regime incompatible with socialism), represented in his view an obstacle to the social changes necessary to supersede the profound inequalities characteristic of the region. Given the liberal-individualistic background of Latin American law, Novoa Monreal expressed a great deal of scepticism about 'whether or not it is possible to fully achieve an authentic socialism by the path of respect for juridical models that emanated from men and institutions who considered socialism a system to be absolutely repudiated'.[20]

The disenchantment with liberal legality among Latin American progressives of the time was also apparent in the writings of the Brazilian jurist Roberto Mangabeira Unger,[21] who, in 1975, went even further in the indictment of legality, by noting its compatibility with authoritarianism: 'A second service which the autonomous legal system renders to the authoritarian government is the provision of a formal normative framework which presents authoritarian power as an impersonal normative order and thereby contributes to the legitimation of government action.' [22]

As can be seen from the writings of these two paradigmatic progressive Latin American jurists, the combination of the traditional dissatisfaction with law and the legal system, and the fascination with Marxist thought and the Cuban Revolution, eventually led those on the left to dismiss liberal legality, including the very backbone of the liberal political system, namely, constitutionalism, which had become associated with all the perceived ills of bourgeois democracy. In the words of a leading French socialist author then working in Latin America, Regis Debray: 'Legality, the Institutions, those were not the work of the proletariat; the bourgeoisie formulated the Constitution to suit its own ends ...'[23]

Complementing this frustration with law, progressive Latin American jurists turned a critical eye, both on themselves as a disciplinary community,[24] as well as on the other central actors in the legal drama, namely, judges, who were regarded as an essentially retrograde set of officials administering an equally conservative set of institutions.

A Tragic Path from the Law as an Obstacle to Law as a Tool for Social Justice

The relationship between Latin America's progressive circles and law was radically transformed during the 1980s and 1990s by a series of interrelated events that drastically changed progressives' perception of the legal system. The first and most dramatic of these events was the brutal repression experienced by most Latin American countries during the wave of military regimes that swept through the region during this time.[25] The inhumane practices of these regimes, which included execution without trial, abduction, and widespread torture, eventually led progressive groups to appreciate the role that such ancient legal institutions as due process and *habeas corpus* play in securing the fundamental rights of life and liberty (even if they play no role in ending economic injustice).[26] At this point, it is important to note that, although there was a history of government abuse of individual rights throughout much of Latin America, on this occasion human rights abuses were thoroughly documented and consistently condemned by the international community, that is, the United Nations and a growing network of domestic and international non-governmental organisations, all of which raised public consciousness concerning the unacceptable nature of such behaviour.

An important consequence of the new awareness of civil and political rights among the left in Latin America was that it became hard to condemn the violations of human rights by right-wing military dictatorships in, say, Chile or Argentina, while keeping silent about the repression of workers and dissidents by left-wing dictatorships in places such as Poland or Cuba. In time, this process led scores of former revolutionaries in the region to abandon their radical views in favour of political liberalism.[27] According to this new appreciation of the inherent value of the rule of law and legality, not even the ideal of social equality promised by a socialist revolution could be attained at the cost of violating fundamental human rights.

By the early 1990s, the political panorama in Latin America had been profoundly transformed. After two decades of repressive military regimes, most of the countries in the region enjoyed electoral democracy. In addition to this, revolutionary guerrilla groups were giving up the armed struggle and entering electoral politics.[28] In an unexpected development, however, the return to democracy in Latin America coincided with the demise of the Soviet Union and the consolidation of an ideological shift toward neo-classical economics, institutionalised through what would be labelled the 'Washington consensus', a programme of political and economic reform emphasising the virtues of the free market and privatisation.[29] As an observer of the region put it, the 'consensus' represented the success of a decade-long process of spreading neo-classical economic thought in Latin America, which had begun in the mid seventies, with the control of Chile's economic agenda by the so-called 'Chicago Boys'.[30] A practical consequence of the ascendancy of this sort of economic thought was that in many Latin American countries social and economic policy was increasingly dominated by 'technopols', that is, highly specialised economists deeply committed to privatisation, deregulation, and the technical management of the state.[31]

At the same time that the policy-making arena was inundated by this sort of economic discourse, progressive circles in the region entered the 1990s in a state of disarray and perplexity, in the context of a rapidly changing world in which the word 'globalisation' seemed best to describe the state of affairs.[32] To make matters worse, the new democratic regimes exhibited a weak inclination to try those guilty of the grave human rights violations committed by the military regimes they had just replaced, out of a concern for the risk of an authoritarian regression, or simply through a desire to move beyond the legacy of that complicated era.[33]

In such a disheartening context, the left – by now completely converted to the creed of human rights – concentrated on attempting to reverse the immunity from prosecution enjoyed by most of the perpetrators of the human rights violations committed by the military dictatorships of the 1970s and 1980s. Joining organisations that had emerged during the authoritarian regimes to defend those persecuted by the military, they turned to the courts to challenge the policies on prosecution that most Latin American governments had adopted. In this struggle, domestic human rights organisations worked in concert with sister organisations in the developed world.[34] Although at first the nature of the collaboration was mostly financial, with the latter channelling economic support to their Latin American counterparts,[35] in time a process of institutional learning by the former became evident as these NGOs began to adopt the discourse and the judicial techniques of their northern partners, such as Amnesty International or Human Rights Watch. This shift from financial and logistical support to the wholesale transplantation of a legal ideology was gradual, but profound. Thanks to this co-operation, the often silent but persistent work against the immunity from prosecution enjoyed by former perpetrators of human rights violations eventually bore fruit, as illustrated by the case of Argentina (where an appellate court declared the laws establishing immunity unconstitutional), and Chile (where General Pinochet was indicted and prosecuted as a result of a lawsuit brought by victims of human rights violations).

The relative success of this strategy of getting from the courts what had been denied by the regular political process encouraged these groups to pursue the same strategy with regard to the promotion of social and economic rights.[36] Thus, toward the mid 1990s, many of the same organisations that had been strong advocates of prosecuting the perpetrators of gross human rights violations decided to use the courts in pursuit of a broader agenda, which included the implementation of constitutionally protected rights to employment, social security, education, housing, environmental protection, and health care.[37] In a scenario in which mainstream political parties had by and large accepted or tolerated neo-classical economic policies, progressive sectors opposed to these policies became attracted to the possibility of framing their social-democratic aspirations as fundamental human rights. The adoption of this strategy to challenge a hegemonic economic ideology also had the following advantage: it transformed what was until then merely a political preference into a moral imperative. Significantly, the arena in which the struggle for these ideas would be played out shifted from traditional party-politics to the courts.

A good example of the new strategy can be found in the writings of Manuel Antonio Garretón, a Chilean sociologist who had been a supporter of Salvador Allende's socialist administration. In a piece written in the mid 1990s, he depicted the expansion of human rights discourse in Latin America from civil and political rights to social and economic rights as a natural progression in the process of democratic consolidation, inevitably following the struggle to defend the right to life during dictatorial times and the fight against impunity in the early transitional era. In his words:

> In democratic consolidation, the issue of finishing immunity ['nunca más'] takes on prospective connotations, encompassing not only the avoidance of authoritarian regressions but also the desire to improve life according to the ethical principles embodied in the concept of human rights ... Another question worth considering is whether it is possible to reformulate the human rights problem beyond the definition – made necessary under military regimes – of the 'right to life' in terms of survival and physical integrity ... Here, questions regarding education, work, poverty, inequality, and access to justice begin to play a primary role in the transcendence of barriers to the extension of human rights to the entire population.[38]

Garretón's call to reformulate the powerful rhetoric of human rights to include not only the defence of traditional civil and political liberties, but also socio-economic rights, had the virtue of giving progressives the upper moral hand vis-à-vis neo-classical economic thought, projecting the moral authority achieved by civil and political rights to those of a social and economic nature.[39] A crucial consequence of this move was that it suddenly transformed what was then regarded as a discredited ideology – social democracy – into a moral truth.

The indictment of neo-classical economic thought implicit in this expanded human rights discourse received international legitimacy in 1993 when, at the United Nations World Conference on Human Rights, the Committee on Economic Social and Cultural Rights issued a statement asserting the fundamental status of 'positive rights'. In the account provided by Makau wa Mutua, an international law scholar critical of this move:

> [The] Committee lamented that the massive violations of economic and social rights would have provoked 'horror and outrage' if they had occurred to civil and political rights ... [and noted] that it was 'inhumane, distorted and incompatible with international standards' to exclude one fifth of the global population which suffered from poverty, hunger, disease, illiteracy, and insecurity from human rights concerns.[40]

This statement is revealing because, after first acknowledging that 'free markets ... have been chosen by a large percentage of the population', it dismisses that democratic preference on the same grounds as traditional human rights doctrine denies the legitimacy of a political majority to, say, order the extermination of a minority. Thus, the argument seems to run, economic and social rights should be considered to have the same status as civil and political rights, and therefore the courts should defend them even against the will of the majority. This would make social and economic rights true constitutional 'trumps',[41] the application of which is not dependent on political power, but on sound judicial interpretation.

The Social-Democratic Basis of Social and Economic Rights

In the preceding sections I have described the process by which Latin American progressive groups shifted from deep scepticism about the emancipatory potential of the law and courts, to the opposite view. This rather remarkable change of perspective – in which the judiciary is expected to deliver the social transformation that the ordinary political system seems unable to provide – is not simply the result of the extension of the previous work done by progressive movements in the domain of civil and political rights to that of social and economic rights, but represents a natural response to a scenario dominated by the ideological and structural constraints which neo-classical thought and economic globalisation currently impose on the countries of the region. While this process accounts for the 'demand-side' of court-triggered social transformation, the 'supply-side' is explained by the remarkable development experienced by international human rights law over the last few decades. Indeed, at the same time as progressive circles in Latin America were being converted to law, the human rights organisations of the United Nations were slowly – but steadily – working on the elaboration of a number of human rights instruments of a social and economic nature, which provided the progressive agenda not only with moral legitimacy, but also with justiciable law.

The construction of a comprehensive institutional framework specifying and providing enforcement mechanisms for social and economic rights (whose origins can be traced to the adoption of the relevant social and economic provisions of the Universal Declaration of Human Rights in 1948), has been remarkably slow, and was only completed toward the late 1980s, when a large number of complementary treaties and protocols entered into full operation.[42] The temporal gap just noted is relevant, since in the forty years that elapsed between the time when social and economic rights were first accepted as fundamental human rights worthy of protection and the time the United Nations enforcement mechanisms were put in place, the ideological environment changed dramatically. In a process reminiscent of Ronald Dworkin's dictum that law is, among other things, 'frozen politics',[43] the set of international human rights norms of a socio-economic nature contained in both the Universal Declaration of Human Rights and the International Covenant on Economic, Social and Cultural Rights, represent the legal expression of the economic thought of an era whose time has passed.

At the domestic level something similar occurred, as those Latin American countries that had not already included social rights provisions in their constitutions[44] have included them in the last few decades,[45] in order to make their domestic constitutional law more compatible with international human rights law on social and economic rights. In consequence, most of the domestic constitutional law in the region now includes social and economic rights, which are incompatible with neo-classical economics, the dominant ideology among the technocratic managers who run economic policy in most countries in the region.

While a rigorous demonstration of the social-democratic roots of human rights law dealing with social and economic issues would require in-depth research on the intellectual and political background of the most crucial actors who participated in the design of the first social and economic rights documents, it seems clear that the intellectual climate prevalent at the time of the drafting of the Universal Declaration of Human Rights was highly sympathetic to the notion that the state ought to intervene in the economy to protect the marginalised.[46] At this point it is important to note that the term 'social-democratic' is not used in a technical way, but instead alludes to the then prevalent notion that it was proper for the government to intervene in the economy in order to ensure full employment and to create the building blocks of a welfare state protecting individuals from such social risks as hunger, old age, poor health, and lack of housing and education. In fact, it is possible to identify a number of intellectual and historical sources other than social democracy that contributed to the consensus regarding the legitimacy and urgency of strong 'positive' state action in favour of the poor, such as Catholic Social Doctrine thought, Bismarkean notions of state-financed social security, and the 'progressive' movement of the United States, among others. For all their differences, these doctrines shared a strong rejection of laissez-faire economics, and agreed that human rights were not limited to civil and political rights, as nineteenth-century liberalism would have it.

In addition to the intellectual sources just mentioned, there was an individual human element in shaping the Universal Declaration of Human Rights' provisions on social and economic rights that is sometimes overlooked. This is the crucial role played by Franklin Delano Roosevelt's wife, Eleanor, in the drafting and following up of the document. Indeed, as has been amply documented, not only did Ms Roosevelt preside over the drafting of the Universal Declaration of Human Rights, but she was also in charge of the process leading to the enactment of the protocols that complemented the text. In fact, her participation represented a direct link between New Deal thinking and the social and economic aspects of international human rights law.

The link between New Deal thought and that of the Universal Declaration of Human Rights is apparent when one contrasts Articles 22 to 26 of the latter, which are precisely those most related to economic rights, with the rhetoric of the American New Deal, as expressed by Franklin Delano Roosevelt's famous speech of 1941, in which he summarised his economic philosophy. Indeed, as we shall see below, Roosevelt's expansion of the liberal idea of 'freedom from fear' (of government abuse, typical of classical political liberal thought) to the economic and social realm, what he called 'freedom from want', permeates the following clauses of the Universal Declaration of Human Rights:

> Article 22: Everyone, as a member of society, has the right to social security and is entitled to realization, through national effort and international co-operation and in accordance with the organization and resources of each State, of the economic, social

and cultural rights indispensable for his dignity and the free development of his personality.

Article 23: (1) Everyone has the right to work, to free choice of employment, to just and favourable conditions of work and to protection against unemployment.

(2) Everyone, without any discrimination, has the right to equal pay for equal work.

(3) Everyone who works has the right to just and favourable remuneration ensuring for himself and his family an existence worthy of human dignity, and supplemented, if necessary, by other means of social protection.

(4) Everyone has the right to form and to join trade unions for the protection of his interests.

Article 24: Everyone has the right to rest and leisure, including reasonable limitation of working hours and periodic holidays with pay.

Article 25: (1) Everyone has the right to a standard of living adequate for the health and well-being of himself and of his family, including food, clothing, housing and medical care and necessary social services, and the right to security in the event of unemployment, sickness, disability, widowhood, old age or other lack of livelihood in circumstances beyond his control.

(2) Motherhood and childhood are entitled to special care and assistance. All children, whether born in or out of wedlock, shall enjoy the same social protection.

Article 26: (1) Everyone has the right to education. Education shall be free, at least in the elementary and fundamental stages. Elementary education shall be compulsory. Technical and professional education shall be made generally available and higher education shall be equally accessible to all on the basis of merit.

(2) Education shall be directed to the full development of the human personality and to the strengthening of respect for human rights and fundamental freedoms. It shall promote understanding, tolerance and friendship among all nations, racial or religious groups, and shall further the activities of the United Nations for the maintenance of peace.

(3) Parents have a prior right to choose the kind of education that shall be given to their children.

These clauses, which comprise the bulk of the social and economic aspects of the Universal Declaration of Human Rights, are in fact strikingly reminiscent of Roosevelt's most famous speech, in which he outlined his New Deal proposal for the United States:

> We have come to a clear realization of the fact that individual freedom cannot exist without economic security and independence ... We have accepted, so to speak, a second bill of rights, under which a new basis of security and prosperity can be established for all – regardless of station, race, or creed. Among these are: The right to a useful and remunerative job in the industries, or shops, or farms, or mines of the Nation; The right to earn enough to provide adequate food and clothing and recreation; The right of every farmer to raise and sell his products at a return which will give him and his family a

> decent living ... The right of every family to a decent home; The right to adequate medical care and the opportunity to achieve and enjoy good health; The right to adequate protection from the economic fears of old age, sickness, accident, and unemployment; The right to a good education. All of these rights spell security. And after this war is won we must be prepared to move forward in the implementation of these rights, to new goals of human happiness and well being.

As can be seen from these two sets of excerpts, both the social and economic clauses of the Universal Declaration and Roosevelt's New Deal agenda represent a stark rejection of laissez-faire economic thought, and the notion that liberalism is only concerned with the potential abuses that government may inflict on individuals. In contrast with this idea, the sort of social-liberalism embraced by the Roosevelts and the United Nations document calls for an active role for the state in helping the disadvantaged and the poor to overcome the fear of want.

At this point, it is worth noting that this agenda, although hegemonic at the time, was not without its opponents, as the rejection by some countries of the social and economic rights provisions in the Universal Declaration of Human Rights demonstrates.[47] More relevant to our discussion, both Roosevelt's speech and the clauses transcribed above would most likely be rejected by Latin American economists and policy-makers today, given the hegemony currently enjoyed by neo-classical economic thought (which owes much to the likes of Friedrich Hayek and Milton Friedman, who spent their intellectual lives opposing state intervention in the economy, as advocated by European social democracy in the case of the former, and New Deal economics in the case of the latter).

At any rate, the intellectual environment has changed so much since the mid-1940s that even the United States (then the leading Western nation championing the incorporation of social and economic rights in the Universal Declaration of Human Rights) now adamantly opposes the ratification of the International Covenant on Economic, Social, and Cultural Rights, as well as other international human rights instruments containing social and economic rights, such as the Convention on the Rights of the Child.

Context and Risks of Court-triggered Social Transformation in Latin America

In the preceding sections I have identified four important elements that in my view explain current expectations about court-triggered social transformation in Latin America. These are: (a) the persistence of widespread poverty and huge social and economic inequalities that have historically characterised Latin America, even after the return to democracy in most countries of the region; (b) the discovery of law and the courts by progressives, and their hope that rights-based litigation can produce the social and economic transformation that the political system has failed to bring about; (c) the completion of a long drawn-out and gradual process of institutionalisation of social and economic rights, both within the United Nations system and in the constitutional law of most countries of the region, providing progressive groups with moral legitimacy and actual legal mechanisms to demand the implementation of these rights; and (d) the hegemony achieved by neo-classical economic thought in policy circles in the region, making the courts an attractive arena to those interested in processes of social transformation.

This rather peculiar combination of legal and political factors explains Latin American progressives' current focus on courts. The remaining question is whether their expectations are likely to be satisfied, in other words, whether social transformation can indeed be achieved through the courts in Latin America. It is, of course, still too soon to know the answer to this question for certain. This should not, however, preclude us from pointing out the risks associated with this strategy. In what follows, I analyse some basic features of the current scenario before concluding on a cautionary note about the possibilities of court-driven social transformation.

The first important aspect of the scenario just described is that it represents a clash of perspectives between those concerned with social and economic rights, typically human rights lawyers and activists, and those concerned with economic development, most of the technopols who dominate policy-making in Latin America. This is not merely a confrontation between two different 'epistemic communities' (lawyers and economists), but also a contest between two views within the discipline of economics itself, given that international human rights law embodies an economic philosophy 'frozen' in time from the mid-twentieth century (in the form of social-democratic, social-Christian, or 'New Deal' thought). This philosophy has been 'transported' into our time by the social and economic provisions of the Universal Declaration of Human Rights and the International Covenant on Economic, Social and Cultural Rights, which are now incompatible with some of the core principles of contemporary mainstream economic thinking.

One practical consequence of this clash of approaches is the difficulty that human rights lawyers have in finding common ground with the army of technopols who populate most Latin American central banks and finance ministries, with the former claiming that social and economic rights are moral imperatives not subject to policy compromise, and the latter arguing that the economic philosophy underlying those rights is either outdated or no longer feasible. In this scenario, when, say, human rights lawyers call for the immediate implementation of the right to employment, neo-classical policy-makers are likely to respond that for full employment to happen, the rights of working people to a living wage ought to be scrapped, because in order to get the former you need to get rid of the latter.

The complexity of this tension can be illustrated by the following example. Suppose a country follows a version of the neo-classical economic model which is actually capable of reducing unemployment and of dramatically reducing poverty, but it does so at the cost of establishing a set of rules, such as labour flexibility, privatisation of social security, and free trade, which leads to wages that maintain most families just above the poverty line with high levels of social insecurity. This is precisely the story of the Chilean economy over the last fifteen years since its return to democracy. When the democratic regime was reinstated in 1990 – after seventeen years of military dictatorship – the proportion of Chileans living in poverty was over 45 per cent of the population (approximately five million people). Over the next 14 years, however, the largely neo-classical economic model inherited by the democratic government managed to reduce the poverty rate to less than 20 per cent, a rather remarkable achievement in a region where most countries have failed to reduce poverty at all.[48] The problem with this picture, however, is that while the Chilean government was able to reduce poverty, the poverty level still remains unacceptably high, especially given that there are very few social safety nets. Still worse, although poverty has been dramatically reduced, the rate of reduction has diminished over the last few years, which suggests that it will be much harder to completely eradicate poverty. Finally, even though there have been important advances in poverty reduction, the embarrassingly high income-inequality that characterises the country remains exactly as it was almost two decades ago.

As the example of Chile suggests, the interaction between social and economic rights, conceived with the economic knowledge of some sixty years ago, and current conditions, makes things complicated, suggesting that a more fluid dialogue between human rights law and economics is necessary. This, however, seems highly unlikely in Latin America, where economists and human rights lawyers do not usually speak to each other. This state of affairs, in which policy-makers impose their neo-classical prescriptions without much public deliberation, prompting human rights lawyers to go to the courts in order to make their case, resembles a creditor who, tired of arguing with a reluctant debtor, utters a defiant 'see you in court', with the hope that the conflict will be settled there once and for all. The problem with this strategy, however, is that, even if on occasion successful, the use by the human rights community of the 'trump' provided by social and economic rights over matters of policy exposes progressive groups to the risk of gradually disengaging from the contemporary economic debate, thus leaving the field exclusively to the neo-classical camp, which is only too happy to avoid substantive debate over the relative strengths of the 'social-democratic' or 'neo-classical' approaches to social and economic problems.

Another element at the background, which complicates court-triggered social transformation in Latin America, has to do with the operation of the judiciary. Given that the very logic of adjudication leads the courts to concentrate exclusively on the legal merit of a claim (in this case, the applicability of a given social or economic right), and not on the economic rationality of a given legal rule, there is always the risk that a judicial decision will have unintended consequences for the economy as a whole, which exposes courts to the accusation by mainstream economists that they are imposing old-fashioned and discredited policies.

Lastly, it is worth noting that, to expect courts to play a central role in processes of social transformation, as if they were completely isolated from their political, social and cultural context is, at least in the case of Latin America, overly optimistic. This is particularly true with regard to economic matters in developing countries, which are usually exposed to devastating crises. If you add to this highly constrained economic and political context an active judicial enforcement of a set of social and economic rights often in contradiction with the policies considered by contemporary policy-makers as sound economic policy, the resulting mixture can be explosive.

Conclusion

The notion that social transformation can be achieved through the judicial enforcement of social and economic rights is now widespread in Latin American law schools and non-governmental organisations. This attitude represents a remarkable shift in perspective within the region's progressive groups, which only a generation ago regarded law and courts as institutions at the service of the powerful and privileged. Such a dramatic change of view is rooted in both the re-valorisation of legality by those sectors in the face of the widespread human rights violations during the brutal military regimes that swept the region during the 1970s and 1980s, and the demonstration-effect of successful experiences of court-triggered social transformation in some developed countries.

Recourse to the courts by groups interested in advancing social justice in Latin America was also prompted by the fact that, precisely when progressive groups had started to look at law and courts with a different eye, international human rights law achieved an unprecedented level of institutional maturity, thanks to the establishment of new enforcement bodies and protocols, and the penetration of social and economic rights into the domestic constitutional law of most countries in the region. This new, more favourable, scenario for the use of the courts in order to achieve social justice severely contrasted with the growing dominance that neo-classical economic thinking achieved within policy-making circles and political discourse, all of which made the appeal to the powerful rhetoric of human rights one of the last viable options for progressive groups in Latin America.

Even if understandable, the appeal of legal mobilisation strategies to those in favour of social transformation may be exaggerated, as the experience of countries with a more extensive history of judicial activism suggests. This seems particularly to be the case with regard to social and economic rights, which are so intimately related to economic policy-making, a domain that has traditionally been left to the political process. Given the current hegemony of neo-classical economic thought within policy-making circles in Latin America, and the fact that this approach clashes head on with the social-democratic ideas embodied in social and economic rights, anyone expecting the courts to bring about social justice should be aware that this is a problematic proposition.

Notes

1 Irwin Stotzky (ed.), *Transition to Democracy in Latin America: The Role of the Judiciary* (Boulder: Westview Press, 1993).
2 I take social transformation to mean 'the altering of structured inequalities and power relations in society in ways that reduce the weight of morally irrelevant circumstances', as Roberto Gargarella defines it in this volume.
3 Juan E. Méndez, Guillermo O'Donnell, and Paulo Sérgio Pinheiro (eds), *The (Un)Rule of Law and the Underprivileged in Latin America* (Notre Dame: University of Notre Dame Press, 1999).
4 Henry J. Steiner and Philip Alston, *International Human Rights in Context: Law, Politics, Morals* (Oxford: Clarendon Press, 1996).
5 Víctor Abramovich and Christian Courtis, *Los Derechos Sociales como Derechos Exigibles* (Madrid: Trotta, 2002).
6 Yves Dezalay and Bryant Garth, *The Internationalization of Palace Wars: Lawyers, Economists, and the Contest to Transform Latin American States* (Chicago: University of Chicago Press, 2002).
7 See Sajó's chapter in this volume.
8 For an account of the way in which law was used by the Spanish Empire to manage its overseas territories, see J.H. Parry, *The Spanish Seaborne Empire* (Berkeley: University of California Press, 1990) and Magali Sarfatti, *Spanish Bureaucratic-Patrimonialism in America* (Berkeley: Institute of International Studies of the University of California at Berkeley, 1966).
9 As people familiar with the history of the relations between the United States and Latin America know, constitutional law lay at the core of the very first contact between them. The American Constitution served as the blueprint for the new republican constitutions adopted by most Latin American nations after gaining independence from Spain.
10 According to an astute observer of Latin America's history, Brian Loveman: 'In the first seventy or more years after independence, Spanish Americans wrote constitutions, proclaiming popular sovereignty while military officers, brigands, would-be national saviors, and aristocrats sought to impose order on peoples tormented by despotism, instability, and misery. Called caudillos, these personalistic leaders of small military bands or national armies came and went in Mexico, Central America, the Caribbean, and South America.' Brian Loveman, *The Constitution of Tyranny: Regimes of Exception in Spanish America* (Pittsburgh: University of Pittsburgh Press, 1993), p. 4.
11 Loveman also points out that in spite of the liberal constitutional rhetoric, during the nineteenth century 'the enumeration of civil liberties and rights was routinely accompanied, in constitutions, legislation, and decrees, by provisions for their suspension or restriction in times of political crises' (ibid., p. 5).
12 For an account of this process as it played out in Chile, see J. Samuel Valenzuela, *Democratización vía Reforma: La Expansión del Sufragio en Chile* (Buenos Aires: Ediciones del IDES, 1985).
13 See David Collier and Ruth Collier, *Shaping the Political Arena: Critical Junctures, the Labor Movement, and Regimes Dynamics in Latin America* (Princeton: Princeton University Press, 1991) and Samuel Valenzuela, 'The Chilean Labor Movement: The

Institutionalization of Conflict', in Arturo Valenzuela and Samuel Valenzuela (eds), *Chile: Politics and Society* (New Brunswick, NJ: Transaction Books, 1976).

14 Of course, such a simplified account of the substantive content of Latin American law does not represent the whole story after more than half a century of social legislation approved by populists or social-democratic administrations all over the region, but was certainly prevalent among the increasingly radicalised left of the 1960s and early 1970s.

15 Such an approach to law would in time be complemented and refined by Marxist thought, according to which the legal system was merely a super-structural feature of a profoundly unjust capitalist regime.

16 The Mexican Revolution (1910), and the populist administration of Juan Domingo Perón (1946-1955) in Argentina come to mind.

17 Marxist thought has had a presence since the turn of the century, when anarchist groups started to dominate the then nascent workers' organisations.

18 The influence of the Cuban Revolution was indeed profound and cut across all Latin America. As Katherine Hite has put it: 'The Cuban Revolution ... influenced political discourse and political behavior in ways unparalleled in the hemisphere. In some Latin American countries, such as Argentina, Uruguay, and Guatemala, the Cuban example inspired revolutionary guerrilla movements. In Chile, the Cuban revolution informed left discourse and debate that questioned the feasibility of a peaceful transition to socialism, as well as the need for a prolonged 'bourgeois democratic' phase to oversee capitalist industrialisation and modernization.' Katherine Hite, *When the Romance Ended: Leaders of the Chilean Left, 1968-1998* (New York: Columbia University Press, 2000), p. 30.

19 Eduardo Novoa Monreal, *El Derecho Como Obstáculo al Cambio Social* (México: Editorial Siglo Veintiuno, 1975), p. 20.

20 Novoa Monreal, quoted in John Gardner, *Legal Imperialism: American Lawyers and Foreign Aid in Latin America* (Madison: University of Wisconsin Press, 1980), p. 180.

21 He later emigrated to the United States to become one of the intellectual leaders of the Critical Legal Studies Movement.

22 Quoted by Gardner, *Legal Imperialism*, p. 122.

23 Quoted by Gardner, *Legal Imperialism*, p. 182.

24 'Lawyers have no solutions to offer', complained Eduardo Novoa Monreal bitterly. 'The lawyer not only remains isolated from the great social movements which are bettering the quality of life for all men but ... the lawyer generally demonstrates a total incapacity to contribute anything to these changes.' Quoted in Gardner, *Legal Imperialism*, p. 146.

25 As Elizabeth Jelin puts it: 'In Latin America states that gained legitimacy and social consensus on the basis of their active role in the provision of services, issues of political democracy and civil rights were pushed into the background. In cultural terms even the tension between civil rights and social rights took on the appearance of antinomy: social justice versus formal justice ... The situation began to change, however, in the 1970s. The struggle against military dictatorships and for democracy created space for the demand of political rights; massive violations of human rights created a new language, a new code. Until this time, the ideal of citizenship had barely extended beyond urban, educated middle class men. But now the surge of popular mobilization and social movements, of feminism and women's movements, of indigenous organizations and urban mobilization.' Elizabeth Jelin, 'Citizenship Revisited: Solidarity, Responsibility, and Rights', in Elizabeth Jelin and Eric Hershberg (eds), *Constructing Democracy:*

Human Rights, Citizenship, and Society in Latin America (Boulder: Westview Press, 1996), p. 108.

26 The levels of state violence reached during the military regimes of the 1970s and early 1980s were in fact unprecedented, or at least they seemed so for those who experienced persecution. This led intellectuals on the left to pay attention to the idea of human rights, in particular the right to life. In the words of a prominent analyst of the region: 'It is worth noting at the outset that human rights are basically historical-cultural constructs centering on the right to life ... [concerning] the problem of life in its elemental, almost biological dimension of survival or physical integrity.' Manuel Antonio Garretón, 'Human Rights in Democratization Processes', in Jelin and Hershberg (eds), *Constructing Democracy*, pp. 39–40.

27 See Jorge Castañeda, *Utopia Unarmed: The Latin American Left After the Cold War* (New York: Alfred Knopf, 1993).

28 Writing in 1992, Skidmore and Smith also recognised the diminishing pull of guerrilla activity in Latin America after the collapse of the USSR: 'To be sure, some [guerrilla] movements remained unflinching in the face of doctrinal adversity – such as Sendero Luminoso in Peru – but most began to revise their outlooks in accordance with the "social-democratic" ideas spread in Europe and elsewhere ... The end of the Cold War implied a change in the ideological content of reformist and radical movements in Latin America. The collapse of international communism struck a near-fatal blow to socialist and communist doctrines and organizations throughout the region. Adherence to Marxism appeared to be a certain prescription for rejection and defeat.' Thomas Skidmore and Peter Smith, *Modern Latin America* 3rd edn (New York: Oxford University Press, 1992), pp. 376–7. Since these words were written, Sendero Luminoso has been disbanded and guerrilla activity has almost completely ceased in Peru.

29 As described by Verónica Montecinos, the 'Washington consensus' reflected 'a widely shared agreement among economists on the desirability of market-oriented reforms'. Paraphrasing J. Williamson, Montecinos reports that 'the consensus stressed the need to secure property rights, reduce government regulations, promote market competition, exports, fiscal discipline and the privatization of state enterprises, and encourage financial and trade liberalization'. Véronica Montecinos, *Economists, Politics and the State: Chile 1958-1994* (Amsterdam: CEDLA, 1998), p. 4.

30 'In the 1980s, militant conservative ideologies invigorated the spread of the neoliberal paradigm. The devastating impact of the debt crisis favored the emergence of pragmatic revisionism among most economists in the region.' Montecinos, *Economists, Politics and the State*, p. 4.

31 Describing these technocratic leaders, Jorge Domínguez writes: 'Democratic technopols in Latin America in the 1990s chose freer markets for both political and economic reasons. In economic terms, freer markets are typically a part of the professional training of most technopols; that has changed little. In politics, democratic technopols have come to appreciate that freer markets permit less room for arbitrary state actions.' Jorge I. Domínguez (ed.), *Technopols: Freeing Politics and Markets in Latin America in the 1990s* (University Park, Penn.: Pennsylvania State University Press, 1997), p. 12.

32 Ricardo Piglia summarised the state of mind of progressives in Latin America at the time when he noted that '[p]ostmodernism means the poor are wrong'. Cited in John Beverley and José Oviedo, 'Introduction', in John Beverley, José Oviedo and Michael Aronna (eds), *The Postmodernism Debate in Latin America* (Durham: Duke University Press, 1995), p. 3.

33 This was the case in Peru, Chile, Brazil and Uruguay, where the new democratic governments did little to prosecute the perpetrators of human rights violations under the military regimes. In Argentina, in which the government of President Alfonsín at first showed a remarkable willingness to try people accused of gross human rights violations, pressure from the military eventually led his government to pass legislation severely limiting this policy.

34 As described by Katherine Sikkink, who has worked widely on the transnational network of human rights NGOs: 'A Latin American human rights network emerged in the past two decades as a response to the increasing level of gross violations of human rights throughout the hemisphere in the 1970s. In particular, the coups in Chile and Uruguay in 1973, the coup in Argentina in 1976, and the upsurge of repression in Brazil in the late 1970s were key turning points for the formation of the human rights network … This process was given impetus by the concomitant emergence and growth of the human rights movement in the United States and Europe.' Kathryn Sikkink, 'The Emergence, Evolution, and Effectiveness of the Latin American Human Rights Network', in Jelin and Hershberg (eds), *Constructing Democracy*, p. 78.

35 As Sikkink points out: 'Other foundations, as well as government funding agencies in Europe and the United States, have also initiated programs funding human rights. By the early 1990s, a group of fifteen to twenty major US private foundations were making regular grants for human rights work, while another twenty foundations gave occasional support.' Ibid., pp. 67–8.

36 In Sikkink's words: 'Today the human rights movement in Latin America is confronting a period of transition and challenge … the challenge facing the network is the need to continually adapt its definitions and strategies to the changing global and regional context. Most of the human rights situations in the hemisphere are no longer gross violations of human rights by a military dictatorship but, rather, the more difficult and complex problem of human rights violations under various types of elected regimes.' Ibid., pp. 68–9.

37 'One dilemma currently facing the human rights movement is that it may have become too dependent on foundation funding … human rights groups in the Southern Cone, which are no longer perceived as priorities in the funding community, have experienced a significant decrease in external funding over the past five years … [N]on governmental human rights organizations have responded to this changing human rights situation by addressing new targets and developing new themes and tactics. New themes that have taken on importance in the human rights movement of the 1990s include issues of impunity, rights violations committed both by governments and by insurgents in situations of armed conflict; and rights violations of especially vulnerable groups such as women, children, homosexuals, and indigenous peoples.' Ibid., p. 70. This was the case with CELS, an Argentinean non-governmental organisation that had been at the forefront of the defence of human rights during the military regime of 1976–83, and showed a remarkable capacity to adjust to the new era, by increasingly expanding its mandate to social and economic rights, while continuing its struggle against impunity.

38 Garretón, 'Human Rights in Democratization Processes', p. 53.

39 Which are typically understood to stand in opposition to neo-liberal economics.

40 See Makau wa Mutua, 'The Ideology of Human Rights', *Virginia Journal of International Law*, 36 (1995–96): 589–657.

41 In Ronald Dworkin's familiar terminology. See Dworkin *Taking Rights Seriously* (Cambridge, MA: Harvard University Press, 1977).

42 For a good description of this process, see Matthew C.R. Craven, *The International Covenant on Economic, Social and Cultural Rights: A Perspective on its Development* (Oxford: Clarendon Press, 1995).
43 Ronald Dworkin, *Law's Empire* (Cambridge, MA: Harvard University Press, 1986) elaborates on the notion of law as 'past political decisions'.
44 Such as Mexico, Chile and Uruguay, which included social and economic rights clauses in their constitutions in the first decades of the twentieth century,
45 Brazil (in 1988) and Colombia (in 1991) enacted new constitutional charters, which included new social and economic rights.
46 This explains why someone like Friedrich Hayek – one of the founding fathers of neo-classical economics – was so isolated from mainstream politics at the time of the writing of his indictment of state intervention in the economy. See F.A. Hayek, *The Road to Serfdom* (London: Routledge, 1944).
47 In fact, the social orientation of those provisions shocked the South African delegation, which abstained in the final vote, arguing that such social and economic rights should never have been part of the Universal Declaration. See Jaime Oraá, 'La Declaración Universal de Derechos Humanos', in Felipe Gómez Isa and José Manuel Puerza (eds), *La Protección Internacional de los Derechos Humanos en los Albores del Siglo XXI* (Bilbao, Spain: Universidad de Deusto, 2003), p. 142.
48 For a good description of Chile's economic model and performance, see Ricardo Ffrench-Davis, *Economic Reforms in Chile: From Dictatorship to Democracy* (Ann Arbor: University of Michigan Press, 2002).

PART 2
Case Studies

Chapter 4

Social Rights as Middle-Class Entitlements in Hungary: The Role of the Constitutional Court

András Sajó

Introduction

This chapter discusses the Hungarian Constitutional Court's jurisprudence on social rights, and argues that it has favoured the post-communist middle classes. By 'post-communist middle classes' I mean those groups that depend on various forms of income redistribution, and do not have sufficient independent means to buy basic services, like healthcare, in case of need.

There are at least two different types of activities that courts might engage in when adjudicating social rights claims:

- A strong centralised constitutional court with the power to review legislative and executive conduct for constitutionality against an entrenched bill of rights may shape social welfare policies.
- In less centralised systems, the ordinary courts may consider specific social rights claims and enforce the existing statutory system of entitlements. Here the courts' primary role is to apply considerations of fairness and due process (as is the case, for example, in the United States).

These two activities, of course, are not mutually exclusive. However, in the post-communist countries, centralised constitutional courts have played a decisive role. The powers conferred on these courts have enabled them, on the one hand, to develop or interpret away social rights, and, on the other, to set conditions for the implementation of such rights (including their non-enforcement). Eastern European constitutional courts have in this way been able to shape social policies but, at least in countries like Hungary, where there is a nearly complete separation between ordinary courts and the Hungarian Constitutional Court, they have not had the power to force the authorities to carry out their policy decisions.

The analysis of the Hungarian Constitutional Court's social rights jurisprudence that follows considers three possible explanations for the direction it has taken: the form of review (that is, abstract or concrete), the Court's understanding of its institutional role, and the substantive values cherished by the Court.

The form of review is an important determinant of a court's approach to social rights. In some countries, constitutional questions arise in the course of an actual case or controversy, where specific remedies, including the supervision of court orders, are almost inevitable. In the case of abstract review, on the other hand, such remedies are unlikely, although courts may go to great lengths in prescribing appropriate methods of carrying out welfare policies.

The Hungarian Constitutional Court (hereinafter 'the HCC' or 'the Court') has abstract review powers only. As a result, it has generally been able to avoid considering the consequences and feasibility of its decisions, in stark contrast to the experience of constitutional courts in countries like India and South Africa, where social rights cases typically arise in the form of concrete disputes. Like other East European constitutional courts, the HCC is not required to evaluate the standard of services provided to actual rights holders, or to consider how its decisions will be implemented. In practice, of course, the HCC's decisions *have* had important consequences, including a dramatic increase in personal income tax.[1] But this result has been the indirect consequence of the Court's preference for protecting existing welfare entitlements rather than the outcome of a deliberate strategy.

Another important determinant of a constitutional court's approach to social rights is its perception of its institutional role, in particular, the view taken by the court of its relationship to the political branches. There are a number of standard objections to judicial policy-making based on the separation of powers doctrine and democratic theory. Additional objections are primarily of a prudential nature, and refer to these courts' lack of human and other resources to develop and administer social welfare policies over time.

A third possible factor explaining judicial treatment of social rights is more substantive, and concerns how judges' value systems, and in particular their conceptions of justice, impact on social rights adjudication.[2]

In this chapter I shall argue that, notwithstanding some activist features in the jurisprudence of certain post-communist constitutional courts, the performance of these courts does not offer much hope regarding the possibilities of judicial anti-poverty politics. In fact, the study of social rights cases in post-communist countries indicates that, where these courts have been sympathetic to such rights at all, their main concern has been to protect existing entitlements. The Hungarian Constitutional Court, in particular, has been reluctant to extend social rights protection to marginalised groups not already protected by legislation (for example, those without housing or permanent shelter).[3]

In order to address the specific question of the judicial role in poverty alleviation in the post-communist context I will in the main discuss the Hungarian experience, with occasional references to other Central European countries that joined the European Union in 2004. The Hungarian experience, as well as that of other post-communist countries, is important because it represents an often-misunderstood instance of judicial social rights enforcement.

The next section of this chapter considers the relevance of the recognition of social rights in emerging democratic constitutions. The third section then offers a brief description of the rulings of the HCC, especially those regarding pensions, healthcare, and the 'appropriateness' of the level of the service provided.

I argue that the form of review (concrete or abstract) makes an enormous difference to the role of courts in promoting social justice. In order to corroborate such claims, I also look at the courts' substantive understanding of social rights.[4] Dignity in particular is a concern that is sometimes used to justify strong judicial intervention in favour of the poor. And yet, as I argue in the fourth section of this chapter, notwithstanding a strong dignitarian concern, substantive assumptions about social rights were not decisive in the Hungarian case. In conclusion, I emphasise that the rule-of-law approach to social rights and their enforcement was the decisive factor in the social rights jurisprudence of the HCC. The value of legal certainty applied to social rights in post-communist countries has resulted in the protection of majoritarian values, primarily the status quo ante of generous welfare provision to the middle classes. This conclusion conforms to the predictions of Thaler's 'endowment effect' theory.[5]

Textual Arrangements in the Hungarian Constitution

In the 1949 Hungarian Constitution and its amendments, which were drafted by the communists, there was a long list of free, state-provided services, mostly related to the sphere of work. Housing and healthcare were defined as state-provided services, without being legally guaranteed. Nevertheless, healthcare, and to a lesser extent housing, were actually provided by the state, although housing was not free and not available to all. The state operated a pension system on a pay-as-you-go basis, relying on the annual budget, though there was some minimal individual contribution to the state-run public pension fund.

The Hungarian Constitution was fundamentally amended in 1989 as part of the transition to democracy (hereinafter, 'the Amendment'). At the time it would have been unthinkable to discontinue the provision of social services, although the language used in the Amendment was rather non-committal. For example, the term 'right' in relation to social services was phrased in an ambiguous way, with wording different from that used to describe the traditional civil and political rights. The standard form used in the Amendment states that the listed social rights are provided by the state, which must take measures to protect them. This wording could have been understood to imply that these rights were not enforceable in the ordinary way. On the other hand, social rights were included alongside other fundamental rights, and there was enough textual support for robust judicial intervention to enforce such rights. As it turned out, these terminological issues did not play a decisive role in the eventual approach taken by the courts.

Of course, the partial imitation of the Soviet-type constitutional language is not to be explained by the 'innocent' survival of the previous legal culture. The decision to repeat certain pre-existing formulae was the result of a social consensus. Nevertheless, the commitment in the Amendment to continue services provided under communism was problematic. After all, the crisis of communism was intimately related to the increasingly unaffordable welfare system. The legal and cost implications of entrenching social rights might have been clear to some of the founding fathers of the 1989 Amendment, but their choices were limited, given the popular expectations developed under communism, and the lack of actual alternative (non-etatistic) solutions to the problem of providing basic social services.[6] In the words of one commentator, '[t]he inclusion of social and economic rights in communist constitutions created expectations and set standards which continue to be approved by a majority of people in post-communist countries'.[7] Post-communist societies moved into capitalism with Scandinavian expectations of equal social welfare (without the expectation of high taxes). Their economies were capable of adjustment but were generally performing 80 per cent below the level of the West European economies.

The language of the Hungarian constitutional amendment relied on the Universal Declaration of Human Rights (in particular by copying the language of 'social security') and the United Nations Covenant on Economic, Social and Cultural Rights (CESCR). (The Covenant was ratified and even promulgated in many communist states.) Given the well-established social protection system inherited from communism, the Covenant requirements were seen as non-onerous and acceptable in 1989. After all, the principal obligation flowing from article 2(1) is merely that the state should take steps 'with a view to achieving progressively the full realization of the rights recognized'. Note that, in 1989, poverty in most communist countries was very limited and certainly not visible. Poverty became visible and dramatic only during the transition to capitalism,[8] when an identifiable group of marginalised people living in abject poverty emerged. For example, Budapest, a city of two million people, now has a homeless population of 30,000 to 50,000, and there are small villages in the northeastern provinces of Hungary where unemployment is at 60 per cent.

The drafters of the Amendment were attracted to market capitalism, and were thus initially reluctant to incorporate socio-economic expectations as full individual rights, because of the financial implications, and because they felt that these issues could not be solved on a case-by-case basis by the judiciary. In the historical moment of transition it was not clear to them how the entrenchment of social and economic rights would affect the operation of the market economy, which was a political and even constitutional goal. Obviously, they were aware that specific constitutional arrangements regarding social rights preclude market solutions. For example, if public higher education is free and prevailing there is little chance for a private educational sector, and a solidarity-based public insurance system provides no encouragement for private pension funds.[9]

In the end, the selection of rights from the CECSR was somewhat arbitrary. Many specific requirements regarding some of the most vulnerable groups were left out from the Amendment, including, for example, the right to shelter, food, and certain gender rights[10] – perhaps because they were believed to be third-world related. The 'right to social security' was, however, retained. After a semicolon, the same provision of the Amendment that guarantees social security provides for welfare services to citizens in certain specific cases: '[Citizens] are entitled to social support in old age and in the case of sickness, disability, the death of a spouse, and being orphaned, and in the case of unemployment through no fault of their own.'

The lack of concern in the Amendment for some of the most vulnerable categories of people is partly attributable to the fact that, at the time, Hungarians had little experience of the suffering of vulnerable and marginalised groups. As noted already, these types of suffering were not a visible social problem in 1989. Paragraph 2 of article 70E thus states that social rights are to be 'provided' through a system of social security insurance and social welfare institutions. The right to health was 'translated' into a similar institutional guarantee without any specifics as to the financial arrangements regarding these services.

The textual choices made in the Amendment were not necessarily decisive. In fact, one might argue that the textual ambiguities were to some extent deliberate: things had to be left undecided during the transition. Certainly, the text provides little guidance on the justiciability of welfare rights. As we have seen, some provisions translated social rights into organisational obligations of free, state-run services and state welfare institutions. For example, there is a constitutional obligation to maintain a social insurance system. In other post-communist constitutions there was considerable textual commitment in this regard and states were driven to a constitutionally mandated welfare path.[11] But even these constitutions were flexible and left considerable room for choice: a public monopoly on service provision does not follow from a reference that social insurance be provided.[12]

Social Rights in Hungarian Constitutional Jurisprudence

The Protection of the Status Quo: 'Social Security'

As mentioned above, the post-communist constitutional texts generally did not dictate the extent to which the new democracies would take social rights seriously. As Wiktor Osiatynski stated: 'The constitutionalization of social and economic rights does not result in their automatic protection, while their absence from the constitution does not prevent some countries from instituting fairly generous welfare policies.'[13]

This openness must be understood in the context of a broader expectation regarding the new constitutions: as the communist constitutions remained written words, the credibility of the new constitutions depended on their practical enforceability. Non-enforceable declarations of intent smelled of communist continuity. It was obvious, however, that the full enforceability of constitutional social rights as individual rights would result in chaos.

The HCC could not avoid facing these issues as it had to decide abstract review requests from members of the general public, even from people without a subjective interest in the matter. Needless to say, both politicians and the general public requested the court to rule on the constitutionality of various enactments.[14] In response, the HCC developed a practice that enabled it to declare constitutional omissions where legislation failed to implement a constitutional right or institution.

The Case of Pension Benefits

In relation to social rights, the immediate issue in the transition process was the extent to which the inclusion of social entitlements in the constitution was to be understood as a precept to maintain the existing statutory services provided by the communist regime. Note, once again, that these services were set at a relatively high level and were non-sustainable given the economic conditions prevailing in these countries. The most common problem emerged in the context of the right to pensions, mainly because economic stabilisation in the early period of transition was accompanied in many East European countries by inflation. In consequence, pensions that were not indexed lost their value dramatically.[15]

The post-communist decline in the value of pension benefits was litigated in many countries, with somewhat conflicting results. In some of its early decisions (1990-93), the HCC found that the monetary value of pension and healthcare contributions was not related to later benefits (that is, contributions made did not result in a specific entitlement) and, therefore, that there were neither legitimate expectations nor property rights in specific forms of benefit. The Court also found that there was no obligation on the state to index pensions during times of inflation. On the other hand, the Polish Tribunal was from the very beginning reluctant to allow austerity measures and plans that did not provide for indexation.[16] The Tribunal's position was, however, *not based on social rights considerations, but on assumptions about the rule of law (that is, the value of legal certainty).*[17]

In 1995, the HCC moved towards and even beyond the Polish position in the extent and scope of protection provided to existing entitlements, relying on substantive (though not individual, 'subjective' rights) considerations. Asked to review a government austerity package, the HCC found that contributors to the national pension plan had a property interest in their pensions, and that the proposed cut in pensions was accordingly unconstitutional. Although still recognising that past pension contributions were not directly correlated to current pension benefits, the Court held that citizens' expectations of continued benefits were legitimate given their basis in past contributions. Once the contributions had been made according to law, the conditions of future or current benefits were to be honoured, irrespective of the value of the contribution. The HCC was also inclined to protect childcare benefits as legitimate expectations on the same basis.

On the other hand, both the Polish Tribunal and the HCC recognised that there was no obligation on the state to maintain the existing level of benefits in the case of non-contribution-based services.[18] The revocation of a service, however, should conform to the rule of law, which required adequate lead-time (due notice). As to non-statutory entitlements, these should receive at least a due-process-type protection.

Healthcare Services

Post-communist constitutions expressly recognise the right to health, or the right to free healthcare. Both the Hungarian and the Polish Constitutional Courts have interpreted these as non-individual rights, which are satisfied where the state provides public services. In the Hungarian case, however, the right to the 'highest level of health' was construed as a duty to maintain, at least for a long transitional period, the existing level of services, even during economic hardship. Contrary to the French approach,[19] the Hungarian Court developed its theory of the so-called 'ratchet effect', which it had originally devised in the context of environmental protection. Of course, a similar result could have been achieved by reference to the CESCR,[20] which has been interpreted to prohibit states from taking retrogressive steps in the provision of welfare services.[21] Interestingly, however, the CESCR approach was not used in Eastern Europe.[22]

One of the main arguments used by post-communist tribunals in their rejection of the reduction of governmental welfare services was that such reductions contradicted the value of legal certainty. Only to a lesser extent did courts argue that such reductions violated the right to social security. The vigorous affirmation of legal security as social security against government austerity packages in Hungary and Poland resulted in a spectacular increase in the popular legitimacy of the courts as protectors of 'ordinary people'. Popular legitimacy, however, came at a price, as the increased protection given to social rights resulted in what has probably been the fiercest political conflict between the three branches of government.

Both the Polish and the Hungarian Courts recognise the need to maintain a balanced budget. Statutory 'promises' may accordingly be modified if required, even where the resulting changes are unfavourable to certain groups. Changes to statutory welfare entitlements are, however, limited by the requirement of legal certainty, which follows from the constitutional commitment to the rule of law.[23] The Polish Tribunal, as early as its decision of 30 November 1988 (K. 1/88), when Poland was still under communist rule, started to develop a theory of social security in ruling that conditions regulating the acquisition of social rights could not be changed ex post, that is, additional conditions could not be attached to services promised by law. In this case, the Court relied on the 'principles of social justice', a term that was to be found in the programmatic provisions of article 5.5 of the 1952 (Communist) Constitution.

In order to face the growing economic crisis, the last communist governments of Poland attempted to rationalise the welfare system. When the anti-communist opposition came to power, it imposed an austerity programme to save the economy destroyed by long years of communist rule. The new measures affected a number of welfare and pension allowances, and were challenged by the trade unions. The Polish Tribunal found that pension benefits were acquired rights and were protected accordingly, while expectations were to be protected as part of the social security system, 'based on the assumption that in exchange for premiums – work input – guarantees of future, gradually increasing rights are created'.[24]

The rule-of-law-based approach to social security protection has not been universally accepted. Reviewing a maternity allowance case,[25] the Croatian Constitutional Court found that the restrictive new legislation was not in violation of the requirement of legal certainty. In particular, the Health Insurance Law that allowed the maternity allowance to be determined in the annual budget[26] (and potentially to be reduced) was found constitutional.

Does membership of a welfare society imply that the right to social security is available to everyone, irrespective of contribution? Here there might be statutorily required contributions to a social-solidarity-based welfare system, but a rule that benefits could not be denied to participants, irrespective of their actual contribution.[27] The post-communist constitutional courts construed pension and free healthcare services as services based on contributions and, at least to some extent, protected in terms of the right to property,[28] and not in terms of membership, dignity, or need. Given the elements of uncertainty in any insurance scheme, the individual contribution to a welfare fund does not establish a right to a specific return. This consideration was, however, not held to be decisive and the value of pensions was maintained, irrespective of contribution. In case of healthcare and sick leave allowances, the HCC insisted that the pre-existing level of contributions and services represents a proportion that cannot be disrupted without amounting to a taking of property.

A distinction regarding the welfare state might be helpful at this point.[29] Welfare measures and policies might be intended to be corrective, that is, intended to help people in need. The system is corrective, too, in the sense that it reduces the overall uncertainty of the market economy and the 'natural' injustice of the world resulting from bad luck and otherwise irreparable social injustice. From a different perspective, it provides the minimal conditions for a dignified life to all. The distributive-egalitarian version of welfare consists in providing services to all, irrespective of need. From a dignitarian perspective, the welfare state is not simply providing the minimum conditions for dignity but *services*, because otherwise the equal dignity of citizens would be violated. The practical difference is indicated in the maternity support policies in Hungary as adjudicated by the HCC in 1995. As part of the austerity measures the government proposed a measure that would have abolished a lump sum maternity support as an entitlement (a subjective right based on citizenship), and replaced it by a means- or income-related support, which was to be given only to the needy. (The lump sum allegedly reflected childbearing expenses.) The first approach is distributive-egalitarian, the second one corrective. The HCC implicitly favoured the first approach, partly because of legal certainty concerns, and partly because the Constitution provides as a state goal that maternity is to be protected, which apparently suggests non-need-based welfare policies. The actual system of child support was a remnant of the state-socialist equality concept.

In state socialism most people were equally needy and dependent on state support, as the economic and political system did not allow them to have their own means of subsistence. Dependency on state-provided services was an important element of social control. In state socialism most families were in need of maternity support, hence the assumption affirmed by the HCC made sense – in state socialism. In a market economy, on the other hand, such a position perpetuates a certain perverse misallocation and misperception, depriving society of resources needed by the poor. The prevailing social mood favours majority welfarism, meaning that marginal groups are neglected, and policies that do not yield benefits to the middle classes are not enforced.

Note that social rights protection, like civil rights protection, is not a neutral recognition of indisputable human rights. As Norbert Reich stated in the context of the European Community, '[t]he idea of fundamental rights protection risks being transformed into a tool for the protection of property rights of special groups, whose interests take priority over "the objectives of general interest pursued by the Community".[30] The judicial selection of the existing social-distributive arrangements in the name of the rule of law gave support to the status quo, which was not necessarily fair.

It seems to me that, given the inherited (socialistic) status quo and the political pressure to preserve existing services, the emerging political systems are middle-class oriented, to the detriment of the poor and victims of the transition. This is further confirmed by the logic of free-elections-based democracy: the vote-maximising political parties are concerned with the interests of those who vote, and the poor and handicapped outcasts do not vote (they would not vote even if their dignity would be enhanced by more generous welfare). Social welfare benefits benefiting the poor are of little use for electoral purposes – hence the return to apparently generous subjective-rights-based social services, which entail barely-hidden criteria that favour the better off. (For example, in Hungary, in a new 'welfare to all' system, unemployment benefit periods are reduced, child support is conditional on school attendance, and so on). The prevailing form of support is provided as a universal service, as is the case with child support, while special programmes (for example, to enable poor children to attend school) are insufficient.

Minimalism: Scrutiny of Appropriateness of Social Services

One way to protect 'acquired benefits' is to actively review the level of social services provided. Such judicial activity would contradict the judicial minimalism that characterises, among others, the German courts' approach to the social welfare state, which is concerned primarily with minimum levels of protection.[31] Many constitutional courts in welfare states tend to leave the determination of the adequate level of social welfare service to legislation. The main concern of the dignity-based judicial approach is that social rights are to be protected to the extent that lack of protection would undermine the individual's personal dignity. The minimalist implications of this approach are illustrated in a decision of the Korean Supreme Court (*Standards for Protection of Livelihood* case). The Korean court found that:

> In a judicial review of whether the state performed its constitutional duty to guarantee people to have living condition worthy of human beings, the state action can be adjudged unconstitutional only where the state did not legislate for livelihood protection at all or where legislation is so irrational that the state abused its discretion. Whether the standards for livelihood protection are reasonable has to be determined by considering all relevant payments for livelihood protection and all reduced or exempted burdens. Taking into account all these elements, i.e., livelihood protection payment, winter subsidy, elderly allowance, free transportation, exemption of charge for TV, reduction of utility fare, etc., the standards in question did not transgress the petitioners' right to pursue happiness and to enjoy life worthy of human beings.[32]

Of course, once a court believes that it is proper to review legislative choices even if these are dependent on available economic resources, the court will rely on its own understanding of the 'appropriateness' of services. A similar conclusion might be reached on grounds of a stronger, substantive concept of dignity.

Notwithstanding the HCC's rather activist position that resulted from its concerns for legal certainty, the post-communist constitutional courts did not attempt to force the legislature and the administration to develop and carry out new state-run services in order to make social rights effective. A more demanding approach would require new, specific government services in order to implement social rights. This is exemplified in the Indian position regarding the right to shelter: here the Supreme Court required the state to provide efficient programs, which are reviewed by the Indian courts.[33] Note, once again, that contrary to the situation in many developing countries, in post-communist countries there were welfare services corresponding to social rights, hence the issue of social rights triggering new state action did not come up, at least not in areas important for the middle classes.

The other side of the constitutional analysis of the adequacy of service provision is this: Are there economic limits to the state's obligations to satisfy social rights? The common minimalist expectation is that the state should provide regulations, which govern access to services. Where there is a social right and/or a positive state obligation to provide services, or organise services, the state should at least take legal regulatory measures.

Even such a minimalist approach may have constitutional consequences, and entails matters subject to constitutional review. As the Czech Constitutional Court ruled (Pl. US 35/95 (1996)), because the right to health is a constitutional right, it can be regulated and restricted by statute only (in the Czech context, regarding the manner in which free healthcare is provided).

A less formalistic review of the appropriateness of the level of services, though still not going into substantive issues, is one that takes into account considerations of equality or fair procedure, that is, the manner in which the service is provided is subject to review with regard to its impact on different groups and the fairness of the procedures followed.[34]

Irrespective of the textual points of departure, the early post-communist legislatures and the constitutional courts (interacting in the political context of the social and economic transition to capitalism) had a considerable margin of appreciation. The lack of established conventions in social relations and legal doctrines left a considerable degree of freedom for the courts and legislators. Interestingly, one cannot explain the emerging arrangements in terms of a clear or coherent social solidarity vs. market liberalism choice. While at least some of the courts tended to protect existing welfare benefits, especially for those people who had strong reliance expectations, the same courts were reluctant to use the constitution to impose new constitutional welfare obligations on the state. The post-socialist courts were reluctant when it came to the possibility of broadening the reach of constitutionally free governmental social services in case the governments were not ready to move in that direction.[35]

The judicial resistance to social rights claims was often based on the narrowest interpretation of the text. This is illustrated in the Czech Textbook case, where statutory denial of free high school textbooks (in the name of the right to free education) was challenged. The Czech government's position was that article 33 para 2 of the Charter of Fundamental Rights and Basic Freedoms ('Citizens have the right to free education in elementary and secondary schools') was to be understood (in connection with the abovementioned § 4 of the Education Act) as referring to the right of students to be provided with instruction in suitable buildings, the wages of qualified instructors and further personnel, the costs of the operation and maintenance of the buildings, free use of educational aids, that is, those which are owned by the school and which it uses for its own instruction (for example, models, chemicals, chalk, wall maps and pictures). Students, or their parents, were to pay for educational materials that were owned and used by the students. This position was challenged, and the court rejected the extension of the free governmental service:

> The mentioned Government Regulation, No. 15/1994 Sb., does not restrict the right to education free of charge nor does it affect it substantially. Education free of charge unquestionably means that the state shall bear the costs of establishing schools and school facilities, of their operation and maintenance, but above all it means that the state may not demand tuition, that is, the provision of primary- and secondary-level education for payment ...The provision on the degree to which the government provides free textbooks, teaching texts, and basic school materials can not be placed under the heading of the right to education free of charge ...
>
> The costs connected with putting the right to education into effect can be divided between the state and the citizen, or his legal representative. It is appropriate to keep in mind that it is in the citizen's own interest to obtain education (and by this way also higher qualifications and better opportunities to make one's way in the labor market) and to make effort himself to achieve it. The expenses connected with putting the right to education into effect are a long-term investment in the life of the citizen. The state bears the essential part of these costs, however, it is not obliged to bear all of them.[36]

The underlying assumption behind the Czech decision is that, although the Constitution sets specific rules obliging the state to provide services, in reality members of society have their own resources, and the state's constitutional obligation is satisfied when there is an appropriate balance between individuals and the state.[37]

Dignity-based Social Rights

The concept of dignity is present in most post-communist constitutions. The Hungarian Constitution refers to the right to inalienable dignity, while the Russian one prohibits the violation of dignity in apparently absolute terms. On the other end of the dignity continuum, dignity is only the foundation of fundamental rights (see for example, article 30 of the 1997 Polish Constitution).[38] The Czechoslovak Charter and the Bulgarian Constitution refer to equality in dignity.

While the prevailing social rights approach of the post-communist constitutional courts is concerned with safeguarding the status quo of the recipients in the name of social security (in expectations) a more aggressive position would dictate that welfare rights are to be positively provided by government action to the extent that this is required by the needs of a *dignified life*. Following the German understanding of the objective hierarchy of values, the HCC committed itself to the unconditional centrality of human dignity. (See the rejection of the right to housing for the homeless in Hungary, below.)[39]

One of the standard justifications of social rights is that they are dictated by the concept of human dignity in a welfare state. The welfare state argument is that, in a condition of need, there can be no use for dignity, or that living in a state of constant need violates dignity. Liberal constitutional theory, too, recognises dignity from a political perspective, indicating that it might trigger constitutional welfarism even in the United States:

> People who cannot buy bread cannot follow the suggestion that they eat cake; people bowed under the weight of poverty are unlikely to stand up for their constitutional rights. Yet the Constitution cannot readily be construed to make income support an affirmative duty of the state. The effort to identify the 'indispensable conditions of an open society' thus proves inseparable from the much larger enterprise of identifying the elements of being human – and deciding which of those elements are entirely to politics to protect, and which are entrusted to protection by judicial decree … [T]he supposed dichotomy between economic and personal rights must fail … The day may indeed come when a general doctrine under the fifth and fourteenth amendments recognizes for each individual a constitutional right to a decent level of affirmative governmental protection in meeting the basic human needs of physical survival and security, health and housing, work and schooling … But … that time has not yet come.[40]

The recognition of dignity as an underlying value in the implementation and enforcement of social rights is not decisive. Both minimalist and social-rights-maximising activist approaches are known in contemporary democracies. Post-communist courts follow in this regard a minimalist attitude, even if their way of thinking about these matters is activist, in the sense of not being interpretivist. The alternative to such dignity minimalism is illustrated in the last two decades of Indian adjudication. Here, a rich constitutional social rights scheme emerged on the basis of a foundational commitment to dignity, and it generated specific, court-mandated state action. For example, the Indian Supreme Court gradually moved towards claiming that the right to shelter obliges the state to develop adequate, judicially supervised programmes to realise this right.[41]

In order to understand the possible implications of human dignity for social rights, a distinction between *welfarist dignity* and *classical liberal dignity* must be made. By welfarist dignity, I mean a concept that: (a) presupposes that a level of poverty/deprivation deprives one of one's human dignity; and (b) claims that it is the duty of the state to eliminate conditions that result in deprivation of dignity. The classical liberal notion[42] is that the state should not contribute to the disregarding of human dignity. Where it provides services, it should respect dignity (not taking humans as means to ends, not depriving individuals of choices respecting equality (in dignity)). The welfarist dignity approach requires that the state should create conditions that enable the individual to make fundamental life choices. Arguably, none of these approaches adequately confronts situations where lack of fundamental services (for example, food or shelter) results in actual *harm*, as is the case in some, but not all, situations of poverty in less developed countries. In all concerns for dignity an element of equality (in the sense of equal dignity) is present.

While the prevailing social rights approach of the post-communist constitutional courts is concerned with safeguarding the status quo of the recipients in the name of social security (in expectations) a more aggressive position would dictate that social rights are to be positively provided by government action to the extent that this is required by the needs of a dignified life. Interestingly, dignity is the central concept in German constitutional jurisprudence, and the *Bundesverfassungsgerichtshof* developed certain dignity-related social existence minimum requirements in the context of child support tax. Nevertheless, dignity is seldom used on its own in Germany – in most cases, one needs a special right to breathe life into it.[43] The lack of a vigorous use of dignity in the welfare context in Germany was probably due to the fact that, in the view of the justices, the rich German welfare state provides the minimum conditions to its citizens anyway.

The standards of human dignity are not satisfied in many instances in post-communist countries (for example, the roma in ghettos, the homeless, pensioners (especially in villages), or refugees in camps). It is not my task to discuss structural violations of welfarist dignity. It seems to me, however, that dignity was not used in Central and Eastern Europe to create new social rights nor to give substantive meaning to the social rights listed in the constitution. It is quite telling in this regard that the HCC in decision 42/2000 (XI.8) AB hat. rejected the ombud's argument that the right to social security entails a right to a dwelling and housing (except the right to shelter in life-threatening situations, on the basis of the constitutional obligation of the state to protect life). The HCC argued that, although it follows from human dignity that an existential minimum is to be provided, this is to be provided by the system of partial rights created under the social welfare system, and it is up to the state to determine how the totality of such rights satisfies the requirements of dignity. Hence, there is no specific individual right to any of the elements of the bundle of rights that provide for social dignity (like housing versus monetary support). To specify any of these elements of the social security system would unconstitutionally fix the legislator's choice.[44]

Conclusions

The prevailing trend[45] in the use of social rights in post-communist Hungary is '*status quo protective*'. This position is exemplarily summarised in a dissenting opinion of Justice Kilenyi of the HCC regarding social security. (The dissent became the majority position in the 1995 austerity measures decision.) Justice Kilenyi argued that the right to social security entails, among other things, the obligation of the state 'to refrain from interfering in the wealth of its citizens through regulation in a way that would impose on the mass of citizens (in the spheres of taxation, raising interests and housing rents) disproportionate burdens that exceed their performance possibilities, without compelling reason.'[46] This is a perfect summary of the expectations of the petty bourgeois legal subject in the late communist Kadar regime: 'leave us in peace and provide us a minimum security of existence'. In my opinion, the post-communist courts did not in fact depart from the above deferentialism. The standard of service existed already at the time the courts had to review the content of social rights. It was not for the court to determine *ex nihilo* the proper level of a government welfare service: the only reason the court insisted that a certain benefit was adequate was that the benefit was already provided, or was expectable, therefore its deprivation has indeed deprived the individual of its welfare. One way to justify this approach might be to argue that not living in good conditions does not violate one's dignity, but to be *deprived* of what one believed to pertain to one already, on the basis of actual services provided, is a violation of the right to a dignified life. After all, such deprivation is the result of (legislative) state action. Alternatively, the judicial position might have been one based on the CESCR's ratchet concern.[47]

In Hungary, social rights were understood as an entitlement of the overwhelming majority. In these circumstances, judicial enforcement of social rights cannot be seen as counter-majoritarian, even if I would argue that the prevailing majoritarian solutions were both inefficient and socially unjust. Unlike the Indian Supreme Court, the HCC's protection of social rights has never been directed at protecting the rights of the most needy against an alienated, non-responsive government. Protection of social rights in Eastern Europe is hardly the protection of the weakest. The HCC (perhaps with the exception of the earliest pension indexation cases) was always in tune with the majority. This became particularly clear when the HCC dared to confront parliament in 1995: in this case, the austerity package was unpopular and did not reflect the majority's view. The majority felt that the taking away of social welfare services in a moment of economic crisis was unacceptable and the HCC took a popular (even populist) stance in favour of preserving the leftover benefits of state socialism. In order to do so it became 'activist' in the sense of departing from its earlier precedents and interpretivism. The 1995 outburst of judicial activism and the resultant striking down of legislation ran the risk of a confrontation with the political branches, but the popular majority stood behind the HCC. The government acquiesced in the rulings and introduced higher personal income tax (punishing those who actually did pay taxes). A year later, however, the HCC accepted welfare-reducing legislative measures. Nevertheless, the impact of the HCC rulings was a lasting one on the value system of the society and political elites: statutory entitlements are understood today as subjective rights and any needs-based social reform that would reallocate resources to the unpopular poor is likely to meet with claims of constitutional entitlements.

A look at alternative uses[48] of social rights might help to corroborate the claim that post-communist welfare protection is status quo oriented. The courts' reluctance to look into the appropriateness of the level of services (except where there were already established standards), their reluctance to consider dignity in the context of social services forcing different levels of support, and so on, indicate that a status-quo-preserving conservativism indeed prevails in the post-communist courts' approach to welfare. Of course, such 'conservativism' operates in a relatively strong welfare state system, and therefore the reluctance of the courts to be socially activist is not apparent.

Notes

1 The 1991 Polish pension indexation case, on the other hand, resulted in a government crisis and increased the costs of transition, but did not, at the end of the day, actually protect the value of pensions.
2 It would require additional research to evaluate the ambivalent judicial attitude of post-communist constitutional judges. To the extent that social rights were seen among the elite as socialist leftovers there was considerable difficulty in openly endorsing such rights. Once dignity became the accepted language it became possible to stand for social rights in a way that was considered legitimate in a liberal or Catholic intellectual environment.
3 The welfare system of socialism was intended to provide services to the most trustworthy groups in society. Contrary to the prevailing misrepresentation of state socialism in most countries, welfare was not provided to all on an egalitarian basis. As a matter of fact, the early Soviet constitutions did not make any such commitments. The former 'class enemies' and the untrustworthy peasants were not entitled to full pension and healthcare benefits, on the technical ground that they had not accumulated sufficient years in employment. The socialist welfare services were not accessible to all, although the beneficiaries were the majority of the society. These people became the new (lower) middle class in the transition to capitalism. A second segment of the population that did not make it into the privileged middle class consisted of those people whose welfare was provided by the socialist state in conditions of full employment. The handicapped and unskilled workers – the future unemployed – including racial and ethnic minorities, were supported through heavily subsidised employment. Once the system of full employment collapsed these groups could not claim that they were entitled to entrenched social benefits and services, as many benefits were employment dependent.
4 Note that in this chapter the term 'social rights' refers narrowly to those rights that enable persons to participate in a meaningful way in social life (including, among others, rights to culture and education). Special, labour-related rights, like the right to strike, are not included. Social rights and welfare service provisions, as used in this chapter, refer to all social services and monetary support provided by the government to individuals related to their social status, including pensions for the retired and the handicapped, sickness benefits (including the universal and free healthcare system), child, maternity and family support (both monetary supplements and special care), and unemployment benefits. All or most of these entitlements are generally referred to as the 'social security scheme'. Very often these services are provided irrespective of the actual participation by the beneficiary in the social insurance plan, and are unrelated to contributions made. Free education, subsidised cultural activities, free or subsidised housing (including low-interest loans) are or were provided as free or heavily subsidised ['social'] government services and are included here, simply because these rights are often treated the way the above benefits were treated, that is, as pertaining to, or required by, one's social status. (In Hungary even broadcasting is provided free of subscription fees as a matter of subjective right.) The similarity in treatment originates perhaps from the assumption that all these services were intended to promote the general welfare and not private

happiness. (Hence there is a residual instrumentalism in these rights). In post-communist countries and in some Western welfare systems, some of the schemes are administered with government-underwritten, non-voluntary 'social insurance funds'. Finally, note that the terminology regarding social rights and welfare rights is blurred. Fundamental preconditions of existence (health, food, water, shelter) are often provided as part of welfare services. Other welfare services (like pensions) are termed social rights in some contexts, although sometimes the term is intended to express an institutional claim and not an individual right.

5 Richard H. Thaler, *The Winner's Curse: Paradoxes and Anomalies of Economic Life* (Princeton: Princeton University Press, 1994).

6 Retrospectively, the constitutionalisation of welfare, which very often consisted simply in the rephrasing of existing welfare promises made in the communist constitutions, seems to be part of the transitional deal between communists and opposition and, more importantly between political elites and their constituencies. The inclusion of the existing welfare services (although in a modified form) was a kind of hidden promise of the transition: by entrenching existing services the transition will have no losers.

7 Wiktor Osiatynski, 'Social and Economic Rights in a New Constitution for Poland', in A. Sajó (ed.), *Western Rights? Post-Communist Applications* (The Hague: Kluwer, 1996), p. 234.

8 Inequality is an often-voiced concern in Hungary. Nevertheless, on the basis of the Gini index, Hungary does not look like a country of social extremes. According to the 1998 data, it had the second lowest index in Europe. See <http://earthtrends.wri.org/pdf_library/data_tables/econ2_2003.pdf>. Source: The World Bank, 2003.

9 To give another example of the anti-market implications of certain public welfare concerns: the Covenant's principle (article 7) that recognises 'equal remuneration for work of equal value' may trigger wage fixing and, therefore, undermine the fundamentals of freedom of contract, choice, and the market economy. The HCC later (in 1994) stated that the principle of equal remuneration cannot mean what it says, if applied as a *rule*: otherwise a bankrupt company would be forced to pay the same salary to its employees that a solvent company pays for the same work, to the detriment of creditors.

10 The Amendment does, however, contain a general non-discrimination clause.

11 Once again, such a constitutional pre-commitment can be disregarded, though at the risk of increased social dissatisfaction. The current attempt in Russia to curtail (undeniably inefficient) social services is a case in point.

12 Of course, the constitutional determination of free services creates a kind of constitutional welfarism: in this regard one can even posit a welfare index of the post-communist constitutions. The index indicates how deeply committed to the past the draftsmen were at the time of making the constitutions. For example, Hungary, Slovenia and Yugoslavia were rather cautious, whereas Kazakhstan was the most committed to free services.

13 Osiatynski, 'Social and Economic Rights', p. 233.

14 Where a provision is found unconstitutional, the provision becomes immediately inoperative, except where the HCC sets a future deadline for invalidation.

15 Pensions, as inherited from socialism, were financed on a pay-as-you-go basis from the budget, although in some communist countries pension deductions were applied to

salaries. However, pensions and deductions (that is, individual contributions) were only marginally correlated, because of egalitarian concerns.

16 Wiktor Osiatynski has kindly explained to the author that the Polish Tribunal's early activism and the positions it took, both against the ailing communist and freshly elected anti-communist governments, were the result of certain peculiar features. First, the pension-value protection was a major requirement of the victorious Solidarity, and had enormous public legitimacy for that reason. Secondly, according to the law in force, the decision of the Tribunal was not final: Parliament could overrule it by a qualified majority. The Tribunal was therefore relieved of final responsibility regarding the economic consequences of its decision and could limit its concern to rule-of-law considerations. The arrangement made it constitutionally possible to disregard the constitutional concerns of the Tribunal for the sake of other imperatives (like economic hardship consequent on the transition). The new Polish Constitution of 1997 provides that the Tribunal's decisions are final. In Russia in the case of Gulag victims' compensation inflation was held not to be a fact to be considered. In Hungary, where the HCC's decisions were final from the beginning, the Court had to consider both legal (constitutional) values and the dictates of the transition. In order to accommodate both, the HCC developed a doctrine of 'exceptionality of transition', which allows a limited departure from the general rules and expectations of the rule of law, subject to constant constitutional supervision.

17 The first case involved the 1990 Pension Act, which reduced the pensions of former high-ranking officials of the communist regime. In its decision, the Tribunal stated that '[n]onretroactivity of law is one of the basic components of the principle of a state based on the rule of law... Another important aspect is citizens' confidence in the State, which requires ... that vested rights be protected from [retroactive application of the law]'.

18 Both the Hungarian and the Polish courts recognised that extraordinary economic circumstances may impose burdens (restrictions) on vested rights. While the Polish Tribunal accepted the 'drastic breakdown of the balance of the budget' test, the HCC did not accept that concern in 1995 when the Minister of Finance tried to show the Court that the budget would not be sustainable without welfare restrictions. In fact, the solvency of the fiscus was saved by an increase in customs, consumption tax and income tax, introduced partly to compensate for the losses incurred by the Court's protection of welfare benefits.

19 The French doctrine of constitutional objectives does not recognise the ratchet effect, which is reserved for fundamental rights and principles.

20 Article 2 of the Covenant expressly sets the level of rights protection 'to the maximum of [the State's] available resources, with a view to achieving progressively the full realization of the rights recognized'. Note that the UN Committee on Economic, Social and Cultural Rights in its General Comment No. 4 on the right to adequate housing (Sixth Session 1991) [UN doc E/1992/23, note 46 at 11] states that 'a general decline in living and housing conditions, directly attributable to policy and legislative decisions by state parties and in the absence of accompanying compensatory measures, would be inconsistent with the obligations under the Covenant'. Is this to say that retrogressive measures are a prima facie infringement of a right? Is a retrogression regarding a special welfare right or expectation justified, if the overall protection of welfare rights through services is achieved through the measure? Ironically, at least some communist constitutions (for example, the 1952 Polish Constitution) contained a form that would

have required the ratchet effect, in line with the 1966 Covenant. The Polish Constitution of 1952 thus talks of 'ever-growing implementation' and 'increase of various forms of social help'. It was, among others, on this basis (article 70, promising 'steady increase of social insurance') that an increase in the number of necessary years for a disability pension was found unconstitutional. (Decision of 30 November 1988 (K. 1/88; see text, above).) The 1996 South African Constitution also uses the 'progressive realisation' formula (section 27(2)).

21 The legal background to the Comments is described in an Introduction by the Committee on Economic, Social and Cultural Rights to a compilation of UN human rights instruments: 'In 1988, the Committee decided (E/1988/14, paras. 366 and 367), pursuant to an invitation addressed to it by the Economic and Social Council (resolution 1987/5) and endorsed by the General Assembly (resolution 42/102), to prepare general comments based on the various articles and provisions of the International Covenant on Economic, Social and Cultural Rights with a view to assisting the States parties in fulfilling their reporting obligations.' *Compilation of General Comments and General Recommendations Adopted by Human Rights Treaty Bodies*, UN Doc. HRI/GEN/1/Rev.5 (2001), p. 12.

This is not the place to discuss the extent to which the Committee had the power to read into the Covenant the 'duty to provide' when they were determining reporting duties. It is clear that this emerging interpretation had a formative impact on the understanding of the meaning of the right to food; in any case, it was certainly more than the personal preference of a small group of respected socio-economic rights advocates.

Obviously, the Comments cannot determine new obligations under the Covenant. The Comments, which were prepared as reporting guidelines for participating states, cannot be seen as the official position of the participating states regarding the Covenant.

It is obvious that the Comments go far beyond what is in the Covenant and that they express expectations where the Covenant talks only about options. Nevertheless, given that the Committee is the body that systematically and with some international official authority deals with socio-economic rights, it has an important voice and has become an independent international actor in socio-economic rights discourse. See further, András Sajó, 'Socio-Economic Rights and the International Economic Order', *New York University Journal of International Law and Politics*, 35 (2002): 221–61.

22 In Argentina, where the International Covenant on Economic, Social and Cultural Rights of 1966 has constitutional force, the Supreme Court of Argentina ruled that family allowances fall within the scope of social rights and that such allowances, although subject to regulation, can never be withdrawn, even in the event of unforeseen circumstances. The right was based on article 14bis of the Constitution, which secures 'full protection for the family', and article 10.1 of the Covenant. 19.08.1999., V.916.XXXII, BCCL 1999. 344. Article 10.1 of the Covenant states that 'the widest possible protection and assistance should be accorded to the family … particularly for its establishment and while is responsible for the care and education of dependent children'. The Argentinean Court obviously interprets 'protection and assistance' as meaning *material support*. The Argentinean decision is based on the idea of 'widest' protection, and not on the broader and non-specific ratchet obligation of the State under article 2 of the Covenant.

23 'The rule of law embodies maintaining the confidence of citizens in the State; the protection of acquired rights (also the non-retroactive effect of law) is tied to the

foregoing according to the principle of instrumental links. Maintaining confidence is the guiding principle serving as the basis of the social security relationship as it is based on the legal structure of maintaining confidence and on the conviction of the insured that upon the performance of defined terms (work, premiums) and upon the elapse of a defined period of time (achievement of the required age) or the occurrence of some other insurance risk (disability), the insured shall receive defined benefits ... which ... means that this will be taken on by the social security system. Thus, the social security system takes on the form of a unique type of social contract governed by the principle of pacta sunt servanda. Equitably (justly) acquired rights [are protected to a limited extent].' (11 February 1992 K. 14/91. In Constitutional Tribunal, *A Selection of the Polish Constitutional Tribunal's Jurisprudence from 1986 to 1999* (Warszawa, 1999), p. 62.) Retraction of allowances acquired under communism if equitable, as is the case with those resulting from extremely hard working conditions (miners), is unconstitutional, although the evaluation of equitability of acquisition is primarily the duty of the legislative body. Both the Hungarian CC and the Polish Tribunal found that certain pension privileges to former communists were not equitably acquired and, therefore, the discontinuation of special benefits was held not to violate the Constitution. Following the Tribunal's decision, the Sejm repealed most of the critical provisions of the 1991 Pension Act, although the Minister of Finance warned that such a provision would 'aggravate the recession', and resigned in protest. He claimed that the repeal would increase Poland's foreign debt by 30 per cent. The President did not sign the law. In a later case the Tribunal overruled certain provisions of the 1993 Tax Act. In this case, the deputies agreed with the position of the Tribunal but overruled the Tribunal in consideration of the possibility of budgetary collapse. See Mark F. Brzezinski and Leszek Garlicki, 'Judicial Review in Post-Communist Poland: The Emergence of a "Rechtstaat"', *Stanford Journal of International Law*, 31 (1995): 13–59, 46–7.

24 11 February 1992 K. 14/91. See further Polish Constitutional Tribunal, 17.12.1997, 22/96, BCCL, 1998. 99.

25 04.03.1998. BCCL 1998. 27.

26 Three dissenters argued that in a social state, where the rule of law and social justice applies, this amounts to retroactive application of the law. When the right is granted to the mothers the necessary funds should be allocated too. Only in this way could future parents have confidence in the law. The dissenters argued, in line with the 1995 Hungarian decisions, that the budget law diminished rights already acquired by the mothers.

27 In *Bowen v. Gilliard* 483 U.S. 587 (1987), in the context of a takings argument regarding a transfer in the government's child support payments scheme, Justice Stevens wrote: 'Congress is not, by virtue of having instituted a social welfare program, bound to continue it at all, much less at the same benefit level. ... It would be quite strange indeed if, by virtue of an offer to *provide* benefits to needy families through the entirely voluntary AFDC program, Congress or the States were deemed to have *taken* some of those very family members' property.'

28 This is the position of the GFCC. (See, for example 1 BvR 609/90 (1996).) Note that the ECHR found in *Gaygusuz v. Austria* (16 September, 1996) that even the right to emergency assistance is a property-like protected possession under article 1 protocol 1 ECHR because it is sponsored by the unemployment insurance fund, which operates from contributions and is not a State-provided emergency service granted on the basis of

need. The Supreme Court of the Nation (Argentina) considers pensions as property rights which are not infringed as long as the reduction is justified by considerations of public policy, and provided the reduction is not such as to be confiscatory or arbitrarily disproportionate (25.08.1998. M.653.XXVIII. BCCL 1998. 373).

29 See Ulrich K. Preuss, 'The Conceptual Difficulties of Welfare Rights', in A. Sajó (ed.) *Western Rights? Post-Communist Application*, p. 216.

30 N. Reich, 'Judge-made "Europe à la Carte": Some Remarks on Recent Conflicts between European and German Constitutional Law Provoked by the Banana Litigation', *European Journal of International Law*, 7 (1996): 103–11, 110.

31 There are some recent examples of *in merito* service level adequacy evaluation by constitutional courts (See the Italian case of *Di Bella* 185/1998). These restricted cases, however, were developed in an equality context. This means that there was an existing level of protection for a certain class that was extended to others on grounds that the social rights of the second class entail equal provision rights.

32 The petitioners, a couple whose livelihood was protected under the Protection of Minimum Living Standards Act, filed a constitutional complaint, alleging that the payment level suggested by 'Livelihood protection standards in 1994' in the 'Directions for Livelihood Protection Project in 1994' notified by the Minister of Health and Welfare, was far short of the minimum livelihood cost. The issue was whether the challenged 'Livelihood protection standards in 1994' transgressed the petitioners' right to pursue happiness and to enjoy a life worthy of a human being, that is, a guaranteed minimal quality of life (9-1 KCCR 543, 94 HunMa 33, 29 May 1997; translation of the summary of the rationale at the Court's web page). The Korean Court dismissed the petition. Likewise the French Constitutional Council avoids the actual scrutiny of the sufficiency of the services provided. When the CC examined the Act establishing universal sickness cover its approach was limited to equality issues, and it was unwilling to examine the merits of the possible unconstitutionality of the Act in regard to the principle of equality. (Here the issue was not what happens to the recipients but to the contributors as recipients.) The Act established an upper wealth limit to the award of a non-contributory benefit. The Council found itself not competent, as long as the details of the Act were not manifestly inappropriate, to examine whether the goals set out therein could have been achieved by other means (99-416 DC).

33 See Sudarshan's chapter in this volume.

34 See for example *Di Bella* 185/1998. The standard position of the Italian CC is that the protection of the right to health is subject to the constraints that are present in the redistribution of the resources available. However, the Court found that the demands of public finance could not destroy the core of the right to health, which is protected as an inviolable part of human dignity. Free healthcare for the indigenous (poorer) citizens was therefore protected.

35 See the right to housing (denial of) decision in Hungary in 2000 (below).

36 Free Textbooks Case, The Constitutional Court of the Czech Republic Pl. US 25/94 (1995).

37 This is different from the situation in South Africa, where the assumption that individuals have considerable resources to complement the state, and that they have individual benefits, may not necessarily work. A general right to education triggers a positive constitutional obligation of the State. Constitutional obligation here means a duty to take legislative and administrative measures. *In re The School Education Bill of*

1995 (Gauteng) 39/95 (1996), the South African Constitutional Court, per Mahomed J, found it necessary to explain that the right to basic education protected in the interim Constitution imposes a positive obligation on the State since certain state-provided conditions are needed in order to effectively enjoy certain individual rights. Contrary to Section 29(1) of the final Constitution (1996), which states that 'the state must take reasonable measures to make [further education] progressively available and accessible', the interim Constitution was silent regarding the role of the state in realising the right to education.

38 Interestingly, individual human dignity does not figure among the fundamental principles that serve as foundational principles of the Republic of Poland; nation and social justice and other collectivistic principles are mentioned. This is not to suggest that in practical terms dignity is not or might not play a crucial role (even against the collectivistic principles, or in a collectivistic understanding of social dignity). The term 'social justice' was known in the pre-1997 texts, and was used as a vehicle of equality-propelled social security in welfare expectations. See text above. For an overview of the use of equality for a disguised extension of welfare rights, see Brezinski and Garlicki, 43. The technique is widely used in Italy. It has more welfare-enhancing impact than most direct welfare-rights-related decisions, as it tends to extend a government-provided service to all who pertain to the socially identical class. Article 1 of the Czech Charter of Fundamental Rights and Freedoms and article 6 of the Bulgarian Constitution refer to dignity in the context of equality, and not in terms of inalienability.

39 One could also refer to the 2004 decision of the Slovak Constitutional Court that rejected a challenge to a healthcare reform that introduced a minimum payment for each visit to the public healthcare system. The relatively small fee that was intended to force people to use medical resources more carefully and rationally, allegedly excluded the poorest Slovaks, and the Roma in particular. The Court did not find the equal access and social rights argument convincing.

40 L. Tribe, *American Constitutional Law* 2nd edn (Mineola, NY: Foundation Press, 1988), pp. 778–9, fn. 15. See for example *Maher v. Roe* 432 U.S. 464, 469 (1977) (upholding a state refusal to fund non-therapeutic abortions): 'The Constitution imposes no obligation on the States to pay the pregnancy-related medical expenses of indigent women, or indeed to pay any of the medical expenses of indigents.'

41 *Ahmedabad Municipal Corporation v. Nawab Khan Gulab Khan* Supreme Court of India (11/10/96).

42 Stephen Holmes argues that there is a place for welfare in classical liberal theory, in the form of just order (*equite* in Montesquieu). However, even this position assumes that welfare rights are different from constitutional rights. See Stephen Holmes, *Passions and Constraint: On the Theory of Liberal Democracy* (Chicago: University of Chicago Press, 1995), pp. 236ff.

43 Of course, the right to free development of the personality might be a source for radical social rights protection, and indeed, certain unspecified government duties were judicially defined on this basis to enhance dignity. The right of occupational choice was developed into a governmental obligation to provide opportunities in free higher education, but only within the limits of the economic capacities of the state. What is economically possible is left to be determined by legislation. (*Numerus Clausus* case, 33 BverfGE 303 (1972).)

44 Seven years earlier, in obiter dicta in a housing privatization case, the right to housing was described as the *crucial* component of the bundle of rights that constitute social security (64/1993. AB hat.). Note that the Polish Tribunal ruled that especially vulnerable people were to be protected against eviction, and found that a statute that did not contain such protective clauses was unconstitutional.

45 How vigorously 'status quo preservation' is carried out depends, of course, of the general separation of powers strategy (activism or deferentialism) of a court.

46 26/1993 AB hat. 'Az Alkotmánybíróság határozatai' (*Decisions of the Constitutional Court* (Budapest, 1993), p. 206.

47 In an earlier article I noted elements of material justice in these trends, which might endanger both legal security and the market economy; at the moment, however, the trend has not gone any further. See András Sajó 'How the Rule of Law Killed Hungarian Welfare Reform', *East European Constitutional Review,* 5 (1996): 31–41.

48 An alternative interpretative use of welfare rights implies that such rights are used for purposes of justifying other rights restrictions, including a departure from general rules. For example, the Greek Council of State recognises that social rights may justify exceptions to general rules favouring the socially protected group. The homeless and the poorly protected are subject to the special attention of the government (not a constitutional right). Lawmakers may allow exemptions to building regulations with a view to meeting housing needs. According to the Greek Constitution, in article 21(4), the homeless and poorly housed are the subject of special care by the state (550/99 BCCL 1999 385). The ICC, which came close to granting individual access rights to governmental welfare service provisions, at the same time recognises certain welfare rights as grounds for *restricting* other rights. The ICC stated that the right to healthcare entails the right to the medical treatment needed to protect it, and is 'guaranteed to every person as a right that is constitutionally dependent on its implementation by law, through the balancing of the interests protected by this right with the other interests protected by the Constitution' (ICC 267/1998, BCCL 1998, 260).

Chapter 5

The Record of the South African Constitutional Court in Providing an Institutional Voice for the Poor: 1995-2004

Jackie Dugard and Theunis Roux

Introduction

This chapter examines the extent to which the Constitutional Court of South Africa can be said to have provided an 'institutional voice for the poor'[1] during the first decade of its operation, from 1995 to 2004. We look at three aspects of the Court's record in particular: (1) decisions affecting the poor's ability to access the justice system; (2) the Court's social rights jurisprudence; and (3) cases in which members of previously advantaged groups have challenged the constitutionality of pro-poor legislation or policies. In respect of each of these areas, we consider whether the principles and rules developed by the Court have tended to enhance or reduce its capacity to be used as an institutional voice by the poor. We then attempt to answer the more controversial question whether the Court might have taken a different path in these cases, both as a matter of doctrine and in relation to the political context in which it found itself.

This way of proceeding provides a partial but nevertheless instructive answer to the institutional voice question. Partial, because, without further empirical research, we do not know how the rule choices we describe here have in fact impacted on the poor. Our methodology is nevertheless capable of exposing for debate the *possible* consequences for the poor of the rule choices made by the Court. By carefully examining these choices, and the extent to which they were dictated by doctrine or political context, we hope to lay the groundwork for a conversation about whether the Court has done all it might have to open its institutional doors to the poor.

The first part of this chapter gives a brief background to the South African Constitutional Court, including its early battle for institutional supremacy with the Appellate Division. The middle part is devoted to analysing the Court's record in the three areas of law described above. In conclusion, we try to draw out some of the lessons learned.

Background to the South African Constitutional Court

The Constitutional Court of South Africa is the country's 'highest court in all constitutional matters'.[2] In comparative-law terms, it is a court of a hybrid character in that it combines aspects of the centralised German model with a system of decentralised review. Its precise jurisdiction has changed over the last ten years, from the position under the 1993 South African Constitution, where ambiguous wording suggested that it enjoyed parallel jurisdiction with the Appellate Division of the Supreme Court, to the position under the 1996 Constitution, where it has clearly been identified as the court of final instance in all matters in which a constitutional point is raised, including appeals from the Supreme Court of Appeal (the new name for the Appellate Division).

Somewhat predictably, given the ambiguous wording in the 1993 Constitution, the first five years of the Constitutional Court's life saw it engaged in a polite but nevertheless serious jurisdictional battle with the Appellate Division over the question whether there were in effect two legal systems in South Africa: a common-law system over which the Appellate Division exercised final decision-making powers, and a body of constitutional law, for whose development the Constitutional Court was solely responsible. In a series of judgments in the area of administrative law, culminating in the *Container Logistics* case,[3] the Appellate Division answered this question in the affirmative. After the enactment of the 1996 Constitution, however, the Constitutional Court conclusively settled the dispute the other way, in favour of the single system of law view.[4] In a subsequent case, it went even further, holding that all courts in South Africa were under a duty to 'refashion' the common law in line with the 'objective value system embodied in the Constitution'.[5]

The Constitutional Court is therefore today the most powerful court in South Africa, and one that has expressly committed itself to overseeing the transformation of the South African legal system so as to reflect the needs, values and aspirations of the country's predominantly poor black majority. The racial composition of the Court itself has changed over the last ten years, from the position in 1994 when seven of the judges were white and four black, to the position today in which that ratio has been reversed. Significantly, too, in a country where the term 'black' can still distort the real demographic situation, six of the eleven judges on the Court are African. The number of women on the court, on the other hand, has remained constant at two, with the same two female judges (Mokgoro J and O'Regan J) having served on the Court throughout.

In the first ten and a half years of its existence, between February 1995 and November 2004, the Constitutional Court delivered 230 written judgments, averaging 23 per year (with a low of 14 in 1995 and a high of 34 in 2002). The total number of cases submitted to it averages 50 per year, and has never been more than 80.[6] The Court therefore hands down a written judgment in roughly half of the cases that come to it. These figures indicate that the Court has a low caseload compared to constitutional courts elsewhere in the world, and also that it hands down written judgments in a comparatively high proportion of the cases submitted to it.[7]

Overview of Constitutional Court Decisions Impacting on the Poor's Capacity to be Heard

Access to Justice

The first hurdle encountered by poor people in any legal system is gaining access to justice. In many countries the poor fall at this preliminary hurdle because they cannot afford legal representation. Recognising this problem, sections 35(2)(c) and 35(3)(g) of the 1996 South African Constitution give arrested, detained and accused persons the right to a legal practitioner at state expense, 'if substantial injustice would otherwise result'. With the exception of children,[8] however, there is no general right to legal representation at state expense in civil matters.[9]

We do not have space in this chapter to assess the extent to which the qualified right to legal representation at state expense is being implemented in South Africa. Rather, we assess the possible impact of the single decision that the Constitutional Court has thus far handed down on this right, before going on to consider another significant body of decisions impacting on poor people's capacity to be heard – the Court's interpretation of its rules on direct access.

The Right to Legal Representation at State Expense The fourth judgment ever handed down by the Constitutional Court, S v. Vermaas; S v. Du Plessis,[10] took the form of a consolidated referral of two criminal cases from the Transvaal Provincial Division of the High Court in which reliance had been placed on the right to legal representation at state expense in section 25(3)(e) of the 1993 Constitution. In both cases the accused, who had at one time at least been financially well off, were facing numerous charges of 'white-collar' theft, fraud, and corruption. After initially paying for their lawyers themselves, the accused ran out of money and applied for an order directing the state to meet the further costs of their defence. The two trial judges separately decided that the accused were not entitled to rely on section 25(3)(e) because their trials had begun before the 1993 Constitution took effect. Nevertheless, both judges referred the possible application of the right to state-funded legal representation to the Constitutional Court in the event that it might take a different view.

Like sections 35(2)(c) and 35(3)(g) of the 1996 Constitution, the right to legal representation in section 25(3)(e) of the 1993 Constitution was not absolute, but qualified by the phrase, 'where substantial injustice would otherwise result'. The judicial enquiry suggested by this qualification, the Constitutional Court held, depended on 'factual findings and assessments' which it, as a court of final instance, was 'ill equipped' to make.[11] The Court accordingly declined to 'venture' an answer to the main question put to it, and remitted the two cases back to their respective trial courts for consideration.[12] In so doing, the Court laid down some guidelines for trial courts when considering whether to order the state to fund the costs of an accused person's defence, including the need to assess 'the accused person's aptitude or ineptitude to fend for himself or herself'.[13] The Court also took the opportunity to express its concern about the steps that had thus far been taken by the state to put in place 'mechanisms that are adequate for the enforcement of the right [to legal representation]'.[14]

The *Vermaas* case is neatly illustrative of the perils facing a constitutional court with a relatively low caseload and an ambitious transformation agenda. Having arisen in the fourth case presented to it, the nature and scope of the right to legal representation has not again arisen for decision before the Constitutional Court. The Court's passing remarks in *Vermaas* therefore constitute the only contribution it has been able to make thus far to the case law on this point. Although the guidelines laid down by the Court are generally favourable to poor litigants,[15] they do not constitute the kind of comprehensive statement that a pro-poor court might have wanted to have made had it known that it would get so few opportunities to pronounce on this issue. And yet the doctrinal arguments and policy considerations that the Constitutional Court took into account in *Vermaas* were sound. The two High Court cases *had* been incompetently referred to it, and trial courts *are* best placed to decide the essentially factual question of whether a 'substantial injustice' will result from a failure to grant the accused legal representation. Could the Court therefore have decided the *Vermaas* case any differently?

The answer to this question depends on one's attitude to what one might call the Court's style of adjudication. All courts develop over time certain internal rules about how much they are prepared to say when deciding legal questions put to them. Although it was not necessarily the case at the beginning of its life, the South African Constitutional Court has settled into an adjudicative style that Iain Currie (following Cass Sunstein) has described as one of 'judicious avoidance'.[16] The characteristic feature of this style is a reluctance on the part of the Court to pronounce on any issue that does not have to be decided for purposes of settling the case.

Though undoubtedly prudent and well intentioned, this approach inevitably limits the contribution that the Court is able to make to important areas of law affecting the poor. As the *Vermaas* case illustrates, because of the Court's relatively low caseload, the opportunity to pronounce on a particular issue affecting the poor may seldom arise. In this situation, judicious avoidance turns out to be, somewhat ironically, a high-risk strategy. On the one hand, the Court carefully avoids pre-empting its approach to later legal questions, some of which may impact on the poor. On the other hand, however, the Court runs the risk that it may forgo its only opportunity in many years to establish a pro-poor legal principle to guide other courts in their interpretation of the Constitution.

In the *Vermaas* case, with the wisdom of hindsight, the Court might have done a little more to give the right to legal representation in criminal cases an expressly pro-poor inflection. Thus, in addition to the accused's 'aptitude or ineptitude to fend for himself or herself', the Court could have referred expressly to the accused's ability to afford legal representation. Although this criterion would have favoured accused persons (like those in the *Vermaas* case) who had simply run out of funds, the two criteria would, in combination, have given a more balanced picture of the circumstances that prevent poor people from being properly heard when charged with criminal offences. In the absence of this additional criterion, it has been left to the lower courts to develop the case law on legal representation, with varying results.[17]

Direct Access After deciding in Vermaas that the two cases at issue had been incompetently referred to it, the Constitutional Court consoled the losing parties with the suggestion that an application for direct access could have been brought in this situation.[18] At that early stage of the Court's jurisprudence, these consolatory words found some support in the Court's decision in S v Zuma and others,[19] in which direct access had been granted in order to rectify a 'serious prejudice to the general administration of justice'[20] arising from a provision of the old-order Criminal Procedure Act.[21] The Court's subsequent jurisprudence on direct access, however, has not been as encouraging.

Section 167(6) of the 1996 Constitution, which replaced section 100(2) of the 1993 Constitution, provides that '[n]ational legislation or the rules of the Constitutional Court must allow a person, when it is in the interests of justice and with leave of the Constitutional Court—(a) to bring a matter directly to the Constitutional Court.'[22] Because of the complexity, cost and time involved in taking a case through the ordinary courts, this provision potentially constitutes an important mechanism through which poor litigants may access the Constitutional Court. In some countries, constitutional courts have attempted to redress exclusion from the ordinary courts through creative interpretation of rules such as this. In India, for example, the large-scale human rights violations experienced under the internal state of emergency from 1975–77 were partly responsible in the post-emergency years for producing activist judges determined to restore public faith in the judiciary through 'achieving distributive justice'.[23] As perceived by the judiciary itself, one of the biggest constitutional problems in the eyes of the majority of Indians was the denial of access to justice, largely owing to the high costs of litigation and strict rules of standing, particularly in Supreme Court cases. In order to rectify this problem, a group of activist judges, including Justice Bhagwati, deliberately facilitated public interest litigation by relaxing the rules of standing and procedure. The end result was that any individual or group could in theory bring a Supreme Court action for themselves or on behalf of others, even by posting a complaint on a postcard.[24]

Despite the existence of rules of standing theoretically favourable to public interest litigation,[25] the South African experience has been to some extent the opposite of that in India. Although the Constitutional Court's direct access rules are premised on an inclusive public interest ideal, in practice (as we explain below) the Court has interpreted these rules very restrictively. Based on the number of cases involving poor people decided by it, and taking into account the vast difference in population-size between the two countries, the South African Constitutional Court is arguably a less accessible institution than the Indian Supreme Court, which is able to treat each letter or petition addressed to it as a writ initiating legal proceedings, allowing direct access by literally hundreds of poor litigants each year. Indeed, in India, the Supreme Court frequently 'actively invites (or induces)' cases to be brought to it as the court of first and last instance.[26]

Under its first set of rules,[27] which were applicable from 1995 until 2003, the South African Constitutional Court refused the vast majority of applications for direct access by finding non-compliance with one or more of the criteria set out in the then applicable rule 17(1) – 'exceptional circumstances', 'urgency' and 'public importance'.[28] Building on this jurisprudence in cases decided under rule 17's successor rule, rule 18 of 2003, the Court has developed the principle that 'this Court should ordinarily not deal with matters as both a Court of first and as one of last resort'.[29] Recently, the Court has added two more restrictive principles governing applications for direct access: first, that applicants for direct access should show that they have 'exhausted all other remedies or procedures';[30] and, second, that the applicant must have reasonable prospects of success based on the substantive merits of his or her case.[31]

Although clarifying the evolving principles in terms of which the Court refuses applications for direct access, a comparison of the total number of direct access applications against the total number of judgments in which direct access was granted would not necessarily reveal anything about the accessibility of the Court to the poor, for several reasons. First, any Constitutional Court must legitimately be able to exclude cases in which the merits are very weak. Secondly, as an overview of applications for direct access to the Court reveals, a substantial number of applications for direct access are 'repeat chancers', that is, applicants who attempt to have spurious applications heard under multiple guises.[32] Thirdly, it would be wrong simply to assume that the majority of applications for direct access (whether successful or not) are brought by poor applicants.

Given these limitations, we decided instead to examine the actual manner in which poor people are treated when they apply directly for assistance from the Court.[33] This research, which consisted of interviews with the officials concerned, revealed that applications presented to the Court's Registry Office by unrepresented applicants (most unrepresented applicants are poor, and are unrepresented precisely because they are too poor to afford legal fees) are typically turned away with the advice to seek legal support elsewhere.[34] More research is needed to ascertain what happens to constitutional complaints turned away in this manner, but it seems from the limited number of cases brought to the Constitutional Court by institutions such as the South African Human Rights Commission that the alternative avenues of redress recommended by the Court do not prove very useful.

Overall, our research on direct access reveals that the Court has been extremely reluctant to act as a court of first and last instance. When coupled with the principle of avoidance that applies in the lower courts,[35] this means that only the most persistent and well-supported litigants are able to access the Court.

Social Rights Cases

The Constitutional Court has decided five social rights cases to date: *Soobramoney v. Minister of Health (KwaZulu-Natal)*[36] (health care rights); *Government of the Republic of South Africa v. Grootboom*[37] (housing rights); *Minister of Health v. Treatment Action Campaign (No. 2)*[38] (health care rights); *Khosa v. Minister of Social Development*[39] (social security rights); and *Port Elizabeth Municipality v. Various Occupiers*[40] (housing rights).

Soobramoney, *Grootboom* and *TAC* all dealt with claims for positive relief against the state based on social rights enumerated in the 1996 Constitution. *Khosa* concerned whether certain provisions of the Social Assistance Act 59 of 1992 that excluded non-citizens from receiving benefits were constitutional. The fifth case, *Port Elizabeth Municipality*, dealt with the negative infringement of the right not to be evicted from one's home without an order of court.

Although the Court decided in favour of the applicants in four of these cases,[41] there are two broad reasons why its social rights jurisprudence is a little disappointing from a pro-poor perspective. First, none of the judgments provided direct, substantive relief to the applicants, an outcome that gives little incentive to poor litigants to seek relief through constitutional litigation. Second, the standard of review adopted by the Court – viz. that the overall policy, legislation and practices of government in the sector concerned should be reasonable – requires litigants to have a sophisticated understanding of often complex policy and budgetary issues. This requirement, too, acts as a disincentive to the poor to bring cases to the Court, unless they have substantial legal and other expert support. The remainder of this section elaborates on these two criticisms.

Relief Section 172(1) of the 1996 Constitution provides that, '[w]hen deciding a constitutional matter within its power, a court—(a) … (b) may make any order that is just and equitable.' In addition, section 38 confers on courts the power to grant 'appropriate relief, including a declaration of rights'. In theory, these provisions give the Constitutional Court scope to develop innovative remedies for the enforcement of constitutional rights, including pro-poor rights.[42] Despite the existence of these powers, however, 'litigation aimed at advancing the rights of the poor has [thus far] resulted in fairly conventional and somewhat limited relief'.[43]

In *Soobramoney*, where the Court found that the right not to be refused 'emergency medical treatment' did not extend to renal dialysis, no relief was granted to the applicant, who died of kidney failure shortly after the judgment. In *Grootboom*, a declaratory order was granted requiring the state to meet its obligations under section 26(2) of the 1996 Constitution to 'devise and implement within its available resources a comprehensive and coordinated [housing] program'.[44] Such a programme, the Court continued, should 'include reasonable measures such as ... [the provision of] relief for people who have no access to land, no roof over their heads, and who are living in intolerable conditions or crisis situations'.[45] Although remarking in passing that the South African Human Rights Commission (which appeared as *amicus curiae* in the case) would in the course of carrying out its constitutional mandate 'monitor and report' on the state's progress in complying with the judgment,[46] the Court did not incorporate this oversight function in its order. In consequence, when the Human Rights Commission attempted to report back to the Court on the intolerable conditions still prevailing in the claimant community, the Court refused to engage with it, saying that it had been divested of jurisdiction in the case.

In the *Treatment Action Campaign* case, the Pretoria High Court had granted a structural interdict requiring the government to revise its policy regarding the prevention of mother-to-child transmission of HIV/AIDS and to submit the revised policy to the court.[47] Whilst deciding in favour of the claimant, the Constitutional Court considered a structural interdict to be inappropriate, and instead granted an order declaring government policy to be unreasonable, coupled with a mandatory order directing that the restrictions on the use of a particular antiretroviral drug outside of selected research sites be removed, and that the drug be made available at all public hospitals and clinics.[48]

In *Khosa*, the remedy chosen by the Court was to provide a curative re-wording for sections of the Social Assistance Act and other legislation and regulations, so as to allow permanent residents the same social assistance benefits as South African citizens.[49]

Thus, in spite of the power given to the Court to fashion appropriate relief, in the four cases where the Court has considered the state's positive obligations vis-à-vis particular social rights, it has refused relief in the one case in which a poor person sought a direct remedy (*Soobramoney*) and, in the other three cases, mandated that the applicable government policy be changed, without, however, granting any direct relief to the affected individuals.[50]

In the most recent social rights case, where the Court was asked to consider the ambit of the state's negative obligation to protect the right not to be arbitrarily evicted from one's home (*Port Elizabeth Municipality*), the municipality sought a ruling that it was not constitutionally obliged to find alternative accommodation or land when seeking to evict unlawful occupiers. The Court rejected this argument, finding that in most circumstances a municipality would be obliged to procure a mediated solution and provide alternative accommodation or land before an eviction could be executed.[51] This decision *does* provide concrete benefits to poor people, in as much as municipal evictions may now not proceed without a proper plan for relocation.

Reasonableness Standard of Review Although it was not the first social rights case to be heard by the Court, Grootboom was the first case in which the Court began to develop a systematic approach to the justiciability of social rights. Declining to accept the minimum core content argument raised by the amicus curiae,[52] the Court chose instead to advance a narrow interpretation of the state's obligations vis-à-vis social rights in which the standard of review was not whether a particular right had been violated but 'whether the legislative and other measures taken by the state are reasonable' in the context of 'the state's available means'.[53] Grootboom established the principle that, to be regarded as reasonable, a government programme must be 'comprehensive' and 'coordinated', and must 'clearly allocate responsibilities and tasks to the different spheres of government and ensure that the appropriate financial and human resources are available'.[54] Furthermore, 'to be reasonable', programmes must be 'balanced and flexible',[55] and measures must take into account 'those whose needs are the most urgent'.[56]

The reasonableness test developed in *Grootboom* was relied on in the *Treatment Action Campaign* case and now appears to be the Court's established approach when it comes to deciding the positive obligations imposed on the state by social rights. Cass Sunstein has described this model of review as one derived from administrative law.[57] Although one recent commentator has questioned this description,[58] it remains broadly accurate given the Court's continued refusal to entertain arguments about the minimum core content of social rights.

The Court has responded more unambiguously when called on to consider the interaction between social rights and the prohibition on unfair discrimination, a civil and political right. This was the case in *Khosa*, where the Court had to decide whether the exclusion from South Africa's social security system of permanent residents 'who, but for their lack of citizenship, would qualify for the benefit provided under the scheme',[59] amounted to unfair discrimination and as such was unreasonable. The Court found in the affirmative, ruling that the exclusion of permanent residents from social security benefits amounted to unfair discrimination, which was neither reasonable under section 27(2) of the Constitution (right to social security) nor justifiable in terms of section 36 (the general limitations clause). In doing so, the Court implied the existence of a new component to the reasonableness test: whether or not the policy amounts to unfair discrimination.[60]

The Court has also been more robust when it has been called on to protect an unqualified right such as the section 26(3) right not to be arbitrarily evicted from one's home, as it did in *Port Elizabeth Municipality*. Beyond clarifying the state's negative obligation correlative to this right, the Court read particular positive obligations into section 26(3), placing an obligation on the state in most cases to provide alternative accommodation or land when evictions are being undertaken. In this regard, the Court held that, in determining in each case whether an eviction order was just and equitable (and consequently reasonable), the trial court would have to take into account 'the reasonableness of offers made in connection with suitable alternative accommodation', with particular reference to vulnerable occupiers (for example, the elderly, children, disabled persons and female-headed households).[61]

Notwithstanding such advances, the failure of the Court to pursue a rights-based analysis of the content of social rights and the nature of the state's obligations vis-à-vis each right has, in the view of several commentators, been detrimental to the development of South Africa's social rights jurisprudence.[62] Instead, the Court has devised a relatively weak standard of review that would not be out of place in an administrative-law setting. This standard has the potential to diminish the capacity of the Court to function as an institutional voice for the poor since it requires expert understanding of complex policy and budgetary issues, making it all but impossible for the poor to bring social rights cases without extensive technical and financial support.

Constitutional Challenges to Pro-poor Legislation, Policies and Practices

In the two areas of law thus far examined, the Constitutional Court has on several occasions chosen rules that have reduced rather than enhanced its capacity to function as an institutional voice for the poor. Its record in the third area of law chosen for discussion in this chapter is radically different. In a series of cases in which pro-poor legislation, policies or practices have been challenged by members of previously advantaged groups the Court has not only dismissed the challenge but also strongly endorsed the political branches' attempts to redress the socio-economic legacy of apartheid. Ironically, the poor were not directly party to any of these cases. Rather, the democratic government played proxy to their interests, either by enacting pro-poor legislation, or by engaging in executive conduct aimed at ameliorating their position. In one other case of a slightly different type, the poor *were* directly represented in a successful challenge to old-order legislation. We include this case here to illustrate another dimension of the Court's pro-poor jurisprudence, and also because it constitutes one of the few cases, outside the Court's social rights jurisprudence, in which the poor have been directly heard.

Pretoria City Council v. Walker[63] concerned an appeal by the Pretoria City Council against a High Court ruling that the cross-subsidisation of the cost of providing municipal services to the poor amounted to unfair discrimination. The Court's decision in this case established the principle that administrative policies and practices aimed at redressing apartheid's socio-economic legacy, even if they impacted negatively on previously advantaged groups, would be constitutionally supported.

In *Walker*, the Court had to consider whether the Pretoria City Council's rates policy, which differentiated between formerly white and formerly black residential areas to the benefit of the latter, amounted to unfair discrimination. The majority of the Court held that, although the levying of differential charges amounted to indirect discrimination on the grounds of race, this discrimination was not unfair[64] given the constitutional imperative to right apartheid's socio-economic wrongs.[65]

In *Premier, Mpumalanga v. Executive Committee, Association of State-aided Schools, Eastern Transvaal*[66] the Court upheld the province of Mpumalanga's decision to discontinue paying bursaries to 'Model C' (that is, formerly white) schools in the province. Agreeing with the provincial government that the payment of bursaries to schools that mainly educated white pupils was one of the unfair legacies of the past that needed to be eradicated, the Court held that the discontinuation of such bursaries was neither unjust nor inequitable.[67] On the other hand, the Court found that the manner of termination of bursaries was procedurally unfair and in breach of the right to just administrative action, and held that the province should have given reasonable notice prior to termination.[68] Overall, however, the Court approved of the executive's policy (if not its precise conduct) in favouring previously disadvantaged groups.[69]

As in *Premier, Province of Mpumalanga*, the appeal to the Constitutional Court in *Bel Porto School Governing Body v. Premier of the Western Cape Province*[70] concerned the validity of a provincial education department's policy aimed at giving effect to the constitutional imperative to introduce racial equity into its educational system. The appellant schools complained that the policy infringed both their right, and the right of the children attending their schools, to equality and dignity, and also that the manner in which the policy was being implemented, particularly the lack of information surrounding the rationalisation process, infringed their right to just administrative action.[71] The specific issue at stake was the redeployment of staff from overstaffed schools to understaffed schools in order to equalise the apartheid-inherited legacy of gross disparities in funding and teaching resources between white schools and black schools.

The Court was divided on the issue of whether the rationalisation policy violated the previously advantaged schools' right to just administrative action (six out of ten judges finding that there was no infringement of just administrative action rights because the appellant schools received adequate notice of the policy).[72] However, the judges were united on the fact that the policy itself was not unfair. This was because, although there were long-standing differences between formerly white and formerly black schools, these differences were on the whole to the benefit of formerly white schools.[73] Taking this legacy into account, the Court found that it could not be said that the formerly white schools had been subject to unfair discrimination.[74]

Minister of Finance v. Van Heerden[75] concerned an application for leave to appeal from an order of the Cape High Court declaring Rule 4.2.1 of the Political Office-Bearers' Pension Fund discriminatory in that it provided for differentiated employer contributions in respect of members of Parliament and other political office-bearers. The appellants in the Constitutional Court, the Minister of Finance and the Political Officer Bearers' Pension Fund, defended the measures on the grounds that they constituted justifiable 'limited affirmative action'. The Court agreed with the appellants, finding that the differentiation in employer contributions was aimed at protecting or advancing previously disadvantaged persons and that such restitutionary measures did not infringe section 9(2) of the 1996 Constitution.[76] Holding that the disputed measures in Rule 4.2.1 were directed at achieving equality between old and new parliamentarians – the majority of the latter group having been disadvantaged by past unfair discrimination and exclusion – the Constitutional Court overruled the High Court.[77]

In *Jaftha v. Schoeman and others; Van Rooyen v. Stoltz and others*,[78] the Court upheld an appeal against a decision of the Cape High Court in favour of the applicants, who were unemployed with few assets and who were threatened with losing their homes because they could not pay small grocery-related debts. In a unanimous judgment, the Court found certain provisions of the apartheid-era Magistrates' Courts Act,[79] which provide for execution against the immovable property of judgment debtors, unconstitutional to the extent that they allow a person's home to be sold in execution without consideration of all the relevant circumstances. Finding that any measure that deprives a person of their existing home without oversight by the courts amounts to an unjustified limitation on the right to housing,[80] the Court held that an appropriate remedy would be to provide judicial oversight of the execution process so that a court could determine in each case whether an execution order was justified.[81] This case, albeit of a slightly different type, provides a further indication of the Court's preparedness to listen and respond to the concerns of the poor where doing so does not involve it in second-guessing the wisdom of post-apartheid transformation policies.

Some Lessons

This overview of the Constitutional Court's decisions in cases impacting on the poor's capacity to be heard reveals a mixed record. In its direct access and social rights jurisprudence, the Court appears to have chosen principles and rules that have made it harder for the poor to litigate cases than the text of the 1996 Constitution would suggest. In the third category of cases, on the other hand, the Court has stridently defended the political branches' social transformation efforts, and has laid down a number of unambiguously pro-poor principles and rules. How can this apparent anomaly be explained? And to what extent were these outcomes dictated by legal doctrine and political context?

In its single decision on the right to legal representation, *Vermaas*, the Court cannot be faulted on doctrinal grounds for having remitted the question of whether the accused should be afforded this right to the trial courts. The Court could also not have known at the time that more ten years would pass without its being given another opportunity to pronounce on this right. Nevertheless, the *Vermaas* case illustrates the danger inherent in the Court's somewhat cautious adjudicative style, that is, that the prudence shown in declining to answer a legal question potentially affecting the poor may be defeated by the length of time that it takes for that question to arise again.

The Court's record in its direct access jurisprudence is also based on sound legal principles, such as the need to have disputes of fact properly ventilated in the trial court, and for cases to be settled on non-constitutional grounds if possible. Had the Court realized what the practical effect of adopting these principles would be, however, it might have phrased them more flexibly. The Court's strict direct access jurisprudence means that it is largely dependent on the lower courts to ensure that cases reach it. Given the notorious aversion of lower-court judges to being overruled on appeal, and the principle of constitutional avoidance, the danger exists that the lower courts might act as gatekeepers to constitutional justice, ensuring that only the most persistent, articulate and financially well-resourced litigants are able to be heard by the Constitutional Court.

Without further empirical research, it is impossible to say whether the Court's direct access jurisprudence has indeed had this effect. Certainly, many other issues, such as the availability of resources for pro-poor litigation,[82] and the willingness of lawyers to take cases *pro bono*, impact on the capacity of the poor to access the Court. All these factors are beyond the Court's control. Nevertheless, the Court could have taken them into account by choosing procedural rules that gave the poor the best possible chance of accessing the Court from within the constraints of their situation. For a Court committed to achieving the Constitution's vision of a transformed society, the practical consequences of its rule choices must surely be of some relevance.

The Court's social rights jurisprudence has also inadvertently impacted on the ease with which the poor are able to voice their concerns. In declining to grant immediate relief to poor litigants in social rights cases, and by setting a review standard that requires the applicant to critique the entire package of policy choices in the sector concerned, the Court has all but precluded poor people from bringing this kind of case on their own. This outcome was not dictated by pre-existing doctrine, since the Court fashioned its social rights jurisprudence from scratch. Rather, it is best explained by the Court's desire to respect the limits of its role within the South African political system. Thus the Court's refusal to grant immediate, concrete relief to poor people is based on its unwillingness to become a forum in which the political branches' decisions on the prioritisation of resources can be overturned. Likewise, its reasonableness standard of review is the product of the Court's apparent aversion to pulling too strongly on the complex web of choices that determine the state's welfare programmes.[83]

In the past, considerations such as these were adduced as reasons for not giving courts the power to enforce social rights. What the experience in South Africa over the last ten years illustrates is that it *is* possible to give a judicious court this power, but that the usefulness of this power to the poor will be constrained by the inherent limits on the judiciary in a system based on the separation of powers. To be sure, the international acclaim[84] that the Constitutional Court has received for its social rights decisions is justified, not least because of the skill it has shown in steering the exercise of its review powers between the Scylla of overzealous enforcement and the Charybdis of non-justiciability.[85] But the conceptual gains made by the Court in this area of its work have yet to result in the increased use of the courts by the poor.

In the third set of cases the Court's pro-poor political convictions are plain to see. On each occasion in which legislation or executive action aimed at redressing apartheid's socio-economic legacy has been challenged, the Court has not only found in favour of the political branches, but also endorsed their transformation efforts in emphatic terms. Interestingly, too, the Court's minimalist style gives way in these cases to extended passages on the evils of apartheid, that system's ongoing socio-economic legacy, and the laudable efforts that the post-apartheid state is making to right historical wrongs. Like the political branches themselves, the Court here acts as a megaphone for the voice of the poor, translating their needs and concerns into the powerful discourse of constitutional law.

The explanation for the Court's record in this set of cases cannot be found in any difference in the composition of the Court or in the quality of the legal arguments presented to it. Rather, it lies in the fact that the political convictions of the judges on the Court lean in favour of social and economic transformation, which in any case finds strong support in the Constitution; and the fact that the separation of powers problem falls away in these cases because the Court is simply required to amplify the reasons already given by the political branches for the action in question.

In short, the lesson to be learned from the South African experience over the least ten years is that pro-poor judges and a pro-poor constitution are necessary but not sufficient conditions for courts in new democracies to function as an institutional voice for the poor. At least in the early part of their life, these courts' need to accept the inherent limits on their powers will prevent them from becoming a forum in which the poor are able to win concrete benefits that they are unable to win in the ordinary political process. This does not mean, of course, that courts cannot function as important sites for communicating the concerns of the poor. It simply means that the use of courts by the poor must be part of a broader political strategy.

Notes

1 We use this term as defined in the chapter by Gloppen in this volume.
2 Section 167(3)(a) of the 1996 Constitution.
3 *Commissioner of Customs and Excise v. Container Logistics (Pty) Ltd; Commissioner of Customs and Excise v. Rennies Group Ltd t/a Renfreight* 1999 (3) SA 771 (A) para. 20.
4 *Pharmaceuticals Manufacturers Association of SA: In re ex parte President of the Republic of South Africa* 2000 (2) SA 674 (CC) para. 44.
5 *Carmichele v. Minister of Safety and Security (Centre for Applied Legal Studies Intervening)* 2001 (4) SA 938 (CC).
6 These figures are based on a hand search of the court's records.
7 The Russian Constitutional Court, for example, received about 15 000 petitions from 1994-1995, of which 98 per cent were declined by the Secretariat of the Court. Of the remaining 2 per cent (300 petitions), 39 were decided on their merits. (These statistics are drawn from Lee Epstein, Jack Knight and Olga Shvetsova, 'The Role of Constitutional Courts in the Establishment and Maintenance of Democratic Systems of Government', *Law & Society Review* 35 (2001): 117–64, 122 fn. 6.) See also Uprimny's chapter on the Colombian Constitutional Court in this volume.
8 Section 28(1)(h).

9 See, however, *Nkuzi Development Association v. Government of the Republic of South Africa* 2002 (2) SA 733 (LCC) (deducing a right to legal representation at state expense in certain civil matters from the right of access to courts in section 34 of the 1996 Constitution). In general on the right to legal representation in South Africa, see Stephen Ellmann, 'Weighing and Implementing the Right to Counsel', *South African Law Journal,* 121 (2004): 318–38 and Geoff Budlender, 'Access to Courts', *South African Law Journal,* 121 (2004): 339–58.

10 1995 (3) SA 292 (CC).

11 Ibid para. 15.

12 The intermediate question whether the rights in the 1993 Constitution applied to pending cases was settled in *S v. Mhlungu* 1995 (3) SA 867 (CC), a decision handed down in between the referral of the two High Court cases to the Constitutional Court and its decision in *Vermaas.*

13 *Vermaas*, para. 15.

14 Ibid., para. 16.

15 Besides 'the accused person's aptitude or ineptitude to fend for himself or herself', the guidelines in *Vermaas* refer to the 'ramifications [of the decision to grant legal representation] and their complexity or simplicity … how grave the consequences of a conviction may look, and any other factor that needs to be evaluated in the determination of the likelihood or unlikelihood that, if the trial were to proceed without a lawyer for the defence, the result would be "substantial injustice"', *Vermaas*, para. 15.

16 See I. Currie, 'Judicious Avoidance', *South African Journal on Human Rights,* 15 (1999): 138–65, drawing on Cass R. Sunstein, *Legal Reasoning and Political Conflict* (New York: Oxford University Press, 1996).

17 See *S v. Moos* 1998 (1) SACR 372 (C); *Mgcina v. Regional Magistrate, Lenasia* 1997 (2) SACR 711 (W); *S v. Mngadi* 2000 (1) SACR 152 (W), *S v. Pienaar* 2000 (2) SACR 143 (NC); and *S v. Manuel* 2001 (4) SA 1351 (W).

18 *Vermaas*, paras 13–14.

19 1995 (2) SA 642 (CC).

20 Ibid., para. 11.

21 Section 217(1)(b)(ii) of the Criminal Procedure Act 51 of 1977 provided that where a confession was made to a magistrate or confirmed or reduced in writing before a magistrate, it should be admissible in evidence against the accused and should be presumed, unless the contrary was proved, to have been freely made.

22 From 1 December 2003, applications for direct access have been governed by rule 18 of the Constitutional Court's Rules (available at <www.constitutionalcourt.org.za>), which were promulgated in terms of Government Notice R1603 in *Government Gazette* 25643 of 31 October 2003. Under the previous Rules of the Constitutional Court, which were promulgated in terms of Government Notice R1584 in *Regulation Gazette* 5394 of 16 September 1994, rule 17 governed applications for direct access to the Constitutional Court. For a comparison of the current and old rules, see note 28 below.

23 P. Bhagwati, 'Judicial Activism and Public Interest Litigation', *Columbia Journal of Transnational Law*, 23 (1985): 561–77, 566.

24 See Tembeka Ngcukaitobi, 'The Evolution of Standing Rules in South Africa and their Significance in Promoting Social Justice', *South African Journal on Human Rights*, 18 (2002): 590–613, 600–601.

25 Section 38 of the 1996 Constitution provides that '(a) anyone acting in their own interest; (b) anyone acting on behalf of another person who cannot act in their own

name; (c) anyone acting as a member of, or in the interest of, a group or class of persons; (d) anyone acting in the public interest; and (e) an association acting in the interest of its members' may 'approach a competent court, alleging that a right in the Bill of Rights has been infringed or threatened …'.

26 M. Dasgupta, 'Social Action for Women? Public Interest Litigation in India's Supreme Court', *Law, Social Justice & Global Development Journal*, 1 (2002) (electronic journal available at <www2.warwick.ac.uk/fac/soc/law/elj/lgd/2002_1/dasgupta/>).

27 Rule 17(1) provided: 'The Court shall allow direct access in terms of section 100(2) of the Interim Constitution *in exceptional circumstances only*, which will ordinarily exist only where the *matter is of such urgency*, or otherwise *of such public importance*, that the delay necessitated by the use of the ordinary procedures would prejudice the public interest or prejudice the ends of justice and good government.' Emphasis added. These 1995 rules pertained until the adoption of new rules promulgated under GN R1603 in GG 25634 of 31 October 2003. Rule 18 of the new rules brought the Constitutional Court Rules into line with section 167(6) of the 1996 Constitution, in terms of which direct access was broadly contemplated when 'it is in the interests of justice'. Between the coming into force of the 1996 Constitution and the adoption of the new rules in 2003, the situation was never clarified as to whether, under the old rules of the 1996 Constitution, there were any circumstances beyond those contemplated by Rule 17 which would justify the granting of direct access under section 167(6) 'in the interests of justice'.

28 See for example *S v. Makwanyane* 1995 (3) SA 391 (CC); 1995 (6) BCLR 665 (CC) paras 4 and 6; *S v. Dlamini* (heard with *S v. Dladla*; *S v Joubert*; *S v Schietekat*) 1999 (4) SA 623 (CC); 1999 (7) BCLR 771 (CC) para. 35; *Moseneke v. The Master* 2001 (2) SA 18 (CC); 2001 (2) BCLR 103 (CC) para. 19.

29 *Brink v. Kitshoff NO* 1996 (4) SA 197 (CC); 1996 (6) BCLR 752 (CC) para. 14; *Transvaal Agricultural Union v. Minister of Land Affairs* 1997 (2) SA 621 (CC) para. 18; *Bruce v. Fleecytex Johannesburg CC* 1998 (2) SA 1143 (CC); 1998 (4) BCLR 415 (CC) para. 8; *Member of the Executive Council for Development Planning and Local Government, Gauteng v. Democratic Party* 1998 (4) SA 1157 (CC); 1998 (7) BCLR 855 (CC) para. 32; *Christian Education South Africa v. The Minister of Education* 1999 (2) SA 83 (CC); 1998 (12) BCLR 1449 (CC) para. 12; *Van der Spuy v. General Council of the Bar of South Africa (Minister of Justice and Constitutional Development, Advocates for Transformation and Law Society of South Africa Intervening)* 2002 (5) SA 392 (CC) para. 19; 2002 (10) BCLR 1092 (CC) para. 18; *National Gambling Board v. Premier, KwaZulu-Natal* 2002 (2) SA 715 (CC); 2002 (2) BCLR 156 (CC) paras 29 and 38; *Satchwell v. President of the Republic of South Africa* 2003 (4) SA 266 (CC); 2004 (1) BCLR 1 (CC) para. 6.

30 *Besserglik v. Minister of Trade, Industry and Tourism* 1996 (4) SA 331 (CC) para. 6.

31 *Dormehl v. Minister of Justice* 2000 (2) SA 825 (CC); 2000 (5) BCLR 471 (CC) para. 5; *MEC for Development Planning and Local Government in Gauteng v. Democratic Party* 1998 (4) SA 1157 (CC); 1998 (7) BCLR 855 para. 32.

32 South Africa's Constitutional Court register reflects three repeat applicants who have each attempted to bring an application in a number of guises on at least three different occasions.

33 Here direct access refers to direct access in the truest sense, that is, applications made to the Court directly 'from the street' as the court of first instance, as envisaged in section 167(6)(a) of the Constitution.

34 Applicants are usually advised to take their complaint to the South African Human Rights Commission or to the Legal Aid Board.

35 This principle holds that a court should attempt first to resolve a dispute by applying ordinary legal principles, before applying the Constitution. See Johan de Waal, Iain Currie and Gerhard Erasmus, *The Bill of Rights Handbook* 4th edn (Cape Town: Juta, 2001), pp. 27–8.

36 1998 (1) SA 765 (CC).

37 2001 (1) SA 46 (CC).

38 2002 (5) SA 721 (CC).

39 2004 (6) BCLR 569 (CC).

40 2004 (12) BCLR 1268 (CC).

41 In its first social rights case, *Soobramoney*, the Court did not find in favour of the applicant, interpreting section 27(3)'s right to emergency medical treatment as not including a right to ongoing renal dialysis treatment for chronic diabetes sufferers such as Mr Soobramoney.

42 T. Bollyky, 'R if C > P + B: A Paradigm for Judicial Remedies in Socio-economic Rights Violations', *South African Journal on Human Rights*, 18 (2002): 161–200.

43 K. Pillay, 'Addressing Poverty through the Courts: How Have we Fared in the First Decade of Democracy?', paper presented at a Conference 'Celebrating a Decade of Democracy', Durban, 23–25 January 2004.

44 *Grootboom*, para. 99.

45 Ibid.

46 Ibid., para. 97.

47 *Minister of Health v. Treatment Action Campaign* 2002 (4) BCLR 356 (T).

48 *TAC*, para. 135.

49 *Khosa*, paras 86–96.

50 Prior to the main decision in the *Grootboom* case, the Court did grant an interim order, on 21 September 2000, in terms of which the Court ordered the government to provide basic sanitation, water and basic waterproofing materials to the applicants (*Grootboom and others v. Government of the Republic of South Africa* (unreported) CCT Case 38/00 paras 1–3). However, this order was only ever partially implemented and its enforcement was not monitored by the Court.

51 *Port Elizabeth Municipality*, paras 29–30, 39–47, 56–9.

52 *Grootboom*, para. 18.

53 Ibid., para. 41.

54 Ibid., para. 39.

55 Ibid., para. 43.

56 Ibid., para. 44.

57 Cass R. Sunstein, *Designing Democracy: What Constitutions Do* (New York: Oxford University Press, 2001), pp. 224–37.

58 M. Wesson, '*Grootboom* and Beyond: Reassessing the Socio-economic Jurisprudence of the South African Constitutional Court', *South African Journal on Human Rights*, 20 (2004): 284–308.

59 *Khosa*, para. 9.

60 To some extent this is a moot point because if any policy is found to violate the section 9 prohibition on unfair discrimination, it will automatically be unconstitutional.

61 *Port Elizabeth Municipality*, para. 30.

62 David Bilchitz, 'Giving Socio-economic Rights Teeth: The Minimum Core and its Importance', *South African Law Journal,* 118 (2002): 484–501; David Bilchitz, 'Towards a Reasonable Approach to the Minimum Core: Laying the Foundations for Future Socio-economic Rights Jurisprudence', *South African Journal on Human Rights*, 19 (2003): 1–26; Sandra Liebenberg, 'The Interpretation of Socio-economic Rights', in M. Chaskalson et al., *Constitutional Law of South Africa* 2nd edn (Cape Town: Juta, 2004), chap. 33; Danie Brand, 'The Proceduralisation of South African Socio-economic Rights Jurisprudence, or "What are socio-economic rights for?"', in Henk Botha, André van der Walt and Johan van der Walt (eds), *Rights and Democracy in a Transformative Constitution* (Stellenbosch: Sun Press, 2003), p. 33.

63 1998 (2) SA 363 (CC). This decision is discussed in greater detail in Theunis Roux, 'Legitimating Transformation: Political Resource Allocation in the South African Constitutional Court', in Siri Gloppen, Roberto Gargarella and Elin Skaar (eds), *Democratization and the Judiciary: The Accountability Function of Courts in New Democracies* (London: Frank Cass, 2004), p. 92 at pp. 98–102.

64 Section 9(3) of the 1996 Constitution (s 8 of the interim Constitution) prohibits the state from *unfairly* discriminating against anyone, whether directly or indirectly, based on race etc. For an analysis of the Court's reasoning as to what amounts to unfair discrimination see *Harksen v. Lane NO* 1998 (1) SA 300 (CC).

65 As per section 9(2) of the 1996 Constitution (s 8(3) of the interim Constitution). On a separate, and less constitutionally important, note the Court found that the Council's selective recovery of arrears debt in white areas did amount to unfair discrimination as it was not the result of a rational and coherent plan with a discernable and pressing transformation objective, but rather of a situation of confusion and uncertainty that unfairly resulted in white defaulters being singled out for legal action while exempting black defaulters.

66 1999 (2) SA 83 (CC).

67 Ibid., para. 47.

68 Ibid., para. 42.

69 For a full assessment of this decision, see Roux, 'Legitimating Transformation', pp. 103–105.

70 2002 (9) BCLR 891 (CC).

71 Ibid., para. 38.

72 Ibid., para. 105.

73 Ibid., paras 8, 36–7.

74 Ibid., paras 39, 48–9.

75 2004 (11) BCLR 1125 (CC).

76 Section 9(2): 'Equality includes the full and equal enjoyment of all rights and freedoms. To promote the achievement of equality, legislative and other measures designed to protect or advance persons, or categories of persons, disadvantaged by unfair discrimination may be taken.'

77 *Van Heerden*, paras 45–57.

78 2005 (2) SA 140 (CC).

79 Act 32 of 1944.

80 *Jaftha*, para. 39.

81 Ibid., para. 54.

82 In general on the importance of this issue to the capacity of courts to function as an institutional voice for the poor, see Charles R. Epp, *The Rights Revolution: Lawyers,*

Activists and Supreme Courts in Comparative Perspective (Chicago: University of Chicago Press, 1998).

83 Lon L. Fuller, 'The Forms and Limits of Adjudication', *Harvard Law Review,* 92 (1978): 353–409.

84 See, for example, Sunstein, *Designing Democracy: What Constitutions Do.*

85 See Theunis Roux, 'Understanding *Grootboom* – A Response to Cass R. Sunstein', *Constitutional Forum,* 12 (2002): 41–51, 41.

Chapter 6

The Enforcement of Social Rights by the Colombian Constitutional Court: Cases and Debates

Rodrigo Uprimny Yepes*

Should courts enforce social rights?[1] This is one of the major questions facing legal theory and theories of democracy today. It is a difficult question because there are strong arguments on either side. For some, if social rights are not judicially enforced, they are not proper rights. For others, the enforcement of social rights leads inevitably to antidemocratic government at the hands of judges.[2] At a theoretical level, this debate appears to be tied, as each side presents strong arguments in support of its case. Nevertheless, in the last two decades, judges in several countries have been quite active in enforcing social rights. For this reason it may be useful to look at the problem of the judicial enforcement of social rights in a new way, that is, by putting on hold, at least for the moment, the more abstract theoretical and normative debates, and proceeding to analyse concrete examples of the judicial enforcement of social rights in different countries. Such comparative studies may provide new perspectives on the question. They may also tell us whether the promise of judicial social rights enforcement has been fulfilled, or whether the fears of those opposed to the judicialisation of social rights were indeed justified.

The Colombian experience is particularly useful for purposes of this discussion as the Colombian Constitutional Court (CCC) has in recent years been fairly active in enforcing social rights in several fields. For example, there has been a significant judicialisation of certain aspects of economic policy in Colombia, which has been supported by some scholars and social movements, but severely criticised by others. This debate has been one of the major political issues in Colombia over the last decade.

This chapter presents and analyses the evolution of the enforcement of social rights by the CCC, and the social and academic discussions it has prompted. The first part sets out the socio-political context in which the activity of the Court has been inscribed, as well as the legal and institutional elements that might have influenced its development. The second part analyses the most representative social rights cases decided by the Court. The third part presents a general overview of the debates that these judicial interventions have aroused. In the fourth part, I try to reach more general conclusions about the relationship between the judicial enforcement of social rights and social emancipation. And, in the last section, I offer some final conclusions.

The Social, Political and Legal Context: A Propitious Setting for the Progressive Enforcement of Social Rights

In Colombia, the judicial enforcement of social rights is closely linked to the enactment of a new Constitution in 1991 and to the work of the CCC in this field. Before 1991, even though Colombia had a long tradition of judicial review and a certain respect for judicial independence, social rights were not judicially enforced.[3]

Many factors explain this lack of enforcement, but I will stress only two: first, the previous Constitution had a rather meagre Bill of Rights; and secondly, the Supreme Court of Justice, which was responsible for judicial review during this period, understood that its function was not primarily to develop and protect rights, but mainly to resolve conflicts between state institutions.

This presentation of the Colombian experience must therefore begin with a short overview of the enactment of the 1991 Constitution, and an analysis of the factors that enabled the CCC to undertake the judicial enforcement of social rights for the first time.[4]

The 1991 Constitution was not the product of a triumphant revolution, but rather grew out of a complex historical context as a consensual attempt to broaden democracy in order to confront violence and political corruption. In these circumstances, some political and social forces that were traditionally excluded from formal politics played an important role in the Constituent Assembly, namely demobilised guerrilla groups, indigenous communities and religious minorities. The Assembly's composition was thus very pluralist by Colombian electoral standards. Indeed, many commentators saw in it the end of the two-party political system.[5]

In that setting, it is not surprising that the 1991 Constitution included the broadening of mechanisms for political participation, the imposition of social justice and equality duties upon the state, and the incorporation of a Charter that is rich in rights and in new judicial mechanisms for their protection. Indeed, it may even be said that the 1991 Constitution is a document that was deliberately intended to transform Colombian society. Using Teitel's terminology, it is a 'forward-looking' rather than 'backward-looking' constitution.[6]

All the above factors explain the generosity of the Constitution on the subject of rights, which, in contrast with the preceding Charter, not only embraces classic civil and political rights, but also gives great legal weight to social rights and collective or third-generation rights. Thus, the Constitution provides that most of the norms that contain these guarantees are directly applicable (CP articles 4 and 85), and establishes that international treaties on the subject are legally binding for national authorities, and constitute criteria for interpreting constitutional rights (article 93). In addition, it provides that human rights may not be suspended during states of emergency (article 214) and that ILO conventions are part of domestic legislation (article 53).

The 1991 Constitution has another characteristic that distinguishes it from the text it supersedes, namely, its direct justiciability. This characteristic is conducive to a certain amount of judicial activism in favour of individual human rights, which, although not impossible, had a weaker legal basis under the former Constitution. In practice, access to constitutional justice is very easy and relatively inexpensive due to the new constitutional design.

Since 1910, every citizen in Colombia has had the right to initiate a public action to demand that a law be declared unconstitutional, without his or her having any particular interest in the issue. The fact that this action has long been available helps to explain why the CCC's activism in the area of social rights dates back to the very beginning of the Court's existence, in 1992. Indeed, even if the Supreme Court had not used its power to decide these kinds of actions in a progressive way, the Colombian legal and political culture was already familiar with judicial review, and the power to annul laws conferred on the CCC could hardly be seen as exaggerated. The Court was thus able to act vigorously from the outset, without having first to establish its legitimacy in the eyes of the other branches of government or political actors generally.

In addition, the 1991 Constitution created the *tutela* action, by which any person may directly demand, with no special prerequisites, the intervention of a judge to protect his or her fundamental rights. By virtue of this action it is relatively easy for citizens to transform a complaint into a legal issue that the justice system has to decide within a short period of time. This is particularly relevant given that comparative studies show that improved access to courts generally enhances their political influence.[7]

Finally, the procedural design of the Constitution confers enormous legal power on the CCC. Because of its ability to annul other judges' decisions on the basis of the Constitution, the Court has in effect become a super-court with authority over the other courts, including the high courts. This facilitates the Court's activism because, once again, as studies in comparative judicial sociology show, there tends to be greater judicial activism in countries where judicial authority is concentrated in a single supreme court.[8]

Beyond these institutional elements, two structural political factors have stimulated the Court's activism: the crisis in political representation, and the weakness of social movements and opposition parties in Colombia.

On the one hand, Colombians' disenchantment with politics has led certain sectors of society to seek solutions from the judiciary to problems that, in principle, should be debated and resolved by other means and channels of political participation. In many situations it is not that the Court takes on other political actors, but rather that it steps in to fill the vacuum they have left. This kind of intervention appears legitimate to broad sectors of the polity, who feel that there exists at least one power that acts progressively and competently.

On the other hand, there is a historical tradition of weak social movements in Colombia. Not only are these movements weak, but also violence has considerably raised the costs and risks of their actions in recent years. Many leaders and activists have been murdered.

These two factors – historical weakness and growing risks – tend to strengthen the judicial role. Indeed, since access to constitutional justice is cheap and easy, and constitutional judges tend to adopt progressive positions, it is natural that many social groups are tempted to resort to legal strategies instead of social and political mobilisation, with all the enormous risks that this implies.

The previous elements may explain why the CCC has adopted an activist attitude, particularly regarding social rights. Nonetheless, an obvious question still remains: why did this Court take on a progressive role, when it could have engaged in activism of another sort, that is, conservative or non-progressive?[9] The answer to this question lies in the nature of the constitutional transition in Colombia.

It is clear that the Court's active intervention in developing social rights might not have been necessary if other political actors had taken on this task. However, many of the actors that dominated the 1991 Constituent Assembly were rapidly weakened in the following years. For instance, the AD–M19 movement (a left-wing, erstwhile armed movement), which won 27 per cent of the votes for the Constituent Assembly, had practically disappeared from the electoral scene four years later. In turn, the National Salvation Movement, a Conservative Party splinter group that initially won 15 per cent of the votes, lost much of its support in subsequent years. In consequence, the forces that have dominated Congress and the electoral scene since 1992, although not clear enemies of the 1991 Constitution, are not committed to its development.

Additionally, there is a strong tension between the social rights thrust of many of the Constitution's clauses and the economic policies implemented by the Colombian government since 1990. Although the Constitution does not expressly prohibit the adoption of neo-liberal policies, many of its norms favour active state intervention in the search for social justice. This immediately led to conflict between the Constitution and the Gaviria government (1990–94), which, after energetically promoting the constituent assembly process, later embarked on an economic liberalisation programme that was clearly neo-liberal.[10]

The weakening of the political coalition that had been responsible for the progressive elements of the 1991 Constitution, together with the government's neo-liberal strategies, meant that, little by little, one of the few institutions capable of applying the Constitution's progressive content was the CCC. And, from the outset, the Court decided to perform this function with vigour, taking its role of upholding fundamental rights, especially social rights, very seriously.

In this way the Court has become practically the only body capable of implementing the original constitutional project, an image that has afforded it significant legitimacy in certain social sectors. However, it frequently walks on a knife-edge because its progressive decisions have resulted in energetic criticism from other social and political sectors. Business groups and government officials regularly attack the Court's jurisprudence, arguing that it is populist and naïve, and that it disregards the real conditions of Colombian society. Thus, there are contrasting trends: on the one hand, several sectors of Congress and the government have tried, so far unsuccessfully, to bring about a number of constitutional reforms to close down the Court or to at least seriously curtail its powers, and on the other, the representatives and leaders of some social movements have showered it with praise and support.

In this piece-meal way a kind of tactical alliance has grown up between the CCC and certain social sectors that have been excluded or hindered from developing the progressive values enshrined in the Constitution.[11] One of the main factors in this evolution has been the enforcement of social rights by the Court.

The Cases: Some Examples of the Judicial Enforcement of Social Rights by the Colombian Constitutional Court

It is difficult to summarise the CCC's jurisprudence on social rights, not only because of the sheer number of rulings on the subject, but also because of the variety of matters the Court has addressed.[12] Nevertheless, it is possible to set out the Court's principal decisions on social rights according to the different forms of protection it has developed, namely, (i) personal protection in individual cases; (ii) protection of similarly situated groups; and (iii) abstract review of economic policies. These different forms of protection have emerged not only from the jurisdictional powers conferred on the Court, but also from the nature of the complaints presented to it and the legal doctrines developed by the Court.

In this context, it is important to bear in mind that the Court has mainly two forms of jurisdiction, and issues basically two kinds of decisions. First, there are rulings on constitutionality, or abstract control of laws, in which the Court declares, with general effect, if a law or certain types of governmental decree are in conformity with the Constitution. These cases arrive at the Court by way of the *actio popularis*. Once the lawsuit has been filed, the Court must issue its ruling within five months.

The second main function of the Court is to review, by way of a kind of *certiorari* jurisdiction, all the *tutela* actions, through which any person may request a judge to protect his or her fundamental rights. The judge must rule rapidly (within 10 days), and all sentences end up in the CCC, which in turn decides, at its own discretion, which ones to review. If the Court decides to review a sentence, its decision has only an *inter partes* effect.[13]

This summary shows that the Court decides individual and concrete complaints about the violation of constitutional rights, but has also developed a mechanism for the abstract review of legislation and economic policies. The legal regulation of the functioning of the Court explains the different ways in which social rights have become justiciable.

Individual Protection of Social Rights

The 1991 Constitution does not clearly allow for the direct judicial enforcement of many social rights. At first sight, the Constitution appears to restrict the use of the *tutela* action mainly to civil and political rights. Nonetheless, from its earliest decisions, the CCC stated that, in accordance with a broad interpretation of the Constitution, the *tutela* mechanism could be used for the protection of social rights, in at least two kinds of situation.[14]

First, whenever the case involves a group that deserves the special protection of the state – for instance, cases involving children – or a social right whose protection does not imply economic expenditure on the part of the state, the Court has asserted that social rights must be treated as fundamental rights, and must therefore be directly applied. Secondly, the CCC has decided to enforce social rights indirectly, via the *tutela*, in accordance with the legal doctrine of 'connection'.

Social Rights as Directly Applicable Rights: The Case of Labour Rights[15] Labour rights, and in particular the rights of workers to form or join labour unions and to go on strike, can only be understood as social rights if the former expression is used in a broad manner. In reality, these rights do not impose a positive obligation on the state to deliver a service or a subsidy, but simply a duty not to hinder their effective exercise.

Yet, given that these rights may be a necessary condition for workers to be able to enjoy their social rights in a strict sense (such as health, education and housing), the way the Court has dealt with them becomes a very relevant subject for this study. This is especially so, because the progressive attitude of the Court regarding these rights has created an important opportunity for social emancipation that is worth describing.

Starting in the 1970s, the Colombian trade unions' political strategy was essentially ideological, confrontational and very influenced by a Marxist concept of class struggle. The 1991 Constitution was enacted at a time when social movements, and the left in general, were in crisis. This moment coincided with the appearance of new social struggles that were oriented towards the recognition of minorities. The trade union movement has had difficulties in adapting to this new form of political struggle, which is more centred on recognition than on economics.[16] However, the Court's decisions on the subject of equality have, more than anything else, facilitated this adaptation to new political contingencies.

Prior to the 1991 Constitution, the trade unions' legal strategy was limited to defending their rights by means of negotiating collective labour agreements. As neo-liberal hiring and firing policies undermined labour law, however, this strategy was reduced to a minimum, and other types of legal strategy gained increasing importance, fundamentally through the *tutela*. These strategies have led to a new negotiating culture for trade unionists, one that is more pragmatic and less centred on staunch ideological principles.

This change of approach was in part sparked by the Court's decision to broaden the legal basis of its decisions on workers' rights from labour law to constitutional principles. By upholding *tutelas*, the Court was in effect ruling on certain discriminatory practices against unionised workers, practices that nonetheless did not violate the labour code.

Thus, for example, the Court ruled against an employer who gave more work to non-unionised workers than to unionised ones.[17] Based on the labour code, the employer argued that this practice was protected by his right to manage his business, but in reality of course his objective was to get workers to leave the union. On another occasion, the Court ordered that 2,000 unionised workers who had been laid off from an electrical company had to be rehired.[18] Despite the fact that the layoff was carried out in accordance with all the legal requirements, the principle of equality was evoked because only unionised workers were laid off. In a similar case, the Court ordered the rehiring of more than 200 unionised workers, based on the ILO principles.[19]

Union leaders generally consider workers' legal battles before the Court as a 'ray of hope' in the midst of a situation in which workers' rights are being undermined as never before due to the ongoing economic crisis in Colombia, cutbacks in the size of the public service, and the situation of violence and insecurity that frame the defence of workers' rights.[20]

The impression that labour activists have is that the Court is the only legal body that has had some success in halting the deterioration of working conditions in recent years. At the same time, however, labour leaders are aware that the Court cannot bring about structural changes. The Court is rather seen as a symbol that trade unions should embrace in the interests of their overarching strategy to defend workers' rights. Furthermore, labour leaders agree that this symbol's importance is circumstantial. In the medium to long term it is the political arena and not the legal arena that will be fundamental and decisive for workers' rights.

Social Rights as Indirectly Applicable Rights by Means of the 'Connection' Doctrine: The Case of the Right to Health The Court has also defended the possibility of judicial protection of social rights in a strict sense, albeit indirectly. In particular, it distinguishes fundamental rights from other rights, such as social rights, which can only be protected if they are strongly connected to the former. For a social right to be protected, the lack of protection alleged before the judge needs to imply the violation of another right that is considered fundamental and immediately applicable, for instance, the right to life, physical integrity or human dignity. In those cases, protection is usually granted through individual *tutela* actions.

In spite of the progressive character of the Court's decisions, up until 1998 the judicial protection of social rights did not produce any major conflicts between judges and other public authorities. In fact, before 1998, the number of *tutela* decisions concerning social rights that were upheld was over two per cent, such that judicial activism appeared unacceptable only to the most obstinate of the 1991

Constitution's opponents. Besides, most of these decisions referred to cases regarding persons who were part of a health, education or social security system, through a contract with the state.[21]

But the situation changed dramatically after 1998, due to the extraordinary surge of *tutela* actions against the state's Social Security Institute (the ISS)[22] claiming protection under the constitutional right to health.

Through these *tutela* actions, people often seek constitutional justice to order the ISS to deliver, at no charge, a health service that is not included in their health plans, either because of its high cost or because of certain legal restrictions imposed on it – such as pre-existing medical conditions. By alleging that adequate protection of their right to health is fundamental in order for their right to life, physical integrity and/or human dignity to be guaranteed, litigants have succeeded in obtaining declaratory orders recognising the state's obligation to provide a particular service, even if the provision of that service is not expressly contemplated by the law.

So, whereas before 1998 only 2,999 actions of this kind were filed against the ISS, in 1998 the number increased to 10,771. And the costs to the state of complying with the resultant orders more than trebled from around $2 million in 1998 to almost $7 million in 1999.[23]

At a general level, *tutelas* in which the right to health – and, by means of the doctrine of 'connection', to life, physical integrity and/or human dignity – were formally invoked represented around ten per cent of all *tutela* actions brought during 1995, and numbered approximately 3,000. In the first Court term of 1999 that percentage had increased to thirty per cent, and the sum of *tutela* actions filed in this area to 20,000, or 40,000 a year.[24]

This tremendous growth in the use of the *tutela* action as an instrument to obtain health services from the state has obviously been hugely controversial. In fact, the utility of judicial intervention of this sort – in terms of its problematic impact on the right to equality in the provision of healthcare, the coherence of policies, and the financial sustainability of the social security system – has become a constant feature of political debate. However, the beneficiaries of these rulings, who find in the Court's progressivism a way of having one of their basic needs satisfied, and thus their quality of life improved, represent the other side of the story.

Protection of Marginalised Groups' Social Rights

In recent years, certain policies related to stigmatised and particularly vulnerable groups have also been judicialised in an important way. This has especially been so in the case of prisoners and forcibly displaced people.

Due to the over-crowded and precarious circumstances of Colombian prisons, prisoners filed numerous *tutela* actions against the state's penitentiary authorities. After upholding a number of them, the Court decided that the situation of prisoners was a general problem in Colombia, and declared the existence of an 'unconstitutional state of affairs' in the country's penitentiary centres.[25]

Consequently, the Court gave general orders to the government, which included putting an end to the situation within a limited period of time, so as to stop the flagrant violation of the rights to life, dignity and health of prisoners. The Court's orders have resulted in significant governmental expenditure directed at building more prisons, modernising existing infrastructure, and hiring more personnel.

An analogous situation, only on a larger scale, has arisen in relation to the forcibly displaced population. In this case, the situation is to a large extent attributable to the intensification of the armed conflict. Colombia has a very large forcibly displaced population, which represents a humanitarian tragedy of alarming proportions. As in the case of prisons, a significant number of forcibly displaced persons started filing *tutela* actions, in the hope that local and national authorities would protect their fundamental rights, and especially their rights to housing and to human dignity.

After upholding various individual *tutelas*, the Court decided once again to declare the existence of an 'unconstitutional state of affairs', given the inconsistencies in and precariousness of state policy regarding forced displacement.[26] In this decision, the Court ordered the national authorities to reformulate and clarify their strategies vis-à-vis forced displacement, in order to attend to the basic needs of this group.

These decisions of the Constitutional Court regarding traditionally marginalised groups show an important judicialisation of certain public policies of fundamental importance, not only because they have had considerable implications for public expenditure,[27] but also because they have conditioned the priorities and orientations of the governmental strategies in these areas.

Few could deny the necessity of the measures ordered by the Court, given the inhuman circumstances in which prisoners and forcibly displaced people live. However, they raise a number of questions as to whether it is convenient and legitimate for the Court to order them. In any case, after years of neglect by the state, the Court was the first and only public authority to seriously take into account the situation of these marginalised sections of the population, and to decide to protect and defend them vigorously.

General and Abstract Review of Economic Legislation: The Case of Mortgage Debtors

The Court has also severely conditioned economic policy in the exercise of its powers of abstract constitutional review, which has led it to declare certain laws totally or partially unconstitutional. In particular, the Court has annulled laws that extended value-added tax to basic goods,[28] has ordered a partial increase in public employees' salaries in line with inflation,[29] has extended certain pension benefits to specific sectors of the population on the basis of the equality principle,[30] and has forbidden the amendment of certain pension regulations so that workers' existing rights would not be affected.[31] All these decisions have entailed significant economic and budgetary costs.[32]

One of the most controversial examples of this judicialisation of economic policy is the Court's intervention in the mortgage debtors' crisis during 1998 and 1999. Given its significance, it is important to describe this episode in some detail.

Starting in 1997, Colombia went into a deep recession that, combined with certain economic policy decisions, plunged thousands of middle-class debtors into crisis. The situation of 800,000 debtors, who had taken loans to buy their homes with the so-called UPAC (Unity of Constant Acquisitive Power) system, was particularly aggravated by certain state measures. Two years later, there was talk of 200,000 families on the verge of losing their homes.

These debtors were largely from the middle class, people who usually do not participate in social protests in Colombia. However, the situation grew to such proportions that debtors began to join together to defend themselves from the financial institutions, and sent petitions to government and Congress, asking that the financing system be changed and demanding some relief. Some even began to propose strategies for civil disobedience and refused to continue making payments on their mortgages or to hand their homes over to the financial institutions.

In a very short period of time, which some commentators attribute to the lack of a response by government and Congress, debtors and their associations resorted to judicial strategies, taking lawsuits before the CCC against the rules governing the UPAC system. Between 1998 and 1999, the Court handed down several judgments on the UPAC system, which, in general terms, favoured the debtors. The Court thus tied the UPAC to inflation, forbade interest from being added to capital debt, and ordered that mortgages be recalculated to relieve the debtors' situation. Furthermore, the Court ordered that, within seven months, a new law be passed to regulate housing finance.[33]

The public and the media focused considerable attention on these decisions, which were lauded by debtors and some social movements, but fiercely attacked by business groups, some government sectors and many analysts. The latter criticised the Court for overstepping its boundaries and for being ignorant of the way in which a market economy operates, and proposed that the Court should not rule on the constitutionality of economic legislation.

In late 1999, Congress debated and passed a new law on housing finance, which incorporated $1.2 billion in relief for debtors, and tied the cost of mortgages to inflation once again.[34] It is clear that without the Court's rulings it would not have been possible to immediately modify the UPAC system, despite the social turmoil it had caused.

Nevertheless, many debtors expressed their partial dissatisfaction with the new law and decided to launch a fresh legal attack on the UPAC system in January 2000.[35] During the first few months of that year, users' associations and individual debtors brought hundreds of cases before civil judges, asking that their mortgages be reduced in accordance with the Court's doctrine, and demanding the relief measures decreed by the law.

The mortgage debtors' organisations were spawned in reaction to a payment crisis that threatened them with losing their homes. Although debtors held street protests and engaged in political action, the legal strategy, especially the cases presented to the CCC, dominated and defined the movement's profile. This strategy combined civil disobedience with constitutional arguments. The transformation of these individual complaints into Constitutional Court cases and the relatively successful use of other judicial instruments have given these rapidly growing organisations a certain amount of success. However, several questions remain about the risks and limitations of the Court's response.

It is not clear that the Court's decisions will translate into greater access to housing for low-income sectors in the future. Indeed, these rulings have primarily protected middle-class debtors at a substantial cost to the state, and it is likely that the measures undertaken will depress the construction sector. On the other hand, the emphasis placed on the legal strategy has limited the potential role of debtors' associations, some of which have simply become centres for receiving complaints about the recalculation of mortgages.

The Social and Academic Debate: Objections to the Court's Progressivism and Responses

The protection of social rights by the CCC, illustrated in the previous section, has had an enormous impact both on the behaviour of certain important economic sectors and the design of economic policies. Increasingly, the government's economic policies and decisions have to abide by the ground rules set by the Court.

This situation has created a great deal of controversy, since the judicial protection of social rights has a profound impact on the economy, public expenditure and the allocation of scarce resources. Many commentators question whether the Court should make final decisions regarding crucial economic matters, and propose that its power to decide these issues should be strictly limited, and that there should be a specialised economic section in the Court in charge of resolving them.

The controversy surrounding the economic decisions of the Court on social rights poses, then, a basic problem. Is the judicial enforcement of social rights possible and legitimate? I will begin this section by reviewing some of the principal arguments that academics adduce against the judicial protection of social rights. I will then attempt to respond to each of them and, in this way, point out the possibilities and limits of the intervention of constitutional judges in this sphere.

Criticisms of Judicial Intrusion in Economic and Social Policy

According to some analysts, constitutional tribunals should not be competent to protect social rights for several reasons, which can be summed up in a number of basic objections regarding the anti-technical, anti-democratic and socially prejudicial character of judicial decisions on economic matters.

The objections concerning the anti-technical character of judicial decisions on social rights take two basic forms. The first questions the technical competence of constitutional judges in this field, arguing that their interventions produce bad economic policies. The second questions the tendency of judges to be profligate, because they do not bear in mind budgetary restrictions. Allowing tribunals to intervene in the enforcement of social rights, these commentators argue, can lead to 'judicial populism'. These risks are bigger in Third World countries like Colombia, since the state's capacity to finance the satisfaction of social rights is still in doubt.

Objections about the anti-democratic character of judicial decisions constitute a second perspective from which some criticise judicial intervention in this field. This perspective is founded on democratic and participatory theory, especially the notion that it is parliaments and governments that have the right to decide a country's economic model. The judicial protection of social rights is anti-democratic from this perspective because constitutional tribunals, which are composed of non-elected judges, impose their economic philosophy and take away the majority's right to choose the country's development path.

A third critical perspective of judicial decisions on social rights is founded on their socially prejudicial character, in two respects. First, these criticisms invoke the perverse effects that these judicial interventions have on the political system and on the administration of justice. In particular, it is said that tribunals' interference in economic policies erodes democratic participation as citizens replace electoral battles and political mobilisation with legal cases. Moreover, this 'judicialisation' of economic policies brings about a 'politicisation' of justice, which in turn affects judicial independence. This process can also overload the judicial apparatus, because the judiciary begins to assume tasks for which it is not primarily responsible and for which it lacks the technical and material means. Transferring responsibility for resolving economic problems to the judiciary can also end up affecting the legitimacy of this branch of government.

The second socially prejudicial result of the judicial enforcement of social rights is alleged to be that it perpetuates – as does law in general – the unequal distribution of power in society. Although couched in progressive discourse, which boosts their legitimacy and popular support, in practice judicial decisions on social rights do not benefit the most needy sections of the population. Rather, these decisions end up protecting middle-class entitlements and defending conservative positions in favour of hegemonic power structures. In this way, instead of being instances of resistance or social emancipation, they reinforce the status quo of social domination.[36]

The strength of the preceding objections should not be underestimated, as they are based on reasonable theoretical arguments and on unfortunate historical experiences. Judges have no special expertise in handling economic matters and tend to ignore the financial consequences of their decisions. It is also true that constitutional tribunals have sometimes intervened in anti-democratic ways, given that they have blocked or obstructed economic changes supported by the majority of the population.[37] Moreover, an excessive judicialisation of economic policy can be negative for democratic dynamics and for the judicial apparatus itself, as not only might it generate excessive expectations about the possibilities of providential tribunals, but it may also accentuate the demobilisation of citizenship.

Does this mean that the CCC's competence to examine the constitutionality of economic policy decisions should be eradicated? Or should this competence be attributed to a special economic section of the Court? I do not think so, because though relevant and important, none of the preceding objections is conclusive, as I intend to argue in the following sections.

Arguments in Favour of the Judicial Protection of Social Rights[38]

The argument about judges' lack of economic expertise is easy to refute, since judges are trained in familiarising themselves with technical concepts in a range of different fields. Whilst it is valid to demand that judges take into account this specialised knowledge, it is not valid to maintain that they can only make decisions about those subjects in which they themselves are specialists. Such an argument would lead to an anti-democratic conception of law, for it would mean that macro-economic decisions should always be left to a select body of technocratic wise men, different not only from judges, but also from congressmen and citizens, who are not experts on economic matters either.

Criticisms based on the lack of sensitivity of judges regarding the financial consequences of their decisions are partly valid, although insufficient, as they fail to recognise certain particularities of the judicial function and the role of law in a democratic society. Undoubtedly, good judges cannot totally ignore the effects of their economic decisions. However, in a regime that recognises individual rights, a certain insensitivity on the part of judges to the financial or political consequences of their decisions is also advisable, because it implies that there is at least one state authority that is ready to protect certain values, even if its decisions are unpopular or expensive to implement.

The CCC's decisions regarding the circumstances of prisoners and forcibly displaced people illustrate this argument. Indeed, the CCC has been the only state authority that has intervened to defend the rights of these marginalised groups – whose fate is not particularly relevant for the polity or the political system – by ordering measures to improve their living standards, regardless of these measures' considerable costs. If judges made their decisions exclusively on the basis of their eventual consequences, they would stop being independent and become political bodies, and the law's function as a normative instrument of social cohesion would be lost.

Objections about the anti-democratic character of the judicial enforcement of social rights are more profound, as they are founded on the so-called 'counter-majoritarian objection', which has been the main basis for challenging the legitimacy of constitutional review.[39] It would be naïve to try to resolve this difficult question in a few lines. In any event, it is not appropriate to embark on a full discussion, since it is not constitutional review in general, but the constitutional review of economic policies that is currently being criticised in Colombia.

However, it is important to mention that, apart from its classic justifications,[40] the legitimacy of a constitutional review is justified by two contemporary arguments from democratic theory.[41] According to these arguments, constitutional review corrects certain 'defects' in and 'paradoxes' of majoritarian democracy by guaranteeing respect for, and the continuity and impartiality of the democratic process, and ensuring the protection of fundamental rights, which is a precondition for the proper functioning of democracy.

Some critics would, of course, fully agree with the preceding considerations and yet still argue that constitutional tribunals should not intervene in economic matters, or that they should only do so in a very prudent and limited way. According to this view, the appeal to social rights is insufficient because these rights cannot be satisfied in the same way that civil and political rights can, for the simple reason that their fulfilment depends on the judicially enforced allocation of scarce resources, whereas the protection of the latter does not. According to this argument, a constitutional tribunal's decision on social rights may generate a macroeconomic disequilibrium in unforeseeable ways, or may diminish resources that were needed to satisfy other social rights, by which the decision paradoxically contributes to the violation of fundamental rights.

For instance, some have criticised the *tutela* decisions in which the CCC ordered the provision of certain medicines – needed by victims of life-threatening diseases, but excluded from the Obligatory Health Plan – arguing that they caused a disequilibrium in the social security system, and resulted in a reduction of resources needed to vaccinate hundreds of children.[42] Because it is impossible to satisfy all social rights at once, this argument runs, decisions about the allocation and distribution of finite economic resources should be left to political organs.

This objection is clearly significant, because no one can deny the enormous difficulties that the judicial protection of social rights poses. Yet, this does not imply the absolute legal inefficacy or the non-justiciability of social rights. On the one hand, without meaning to deny the specificity of social rights, the difference between civil and social rights is quite nuanced. It is not the case that all social rights impose positive obligations on the state, nor do civil and political rights require only state abstention.[43] The protection of all kinds of rights involves economic costs and requires arbitration between alternative uses of scarce resources.

On the other hand, the argument about the absolute freedom of political organs to choose any economic model is founded on a desire to eliminate the normative force of the Constitution's social rights clauses and international treaties that recognise social rights. This is unacceptable because, just as there can be no democracy without guaranteed rights of freedom of expression and due process, the incorporation of social rights supposes that there cannot be real democratic deliberation unless there is a certain level of social and economic equality and basic satisfaction of people's needs.

In these circumstances, the different economic strategies chosen by the political organs must be oriented towards progressive fulfilment of social rights. And the role of a 'countermajoritarian' authority, like the CCC, should be to guarantee the normative limits constituted by social rights, so that they do not end up being merely rhetorical.

In summary, the difficulties accompanying the judicial enforcement of social rights should not impede the CCC from deciding such cases. By the same token, however, those difficulties do have implications for the proper performance of the judicial function that should not be ignored.

First, the progressive character of the state's duty to fulfil social rights implies that the satisfaction of these rights depends on the availability of resources. Therefore, the interpretative task of the judge is certainly more difficult, because judges must not only take into account the problem of limited resources, but also the progressiveness principle.

Secondly, given that social rights entail public expenditure, the state must determine the way in which it will render services or supply subsidies. Therefore, constitutional control cannot ignore the vital role that law plays in the definition of social rights' content and protection mechanisms, and must recognise the ample freedom of congress to develop strategies for the satisfaction of these rights.

In other words, the constitution must be interpreted as 'open' but not 'neutral'; its pluralist character should still direct judicial decisions, but these should avoid adopting rigid formulas and should maintain the possibility of vigorous democratic deliberation about social rights.

Criticisms of the negative effects of the judicial enforcement of social rights on the judicial and political system should not be ignored. An excessive 'judicialisation' of social rights can certainly be detrimental, both to a participatory democratic culture, and to the cause of social justice, which would tend to become 'politicised' and overloaded.

On the one hand, lawyers and judges should be aware of these dangers and actively contribute to their neutralisation. Thus, lawyers should be conscious of the fact that their task is not to substitute but to complement or reconstitute social movements. Simultaneously, to prevent the excessive 'politicisation' of their activity and the overloading that it may imply, judges should be willing to develop flexible decision techniques that allow for further democratic discussion, instead of foreclosing it. In addition, in order to contribute to the strengthening of social movements, judges should fortify these movements' arguments whenever they are the weak component of a legal dispute, without ever taking the discussion away from them.

On the other hand, we should not forget that the legal battle is only a part of the wider struggle for social transformation or emancipation. No transcendental and lasting change is likely to be achieved if law is the only weapon used to that end.

Objections about the conservative impact that judicial decisions on social rights may have on the distribution of power and wealth in society are also relevant but not conclusive. It is impossible to deny that the role of law in general, and of judicial decisions in particular, as an instrument for social emancipation is quite questionable, given that law can easily also be used as a tool of domination that perpetuates existing power relations. Thus, in principle, social transformation can never be achieved by means of the law.[44] However, in the Colombian case, this perspective has to be refined for two reasons.

First, given its condition as a semi-peripheral country, the law and social change debate in Colombia may be posited in less instrumental terms, since the autonomy of the legal system is reduced, not only with respect to the political system – as an outcome of the political instrumentalisation of law – but also with respect to the social system – as a result of legal inefficacy and the prevalence of legal pluralism over official law. Thus, law is often utilised for institutional legitimisation rather than social regulation.

However, the production of law with legitimising intentions is a double-edged sword. In fact, the symbols of social change and protection of rights that law embodies may be appropriated by citizens, social movements and state institutions that could take law seriously and use it as an instrument of resistance to the hegemonic power.

This is precisely what has happened with some of the CCC's decisions, which have produced significant social mobilisation. As the cases analysed in this chapter show, the emancipatory power of the Court's decisions lies in the fact that they contain a political message; they render effective the expectations encoded in the constitution so that actors find in their message a pretext for political action.

Secondly, given that the idea of revolution as the only means for social emancipation is in crisis nowadays, it is not as problematic to believe in law's social transformation potential anymore. This is especially so in chaotic and anomic societies like Colombia, where neither control nor discipline have ever been specific traits of the legal system. Therefore, it is possible to state that emancipatory results can be achieved through the judicial battle if, as we already mentioned, they are part of a wider social struggle.

Furthermore, over the course of the last decade, legal strategies have become an essential element of the Colombian social movements' political struggle, overshadowing the classical political confrontation between left and right. This is especially clear in the case of the so-called *new social movements*, which are usually related to cultural concerns and demand social and political recognition,[45] and are therefore notably different from the old social movements, which are generally tied to class interests.[46] But the Colombian trade union movement also illustrates this new situation. In fact, despite being a movement with classical features and aspirations, the union movement has found in its legal strategy an essential element, not only for its emancipatory struggle, but also and especially for its revival.

The Constitutional Court and Social Emancipation in Colombia

The previous sections show that it is possible for a constitutional tribunal to produce progressive decisions that, although presenting some contradictions, have an emancipatory impact. Nevertheless, some factors can undermine the emancipatory potential of judicial decisions on social rights. For this reason, it is useful to develop a contextual analysis to establish which conditions allow progressive constitutional practices to have emancipatory or democratising effects, and which conditions impede such effects. These variables should be identified and sharpened, to help us recognise and take advantage of potentially emancipatory judicial decisions regarding social rights.[47]

The relationship between judicial decisions and social practices is of course a complex phenomenon, which cannot be reduced to a simple causal connection. The social influence of judicial decisions alone is not sufficient to produce direct and effective instances of social change; neither is it irrelevant, however, for the evaluation of these changes. Recognising this, the factors I propose to take into account should not be understood as 'causes' that explain the emancipatory potential of the judicial protection of social rights. Rather, they are factors that, according to my empirical analysis, could strengthen or, on the contrary, undermine this emancipatory potential. In my view, at least four elements are important: the type of judicial decision, the social context, the nature of the beneficiaries, and the role of the legal strategy.[48]

Type of Decision

The impact of a judicial decision depends on the nature of the order handed down by the judge.[49] We can differentiate two forms of progressive judicial activism, each of which presents two types of decision.[50]

First, a judge can recognise certain rights whose existence is disputed by political forces. This activism, which I propose to term ideological, consists of legally conferring specific rights on certain social groups. There are two different forms of ideological activism: 'innovatory' ideological activism, which consists of judicial decisions that go against the majority to 'create' rights that have never before been recognised; and 'preservationist' ideological activism, which includes those judicial decisions that tend to preserve a guarantee for which precedents clearly exist but whose existence is threatened by political forces.

Secondly, in cases where the existence of a right is incontrovertible, but the judicial decision that challenges its violation may be criticised by those who think the legal remedies handed down invade the competencies of other branches of government, we have to do with instances of remedial activism. There are negative and positive forms of remedial activism. While the former consists of the judicial enforcement of prohibitions and is easier to execute, the latter consists of judicial mandates to do something, and may encounter greater resistance, since authorities can obstruct enforcement by various means, such as adducing budgetary restrictions or administrative difficulties, without openly committing contempt.

Usually, it can be presumed that negative remedial orders (prohibitions) have a greater emancipatory potential, while enormous controversy and opposition might be generated through innovatory ideological activism. Thus, given that most of the emancipatory impulse in the cases studied originated in either ideological activism (both preservationist and innovatory) or positive remedies, that impulse runs the risk of being hindered or eliminated by the political forces that actively oppose and resist it.

The following table summarises the types of decision that can be made by a progressive Court and relates them to the discussion of the cases in the previous section:

Table 6.1: Type of Progressive Activism

Type of Progressive Activism			
Ideological Activism		**Remedial Activism**	
Innovatory Activism	**Preservationist Activism**	**Positive Remedies**	**Negative Remedies**
Protection of the right to health *Modification of the UPAC system*	*Protection of union members' job stability against discrimination*	*Improvement of prisoners and forcibly displaced people's life conditions*	*Prohibition of taxes on first necessity products*

The Decision's Political Costs

Progressive decisions usually bring with them high political costs for courts. These costs are difficult to evaluate in a context of institutional, social and political fragmentation, such as the Colombian one, and should therefore be carefully weighed in each case.

Yet, beyond the specific dangers originating in concrete decisions of the CCC that oppose the interests of specific actors, the Court is subjected to a general danger that operates as a kind of backdrop against which it acts. This danger consists of the more or less latent possibility that political forces may unite to eliminate the Court by reforming the Constitution or by pressuring it in such a way that, for its own protection, the Court's decisions end up following a conservative line.

This general danger acquires a similar, if less dramatic, connotation when the election of new judges takes place, as this situation posits the risk of a neutralisation of the Court's activity through the appointment of conservative judges. Nonetheless, this danger seems to be notably reduced by the fact that the Court's progressive orientation has become one of its principal sources of legitimacy, so that now there is a wide social understanding that the Court's principal mission is to protect and expand the Constitution's progressive content. Thus, after the 2001 replacement of seven of the nine judges on the Court, its general political orientation has remained unchanged.[51]

What, then, is, the relation between the political costs of progressive decisions and social effects? The emancipatory possibilities of the Court's progressive decisions seem to be greater in contexts in which a consensus has been formed on the values and principles defended by the Court.

Of course, it is difficult for actual cases to conform exactly to an ideal type; our case studies are actually located along a spectrum of intermediary possibilities. For instance, the cases regarding the UPAC movement and forcibly displaced people seem to enjoy broad public support. In contrast, the trade union and prisons' cases operate in a less favourable political climate, since the former face significant opposition, and the latter have extremely weak public support. Cases regarding the right to health are located in an intermediate position, given that they are inscribed in a favourable ideological context, but their judicial resolution tends to be divisive.

The Nature of the Beneficiaries

The emancipatory potential of a judicial decision is also linked to its reception by social actors. Perhaps the most important factor for our model is the degree of internal cohesion among the decision's beneficiaries. Here, we will distinguish three types of social actors.

First, we find the more dispersed actors, who usually seek to assert individual interests and who only choose collective action when it works to the advantage of their own individual strategy. An example of this type of actor is found in the mortgage debtors' movement, which, despite its strength, could easily fall apart were the implementation of the Court's decisions to present difficulties. Prisoners and forcibly displaced people are examples of this type of actor as well, although their dispersion is much more acute, as these two groups cannot even be considered social movements.

Social actors who are strongly tied together through their community links and values constitute the second type of beneficiary of the Court's decisions. The example of several Colombian indigenous communities whose rights to autonomy have been protected by the CCC illustrates this situation.

Finally, social movements whose internal cohesion depends on the shared political interests of their members constitute a third type of actor. The case of the trade union movement is a typical example of this, because its internal cohesion does not depend exclusively on the Court's decisions, although these can inject new life and energy into its political struggle.

The Relative Weight of a Legal Strategy

We should also ask what kind of influence the Court's decisions have on the strategy of counter-hegemonic struggle of social actors. Two possibilities are of interest for our purposes.

The first arises when the judicial decision explains not only the emancipatory struggles of social actors, but also their existence, combativeness, achievements, and so on. This is the case of the UPAC debtors, who found their most important element of cohesion and struggle in the Court's decision. Something similar can be said about the prisoners, the forcibly displaced people, and the claimants in the health rights cases, for whom the Court's decisions were a fundamental source of social emancipation, but whose dispersion could hinder their legal strategies' ability to produce a profound social transformation.

The second possibility occurs in cases in which the legal strategy, although not perceived as a relevant element of the political struggle in the past, acquires an unusual importance in a specific moment. This often coincides with a moment of crisis in the political strategy, or comes at a time when the movement is in danger of disintegration, such as the present situation of trade unions.

In summary, the effectiveness of the Court's progressive decisions is increased when the following factors coincide: remedial judicial decisions – preferably taking the form of prohibitions – put forth in consensual contexts, which social movements, whether dispersed in nature or community-based, can politically appropriate and utilise a legal strategy that becomes part of a broader political struggle and is also part of the construction of their identity.

I believe this postulate contains the ideal combination of factors for progressive judicial activism to bring about social emancipation. This is not a proposition cast in stone, however, but a tendency. It is thus not necessary that this combination of factors be present in their entirety in order for social emancipation to result.[52] Nor does the presence of these factors necessarily guarantee emancipation.[53] Since it is a model that indicates tendencies, further empirical research is indispensable for corroborating the veracity of the tendency in concrete cases.

Some Final Conclusions

This chapter confirms a quite modest but at the same time important idea. Progressive judicial decisions on social rights may or may not become an adequate instrument for social emancipation. It all depends on the context in which these decisions are handed down and on whether certain factors are present or not. This simple conclusion sets the parameters of how empirical research, legal theory and political action need to move forward in the pursuit of a better understanding of the role of the judiciary in social transformation.

The research challenge requires the development of rigorous socio-legal empirical and comparative studies aimed at better understanding the contextual limits and possibilities of progressive judicial strategies. These studies should produce more precise variables for the identification of judicial decisions on social rights with the potential for social transformation.

The theoretical challenge is the need to formulate specific legal concepts capable of responding to the complexities posed by social rights and of enhancing the progressive potential of judicial decisions on these issues. Indeed, as we have seen, the protection of social rights poses many obstacles in contexts in which, like Colombia, poverty and inequality dominate the social scene. This situation requires 'a new theoretical construction'[54] that can adapt constitutional activism on social rights to the specificities of the country's context, and the development of new judicial hermeneutical tools to defend the normative force of social rights.

Finally, the political challenge implies the re-articulation of legal and social struggles, because neither exhaustive empirical investigations nor arduously constructed legal concepts are capable of solving the problem of social rights and emancipation. In fact, constitutional justice can become an important instrument for democratic progress only if we think of it as part of broader social struggles. The fulfilment of the emancipatory promises made by the Constitution is too serious a matter to leave to judges; citizen participation is essential for the realisation of democracy.

Notes

* I want to thank my research assistant, Ms Maria Paula Saffon, for her important contributions to the final version of this chapter.

1 The expression 'social rights' is an ambiguous one. Some include in this concept not only welfare rights (such as rights to education, health or housing), but also labour rights (such as the right to form labour unions or to go to strike), economic liberties (property or freedom to contract), or even cultural rights (the right to speak one's own language). There are good reasons to link, in some respects, all these rights. Nevertheless, in this chapter I restrict the meaning of social rights to welfare rights, that is, rights that imply a positive obligation on the state to deliver a service or an economic subsidy to citizens, in order that they can enjoy some goods considered necessary to live with dignity and real freedom. I think the justiciability of these rights is the issue that provokes the sharpest academic and political debates. However, I do analyse the case of labour rights as a case of social rights for, even if they do not imply *per se* a positive obligation on the State, their protection is a determining factor for workers to be able to claim their welfare rights.

2 Academic literature about this subject is extensive. For approaches in favour of justiciability, see Robert Alexy, *Teoría de los Derechos Fundamentales* (Madrid: Centro de Estudios Constitucionales, 1997); Víctor Abramovich and Christian Courtis, *Los Derechos Sociales como Derechos Exigibles* (Madrid: Trotta, 2002). For critical and more sceptical standpoints vis-à-vis justiciability, see Gerald N. Rosenberg, *The Hollow Hope* (Chicago: University of Chicago Press, 1991); Mark Tushnet, 'An Essay on Rights', *Texas Law Review,* 4 (1984): 1363–402; Friedrich Von Hayek, *Law, Legislation and Liberty* (London: Routledge and Paul Kegan, 1973). For approaches in favour of justiciability in Colombia, see Rodolfo Arango, 'Los Derechos Sociales Fundamentales como Derechos Subjetivos', *Pensamiento Jurídico,* 8 (1991): 138 ff.

3 For a general overview of judicial review in Colombia in the twentieth century, see Manuel José Cepeda, 'La Defensa Judicial de la Constitución', in Fernando Cepeda (ed.), *Las Fortalezas de Colombia* (Bogotá: Ariel, BID, 2004), pp. 145–87.

4 The following is based on Mauricio García and Rodrigo Uprimny, 'Tribunal Constitucional e Emancipaçã Social na Colombia', in Boaventura de Sousa Santos (ed.), *Democratizar a Democracia. Os Caminhos da Democracia Participativa* (Rio de Janeiro: Editora Cvilizaçao Brasileira, 2002), pp. 298–339.

5 In fact, the Constituent Assembly was composed of seventy delegates, of which nineteen represented the Democratic Alliance–April Nineteen Movement (AD-M19 in Spanish), a political party created by former guerrilla group M-19 after the peace process; two came from the Patriotic Union, a left-leaning political party that was drastically targeted by paramilitary violence; two represented children and students; two came from indigenous communities; and two others represented non-Catholic Christians. See Jaime Buenahora, *El Proceso Constituyente* (Bogotá: Tercer Mundo, 1992). As a result, more than 40 per cent of the delegates to the Assembly did not belong to the Liberal and Conservative parties, which until that day had dominated the political scene.

6 Ruti Teitel, 'Transitional Jurisprudence. The Role of Law in Political Transformation', *Yale Law Journal,* 106 (1997): 2009–80, 2014.

7 Herbert Jacob et al., *Courts, Law and Politics in Comparative Perspective* (New Haven: Yale University Press, 1996), pp. 396 ff.

8 Jacob, *Courts, Law and Politics*, p. 389.

9 This question presupposes that there is a difference between judicial activism and progressiveness, since there may be conservative judicial activism, like that of the US Supreme Court in the early twentieth century.

10 See José Antonio Ocampo, 'Reforma del Estado y Desarrollo Económico y Social', *Análisis Político,* 17 (1992): 5–40.

11 Manuel José Cepeda, 'Democracy, State and Society in the 1991 Constitution: The Role of the Constitutional Court', in Eduardo Posada Carbó (ed.), *Colombia: The Politics of Reforming the State* (London: Macmillan Press, 1998), p. 76.

12 For a general overview of the Court's work, see ibid., p. 91. The Court has produced an average of 1,000 rulings a year in very different fields; decisions on social rights are undoubtedly one of its main jobs.

13 While all members of the Court decide constitutional cases, *tutela* cases are regularly decided by its different sections, each composed of three judges. Nonetheless, whenever a *tutela* subject has a special relevance, all the judges meet to decide it. According to the Court's conventions, the first type of case is identified with a C letter, the second with a T letter, and the third with the letters SU. Each of these letters is followed by the number

of the decision, and the year it was handed down. The decisions discussed below will be so identified.

14 For a development of the legal discussion, see Tulio Elí Chinchilla, *¿Qué son y Cuáles son los Derechos Fundamentales?* (Bogotá: Temis, 1999).

15 Much of the information contained in this section was obtained from the empirical research conducted for García and Uprimny, 'Tribunal Constitucional e Emancipaçã'. For the difference and relations between welfare rights and labour rights, see note 1 above.

16 Nancy Fraser, 'Social Justice and the Age of Identity Politics: Redistribution, Recognition, and Participation', in Grethe Paterson (ed.), *The Tanner Lectures On Human Values* (Utah: University of Utah Press, 1998), vol. 19, pp. 3–67.

17 Ruling T-230/1994.

18 Ruling T-436/2000.

19 Ruling T-568/1999.

20 According to personal information given by union leader Luis Eduardo Garzón, during the past 10 years, 2,500 labour leaders have been killed throughout the country.

21 People who were not a part of this field of rights protection, that is, the socially marginalised, were not the object of any sort of protection. Greater needs came along with a more restricted use of the *tutela* action. Sections of the population excluded from the circles of protection of social rights do not consider the *tutela* to be an adequate instrument for guaranteeing their constitutional rights. There is a sort of scepticism on the part of the excluded population regarding the vindicatory possibilities of the *tutela* action. This attitude can be explained by a lack of information or, perhaps, knowledge of the restrictive character of judicial decisions. See Mauricio García Villegas, 'Derechos Sociales y Necesidades Políticas. La Eficacia Judicial de los Derechos Sociales en el Constitucionalismo Colombiano', in Boaventura de Sousa Santos and Mauricio García (eds), *El Caleidoscopio de las Justicias en Colombia* (2 vols, Bogotá: Uniandes, 2001), vol. 1, pp. 455–83.

22 The ISS is a state public corporation in the national sphere. Since 1995, it has been authorised to compete in the health services market.

23 See Luis Carlos Sotelo, 'Los Derechos Constitucionales de Prestación y sus Implicaciones Económico-políticas', *Archivos de Macroeconomía* Working Paper 133 (2000).

24 See Corte Constitucional and Consejo Superior de la Judicatura, *Estadísticas sobre la Tutela* (Bogotá: Autores, 1999).

25 Ruling T-153/1998.

26 Ruling T-025/2004.

27 For instance, according to some preliminary calculations, the recent decision about forced displacement could cost approximately $425 million, and the Court's decision about prisons has already cost approximately $240 million. General Budgetary Direction of the Ministry of Treasure, unpublished document (2004).

28 Ruling C-776/2003.

29 Rulings C-1433/2000, C-1064/2001 and C-1017/2003.

30 Ruling C-409/1994.

31 Ruling C-754/2004.

32 Two examples: since 1995, decision C-409/1994 has cost several hundred million dollars, and continues to cost approximately $340 million a year. Decision C-776/2003, reduced fiscal revenue by approximately $320 million.

33 Rulings C-383/1999, C-747/1999 and C-700/1999.

34 Law 546 of 1999.

35 Ruling C-959/2000.

36 I believe this is the perspective from which András Sajó critically analyses the Hungarian Constitutional Court's decisions on social rights in the chapter included in this book. For an application of these criticisms to the specific case of the CCC's decisions about prisons, see Libardo Ariza, 'La Prisión Ideal: Intervención Judicial y Reforma del Sistema Penitenciario en Colombia', unpublished paper, Universidad de los Andes (2004).

37 The classic example, although not the only one, is the US Supreme Court's attitude in the first decades of the twentieth century.

38 This section is based on Rodrigo Uprimny, 'Legitimidad y Conveniencia del Control Constitucional de la Economía', *Revista de Derecho Público*, 13 (2001): 145–83.

39 For a summary of the debate, see Eduardo García de Enterría, *La Constitución como norma y el Tribunal Constitucional* (Madrid: Editorial Civitas, 1985); Roberto Gargarella, *La Justicia Frente al Gobierno* (Barcelona: Ariel, 1996).

40 See Alexander Hamilton, James Madison, and John Jay, *The Federalist Papers*, ed. G. Wills (New York: Bantam Books, 1988), no. 78; *Marbury v. Madison* 5 US 137 (1803).

41 See, for example, Alexander Bickel, *The Least Dangerous Branch: The Supreme Court at the Bar of Politics* (New Haven: Yale University Press, 1986); Mauro Cappeletti, 'Necesidad y Legitimidad de la Justicia Constitucional', in Louis Joseph Favoreu (ed.), *Tribunales Constitucionales Europeos y Derechos Fundamentales* (Madrid: Centro de Estudios Constitucionales, 1984), p. 618; Jon Elster and Rune Slagstad (eds), *Constitutionalism and Democracy* (Cambridge: Cambridge University Press, 1988); John Hart Ely, *Democracy and Distrust: A Theory of Judicial Review* (Cambridge, MA: Harvard University Press, 1980); and especially Carlos Santiago Nino, *The Constitution of Deliberative Democracy* (New Haven: Yale University Press, 1996).

42 Kalmanovitz, 'Consecuencias Económicas Fallos', p. 124.

43 An example of the first case is the right of workers to form unions, which basically entails an obligation on the state not to interfere in their development. An example of the second case is the right to a public legal defence for those who cannot afford one.

44 See Tushnet, 'An Essay on Rights'.

45 Fraser, 'Social Justice'; Boaventura de Sousa Santos, *De la Mano de Alicia; lo Social y lo Político en la Post-modernidad* (Bogotá: Siglo del Hombre, 1998).

46 Anthony Giddens, *The Constitution of Society* (Berkeley: University of California Press, 1984); Alain Touraine, *The Self-Production of Society* (Chicago: University of Chicago Press, 1977).

47 I believe this is what Siri Gloppen does in her chapter in this volume.

48 These variables are taken from García and Uprimny, 'Tribunal Constitucional e Emancipaçã'.

49 Erwin Chemerinsky, 'Can Courts Make a Difference?', in Neal Devins and Davidson Douglas (eds), *Redefining Equality* (New York: Oxford University Press, 1998), pp. 191–204.

50 I partly follow the terminology proposed by William Wayne, 'The Two Faces of Judicial Activism', in David O' Brien (ed.), *Judges on Judging: Views from the Bench* (New Jersey: Chatham House Publishers, 1997), pp. 302 ff.

51 This demonstrates that the socially perceived mission of an institution influences the behaviour of its members. Following Howard Gillman, I formulated this idea in Rodrigo

Uprimny, 'The Constitutional Court and Control of Presidential Extraordinary Powers in Colombia', *Democratization*, 10 (2003): 46–69.

52 Even if they all brought about emancipatory practices, the cases we studied lack one or more of these factors. Thus, in the right to health cases, the consensual element is missing; the prisoners and forcibly displaced people's cases are not community-based; and the trade unions' case appears to lack at least three factors – a consensual audience, the movement's characterisation as either disperse or community-based, and a constitutive legal strategy – but because of its specificity as a classic social movement willing to survive through legal strategy, it still presents an interesting emancipatory potential.

53 None of the case studies serves as an example of this situation. However, it is clear that not every progressive decision leads to social emancipation. An interesting supplement to this research would be to expand the number of cases and to include progressive decisions that have not led to emancipatory practices.

54 Eduardo Cifuentes, 'El Constitucionalismo de la Pobreza', *Direito: Revista Xuridica da Universidade de Santiago de Compostela*, 4 (1995): 53–78.

Chapter 7

Courts and Social Transformation in India

R. Sudarshan

Introduction

The social transformation that India has aspired to achieve since independence in 1947 has been to change a society based on the principle of *homo hierachicus* (the title of Louis Dumont's classic work on India's caste system[1]) into one of *homo equalis*. Hindu society is a harmonic system where inequality exists and is perceived to be legitimate. The Constitution, which was brought into force in 1950, ushered in a diachronic system where inequalities persist, but are no longer regarded as lawful and legitimate. During the drafting process, India's Constituent Assembly succeeded in reaching a consensus on the need for a 'social revolution' through two main devices: the inclusion of fundamental rights, broadly corresponding to the traditional civil and political liberties, and a separate chapter on Directive Principles of State Policy, containing social, economic, cultural and environmental rights.[2] The Assembly also integrated a declaration in the Constitution stating that 'untouchability is abolished', and proclaimed it an offence for anyone to practise it in any form. The effort made to launch a 'social revolution' in India resulted in a Constitution that was oriented towards socio-economic justice in a society characterised by sharp inequalities of status, caste and class.

Fifty-five years after the adoption of the Constitution, what has happened to the 'social revolution' in India, understood for purposes of this chapter as 'the altering of structured inequalities and power relations in society in ways that reduce the weight of morally irrelevant circumstances'?[3] While one cannot offer a comprehensive account of the changes that have indeed come about, it is possible to illustrate what has not yet been done by looking at the case of the 'untouchable' castes in India, referred to in official discourse as the 'scheduled castes'. '*Dalits*' (the term preferred by members of the group, meaning 'downtrodden') constitute about 170 million people. In many parts of India they continue to be employed in jobs that are regarded as defiling – scavengers (some 800,000 persons carry human excrement on their heads every day), cremation ground attendants, and removers of carcasses of dead animals. *Dalits* are still served tea in separate glasses in many tea-stalls across the country, for fear of losing the custom of the more numerous higher-caste patrons. Poverty remains the predominant affliction of *dalits*, despite the reservation of seats for them in provincial legislatures and in India's parliament, and employment quotas proportional to the population of *dalits* and other 'backward' castes. The beneficiaries of these affirmative action policies, it is clear, constitute a 'creamy layer', leaving their brothers and sisters in the same predicament that the constitution-makers wanted to address.[4]

Focusing on the period after 1973, and applying the helpful analytical framework proposed by Siri Gloppen in this volume, this chapter analyses the role of the judiciary, as the custodian of the norms of the Constitution, towards achieving social transformation in India.

Courts in India

It is a common belief that there can be no fate worse than becoming a litigant in India's courts. Law, lawyers, and courts are not held in high esteem by the general public. Penderel Moon of the Indian Civil Service wrote: 'The whole elaborate machinery of English law, which Englishmen tended to think so perfect, simply didn't work and has been completely perverted.'[5] Lawyers and courts deliver little by way of justice. Courts are used not so much with the expectation of settling disputes, but rather to keep an issue in dispute, for as long as possible, as a way of harassing an adversary. Courts are useful to 'stay' matters – such as the payment of taxes and debts – and to restore the *status quo ante*. 'We tell our clients to settle if they have a strong case and to go court if it's weak', said one Indian bank official.[6]

People in India are ill served by courts, especially the lower courts at the district and municipal levels. India's courts are congested with cases, not because people resort to them excessively, but because, relative to the size of India's population, there are few courts and fewer judges (about one judge per 100,000 people). The lower courts, or subordinate judiciary as they are called in India, have a large proportion of cases that have been pending for a decade or more. It is not surprising, therefore, that much of the literature that paints a positive view of India's judiciary is focused on the Supreme Court, located in the country's capital, New Delhi, and the High Courts, located in the state capitals. The people who have access to these courts are necessarily elites, although some of the members of this elite group do act on behalf of the poor and disadvantaged people, and seek to secure their rights and entitlements.

The greater part of the time of the higher courts is taken up by litigation that seeks to activate the writ jurisdiction of these courts to stall actions taken by state governments, and a very large part of the docket in these courts includes appeals by state governments against adverse judgments passed by lower courts.[7] Even though the appeals may have little merit, state officials are expected to act in the interests of saving taxpayers' money. In the process, of course, they expend a good deal of that money, enriching counsel engaged by governments, and eventually losing the appeals.

Structure of the Higher Judiciary, Fundamental Rights and Locus Standi

The lower courts in India offer little succour to the poor and other disadvantaged groups in their quest for social transformation. However, the Supreme Court and the High Courts have the power to issue writs for the enforcement of fundamental rights. This makes recourse to these courts, by framing one's case as a violation of fundamental rights, an attractive option. The Supreme Court (under article 32 of the Constitution) and the High Courts (under article 226) are empowered to issue writs and orders 'in the nature' of *habeas corpus, mandamus, certiorari,* prohibition, and *quo warranto*. They can issue these writs for the enforcement of fundamental rights and, in the case of the High Courts, for 'any other purpose' as well, such as enforcement of any statutory or common-law right. The writ jurisdiction of the higher courts has been frequently invoked, and these courts generally set aside a whole day to hear 'special leave petitions' seeking to admit writ claims.

Until 1978, the beneficiaries of the writ jurisdiction were generally 'men with long purses', landlords, owners of banks and businesses. After the resounding rout of the Congress party led by Prime Minister Indira Gandhi, who had imposed a state of emergency (26 June 1975–21 March 1977), the higher judiciary in India entered into a new phase of activism in the use of its writ jurisdiction, in defence of the poor and disadvantaged groups. As a result of this new activism, the institution of Public Interest Litigation (PIL) emerged,[8] as more fully explained below.

While the emergency was in force, the Supreme Court declared that fundamental rights were suspended, and a person detained during that period was not entitled to *habeas corpus*, and the courts could not examine the basis of the detention and pronounce on its legality.[9] The High Courts of Allahabad, Andhra Pradesh, Bombay, Delhi, Karnataka, Madras, Madhya Pradesh, Punjab, and Rajasthan had all held that despite the suspension of fundamental rights, a person detained could demonstrate that his or her detention was not in compliance with the law (under which he or she was detained), or that the state action was *mala fide*, or that there was a mistake of identity. There is little doubt that the Supreme Court had no wish to confront an executive armed with emergency powers.[10]

The verdict of people in the 1977 general elections gave new courage to the Supreme Court. Two of its judges, P.N. Bhagwati and V.R. Krishna Iyer, submitted a report in 1977 making a case for a paradigm shift in judicial procedures and enabling access to all, especially the poor and other disadvantaged groups.[11] While the government of India does not appear to have taken much notice of the recommendations in this report, the two judges teamed up on the bench of the Supreme Court to give effect to some of them, exercising the extraordinarily large writ jurisdiction of the court. A leading authority on Indian jurisprudence remarked:

> Post-emergency judicial activism was probably inspired by the Court's realization that its elitist social image would not make it strong enough to withstand the future onslaught

> of a powerful political establishment ... [T]he Court adopted two strategies: (1) it reinterpreted the provisions for fundamental rights in a more liberal manner in order to maximize the rights of the people, particularly the disadvantaged; and (2) it facilitated access to the courts by relaxing its technical rules of *locus standi*, entertaining letter petitions or acting *suo moto*, and developing pro-active public law technology for the enforcement of human rights.[12]

In 1978, an inmate of the central prison in New Delhi, Sunil Batra, scribbled a letter to Justice V.R. Krishna Iyer claiming that a fellow-prisoner had been subjected to torture. Justice Iyer was persuaded to regard this letter as a petition for the enforcement of fundamental rights of prisoners. This was the beginning of what has been termed the Supreme Court's 'epistolary jurisprudence'.[13] Justice Bhagwati, in a case involving stone-quarry workers brought to the Supreme Court by the Bonded Labour Liberation front, stated that:

> There is no limitation in the words of clause (1) of Article 32 that the fundamental right which is sought to be enforced by moving the Supreme Court should be one belonging to the person who moves the Supreme Court nor does it say that the Supreme Court should be moved only by a particular kind of proceeding.[14]

The nature of public interest litigation was further elucidated by Justice Bhagwati in the following observations in the case of *People's Union for Democratic Rights v. India*:[15]

> We wish to point out with all the emphasis at our command that public interest litigation which is a strategic arm of the legal aid movement and which is intended to bring justice within the reach of the poor masses, who constitute the low visibility area of humanity is a totally different kind of litigation from the ordinary traditional litigation which is essentially of an adversarial character where there is a dispute between two litigating parties, one making claim or seeking relief against the other and that other opposing such claim or resisting such relief. Public interest litigation is brought before the Court not for the purpose of enforcing the rights of one individual against another as happens in the case of ordinary litigation, but is intended to promote and vindicate public interest which demands that violations of constitutional or legal rights of a large number of people who are poor, ignorant or in a socially or economically disadvantaged position should not go unnoticed and unredressed.

During the initial phase of expansion of *locus standi* and 'epistolary jurisprudence' individual judges treated letters addressed to them as writ petitions. However, as this could have been construed as enabling the petitioner to choose a judge, a Public Interest Litigation Cell was established to go through the letters, and enable the Chief Justice to assign selected cases to appropriate benches.[16]

Even though India's higher judiciary has altered the traditional rules of *locus standi* as described above, disadvantaged groups still depend on a handful of civil society organisations, and a smaller number of public-spirited lawyers (who have to be well-established in the Bar to be taken seriously in such matters by the courts) to take up their cases. India does not have law firms that specialise in public interest litigation. Lawyers who argue public interest cases are also those most sought after by rich corporations and leading politicians. Therefore, it would be wrong to conclude that the Supreme Court's liberal rules of standing have made it easy for the voiceless and deprived sections of the population to seek legal redress for violations of their fundamental rights.

Responsiveness of Courts

In Siri Gloppen's framework for determining the transformative potential and impact of courts, their responsiveness – comprising receptivity to modes of interpretation intended to advance the court's transformative potential, and sensitivity as determined by value-orientations, backgrounds and ideology – is all important.

How sensitive are judges to the need to bring about social transformation and redress some of the wrongs that are done to people who are not even regarded as human? Undoubtedly, some judges in India have displayed the requisite sensitivity for them to be successful crusaders in the cause of justice on behalf of the poor and other disadvantaged groups.

Justice Krishna Iyer's sensitivity is evident, for instance, when long after his retirement, he called upon judges to ask themselves:

> Who are our people? Where is their habitat? What, in human terms, does justice mean to them? How can law and its administration, through conventional court processes, fulfill the hunger of the common man for simple, quick justice, which assures him a fair share of the good things of life? ... By what means does the law in the books communicate with life in the raw? Can the gap between lawyer's law and the rule of life be bridged?[17]

Judicial Creativity and Capability

The higher judiciary in India has demonstrated its ability to be creative in its interpretation of constitutional provisions in order to bring social, economic, cultural, and environmental rights into the realm of justiciable issues. In the initial years, the Supreme Court maintained that the Directive Principles were not justiciable, but in the post-emergency phase, the Court found ways of making those principles justiciable by 'reading them into' article 21 (right to life and personal liberty).[18] Justice Bhagwati defended this move with the following reasoning:

> This principle of interpretation which means that a constitutional provision must be construed, not in a narrow and constricted sense, but in a wide and liberal manner so as to anticipate and take account of changing conditions and purposes so that the constitutional provision does not get atrophied or fossilised but remains flexible enough to meet the newly emerging problems and challenges, applies with greater force in relation to a fundamental right enacted by the Constitution.[19]

In this case the Court claimed that 'life' in article 21 could only mean a life with dignity that acknowledges the worth of the human person.

Article 21 has been held to affirm that life does not mean merely animal existence or continued drudgery but the finer aspects of human civilisation, which make life worth living.[20] The right to life and personal liberty has also been held to encompass rights to privacy; development of urban areas; fresh water and air; protection against environmental degradation; food, clothing and shelter; health; education; roads in hilly regions; conservation of the physical environment; and even protection against the importation of injurious chemicals.[21]

Apart from creativity in interpretation, the higher judiciary in India has also been creative in attempting pragmatic solutions to public interest cases adjudicated by it. The Court has been prepared to abandon the common-law view of the judge as a neutral umpire concerned with the merits of the arguments advanced by contended parties. It has assumed the role of an investigator, adopting the inquisitorial stance of judges in the civil-law tradition, to investigate violations of human rights, subversion of the rule of law, or disregard for the environment.

The Court has demonstrated its capacity to come up with creative solutions to problems, as illustrated by the case of *Azad Riksha Pullers Union v. Punjab*.[22] The Punjab Cycle Riksha, or Regulation of Rikshaws Act of 1975, licensed only owners of rickshaws to ply their trade. This meant that persons who rented these vehicles faced the risk of losing their livelihood. Their union challenged the Act on the ground that it would affect the right to carry on any trade, business, or occupation guaranteed by article 19(1)(g) of the Constitution. Sympathetic to the predicament of those who could not afford to own their own rickshaws, Justice Krishna Iyer came up with a solution under which the Punjab National Bank agreed to provide them loans, with easy repayment requirements.

Judicial Co-governance

In the post-emergency period, India's higher judiciary has been engaged in co-governance with the other branches of government, and the distinctions between making policy, implementing policies, and interpreting the law have become blurred.[23] A recent order issued by the Supreme Court in *People's Union for Civil Liberties v. Union of India*, illustrates the continuing activism. This was a case filed in 2001, for enforcement of the famine code, release of surplus food in the government's buffer stock to drought-affected areas, and directions for reforms in the public distribution system. On 29 April 2004, the Supreme Court issued the following order, among several others:

> Food is supplied to children through Anganwadi Centres (AWCS). In all there are about 6 lakh (600,000) centres. The norms of Government of India provide for one centre for a population of 1000 (700 in the case of tribal area). According to the petitioner, going by the said norms, there should be 14 lakh ACWS. It appears according to the calculation of Government of India the AWCS would be 12 lakh. We direct the Government of India to file within 3 months affidavit stating the period within which it proposes to increase the number of AWCS so as to cover the 14 lakh habitations. We notice that the norm for supply of nutritious food worth rupee one for every child was fixed in the year 1991. The Government of India should consider the revision of the norm of one rupee and incorporate their suggestions in the affidavit.

Prior to this order, cited here to demonstrate the degree to which the Court trespassed into what in other countries might be regarded as the territory of the executive branch, the Court issued an order on 28 November 2001. This order stipulated that benefits available under eight nutrition-related schemes were entitlements, directed all state governments to provide cooked mid-day meals for all children in schools financed by the government, and directed the governments to adopt specific measures for ensuring public awareness and transparency in the nutrition programmes. Moreover, the Court specified the minimum quantities of calories and protein that should be in the diet provided. In May 2002, the Court directed elected village assemblies (*gram sabhas*) to provide information on entitlements to people, and to empower democratic institutions to manage and control food supplies and hold the state government to account for failure to provide basic minimum food requirements. The Court also directed the heads of state administrations to file affidavits showing how many children, adolescent girls, and pregnant and lactating women were supplied nutrition supplements from the sanctioned AWCS, and for how many days, during the period 1 April 2003 to 31 March 2004. When the Court learned that some of the schemes covered by its orders had been discontinued, it directed that no scheme covered by its orders, including the National Old Age Pension Scheme, Family Benefit Scheme, Maternity Benefit Scheme, should be discontinued or restricted without prior approval of the Court.[24]

Clearly, the Court has had no compunction about placing itself in the position of a super-executive exercising oversight powers over executive action. The Court has the power to sentence errant officials to prison for contempt of court if they fail to obey its orders. However, adopting a more realistic and pragmatic approach, the Court has tried to galvanise the conscience of the executive to emulate its humanitarian and sympathetic approach to the right to food. At the end of the day, if the right to food is to be realised, it will depend on the legislative and executive branches complying with the orders of the Court. The orders by themselves cannot deliver food to the hungry.

Composition of the Judiciary

Patriarchy is predominant in Indian society. The higher judiciary, for all its activism, remains a male-dominated institution. There are 20 female judges in the Supreme Court of India and the High Courts, including one female judge on the Supreme Court of India out of a total of 26 judges. The number of female judges in the 21 High Courts is 19 out of a total of 647. The Bombay High Court has four female judges followed by three female judges in the Madras High Court, three female judges in the Kerala High Court, two female judges in the Delhi High Court, and one each in the Gujarat, the Himachal Pradesh, the Karnataka, the Madhya Pradesh, the Patna, the Punjab and Haryana and the Rajasthan High Courts.

India's higher judiciary is also upper-caste dominated. The Supreme Court has only one Scheduled Tribe and one Scheduled Caste judge. There are no judges belonging to the so-called 'Other Backward Communities'. The situation in the High Courts, in the matter of giving representation to the disadvantaged sections of the society, is worse. In November 1998, India's President, K.R. Narayanan (the first *dalit* President in India) made an extraordinary noting on a file seeking his assent for the appointment of four Supreme Court Judges.

Granting approval, the President observed: 'While recommending the appointment of Supreme Court judges, it would be consonant with constitutional principles and the nation's social objectives if persons belonging to weaker sections of society like Scheduled Castes and Scheduled Tribes, who comprise 25 per cent of the population, and women, are given due consideration.' He added: 'Eligible persons from these categories are available and their under-representation or non-representation would not be justifiable. Keeping vacancies unfilled is also not desirable given the need for representation of different sections of society and the volume of work which the Supreme Court is required to handle.'[25]

The Chief Justice's response to this noting, as reported in a newsmagazine, was the following:

> I would like to assert that merit alone has been the criterion for selection of Judges and no discrimination has been done while making appointments. All eligible candidates, including those belonging to the Scheduled Castes and Tribes, are considered by us while recommending names for appointment as Supreme Court Judges. Our Constitution envisages that merit alone is the criterion for all appointments to the Supreme Court and High Courts. And we are scrupulously adhering to these provisions. An unfilled vacancy may not cause as much harm as a wrongly filled vacancy.

In what is known in India as the *Second Judges Case*,[26] Justice Pandian wrote in his opinion:

> It is essential and vital for the establishment of real participatory democracy that all sections and classes of people, be they backward classes or scheduled castes or scheduled tribes or minorities or women, should be afforded equal opportunity so that

> the judicial administration is also participated in by the outstanding and meritorious candidates belonging to all sections of the society and not by any selective or insular group.

In the *Judges Case* decided earlier,[27] Justice Bhagwati wrote:

> What is necessary is to have Judges who are prepared to fashion the new tools, forge new methods, innovate new strategies and evolve a new jurisprudence, who are judicial statesmen with a social vision and a creative faculty and who have, above all, a deep sense of commitment to the Constitution with an activists approach and obligation for accountability, not to any party in power nor to the opposition nor to the classes which are vociferous but to the half-hungry millions of Indians who are continually denied their basic human rights. We need Judges who are alive to the socio-economic realities of Indian life, who are anxious to wipe every tear from every eye, who have faith in the Constitutional values and who are ready to use law as an instrument for achieving the Constitutional objectives. This has to be the broad blueprint of the appointment project for the higher echelons of judicial service.

Despite these wise words from the Bench, the composition of India's judiciary is far from satisfactory. Judges both interpret and make the law. The judiciary, as a co-governing institution, needs to be democratic in the sense of representing fairly the diversity of society, not only among its social groupings but also ideologies that have significant adherents.

Compliance

The crucial component in Gloppen's framework is compliance: 'For litigation to improve the rights situation on the ground the relevant authorities must comply with the judgment and political action must be taken to implement the ruling.'[28] A number of factors have a bearing on compliance, including the dimensions that have been considered above.

As already noted, even though there are significant obstacles in the way of access to justice on the part of disadvantaged groups, the availability of a good number of civil society organisations and lawyers willing to take up pro bono PIL cases mitigates to some extent shortcomings in voice. The higher judiciary's efforts to liberalise the rules on *locus standi*, willingness to investigate violations of human rights by appointing special commissions, readiness to issue detailed directions, and creativity in constitutional jurisprudence, are all positive features. Yet, when judged from the standpoint of the extent of difference that judicial activism has made to the lives of the poor and other disadvantaged groups, there is little to cheer.

Paradoxically, it is possible that when the Court fails to live up to the expectation that it would do justice by vindicating the rights of the poor and disadvantaged, it could result in triggering protest movements that could force the legislature into amending the law, and lead to greater public awareness regarding the relevant issue. All this happened as a consequence of an infamous verdict of the Supreme Court that overturned the conviction of two police officers who had been convicted and sentenced for the rape of a minor in the premises of the police station.[29] Professor Upendra Baxi from the Law Faculty of Delhi University, and some of his academic colleagues, wrote a letter to the Chief Justice protesting against this verdict, and galvanised countrywide protests by circulating the letter to civil society organisations and the media.[30] The public at large demanded amendments to the antiquated provisions of the Indian Penal Code enacted in 1860. In 1983, the Criminal Law Amendment Act prescribed the minimum punishment for rape as 10 years for 'custodial' rape, gang rape, rape of minors (under 12 years) and pregnant women. The onus of proving his innocence was placed on the accused in cases of custodial rape (in police custody, hospitals, remand homes and jails). These amendments have led to much awareness and, in a few rare cases, a new sensitivity among the judiciary.

In 1997, an organisation involved in issues affecting women and children approached the Supreme Court through a writ petition, asking for directions concerning the definition of rape in the Indian Penal Code. The Supreme Court directed the Law Commission of India to respond to the issues raised in the petition. The Law Commission responded by saying that the 156th Law Commission Report had dealt with these issues. The Supreme Court held that the 156th Report did not deal with the precise issues raised in the writ petition. In August 1999, it directed the Law Commission to look into these issues afresh.

In 2000, the Law Commission released its 172nd Report on the Review of Rape Laws. The report recommended the deletion of section 155(4) of the Indian Evidence Act, so as to prevent a victim of rape from being cross-examined about her 'general immoral character' and sexual history. It suggested graded sentences, with higher punishment for rape committed by the relatives and persons in 'trust or authority', public servants, and superintendents, management and staff of hospitals, and the insertion of a new section 376(E) covering sexual harassment at the workplace. The Commission further suggested that the law relating to sexual assault be made gender neutral, that is, that men and women should be capable of being charged with the rape of men, women and children. If adopted, this recommendation would have meant that for the first time the sexual assault of minor boys would have been prosecutable under the law. Finally, the Commission asked for section 377 of the Indian Penal Code to be dropped, thus decriminalising sodomy. The recommendations did not, however, take into account marital rape.

In 2002, based on the Law Commission's recommendations, Parliament deleted section 155(4) and inserted a proviso to section 146 of the Indian Evidence Act. In consequence of these amendments, a victim of rape may no longer be questioned about her past sexual conduct and her 'general immoral character'. The rest of the Law Commission's recommendations were not, however, implemented.

The point of this narrative on developments in the law on rape is to highlight the importance of public action in a democracy to bring about necessary and desirable changes in the law. In this case, the public was shocked by a decision of the Supreme Court because it was expected to be on the side of the underdog. It is, on the whole, better that the judiciary so interprets laws as to favour the voiceless and the weak. Even if the directions of the Court are not fully complied with, having the law on their side is a form of empowerment for the powerless.

By and large, going by the criterion of little and slow positive changes in the lives of India's *dalits* and other downtrodden people, it may be said that the decisions of the higher judiciary in public interest litigation have been more *symbolic* and less *instrumental*. Moreover, there are indications that the focus on the poor and other disadvantaged groups in public interest litigation has been diluted with the development of 'publicity interest litigation' (this phrase was used by the Delhi High Court when it dismissed a petition seeking to prevent General Parvez Musharaff, President of Pakistan, from visiting India, and by the Madras High Court when dismissing a petition that sought a direction that India's president should be directly elected). 'Publicity interest litigation' can crowd the judiciary's already over-crowded docket, and preclude the possibility of reasonable redress of grievances of victims of exploitation and violation of human rights.[31]

For the full realisation of their social and economic rights, the poor and other disadvantaged groups need a lot more than favourable verdicts handed down by the Supreme Court and the High Courts.

There are anecdotal reports that many of the bonded labourers freed from servitude, following the orders of the Supreme Court, continue to be victimised and exploited elsewhere, since they could not get gainful employment as free labourers. It was also reported that the appalling conditions in the facility provided for destitute women in Agra – a matter that the Supreme Court improved during five years of monitoring – are now little better than they were when the case was first heard.[32]

A proper assessment of the impact of the role of courts in the achievement of social transformation will require the development of the key indicators that have been proposed by Gloppen. Unfortunately, the data needed to develop most of these indicators is not readily available in the case of India.

Courts and the Democratic Process

Even though we cannot, on the basis of data available, provide a verdict on the direct and indirect impact of the involvement of courts in vindicating rights and entitlements of the weak, we must acknowledge the crucial role played by the Supreme Court in protecting the democratic process in India.

The *Privy Purses* case is a good example of this. The Court struck down a 'midnight executive order' that 'derecognised' the former Rulers of Princely States, after a constitutional amendment to terminate their privileges fell short of the required majority by one vote. The judges struck down the order, but not because their class bias inclined them to think that *maharajas* should continue to have anachronistic privileges. Rather, they struck it down because the commitments made to Rulers in the Constitution, whose territories were merged into the Union of India, could not be revoked by executive fiat. Respect for the rule of law required that the abolition of the privileges of former Rulers had to be done properly, through an amendment of the Constitution.

In 1973, a landmark decision[33] of the Supreme Court of India introduced the so-called 'basic structure doctrine'. This doctrine stated that the Constitution could be amended only in ways that did not alter its basic structure or framework.[34] It acquired real teeth in November 1975 when the Supreme Court relied upon this doctrine to strike down clause 4 of the Thirty-ninth Amendment. This amendment was passed by a parliament that had become subservient to a prime minister who had suspended the chapter on fundamental rights, having declared a state of internal emergency in June of that year. The Allahabad High Court had set Prime Minister Indira Gandhi's election to the Lok Sabha aside. She feared that the 'total revolution' call of Jayaprakash Narayan would remove her from office even before the Supreme Court could hear appeal against that judgment. The Thirty-ninth Amendment inserted a new article 329A into the Constitution. It removed the jurisdiction of the Supreme Court over election disputes involving the Prime Minister, the Speaker of the Lok Sabha, as well as the President and Vice-President. It vested that jurisdiction in an 'authority' or 'body' yet to be established by Parliament for that purpose. The amendment was intended to set aside the Allahabad High Court's decision, and furthermore, rule out the possibility that the Supreme Court could reject her appeal against that decision.

Each of the five judges constituting the majority in the *Indira Nehru* case cited a different element of the *basic structure* violated by the constitutional amendment – rule of law, principle of free and fair elections, judicial review and equality. But the Supreme Court reached the correct conclusion on an amendment that is a blemish on India's parliamentary democracy.

The Supreme Court used the *S.R. Bommai* case to strengthen democracy by affirming that the President's order under article 356, although 'subjective', was subject to judicial review. The Court said that if a state government's actions militated against the principle of secularism that would be tantamount to violating the *basic structure* of the Constitution. Violating a basic tenet of the Constitution could be construed as creating a situation in which it could reasonably be held that that the government of that state could not be carried on in accordance with the Constitution.

In 1980, the Supreme Court relied on the *basic structure* doctrine for the second time and struck down some provisions of the Forty-second Amendment.[35] These clauses had been passed during the Emergency, but they could not be revoked by the Forty-fourth Amendment meant to undo the damage done by emergency rule to India's Constitution. Although it had been routed in the 1997 elections by the Lok Sabha, the Congress majority in the Rajya Sabha had not been diminished by then. Whether out of conviction, or just to save face, the Congress insisted on the retention of some provisions of the notorious Forty-second

Amendment. The Supreme Court struck down the amended provision in article 368 that 'there shall be no limitation whatever on the constituent power of Parliament' to amend the constitution. It also struck down another provision of article 368 that held that no amendment made before or after the Forty-second Amendment could be questioned in court. These two provisions, the Court held, were bad because they enabled Parliament to amend the Constitution 'so as to damage or destroy its basic or essential features or its basic structure'.[36]

Fifty years of constitutional interpretation by the Supreme Court have led to a better understanding of the relationship between the form of the Constitution and the substance of politics. The *basic structure* doctrine has taken root. It is now better understood, not only in Indian constitutional law, but also in international human rights law, that fundamental rights are as indivisible as the idea of the state is holistic.

The Constitution anticipates the transformation of India, not of itself. Its form undoubtedly influences the substance of politics, but only to a limited extent. But that limited influence of constitutional form over the substance of politics is critical. Without the force of form over substance the Constitution could not have lasted until now, animating as it has done a great deal of debate and discourse.

The *basic structure* doctrine remains a shield against predatory subversion of constitutionalism of the kind that was attempted during the Emergency. Democratic politics must be allowed to do what it is meant to do, that is, establish ideological goals and policies based on the preferences of people at any particular point in time. This need not give rise to anxieties that the Constitution will be subverted. The judiciary has played its part, attempting to inculcate the importance of the impersonality of public office, and separation of the public interest from the private interests of rulers.[37]

The realisation of the transformative *telos* of the Constitution depends on the shape and substance of democratic politics. It is only democracy that can provide the best institutional voice for the poor, even though courts can contribute, to an extent, to reducing or overcoming some of the deficits of democracy as we have come to know them.

Courts by themselves cannot bring about social transformation. If India today has a Prime Minister drawn from a small minority (Sikh), a President who is a Muslim in a polity where the vast majority is Hindu, and had until recently a President who hailed from a caste regarded as 'untouchable', the credit should go to its democracy.

Courts can act as the conscience of governments, drawing their attention to neglect, and the shortfalls in realisation of the vision of the Constitution. But courts are, after all, courts, and they cannot be expected to bring about all of the desired social transformation on their own.

Notes

1 Louis Dumont, *Homo Hierarchicus,* 2nd edn (Chicago: University of Chicago Press), p. 51.
2 While legislation inconsistent with the Fundamental Rights is void, the Directive Principles (Chapter IV of the Constitution) serve only as guidelines for the legislators. When Parliament and the state legislatures legislate, they have to take the Directive Principles into consideration, but the Principles are not binding on the legislature branch.
3 See Siri Gloppen's chapter in this volume.
4 The chair of the drafting committee of India's Constitution, Dr B.R. Ambedkar, was an 'untouchable' who had to sit outside the classroom at school, but went on to earn doctoral degrees from the London School of Economics and Columbia University.
5 Penderel Moon, *Strangers in India* (New York: Reynal and Hitchcock, 1945), p. 22
6 David Gardner, 'Weighed Down by an Old Economy', *Financial Times*, 17 October 2000, p. 21.
7 Charles R. Epp, *The Rights Revolution: Lawyers, Activist, and Supreme Courts in Comparative Perspective* (Chicago: University of Chicago Press, 1998), chap. 6 has data showing that only a very small percentage of cases in the Supreme Court are rights-based claims.
8 PIL has been described as the device by which public participation in judicial review of administrative action is assured (Personal Website of R. Kannan, *Remedies, Public Interest Litigation* at <www.geocities.com/kstability/projects/safeguards/pil1.html>). Under PIL, courts take up cases concerning the public at large, not the petitioner. For instance, a slum dweller cannot file a PIL to promote his own fundamental rights, but it will be possible for him to file a PIL case to ensure the fundamental rights of slum dwellers as a group. Partly due to the heavy load of PIL filings, the courts have lately been insisting that the complaints be made by the affected parties themselves.
9 *Additional District Magistrate Jabalpur v. Shivakant Shukla* 1976 AIR (SC) 1207.
10 Justice P.N. Bhagwati (who, together with Justice V.R. Krishna Iyer, pioneered a paradigm shift in advancing public interest litigation in defence of the disadvantaged) said in his judgement: 'I have always leaned in favour of upholding personal liberty, for, I believe, it is one of the most cherished values of mankind, without it life would not be worth living. It is one of the pillars of free democratic society. Men have readily laid down their lives at its altar, in order to secure it, protect it and preserve it. But I do not think it would be right for me to allow my love of personal liberty to cloud my vision or to persuade me to place on the relevant provision of the Constitution a construction which its language cannot reasonably bear.'
11 P.N. Bhagwati, V.R. Krishna Iyer, *Report on National Juridicare: Equal Justice-Social Justice* (Ministry of Law, Justice & Company Affairs, 1976).
12 S.P. Sathe, 'Judicial Activism: The Indian Experience', *Journal of Law and Policy*, 6 (2001): 29–107, 51.
13 *Sunil Batra v. Delhi Administration* 1978 AIR (SC) 1675.
14 *Bandhua Mukti Morcha v. India* 1984 AIR (SC) 802, 813.
15 *People's Union for Democratic Rights v. India* 1982 AIR (SC) 1473, 1476.
16 Not all judges of the Supreme Court were as activist and liberal regarding the judicial role as Justices Iyer and Bhagwati. Justice Pathak (who later became Chief Justice and a judge of the International Court of Justice) warned: 'I see grave danger inherent in a

practice where a mere letter is entertained as a petition from a person whose antecedents and status are unknown or so uncertain that no sense of responsibility can, without anything more, be attributed to the communication. There is good reason for the insistence on a document being set out in a form, or accompanied by evidence, indicating that the allegations made in it are made with a sense of responsibility by a person who has taken due care and caution to verify those allegations before making them.' *Bandhua Mukti Morcha v. Bihar* 1984 AIR (SC) 802, 840.

17 V.R. Krishna Iyer, 'Judiciary: A Reform Agenda I & II', *The Hindu*, 14–15 August 2002.

18 *Minerva Mills v. Union of India* (1980) 3 SCC 225.

19 *Francis Coralie Mullin v. Administrator Union Territory of Delhi* 1981 AIR (SC) 746.

20 *Board of Trustees of the Port of Bombay v. D.R. Nadkarni* (1983) 1 SCC 124.

21 See the following cases: *Kharak Singh v. State of U.P.* (1964) 1 SCR 332; *Municipal Council, Ratlam v. Vardichand* (1980) 4 SCC 162; *M.C. Mehta v. Kamal Nath* (2000) 6 SCC 213; *A.R.C. Cement Ltd. v. State of U.P.* 1993 Supp (1) SCC 426; *Shantistar Builders v. N.K. Totame* (1990) 1 SCC 520; *Vincent v. Union of India* (1987) 2 SCC 165; *Mohini Jain v. State of Karnataka* (1992) 3 SCC 666; *State of Himachal Pradesh* v. *Umed Ram Sharma* (1986) 2 SCC 68; *M.C. Mehta v. Kamal Nath* (1997) 1 SCC 388; *Ashok (Dr) v. Union of India* (1997) 5 SCC 10.

22 1981 AIR (SC) 14.

23 'The court has been charged not only with exceeding its institutional capacity, but with reversing constitutional priorities, usurping both legislative and administrative functions, violating the rule of law, riding roughshod over traditional rights and succumbing to the corrupting temptations of power.' Jamie Cassels, 'Judicial Activism and Public Interest Litigation in India: Attempting the Impossible?', *The American Journal of Comparative Law*, 37 (1989): 495–519, 509.

24 *PUCL v. Union of India* 2004 (2) SCC 476.

25 Report in *India Today*, 15 January 1999.

26 (1993) 4 SCC 441.

27 1981 Supp SCC 87, 222.

28 See Gloppen's chapter in this volume, p. 53.

29 *Tukaram v. State of Maharashtra*, (1979) 2 SCC 143.

30 Baxi et al.'Open Letter to the Chief Justice of India', (1979) 4 SCC (Journal) 17.

31 Cassels, 'Judicial Activism and Public Interest Litigation in India', 508 reports that between January 1987 and April 1988, the Supreme Court of India received 23,772 PIL petitions in the form of letters alone.

32 *Upendra Baxi v. State of Uttar Pradesh* 1987 AIR (SC) 191.

33 The *Kesavanada* case (1973) 4 SCC 225.

34 This 'basic structure' theory propounded by the Court was revolutionary and perhaps without parallel anywhere in the world. The content of the 'basic structure' was left for determination in the hands of the Court itself. (H.S. Mattewal, 'Judiciary and the Government in the Making of Modern India' 1 (2002) SCC (Jour): 19.

35 *Minerva Mills Ltd v. Union of India* 1980 AIR (SC) 1789.

36 Order read out by the Chief Justice Chandrachud before delivering the full judgement. Supreme Court Report, 1981, 263–4.

37 Among the judges whose opinions have helped in articulating the teleology of India's Constitution, Justice V.R. Krishna Iyer stands out. See R. Dhavan, S. Khurshid and R. Sudarshan (eds), *Judges and the Judicial Power: Essays in Honour of Justice V.R.*

Krishna Iyer (London: Sweet and Maxwell, 1981). See also B.N. Kirpal, Ashok H. Desai, Gopal Subramanium, Rajeev Dhavan and Raju Ramachandran (eds), *Supreme But Not Infallible: Essays in Honour of the Supreme Court of India* (Delhi: Oxford University Press, 2000), especially Raju Ramachandran, 'The Supreme Court and the Basic Structure Doctrine', pp. 107–33) where he concludes that the doctrine should be buried now in order to enable the democratic process to 'to put half a century of politics and economics into the Constitution'.

Chapter 8

Judicial Enforcement of Social Rights: Perspectives from Latin America

Christian Courtis

Introduction

This chapter offers an overview of the state of the discussion and practice relating to the judicial enforcement of social rights in Latin America. It does not purport to trace a comprehensive picture. Rather it highlights some of the most controversial issues, obstacles and challenges, and describes how different national courts in the region have dealt with these rights.

Social Rights as Rights

While some Latin American constitutionalists have maintained a traditional approach to social rights, constitutional changes over the last 25 years have fostered new ways of enforcing these rights, and some activism on the part of judges. At least two important normative developments have led to changes in the field. First, in a process broadly connected to the revival of democracy and the rule of law, several Latin American countries have amended their constitutions or passed new ones. Most of the new constitutional texts have included social rights of various kinds: workers' rights, the right to social security, the right to education, the right to healthcare, the right to housing, and, occasionally, rights relating to the situation of vulnerable groups or minorities, such as women, children, indigenous people, and people with disabilities.[1] The second development involves the widespread ratification of international human rights treaties – both regional and universal – including, inter alia, those recognising social rights, such as the International Covenant on Economic, Social and Cultural Rights; the Convention on the Rights of the Child; the Convention on the Elimination of All Forms of Discrimination against Women; and the regional Protocol of San Salvador. Some countries have gone further along this path, granting international instruments a privileged legal status – higher than national laws, and sometimes equivalent to the constitution.[2] At the same time, the legal tradition in most of the countries of the region has been monist, meaning that international treaties, once ratified, are considered to be part of domestic law.

These two developments have opened up new debates on the meaning and extent of social rights all over the region. The first point of discussion concerns what may be described as the classical question in the field of social rights, that is, whether these rights are really best described as rights or as other kinds of legal norms, such as institutional guarantees, principles, directives or legal goals or standards.

Any approach to this question should focus first on textual matters since arguments about the meaning of social rights need at least to respect the language chosen by the drafters of the different constitutions. There are thus instances where constitutional provisions dealing with social rights were clearly not drafted in the language of rights, but rather in the language of goals, principles or directives purporting to guide social policies. For example, the Dominican Constitution provides that: 'The State will stimulate the progressive development of a social security system, so that every person can enjoy adequate protection against unemployment, illness, disability and old age.'[3] The Honduran Constitution, for its part, provides that: 'Education is an essential function of the State. It shall be aimed at the conservation, promotion and diffusion of culture, which shall benefit society without discrimination.'[4] This Constitution then goes on to provide that: 'The eradication of illiteracy is a primary function of the State.'[5] The Colombian Constitution includes, under a title 'On Economic, Social and Cultural Rights', a provision that refers to the goals of public policies regarding persons with disabilities.[6] Countless other examples of a similar kind could be cited here. On the other hand, many constitutional norms, and definitely those contained in international human rights instruments, are actually written in the language of rights – such as the right to healthcare, the right to education and the right to adequate housing.[7]

Even when drafted in the language of rights, the question of how best to conceive of social rights remains controversial. Putting aside workers' rights and social security rights – whose status as judicially enforceable rights was hardly ever contested – social rights were traditionally treated in constitutional doctrine as 'programmatic' rights, that is, as mere statements of goals to be pursued by the political branches, not as judicially enforceable individual or collective entitlements. The renewed recognition and expansion of social rights in Latin American constitutions, and to a certain extent the influence of the jurisprudence of international treaty-monitoring bodies such as the UN Committee on Economic, Social and Cultural Rights, has led to a less monolithic view, and to a growing discussion about the possibilities and limits of the judicial enforcement of these rights. In the same vein, concrete judicial experiences in different countries have challenged the idea that social rights are not judicially enforceable, and in some contexts, there is a growing case law showing exactly the opposite trend. Generally speaking, one can identify some countries where the traditional doctrine still prevails among courts and academia – Chile, Mexico and the Central American states[8] – and countries where there is a growing acceptance of the possibility of invoking social rights before courts – Argentina, Brazil and Colombia being good examples of this trend.

Obstacles Confronting the Judicial Enforcement of Social Rights

Even in countries where there is a favourable trend towards the consideration of social rights as rights, and towards the judicial enforceability of some social rights, it is possible to identify certain issues that have limited the full development of this trend. This section will focus on some of these obstacles, and discuss different responses to them.[9] I will also try to situate these difficulties within the theoretical framework offered by Siri Gloppen in her contribution to this volume.

The Content of Social Rights and the Identification of the Action Required

The first difficulty regarding the judicial enforcement of social rights is linked to the specification of their exact content, and therefore to the legal obligations that flow from them. This is not surprising, as the long-standing view of social rights as non-enforceable rights has delayed jurisprudential efforts to define and build principles to aid the interpretation of these rights. Due to the rhetorical value ascribed to these rights, and to the lack of interpretive practices regarding them on the part of the judiciary and legal academia, few principles have been developed to cope with rights such as the right to education, the right to health, the right to adequate housing and the right to food.[10] In terms of Gloppen's framework, this obstacle may be associated with the nature of the legal system: even if social rights are recognised at a constitutional level, that recognition is not backed up by a legislative, judicial or doctrinal effort to develop their conceptual basis and content. The inadequate development of the content of social rights poses problems both for the channelling of victims' voices – imposing on the victims the additional burden of defining the content of these rights – and to the courts' responsiveness to these claims – forcing courts to adopt an activist stance they may not be able or willing to take.

It seems clear that, in the absence of clarity on the content of a right, and the identity of the right holder and the duty bearer, judicial enforcement becomes a difficult task. The adjudication of a right presupposes a relatively clear 'rule of decision' enabling the judge to assess compliance or non-compliance with the obligations stemming from the right. Absent this 'rule of decision', it may be impossible to distinguish adjudication from impermissible judicial law making.

This obstacle, however, requires further comment. In the first place, it is not a problem exclusively associated with social rights: the determination of the content of *every* right – regardless of its classification – is affected by the same flaw, given the fact that legal rules are expressed in unavoidably vague language.[11] Thus, 'classical' rights, such as the right to property, freedom from censorship, equal treatment or due process of law, are subject to the same difficulty. And yet, this difficulty has never resulted in the conclusion that 'classical' rights are not rights, or that they are not judicially enforceable. Rather, it has led to ongoing work on the specification of their content and limits, through a series of mechanisms aimed at defining their meaning, such as the development of statute law, administrative regulation, and case law.[12]

It seems clear that the main work in defining the content and extent of rights should be carried out by the legislative branch and, subsequently, through administrative regulation. The nineteenth-century civil codes could thus be seen as a sustained attempt to define the content, extent and limits of property rights. Nothing prevents the legislature and executive from engaging in a similar effort to define social rights on a similarly general, abstract and universal basis. Indeed, some countries in the region are already leading the effort to specify the content of some social rights. For example, Argentina and Mexico have tried to give content to the right to health through defining the kind and extent of treatment that any health service should provide.[13]

International efforts have also contributed to this effort. The General Comments of the UN Committee on Economic, Social and Cultural Rights and of the UN Committee on the Rights of the Child are examples of attempts to specify the rights set forth in the respective treaties to which they are directed.[14]

While the absence of international case law in this area obviously creates difficulties, a growing body of domestic case law is starting to offer criteria for the specification of the content of social rights. Supreme and lower-court precedents regarding the right to health in Argentina,[15] and a number of constitutional court cases on various rights in Colombia[16] have fostered litigation in this field that would have been unthinkable twenty years ago. Consumer and environmental protection jurisprudence in Brazil has followed a similar trend.

The same could be said of the absence of jurisprudential work on social rights: the task of building a systematic body of jurisprudence in this area is no different from the task of building a body of jurisprudence in any other area. Labour law and consumer law offer good examples of the possibility of developing jurisprudence in new areas of law. A growing body of doctrine on Brazilian environmental and consumer law, Colombian social rights law and Argentinean health law, are good examples of the development of new fields[17] that provide operative criteria and standards for lawyers and judges.

The absence of a coherent body of legal regulations, case law and jurisprudence in the area of social rights does not follow from any metaphysical impossibility. Rather, it has ideological origins: symbolic and material resources were disproportionately allocated to the development of the legal basis of the nineteenth-century capitalist market structure, which still dominates the core legal academic curriculum in Latin America. Even if part of the development of nineteenth-century legal culture focused on the development of a legal basis for the welfare state, the lack of development of constitutional and statutory law on social rights, together with a body of case law and jurisprudence, is partly the result of a self-fulfilled prophecy: the ideological operation of the theory of social rights as 'programmatic' rights.

Another historical issue that helps to explain the gap between the constitutional recognition of social rights and the coherent theoretical development of their content is that the growth of the welfare state was mainly centered on labour relations. The position of workers in the labour market has strongly influenced the assignment of rights, income transfers and access to other socially oriented services, such as housing, consumer credit, social insurance and health services. There was no space for the autonomous development of rights such as the right to health, the right to nutrition and the right to adequate housing because they were seen as supplementary workers' entitlements.[18] This situation, however, is gradually changing.

Secondly, the lack of specification of the content of rights is a typical problem of constitutions and human rights treaties, due to the fact that these kinds of instruments prescribe the general norms of the legal order. There are a number of reasons for this: general norms are more flexible and adaptable to change than ordinary legislation; they allow the bodies in charge of specifying the content of these norms a greater margin of discretion, which is both prudent and necessary to contextual political decision-making; and their brevity is appropriate to the statement of the fundamental legal principles of state and society.[19]

Recognising the desirability of drafting a constitution or human rights treaty in general language does not mean that, without further specification of its content, it is impossible to say that a right has been breached. If this were the case, it would be impossible to argue that a particular limitation of a right was unconstitutional: the whole language of constitutional and international human rights law would be meaningless. The existence of a tradition of judicial review in several countries in the region, and in international human rights courts – such as the European or Inter-American Court of Human Rights – are in fact examples of the possibility of verifying the compatibility of an act or omission, or inferior norm, with a right expressed in general terms. If this is the case with civil rights, there is no reason not to reach the same conclusion with regard to social rights. In both cases, the task of assessing whether a right has been violated is of course much easier when the content of the right has been further specified by statutory regulation. But when the formulation of a right in a constitution or a human rights treaty is clear enough, the objection based on indeterminacy misses its point.

In some countries in the region – for example, most of the Central American countries – the power of constitutional judicial review existed on paper, but for various reasons (lack of judicial independence and impartiality, authoritarian regimes, extreme deference to the political branches), this power was never exercised. In the result, in these countries, there is no tradition of constitutional rights enforcement, either of civil and political rights, or of social rights. In other countries, there is no tradition of judicial control of administrative action. Under these circumstances, it is obviously difficult to develop case law. Once again, however, these difficulties not only affect social rights, but also civil and political rights.

The third observation has to do with the need to consider two different issues when determining the duties imposed by social rights. I have already referred to the problem of the *semantic* determinability of the content of rights. As noted above, the specification of the duties imposed by social rights in statutory regulations, case law and academic writing constitutes one means for determining their content. However, another means of determining the content of social rights has to be considered. I am referring here to the possibility of *factual* determination: in many cases, even if the duty that flows from a right is not fixed by a legal text, there is only one way, or a limited number of ways, in which the right may be respected, protected or promoted. For example, in the context of the right to healthcare, the factual classification of the dispute into an area, such as medical treatment or vaccination, clearly narrows the duty-bearer's discretion to choose between competing options. Argentinean and Colombian courts have followed this path by taking into consideration the state's previous conduct when considering whether there has been a breach of a social right. For example, the fact that the state had started producing a vaccine or begun providing medicine to an infant suffering from a serious illness, was held to restrict the state's choices, and prevent it from arbitrarily stopping treatment, even where treatment was not mandatory under the Constitution.[20]

Lastly, when judges examine whether a right has been violated, they do not necessarily prescribe the specific course of conduct that the state or individual must follow. Judges usually assess the action required of the duty-bearer in terms of legal standards, such as 'reasonableness', 'proportionality', 'adequacy', 'appropriateness' or 'progressive realisation'. These standards are not alien to the tradition of judicial review of decisions of the political branches.[21] Judges also do not necessarily substitute their views for those of the political branches in deciding how a right should be fulfilled, but often examine the effectiveness of the chosen measures in achieving their stated goals. Although the state's margin of appreciation may be wide, certain types of conduct, such as the exclusion of specially protected groups, the failure to satisfy needs associated with the minimum core content of a right, or the adoption of retrogressive measures, are likely to be subjected to judicial review in terms of 'reasonableness' or similar standards. Once again, there are some good examples of this point from Argentinean courts in the housing rights context.[22]

Judicial Self-restraint in the Face of 'Political' and 'Technical' Questions Another set of obstacles confronting the judicial enforcement of social rights has to do with different interpretations of the constitutional principle of 'separation of powers'. Traditionally, Latin American judiciaries have been reluctant to review matters considered to be the result of 'political' decision-making by the political branches of government. Although the nature of this argument varies, judges tend to be reticent to make decisions that affect issues such as the allocation of resources, the design or implementation of public policies and the setting of priorities.[23] This difficulty is related to two of the categories proposed in Gloppen's paper: court *responsiveness and judges' capabilities.*

In the same vein, the margin of discretion enjoyed by the executive is thought to be broader – and thus, the space for judicial control reduced – when a decision is made on the basis of technical expertise or criteria, which are deemed to be part of the executive's special sphere of knowledge.

There is obviously some truth to this point: trials – at least in their traditional bilateral format – do not constitute the best forum for deciding some of these issues, not least because they involve a multiplicity of actors and interests. Our discussion here, however, focuses on the extent to which this argument relates to the reluctance of judges to enforce social rights. Court responsiveness to claims based on social rights could thus be conditioned by judges' perception of their role, and by a corresponding lack of sensitisation regarding the legal character of social rights. Conversely, even if judges considered themselves able, as a formal matter, to decide on social rights issues, they might feel that their capacity to impose duties on the political branches was weak, and that venturing their opinions in this uncertain field might undermine their authority.

One initial comment is self-evident: the broader the margin of discretion about questions that could be considered 'political' or 'technical', the less likely it will be that judges will be tempted to enter into the discussion. However, one must first inquire into the conceptual basis for defining a question as 'political' or 'technical'. There are no essential or absolute notions of what questions fall into these two categories, so the borderline between these kinds of questions and 'merely legal' questions is actually constantly moving. For example, the application of the 'political question' doctrine in US constitutional law – and in Latin American countries influenced by this tradition – has dramatically varied over the last century: matters that were previously considered 'political' have changed, and the judiciary has broadened its review powers over acts or omissions by the political branches.[24]

Moreover, not every state or private obligation in the area of social rights involves a 'political' or 'technical' question: when the 'rule of judgment' is fixed by the constitution, a human rights treaty or a statutory provision, there is less space to argue that decisions made under that rule should be exempted from judicial review. A considerable number of cases involving the violation of social rights deal with situations where the executive is sued for not complying with statutory regulations passed by the legislature. In these cases, adjudication could be seen as reinforcing – and not undermining – the separation of powers.

Even where the rule of judgment is not fixed, there are plenty of examples of legal standards – such as the reasonableness, proportionality and adequacy principles already mentioned – that are regularly applied by the judiciary in many areas.

Last, but not least: while the margin of discretion enjoyed by the political branches could be broad in the abstract, judges have developed other ways of assessing state compliance with a legal standard or rule, for example, taking into consideration the state's past behaviour, as noted in the previous section. In this fashion, courses of action that were potentially 'open' get 'narrowed' by the state's past behaviour, and thus there is often a more concrete basis on which the courts may decide questions of compliance and non-compliance.

While 'political' or 'technical' question doctrine is still powerful in some courts of the region – for example, in Mexico, Central America, and Chile – other Latin American countries are gradually overcoming the effect of this doctrine. Most judicial decisions in any sphere have a budgetary impact, so arguments about the effect of a decision on the allocation of resources are not decisive. Constitutional and statutory rules offer standards that allow public policy choices enshrined in regulations to be evaluated from a legal standpoint. Although it may take some time to develop these criteria properly, comparative examples provide a good starting point.

Procedural Limitations and the Inadequacy of Some Traditional Procedural Mechanisms for Protecting Social Rights

Another important obstacle in the way of the judicial enforcement of social rights is the inadequacy of traditional procedural mechanisms for protecting them. Traditional rights-enforcement mechanisms were devised within the paradigm of nineteenth-century property rights.[25] The hegemonic allocation of legal resources to property rights, to which I referred above, did not only affect the content of the legal curriculum, but also the design of apparently 'neutral' legal institutions, such as procedural mechanisms to guarantee rights. Thus, traditional forms of procedure privilege bilateral trials and narrow rules of standing related to individual grievances, and have been developed mainly for conflicts between private individuals. This question again raises concerns about the nature of the legal system, in particular the existence of barriers between the victims' voice and the courts' response. Some procedural problems are also linked to limitations on judges' capacity to enforce rights against the political branches of government.

The absence of an adequate procedural framework for the judicial enforcement of social rights is also connected to the broad discretion granted to the political branches – especially the executive – in the implementation of social services. One of the features of this discretion has been the absence of causes of action or grounds of review in statutes regulating the provision of social services such as healthcare, education and housing. Instead of giving content to the rights they are intended to regulate, these statutes are mostly concerned with designing the administrative structure behind the provision of these services. Once again, Mexico, and some Central American countries, such as El Salvador and Panama, are good examples of this trend.[26]

Some examples might assist in illustrating these difficulties:[27]

- Procedural mechanisms designed for hearing individual grievances are not suited to the resolution of collective claims, such as those involving group rights, massive rights violations or situations that require a collective remedy. Requirements such as the need to show a sufficient individual interest in the case for the purposes of establishing *locus standi* or the limitation of remedies to those that address the concerns of the individual plaintiff, and the lack of collective representation mechanisms characteristic of civil procedure in many countries in the region, clearly exclude the possibility of challenging measures that affect a whole group.[28] This is precisely the situation in many cases involving the enforcement of social rights.

- Violations of social rights often require simultaneous urgent satisfaction *and* ample proof, but these requirements tend to be mutually exclusive in traditional procedural mechanisms. Constitutional actions (such as *amparo, acción de tutela* and *recurso de protección*), injunctions and preliminary measures often impose a burden of proof on the complainant at the admissibility stage to produce evidence of a clear violation or probability of a violation, but thereafter keep the discussion of factual issues to a minimum. However, cases involving the violation of social rights often involve complex factual or legal problems, which require more extensive argument on factual issues and proof.
- The state often has procedural advantages over private individuals. This feature has been inherited from French administrative law, whose influence is pervasive in the whole region. For example, the state has more time to respond to pleadings, it can bring its own administrative dossier as proof, and it has privileges that individuals do not have. Judgments against the state ordering the fulfilment of its positive obligations are often merely declaratory, do not come with sufficient procedural safeguards, and are regularly difficult to implement. This issue could be simultaneously seen as a problem related to the nature of the legal system, and as a legal obstacle that limits judges' capacity to enforce these rights. It may also raise problems of compliance and implementation: judgments that impose duties on the state may by postponed or subjected to cosmetic compliance.

Even acknowledging these problems – which obviously do impose some limits on the judicial enforcement of social rights – it is perfectly possible to identify types of situations where the present procedural mechanisms do allow judicial review of alleged violations of social rights. In many cases involving health rights – particularly in the area of HIV/AIDS – in different countries in the region, courts have imposed on public and private healthcare givers obligations to provide treatment that were already specified in legislation.[29]

Moreover, the absence of adequate procedural mechanisms does not mean that it is impossible to overcome the framework of bilateral/property-oriented suits by devising new procedural mechanisms. The argument concerning procedural mechanisms merely highlights a certain state of affairs,[30] which in fact *prima facie* violates the state's obligation to provide procedural guarantees when recognising a constitutional right, including social rights.[31] It says nothing about the conceptual impossibility of enforcing social rights. On the contrary, the above argument actually calls for imaginative and creative thinking on how to provide procedural mechanisms to enforce these rights.

While the issues discussed above certainly pose obstacles, they do not create an insurmountable barrier in the way of the judicial enforcement of social rights. Part of the contemporary evolution of procedural law has taken into account some of these difficulties, pointing out the need to adapt the old model of individual/bilateral actions to new challenges, such as the collective incidence of some wrongs, or the need for urgent protection of fundamental legal rights before the violation takes place. Environmental, consumer and mass tort procedural mechanisms have opened up some new paths in this direction. Comparative law also offers many helpful examples, such as class actions; collective *amparo*; new standards in preliminary measures (for example, the precautionary principle); the Brazilian *ação civil pública, mandado de segurança* and *mandado de injunção*; *locus standi* for public prosecutors, the office of the Attorney General or Ombudsperson to represent collective complainants; *qui tam* actions; and so on.

Constitutional, legislative and judicial evolution in this field has been notorious in some Latin American countries, such as Argentina, Brazil, Colombia and Costa Rica. In Argentina, the judicial development of a new constitutional action provided by the 1994 constitutional amendments, collective *amparo*, even without statutory regulation, is surprising.[32] In Brazil, the use of a novel procedural mechanism called 'public civil action' (*ação civil pública*) to trigger judicial protection in environmental, consumer and occupational safety and health cases has been generalised since its regulation in 1985.[33] In Colombia, a number of new procedural mechanisms – namely, *acción de tutela* before the Constitutional Court, *acción popular* before ordinary courts, and *acción de cumplimiento* – has radically changed the possibilities of challenging state activities or omissions before the judiciary. In Costa Rica, a centralised and rather simplified *amparo* jurisdiction before the Constitutional Section of the Supreme Court has led to noteworthy results – for example, oral suits brought by children challenging educational decisions by school directors. Even acknowledging all the difficulties that every innovation presupposes, the doctrinal and institutional evaluation of these new procedural mechanisms has been positive, and countries where they still have not been adopted are pushing for change.[34] Many of the signals detectable in this field today are rather promising.[35]

My last comment in this regard is directed at the difficulties of executing orders against the state and, generally, at the particular position of the state before local courts. The state's procedural advantages, which would be considered unjust or intolerable in private suits, have also been the rule in the continental administrative tradition. While some of these advantages could be justified, in many other cases complete discretion, lack of impartiality, breach of the 'equality of weapons' principle and other features could be considered violations of due process, and may also require legislative reform and jurisprudential development. Cases involving judicial review of the legal procedures established to grant, adjust or terminate labour rights, pensions, social security benefits and other social rights are not uncommon in a number of countries in the region, including Argentina, Colombia, El Salvador, Peru and Venezuela, and have been the subject of litigation before international human rights bodies.[36]

The Lack of a Judicial Tradition of Protecting Social Rights

Finally, I would like to emphasise a kind of cultural obstacle, which is likely to aggravate the above-mentioned difficulties: the lack of a longstanding tradition of judicial enforcement of social rights in the region, especially with regard to those rights that require positive action on the part of the state, such as the right to health, education, nutrition and housing.[37] Although some of these rights enjoy a high constitutional status, traditional conceptions of the role of the judiciary and of the separation of powers have hampered judicial discussion of these rights, and have fostered disdain for the legal value of the constitutional provisions concerned. This issue, as previously discussed, may affect court responsiveness by entrenching negative perceptions of the role judges should play in the enforcement of social rights.

Due to the absence of a tradition of enforcement, not only have few cases been decided in this field, and few jurisprudential criteria developed, but also courts are not perceived as a mechanism through which social rights may be claimed.

In the same vein, victims either do not perceive violations of social rights as rights violations, or they tend to prefer other enforcement mechanisms – such as public demonstrations, petitions, negotiations with the executive and lobbying before the legislature. This reluctance is sometimes caused by the lack of trust that lower-income social groups have in courts and lawyers. This is clearly a matter linked to the channelling of victims' voice: it may involve problems of awareness, practical barriers to access, lack of resources to articulate a legal claim, and lack of motivation to undertake a judicial strategy.

One should not underestimate this difficulty, but there is no reason to think that things cannot change: traditions, with all the weight they may carry, are no more than an entrenched set of contingent attitudes and beliefs.[38] Part of the problem has to do with lower-income social groups' lack of access to legal services, and to the exaggerated prevalence of private property claims in the legal system, which is unfortunately a widespread problem in the region, and tends to shape the judiciary as an institution solely oriented to serve middle- and upper-class interests.

Reversing this trend would entail, among other strategies, selecting and taking to courts solid cases in which social rights violations are alleged. The accumulation of precedents and the development of jurisprudential criteria from which to establish standards for similar cases will help to change the attitude of courts, and to make the judicial enforcement of social rights more visible as an option for the victims.[39] Improvement in access to public and private legal aid services and other mechanisms to represent lower-income groups before courts, such as legal clinics, recognition of *locus standi* for NGOs or trade unions, representation of collective cases by Ombudspersons or public defenders, *pro bono* arrangements, and mandatory provision of legal services by bar associations, would also be helpful in overcoming this obstacle.

Closing Remarks

The judicial enforcement of social rights is a wide open question in Latin America. While some countries still stick to a traditional view of social rights as mere political declarations, in some others there is a growing trend of granting these rights legal status, at least *prima facie*, and confronting the challenges of making them operative before the courts.

Judicial enforcement faces a number of 'technical' obstacles, namely doctrinal, procedural and cultural barriers, most of which are founded on the idea that courts should mainly be devoted to settling property rights disputes between individual private parties, and that the state should be granted wide discretion in the design and implementation of social policies. Most of these arguments, while influential in local legal cultures, are ideological reflexes of the nineteenth-century hegemonic legal model; as such, their 'necessity' is open to conceptual challenge.

However, judicial enforcement of social rights – as is the case with any other category of rights – requires the development of standards, criteria and practices, without which the operation of abstract legal norms is impossible. The recent experience of some Latin American countries – such as Argentina, Brazil and Colombia – has seen the gradual creation of this set of standards, criteria and practices. This experience is too new to be fully evaluated, but the prospects look promising.

Notes

1 See, for example, Argentina (amendments of 1994), Bolivia (amendments of 2002), Brazil (1988), Colombia (1991), Dominican Republic (2002), Ecuador (1998), Guatemala (1992), Mexico (several amendments), Paraguay (1992), Peru (1993), and Venezuela (1999).
2 This is the case, for example, in Argentina, Bolivia, Colombia, Costa Rica, Ecuador, El Salvador, Guatemala, Honduras, Paraguay, Peru, and Venezuela
3 See Dominican Constitution, art. 8.17.
4 See Honduran Constitution, art. 151.
5 See Honduran Constitution, art. 154.
6 See Colombian Constitution, art. 47: 'The State shall promote a social insurance, rehabilitation and social integration policy for persons with physical, sensorial and mental disabilities, to whom it shall provide special assistance.'
7 See, for example, Brazilian Constitution, art. 6: 'Education, health, work, housing, leisure, security, social insurance, protection of maternity and childhood, and assistance to indigents are social rights, according to this Constitution.'
8 For Mexico, see the comments of J.A. Cruz Parcero, 'Los Derechos Sociales como Técnica de Protección Jurídica', in M. Carbonell, J.A. Cruz Parcero and R. Vázquez, (eds), *Derechos Sociales y Derechos de las Minorías* 2nd edn (Mexico: UNAM-Porrúa, 2001), pp. 89–112; J.R. Cossío, 'Los Derechos Sociales como Normas Programáticas y la Comprensión Política de la Constitución', in E.O. Rabasa, (ed.), *Ochenta Años de*

Vida Constitucional en México (Mexico: Cámara de Diputados-UNAM, 1998), pp. 295–328.

9 I devote more space to pointing out different strategies to overcome these obstacles in Víctor Abramovich and Christian Courtis, *Los Derechos Sociales como Derechos Exigibles* (Madrid: Trotta, 2002), chap. 3.

10 See, for example, the Chilean Supreme Court decision of 6/11/2000, stating that it is not the lack of healthcare by state authorities that puts the plaintiff's health at risk, but the unfortunate fact that the plaintiff is ill.

11 See H.L.A. Hart, *The Concept of Law* (Oxford: Oxford University Press, 1961), chap. VII; G. Carrió, *Notas sobre Serecho y Lenguaje* (Abeledo-Perrot: Buenos Aires, 1964), pp. 45–60; I. Trujillo Pérez, 'La Questione dei Diritti Sociali', *Ragion Pratica*, 14 (2000): 50–54.

12 For the right to work see, for example, R. Sastre Ibarreche, *El Derecho al Trabajo* (Madrid: Trotta, 1996). For the right to health, see Barbara Pezzini, 'Principi Costituzionali e Politica della Sanità: Il Contributo della Giurisprudenza Costituzionale alla Definizione del Diritto Sociale alla Salute' and Massimo Andreis, 'La Tutela Giurisdizionale del Diritto alla Salute', both in in C.E. Gallo and B. Pezzini (eds), *Profili Attuali del Diritto alla Salute* (Milan: Giuffrè, 1998).

13 See, Argentina, Laws 23.660 and 23.661, Presidential Decrees 492/95 and 1615, Ministerial Resolutions of the Ministry of Health and Social Action, 247/96 and amendments (542/1999, 157/1998, 939/2000 and 1/2001); Mexico, General Health Law. These statutes and regulations purport to establish the basis of the health system, defining its general goals and objectives, the standards that should govern the health services, and the identification of the type, content and coverage of the services. In the Argentinean case, a minimum common medical plan also applies to private healthcare givers.

14 See UN Committee on Economic, Social and Cultural Rights, General Comment 3 on general obligations imposed by the Covenant (1990); General Comment 4 on the right to housing (1991); General Comment 5 on the rights of persons with disabilities (1994); General Comment 6 on the rights of older persons (1995); General Comment 7 on forced evictions (1997); General Comment 9 on the domestic application of the Covenant (1998); General Comment 11 on primary education (1999); General Comment 12 on the right to food (1999); General Comment 13 on the right to education (1999); General Comment 14 on the right to health (2000); and General Comment 15 on the right to water (2003). For an overview of the international efforts to define the content of social rights, see the different essays in V. Abramovich, M.J. Añón and C. Courtis, *Derechos Sociales:Instrucciones de Uso* (Mexico: Fontamara, 2003).

15 See, for example, among many others, Argentinean Supreme Court, *in re Campodonico de Beviacqua, Ana Carina*, 10/24/2000; *in re* Laudicina, Ángela Francisca, 3/9/2004; *in re Lifschitz, Graciela Beatriz*, 6/15/2004; *in re Martín, Sergio Gustavo*, 6/8/2004, where the Supreme Court filed injunctions to order the administration and other health care providers to cover the treatment of, or to deliver medication to, the plaintiff. See also Bahía Blanca Civil and Commercial Court of Appeals, Section II, *in re C. y otros v. Ministerio de Salud y Acción Social de la Provincia de Buenos Aires*, 2/9/1997, where a local appellate court order the provincial government to provide medication to 34 HIV/AIDS patients; Argentine Federal Administrative Court of Appeals, Section IV, *in re Viceconte, Mariela*, 6/2/1998, where a federal appellate court filed an injunction to ensure the production of a vaccine when the interruption of funding threatened it.

16 Colombian examples include cases dealing with the right to health, right to social security, right to education, right to housing, rights of indigenous people, among many others. For an account of the cases regarding the right to health, see, for example, M. Mónica Arbeláez Rudas, 'Diez Años de Protección Constitucional del Derecho a la Salud: La Jurisprudencia de la Corte Constitucional Colombiana', in Comisión Andina de Juristas, Red de Información Jurídica, <www.cajpe.org.pe/rij/bases/jurisnac/arbelaez.pdf> (2002), and Rodrigo Uprimny Yepes, 'El Derecho a la Salud en la Jurisprudencia Constitucional Colombiana', in S. Franco Agudelo (ed.) *La Salud Pública Hoy: Enfoques y Dilemas Contemporáneos en Salud Pública* (Bogotá: Universidad Nacional de Colombia, 2003). For a general account of the protection of social rights by Colombian courts, including statistical data, see Mauricio García Villegas, 'Derechos Sociales y Necesidades Políticas. La Eficacia Judicial de los Derechos Sociales en el Constitucionalismo Colombiano', in Boaventura de Sousa Santos and Mauricio García (eds), *El Caleidoscopio de las Justicias en Colombia* (2 vols, Bogotá: Uniandes, 2001), vol. 1, pp. 455–83.

17 Some excellent examples of recent doctrinal development of social rights are provided by E. Góngora Mera, *El Derecho a la Educación en la Constitución, en la Jurisprudencia y en los Instrumentos Internacionales* (Bogotá: Defensoría del Pueblo, 2003) (regarding the right to education), O. Parra Vera, *El Derecho a la Salud en la Constitución, la Jurisprudencia y los Instrumentos Internacionales* (Bogotá: Defensoría del Pueblo, 2003) (regarding the right to health); G. Pisarello, *Vivienda para Todos. Un Derecho en (De)construcción* (Barcelona: Observatori DESC-Icaria, 2003) (regarding the right to housing).

18 For a more extensive discussion of this point, see V. Abramovich and C. Courtis, *Los Derechos Sociales en el Debate Democrático* (Madrid: Bomarzo, 2006), chap. 1.

19 See C. Fabre, *Social Rights under the Constitution* (Oxford: Clarendon Press, 2000), pp. 156–7.

20 See, for example, Argentine Supreme Court, *in re Campodonico de Beviacqua, Ana Carina*, 10/24/2000, where the Supreme Court took the state's previous conduct of delivering medication to a child with disabilities as an indication of a self-assumed duty; Argentine Federal Administrative Law Court, *in re Viceconte, Mariela*, 6/2/1998, where a Federal Appellate Court considered that the previous conduct of funding research and purchasing doses of an experimental vaccine bound the state.

21 See, for example, C. Bernal Pulido, *El Principio de Proporcionalidad y los Derechos Fundamentales* (Madrid: Centro de Estudios Políticos y Constitucionales, 2003).

22 See Buenos Aires Administrative and Tax Trial Court N°1, *in re Aguero, Aurelio Eduvigio*, 2/27/2002; Buenos Aires Administrative and Tax Law Court of Appeals, Section II, *in re Ramallo Beatriz*, 3/12/2002; Buenos Aires Administrative and Tax Law Court of Appeals, Section II, *in re Comisión Municipal de la Vivienda v. Saavedra, Felisa A.*, 4/9/2002; Buenos Aires Supreme Court, *in re Pérez, Víctor*, 6/21/2002. In most of these cases, local courts reviewed the reasonability of housing policies carried out by the Buenos Aires government, screening out cases of unreasonable or deliberately retrogressive measures.

23 See, for example, Chilean Supreme Court decision of 9/10/2001, deciding that health issues are to be regulated by the political branches, and thus rejecting a case in which the claimants required HIV/AIDS treatment as defined in the law. For a critical comment, see 'Informe Annual sobre los Derechos Humanos en Chile 2003. Hechos de 2002' (Santiago: Facultad de Derecho, Universidad Diego Portales, 2003), pp. 390–93.

24 The list of matters previously considered 'political' that became judicially enforceable is large: the delimitation of electoral districts, control of the exercise of powers exclusively attributed to the political branches, and due process in case of impeachment. In Argentina, the Supreme Court declared unconstitutional a constitutional amendment, for breach of the limits imposed by a statute that declared the need for an amendment. See Argentine Supreme Court, *in* re Fayt, Carlos S., 8/19/1999.

25 See, for example, J.R. Lopes, 'Direito Subjetivo e Direitos Sociais: O Dilema do Judiciário no Estado Social de Direito', in J.E. Faria, (ed.), *Directos Humanos, Directos Sociais e Justiça* (São Paulo: Malheiros, 1994), pp. 114–38.

26 For Mexico, see J.A. Cruz Parcero, 'Los Derechos Sociales como Técnica de Protección Jurídica', pp. 103–104.

27 Many of these difficulties are not exclusive to social rights, but are also typical of contemporary contract and tort law. For example, the inadequacy of traditional bilateral/individual procedural mechanisms also affects mass contracts, prevention and reparation of mass torts, damage to collective goods such as the environment, public health, cultural or historical heritage, and so on. Some scholars have developed the notion of 'collective private law' to refer to this field. See R.L. Lorenzetti, *Las Normas Fundamentales del Derecho Privado* (Santa Fe: Rubinzal-Culzoni, 1995).

28 For Mexico, see E. Ferrer Mac-Gregor, *Juicio de Amparo e Interés Legítimo: La Tutela de los Derechos Difusos y Colectivos* (Mexico: Porrúa, 2003); A. Zaldívar Lelo de Larrea, *Hacia una nueva Ley de Amparo* (Mexico: UNAM, 2002), pp. 41–64, commenting on many rejected cases. For El Salvador, see M.A. Montecino Giralt, 'Defensa de la Constitución', in S. Anaya, et al., *Teoría de la Constitución Salvadoreña* (San Salvador: Unión Europea-Corte Suprema, 2000), pp. 322–3.

29 See, for example, Bahia Blanca (Argentina) Court of Appeals, Section II, *in re C. v. Ministry of Health and Social Action*, 9/2/1997; Federal Civil and Commercial Court of Appeals, Section I, *in re S/N s/amparo*, 8/21/2003; Argentine Supreme Court, *in re Asociación Benghalensis*, 6/1/2000. These cases deal, individually or collectively, with the state's lack of compliance with its statutory duty to provide medication or treatment.

30 A 'legal gap' which derives from the lack of plenitude in the legal order. See L. Ferrajoli, 'El Derecho como Sistema de Garantías', in Luigi Ferrajoli, *Derechos y Garantías. La Ley del Más Débil* (Madrid: Trotta, 1999), p. 24.

31 See, for example, UN Committee on Economic, Social and Cultural Rights, General Comment 9 on the domestic application of the Covenant (1998), paras 9–10.

32 Directly applying section 43 of the Constitution (as amended in 1994), Argentinean courts have overcome the traditional narrow approach to *locus standi* in constitutionally based actions. Courts have granted, for example, *locus standi* to a subway user, for challenging an illegal increase in ticket prices; to a user of the telephone service, for demanding a public hearing before increasing prices; to a neighbour, for challenging the building of a toxic treatment plant without an environmental impact assessment; to an inhabitant of an area affected by an epidemic disease, for requiring the production of a vaccine; and to a disabled user of the suburban train service, for challenging the introduction of architectural modifications in train stations which made them inaccessible. None of these cases would have been admissible under the previous doctrine, which required proof of an individual grievance.

33 See, for example, R. de C. Mancuso, *Açao Civil Pública* (São Paulo: Ed. Revista dos Tribunais, 1999), pp. 46–55; M.F.M. Leal, *Açoes Coletivas: História, Teoria e Prática*, (Porto Alegre: Sergio Fabris, 1998), pp. 187–200.

34 For example, Mexico is witnessing an extensive debate about the need for a change in the *amparo* regulations. The experience of some other countries, such as Brazil, constitutes an important contribution to this debate. See E. Ferrer MacGregor, *Juicio de Amparo e Interés Legítimo*; A. Gidi, and E. Ferrer MacGregor, (eds), *La Tutela de los Derechos Difusos, Colectivos e Individuales Homogéneos. Hacia un Código Modelo para Iberoamérica* (Mexico: Porrúa-Instituto Iberoamericano de Derecho Procesal, 2003); A. Gidi, and E. Ferrer MacGregor, (eds), *Procesos Colectivos. La tutela de los Derechos Difusos, Colectivos e Individuales en una Perspectiva Comparada* (Mexico: Porrúa, 2003).

35 See L. Bujosa Vadell, *La Protección Jurisdiccional de los Intereses de Grupo* (Barcelona: J. M. Bosch, 1995), chap. III.

36 See, for example, Inter-American Court of Human Rights *in re Baena v. Panama*, 2/2/2001, paras 124, 126 and 127, where the Court considered the right to a fair trial to be applicable to an administrative procedure for dismissal of trade union workers; *in re 5 Pensionistas v. Peru*, 28/2/2003, paras 116 and 135, where the Court granted judicial review in a case dealing with administrative measures reducing pensions; Inter-American Commission on Human Rights, Report 03/01; case of *Amílcar Menéndez, Juan Manuel Caride, et al. (Social Security System) v. Argentina*, Admissibility Report, case 11.670, 19/1/2001, where the Commission considered that a complaint based on the alleged violation of procedural rights in the area of social security pensions was admissible. The case ended with an amicable settlement.

37 The exception to this account is litigation in the area of labour rights and social security rights, which is widespread in the region.

38 See R.W. Gordon, 'Nuevos Desarrollos de la Teoría Jurídica', in C. Courtis, *Desde otra Mirada. Textos de Teoría Crítica del Derecho* (Buenos Aires: EUDEBA, 2000), pp. 333–6 (Spanish version of 'New Developments in Legal Theory', in D. Kairys, *The Politics of Law* (New York: Pantheon, 1982), pp. 281–93).

39 The case of collective *amparo* in Argentina offers a good example. The first judicial decisions were related to environmental rights. The principles drawn from these cases were then applied to consumer rights. Once this trend was consolidated, they were employed in health rights, anti-discrimination litigation, and so on.

Chapter 9

Brazilian Courts and Social Rights: A Case Study Revisited

José Reinaldo de Lima Lopes

Introduction

This chapter reassesses one form of social rights litigation in Brazilian courts. A previous survey of cases dealing with the right to education and health showed that the Brazilian class action (*ação civil pública*) was filed mostly against private providers of health and educational services. At that point in time (1997) one could see that the public prosecutors who filed these suits were especially sensitive to 'middle class' issues, and that better-organised middle-class groups could voice their complaints more effectively than disadvantaged groups. Cases studied since 1997, however, show an increasing number of suits filed by poor people accessing services in the public sector, suggesting a new approach to social rights in Brazil.[1]

The chapter begins with a short description of the institutional setting of courts in Brazil in order to justify the selection of courts and sources of information. It goes on to inquire about the symbolic effect of these social rights cases and their originality in Brazilian legal culture. Historically, ours is a time of shrinking social legislation,[2] and one may recall Hegel's phrase on Minerva's owl, which only starts to fly when the sun sets (that is, too late). I believe, however, that social rights constitute one chapter in the story about distributive justice, and an important one in democratic societies. Even when considered in comparison with individual rights (civil and political), social rights depend on a modern concept of right (that is, a vested interest with a given remedy, 'remedy precedes right'). They have become a major point of debate within constitutional welfare states, in which a charter of individual rights is complemented by a charter, or bill, of social and welfare rights, so that social rights have had to co-exist side by side with property rights, or 'traditional' vested interests. In political terms, education and healthcare are especially meaningful. Not only are they the most traditional social rights,[3] but they have also given rise to large public service sectors. Legislation regarding them includes regulation of private business in these sectors, in the widest possible sense. As they are a traditional factor believed to increase social mobility, access to good education and public healthcare have been regarded as part of the democratic social order. Democratisation in Brazil (in the 1980s) took place with the support of social movements, some of which directly organised sectors of the urban poor to reclaim their rights to health and educational services. Mothers in poor neighbourhoods (in the late 70s and early 80s) demanded district healthcare centres (*postos de saúde*) and nurseries (*creches*) in their districts, and combined their efforts into a citywide network of grass-roots movements. These groups had an important role in re-evaluating the importance of democratic rules (freedom of association, electoral process, and so forth) in the belief that greater democracy could mean greater material benefits.

Many distinctions are relevant here. Working class movements of the 1980s are quite different from the middle-class plaintiffs we will find more frequently in the cases selected for this chapter. The instrumental use of democratic means to achieve economic democracy has to be seen *cum grano salis*, since a larger consumption of collective goods may be directly related to greater participation in policy-making. These and many other objections notwithstanding, social rights and democracy have been closely connected for much of Brazil's recent history.

I have restricted my inquiry to court decisions. However, many cases do not reach the courts. In some instances they are the subject of a compromise settlement prompted by the *ministério público* (public prosecutor's office) during the civil investigation (*inquérito civil*), a preliminary procedure in which a class action is prepared and evidence is gathered. It is also very difficult to assert the 'social validity'[4] of legal norms by counting numbers at courts. From court cases one may have an idea of what the mainstream legal culture says. On the other hand, if courts are naturally only 'reactive' and not 'proactive' (*ne procedat iudex sine auctorem*), successful adjudication depends on adequately framing the cases.

Institutional Setting

Judicial Review and Social Rights in Brazil

Since her first Republican Constitution in 1891, Brazil has had a federalised judiciary with general judicial review powers conferred on both state and federal courts and judges, at trial and appellate levels. Administrative courts (*contencioso administrativo*) were abolished, much in line with the Dicey-model.[5] The Constitutions of 1946, 1967 and 1988 have all included charters of welfare and social rights.

If we wonder what has really changed in Brazilian legal practice of late, we must look at other institutional arrangements (such as the issue of *standing*) and the growth of social movements under military rule. The curtailment of representation, both in the legislative and the executive branch, channelled many disputes into the judicial arena. This is reflected in the 1988 constitutional design, which allows for greater public interest litigation.

The Selection of Courts

The field for this study included cases decided by the High Court of Justice (*Superior Tribunal de Justiça*, or STJ) and the São Paulo State Court of Justice (the *Tribunal de Justiça do Estado de São Paulo,* or TJSP) due to their jurisdiction.

The STJ has special jurisdiction (*recurso especial*) to ensure uniform enforcement of federal statutes (article 105, III of the Constitution, or CF). Many social rights depend on the federal level for their statutory provisions, funding and policy framework. States have concurrent powers on health and education (article 24, IX, XII, CF), and it is natural that some cases reach the STJ seeking uniform interpretation of federal and state statutes. The STJ is also entrusted with jurisdiction to issue injunctions against federal authorities (article 105, I, h, CF).

As states have concurrent power to legislate and the primary responsibility for the provision of schools and healthcare, a state court also rules on these matters. That is why the TJSP is also an important source of social rights litigation. State courts are the ordinary courts of the legal system, since federal courts are only involved in cases where one of the parties is the federal government, a federal agency or federal authority. Most regular court business is dealt with by state courts. The state of São Paulo, which has the largest population and produces the biggest proportion of Brazil's GNP, is also an important locus of political experiment.

The STJ has 33 justices, and the TJSP has over one hundred. All of the courts sit in panels of three or five judges. Matters are decided by the full panel, except when the *Tribunal de Justiça* sits in plenary session and actually becomes an assembly. The federal judicial branch also comprises five regional courts of appeal (*Tribunais Regionais Federais*). There are also federal trial judges in the larger cities of all states. With these numbers, courts (and judges) tend to operate and work with a degree of anonymity, in sharp contrast to US courts. Panels sit in public sessions and there is no official 'conference' outside the public panel.

A final word on the selection of judges: Trial judges (at both federal and state level) are selected in public competitions. Exams are organised and conducted by the higher courts of each state (for state judges) and the higher federal appellate court of the region (for federal judges). The only court in which there is no judicial participation in the nomination process is the Supreme Federal Court (*Supremo Tribunal Federal*, or STF), whose members are appointed by the president from nominations approved by absolute majority in the senate. Professional insulation is a marked characteristic of the judicial branch. Political and economic influences are not directly present in most of the selection procedures.

The Dockets

We have obtained the following numbers directly from the statistical bureaux of the courts, the National Data Bank of the Judicial Power maintained by the

Supreme Federal Court,[6] and the statistical web page of the *Superior Tribunal de Justiça*.[7]

Ten years ago, in 1994, when the data for this study was first collected, the TJSP enrolled a total of 87,504 cases and the STJ 68,576. In 2003, the TJSP enrolled 169,303 cases and STJ a total of 226,440 cases.

How Do Decisions Reach the Public? Selecting the Sources

In asking what criteria are used to select decisions that are published in the court reviews we were given rather impressionistic and personal replies.[8] At the TJSP we learned that all decided cases are first sent to a 'jurisprudential' division.[9] An ordinary clerical employee of the court is in charge of the review (or *Revista*). Her selection of cases follows the advice of one of the court's judges, who recommends the inclusion of a decision in the review, marked with a 'J' stamp. These decisions are grouped into large fields (civil, criminal, public law, and so forth) and sent to the six judges of the editorial board. However, in some cases, the employee selects the cases herself. Given the figures mentioned above, it is clear that a remarkably limited number of cases reach publication. However, these are the cases that will eventually inform the professional public in general.

It is clear that legal culture goes through a series of 'filters'. Precedents depend on the existence of cases that successfully reach the higher courts ('successfully' meaning that they can be heard at the higher courts). They also depend on the good will and sensitivity of the members of the editorial boards of the reviews. Not all court opinions are published in the same review, and some of the reviews (or *Revistas)* have greater circulation in some parts of the country than in others. Thus, many factors influence the development of this specific body of knowledge.[10] This is why some interest groups play an important role in both bringing the cases to public knowledge and in distributing copies of decisions that have not been recorded in the court reports. The priority given in this study to court *Revistas* is due to their being the primary resource used by lawyers and judges. They are also an official resource. In certain appeals, evidence of contradictory precedents is produced by citing or copying official court reviews.[11] This is the easiest and most inexpensive way.

Wide access to the Internet is changing things very fast. Most, if not all, courts have web pages in which search services are available, so that a larger number of decisions can be read. But, as not all courts publish all of their decisions on the Internet, controlling what is published is even harder than in the case of the *Revistas*.

For the STJ, we considered the *Revista de Jurisprudência do STJ e Tribunais Federais*; for the TJSP we considered the *Julgados do Tribunal de Justiça do Estado de São Paulo*. This selection applies to all tables and references in this chapter, unless otherwise indicated.

Social Rights Litigation: The Numbers

We have selected cases according to two criteria in order to have an idea of the courts' general profile. The first criterion was formal (procedural), restricting our research to class actions (*ações civis públicas*).[12] The second was material (subject matter), restricting our search to cases dealing with education and healthcare.

Since class actions can only be filed by organisations representing some sort of public-collective or diffuse interest, that is by public prosecutors – in their capacity as defenders of diffuse interests and rights – they may serve to indicate the extent to which social rights are claimed as collective goods. Individual litigation, even if in the form of mass individual litigation, does not present any greater legal problem to professionals, as they would tend to consider it in terms of traditional individual rights language (especially in contractual or property language).[13]

Education and healthcare were chosen because they are both the most traditional social rights and probably represent a very clear economic and class-cut. They correspond to the older form of providing lower classes with services that were affordable on an individual basis, and which were believed to be instrumental to social mobility. They also refer to collective goods that cannot easily be provided to people on an individual basis (parents, at least until now, have not required private tuition for their children). The Brazilian Constitution has a long bill of rights, under Title II (Fundamental Rights and Guarantees). Article 5 provides for traditional individual rights as well as newer ones (such as consumer protection); article 6 gives a general list of 'social rights'; articles 7–11 provide for workers' rights (the basis of labour law); and articles 12–16 deal with political rights.

Table 1 AÇÃO Civil Publica (class action)

Court	Health or education*
STJ	8
TJSP	36
Total	44

* Published in *Revistas* (law reports).

Social movements, as stated above, have played a role in publicising decisions in their areas of interest both at a grass-roots level and through the media, much beyond official reviews. However, in order to file certain appeals, parties must show evidence of controversy in rulings, either by citing official court reviews or reports, or by producing and filing an authentic copy of the court records of the decision. The first choice is clearly easier and less expensive.

Table 9.2: AÇÃO Civil Publica (class action) Health

Court	Published
STJ	7
TJSP	15
Total	22

Table 9.3: AÇÃO Civil Publica (class action) Education

Court	Published
STJ	1
TJSP	21
Total	22

When compared to the general docket of the courts it is clear that only a small number of cases ever become public knowledge (the legal profession is the most relevant public for these editions).

Nature of Social Rights Litigation

Until recently, social rights were seldom the subject of litigation. Military rule curtailed the legislative process and interrupted the traditional means of obtaining social benefits, namely through legislation and public policies defined through budgetary considerations. This led some social movements to force their way through court procedures. This is also true of the many groups that used court procedures to create obstacles to individual action against the impoverished.[14] Social rights litigation is a by-product of military rule in this respect. Courts have played no active role in it. Courts do not have jurisdiction over moot cases and they lack standing to initiate a suit. They can, at best, be receptive to such claims.

Courts played a very limited role in resisting the military. Only a few justices of the Supreme Federal Court challenged the regime in its core political abuses: Vitor Nunes Leal, Hermes Lima, Evandro Lins e Silva and Antonio Gonçalves de Oliveira. Ordinary courts continued to decide cases in which the government (at federal, state or city level) was regularly held liable to pay damages. There was no limitation whatsoever on imposing financial burdens on the state in this respect. In fact, a number of powerful economic groups, for instance those in charge of public works (such as contractors), had free access to courts and could receive generous damages. The fact that the government was found liable in civil cases, however, did not represent any challenge to the political abuses of the regime. A large number of courts, judges and lawyers willingly accepted breaches of the constitutional order in the name of national security. Theirs was an ideology of the defence of private vested interests and property, and the 'coup d'état' was exactly that: a breach of the political order in the name of citizens' personal rights.[15]

Specific Aspects of Social Rights Litigation

The most striking difference between social rights litigation and ordinary litigation lies in the multi-polar or pluri-lateral structure of the first, and the bi-polar design of the latter. Traditional lawsuits, both civil and criminal, are bi-polar and can be compared to a zero-sum game or winner-takes-all. Traditional adjudication consists of deciding who is right or wrong on some given act or matter and who will pay (bear responsibility) for some past event. It involves different sorts of conflicts: commutative (or retributive) and distributive matters. Some distributive cases may end up being treated as retributive conflicts once the law provides certain institutional structures. Discrimination is one such case. Anti-discriminatory legislation can be passed and racism, sexism, homophobia, hate-speech, and so forth, can become punishable (as criminal offences or torts). Public recognition is a distributive issue because it deals with a collective good called mutual respect owed to any human being or fellow citizen. Welfare can also be converted into a justiciable question: budget provisions and statutory acts may assign each citizen a certain claim to given amounts of wealth, in the form of pensions, healthcare, minimum family income, and so on. In many respects, social rights litigation has evolved towards empowering each citizen and groups of citizens to claim, as individual rights, what is owed to them as a matter of *distributive justice*.

There are some instances in which adjudication shows important limitations. These are not personal limitations of the judges or courts involved (although they may be). I prefer to look at them as institutional constraints, given the nature of distributive disputes. Some aspects of distributive disputes require explanation.

First, in distributive disputes – roughly the equivalent of *non-zero sum games* – conflicts can be settled by compromise, especially when the business that brought the parties together is an ongoing matter.[16] In many cases, splitting the group is no solution, either because it is not feasible, or because it is not what the parties want. It is not feasible, for example, to put an end to a society as a whole (the Brazilian society, the US society) in order to apportion different shares for different groups or classes. The same is true in smaller groups (public hospitals in a given city or district, the production of medicine, or the provision of health insurance). Traditional adjudication is useless in these cases, unless it is turned into mediation or conciliation. Non-voluntary groups do not usually seek the splitting of the group either, and they usually want a different sharing of the common goods or burdens.

Courts in the last two centuries have not been not institutionally designed to mediate; they do so under the pressure of circumstances and if they are flexible enough to recognise that the conflict at their door does not require actual adjudication.

Examples of the Brazilian courts' lack of sensitivity to these issues have occurred in land reform conflicts. When farms were occupied by the landless (*sem-terras*), injunctions were immediately issued in favor of the presumptive owners and, in trying to enforce evictions, some defendants (*sem-terras*, or landless workers) were killed or injured. The cases were not just a matter of protection of private vested rights, but a protest against land policies. They were distributive disputes. In such cases, a compromise should not be understood as a second-best choice. If adjudication means a *zero-sum* decision, and if *bi-polar* adjudication is perfectly suitable for 'oppositional contracts' (for instance one-shot businesses, in which parties have opposing interests, such as *sales*, in which no 'common good or purpose' binds them in a lasting relationship), it is not the case for 'co-operational contracts, such as partnerships.[17] It is no wonder that the partners in a partnership agreement work out some compromise. The judge will be called upon only to preside over a *fair* dissolution of the partnership. The latter option, of course, is not open to citizens (they can become emigrants or refugees at best, or engage in civil war, at worst) or members of non-voluntary groups.

Secondly, social rights legislation, contrary to private law, is not a means of preserving vested interests – quite the contrary. It is passed in order to put an end to a 'caste system'.[18] This is probably its greatest theoretical challenge to traditional legal reasoning. Social rights at the constitutional level are written in the words of principle.[19] They refer to those ends that are to be achieved in the future, and not to the preservation of the status quo. Thus, they are instruments of social reform. Are courts equipped to conduct social reform programmes? Clearly they are not. They can once again be used to mediate disputes, or to act as a public arena in which debates take place, but traditional judicial structures cannot respond to social reform programmes. An important contrast may be drawn between the US and the Brazilian legal systems in this respect. US courts have relied heavily on equity and equitable remedies to push the 'rights revolution'.[20] Brazilian law does not have an equivalent to equity. Very few provisions in statutory law give the courts the option to elaborate equitable remedies, and in only a few instances are they expressly allowed to appoint administrators to ongoing businesses (examples are the judicial pledge of ongoing concerns and the appointment of administrators by CADE-Conselho Administrativo de Defesa Econômica).[21]

More often, courts have to decide the claims put forward by parties on a simple yes-or-no basis. The caseload of the courts (see earlier discussion), when compared with the number of class actions dealing with education and healthcare as social rights, is evidence of the enormous load of traditional zero-sum, commutative disputes. Traditional thinking and lack of familiarity with equitable remedies will push judges toward a *non-compromise* solution.[22] Cases in which the only feasible solution is compromise or long-term compliance with the ruling tend to lead to threats of criminal prosecution against civil servants or the death of people, as in the case of land reform movements.

The Brazilian courts lack familiarity with the drafting of mutually agreed injunctive relief. They issue injunctive orders but impose them on an 'all-or-nothing' basis. Administrative officers, on the other hand, are bound by a general prohibition on negotiating decisions. The doctrine of 'public service strict morality', supported by the courts in administrative law, states that 'public cases' cannot be the subject of trade-offs. So the very administrative law created by the courts tends to be paradoxical at some points. By reinforcing the idea that public officials cannot negotiate anything, they tend to assume a final decision on allocational and distributional processes.

Thirdly, distributive conflicts require decisions about what to do in the future. These are not simple decisions on what is right or wrong, but rather decisions on what is better or worse in the long run. It is not a choice between two opposing qualifications of past actions, but a choice between an open number of courses of action possible to attain fair and efficient results.[23] Compliance with decisions will be measured, but only on the basis of a general approximation. For instance, a judge may order a public officer to provide a given number of school places within a predicted period. Compliance with such an order may be absolute, but it may also be less than absolute, provided that good reasons are given.

Distributive disputes, therefore, often require mediation and negotiation, while typical retributive disputes require straightforward adjudication. Mediators do not decide the case but lead the parties to negotiate a solution. Mediators may be needed before the parties enter into any sort of business; they can be compared to brokers, that is, people who carry back and forth the offers made by the parties in order to accomplish some mutually advantageous business. Mediation is a *rule-building* procedure. If a mediation procedure is successful, the parties will accept the rules and behave accordingly. Adjudication (or arbitration) is a *rule-applying* procedure. If the parties already know what is owed to them (what their *right* is), they will claim the enforcement of that right in the adjudication. If they are not strong enough to enforce their right, they may have (or be forced) to accept less than what they are due, but this is not a case of mediation (*transaction*).

Fourthly, one must acknowledge that there are conflicting principles in the constitution and be aware that they apply to different spheres. In Walzer's opinion, the use of one principle (one 'social good') as the final and exclusive rule for all cases leads to the dominance of one 'social good' over all others.[24] On the other hand, principles are not as clear as one would expect. Principles (as general rules) have to be 'redefined' in every case: in every case one has to consider (that is, one has to 'judge', in the Kantian sense of judging) whether recourse to that principle is appropriate.[25] The easiest way to decide cases is to interpret the constitution from a point of view where one single principle is paramount. In many jurisdictions in Brazil, the predominant principle has been private property and freedom of contract.

Fifthly, social rights (at least the traditional rights to healthcare and education) concern the provision of collective goods.[26] If we understand recognition to be a collective good – self-image and mutual respect as social products of human interaction[27] – anti-discrimination law is one type of distributive field. Anti-discrimination law has been thought of as a means of empowering citizens with greater social mobility and equalising opportunities, if not resources. Welfare rights in the US (economic and social rights) were advanced by legislation during the New Deal, and by the end of the 1930s the Supreme Court had abandoned most of its earlier laissez-faire opposition to these reforms. Anti-discrimination litigation, therefore, was a secondary step in some respects.

Even if Brazilian society may be seen as highly discriminatory against certain groups, economic and social rights had a different point of departure. What were the collective goods to be provided in Brazil? It was not only welfare but *development* as well. For a considerable period of time, development in Brazil meant industrialisation. So public policies in Brazil took the form of regulation and legislation sponsoring industrialisation, the concentration of capital resources and minimum social welfare.[28] Public policies translated into mandatory insurance and savings (welfare, healthcare, housing programmes and credit), regulation of economic activities by police power (regulated industries, such as the banking, transportation, insurance, nuclear, chemical and pharmaceutical industries), and statutory limitation of contractual freedom (for instance, urban lease agreements).

Sixthly, collective goods may have to be created or improved through budgetary devices and regulation. The provider of the public good must have both material and authoritative resources to enforce compliance and avoid the free-rider effect. Brazilian courts have been reluctant in recent years to confer either of these on the other branches of government. Increasing restrictions on the exercise of the police power and tax collection now play an important role in the legal discourse of the courts, together with a laissez-faire economic philosophy, which seems to have exerted a stranglehold on the courts from the early years of the Republic.[29] Re-distributive policies have thus been subjected to strict scrutiny by the courts in challenges brought by corporations over alleged violations of property rights and in cases concerning progressive taxation policies. This development may have the effect of freeing the *haves* from subsidising the *have-nots*, thereby complicating the implementation of re-distributive policies, when and if endorsed by the political branches.

It is therefore not surprising that Brazilian legal scholars and courts never discuss the nature of distributive conflicts. Legal history shows that these conflicts were considered and given a fair amount of attention before modern contract and property doctrines became dominant in private law. The turning point in legal thinking may be found in the work of Hugo Grotius, although he still makes a clear distinction between commutative and participatory contracts. Pufendorf also refers to distributive justice. Both authors, writing in the seventeenth century, emphasise the promissory nature of contracts. The liberal judiciary is structurally designed to deal with commutative conflicts. Only recently, with the welfare state, have distributive conflicts once again become the subject of legal reasoning.[30]

The Limits of Social Rights Litigation

The critique of judicial involvement in matters of distributive justice takes different forms. Some refer to the institutional deficiency of courts in dealing with complex cases. This is a predominantly US 'New Deal' point of view. In Brazil, this point was made, in general, by Oliveira Vianna in the 1930s,[31] but is insisted upon by very few legal scholars today. Rather, the trend has been, ever since the Vargas period, to create *specialised jurisdictions*. The most important example is that of labour courts, which eventually became an independent judicial structure. The most recent example may be that of trying to create specialised courts for land reform cases. However important, this solution misses the point. Of course, specialised courts may have greater knowledge of certain cases and a lighter caseload, but their effectiveness depends upon the cases being tried as bilateral conflicts, which most often does not happen.

Some will advocate judicial reforms, calling for greater autonomy for the judicial branch, usually from a standard nineteenth-century liberalist point of view. The Brazilian system, however, already gives the judicial branch considerable autonomy. The judiciary manages its own budget (once it has been approved by the legislative branch); it selects its own members through independent public competitions (*concursos*); and it settles its internal administrative rules and business. In addition, there is no doctrine of precedent, so lower courts and single trial judges are free to decide cases without regard for higher court rulings. The traditional evaluation tends to stress the courts' lack of financial and human resources (which is true), so that little or no attention is given to the nature of cases.

A different group in favour of judicial reform comprises those who stress the judiciary's inability to deal with 'collective' conflicts. For this group, it is mainly a matter of culture change that is required, including the development of a greater sensitivity on the part of judges and courts to the social struggles that are brought before them in the form of litigation. This second approach includes people of very different political and theoretical positions. They do not deal with the rationality of distributive justice or of collective action. They all acknowledge that the new litigation has a social character, but they do not seem to give full recognition to the structure of 'multilateral' litigation.

Another approach may be that represented by US thinkers such as Rosenberg, Sunstein, Chayes, Fiss and Fuller.[32] Although they differ amongst themselves, it is clear that the focus of their analyses is the structure of the conflicts that reach the judicial branch. Distributive conflicts do not only require the adjudication of vested interests, but an effort to change social structures (the distribution of power, wealth, and recognition) inside one group (which may be as large as a 'national' society). Rosenberg stresses that courts do not have the resources to do this, for a number of reasons: first, judges tend to accept mainstream public opinion; secondly, distributive conflicts advance social reforms, and not simply adjudication; thirdly, courts lack the institutional means (an administrative apparatus) to implement and monitor decisions that imply some continuous programme or public policy; fourthly, the absence of any power to initiate cases (*ne procedat iudex sine auctorem – jurisdictional inertia*) puts the judiciary in a merely passive position, unable to control its own reform agenda; and fifthly, courts cannot appropriate resources, levy taxes or finance their own decisions affecting the direction of public policy or social reforms. In the case of civil-law countries, one may add that courts also lack general 'equitable jurisdiction', which has been used widely by US courts in racial conflicts in recent decades.[33] This sort of critique has not had any real significance in Brazil as yet, mostly because, as we shall see, welfare rights cases have been decided under consumer protection law. In this respect, they have not actually been involved in any large reform action: the traditional principles of litigation have generally served them well enough.

However, public interest litigation has been a major arena for civil procedure lawyers. Great legislative effort has been dedicated to legal reform, finally resulting in the creation of the Brazilian class action (*ação civil pública*) in 1985, the injunction (*mandado de injunção*) in 1988, as well as some 'equitable' powers (in 1994–95) by extending judges' power to issue preliminary injunctions (article 273, article 461 CPC) and other injunctive relief (article 1102a, CPC). The full consequences of these innovations remain to be seen. The following section merely presents a preliminary assessment of the procedural reforms. It is already clear, however, that these changes have not altered the general design of the judicial branch. Their impact on matters of collective action is also briefly assessed. So far, it is clear that courts have tended to issue orders that require immediate compliance and have not created any place for long-term reform devices.

Analysis of Court Decisions

Healthcare: 1989–1996

State Court Between 1989 and 1995 we found only one decision (within the limits of the publications mentioned before) directly concerning the right to healthcare decided by the TJSP. It was disposed of as a matter of *consumers' rights*, not as an issue of constitutional social rights. Some other cases discussed environmental issues, such as garbage disposal by cities and industrial plants. We also found cases dealing with private health insurance and healthcare outside the review areas we had chosen.

Federal Court Six other cases (35.29 per cent) in the STJ deal with environmental protection (indirectly with health, but the protection of the environment is in itself a sufficient cause of action in Brazil). The question regarding the standing of the public prosecutor was not raised in any of the cases, since it is specifically provided for in a federal statute, but in four cases (66 per cent) the decision was concerned with the standing of the defendant.

Healthcare: 1997–2003

State Court Things have changed in the last few years. In the case of the State of São Paulo (TJSP), we found 14 cases dealing with health rights, of which only four dealt with private healthcare or insurance. This means that 70 per cent of the cases involved challenges to the public healthcare system, claiming universal rights rather than consumer's rights. Among these 14 cases, it is remarkable that public prosecutors used the class action to claim treatment or the provision of medicine for individual patients. The claim directed against the public sector is for the individual provision of healthcare. Decisions varied as some of them took into consideration the fact that the sort of treatment the public prosecutor was claiming could not be extended to all patients in equal conditions except by infringing the budgetary allocations decided by the legislative body. In some cases, however, the claims were successful.

Federal Court The STJ decided one case on a question of standing, but the case dealt with the public healthcare system. The court decided that the public prosecutor had standing to challenge dealings between the Public Health System (SUS – *Sistema Único de Saúde*) and the private sector. Even if the case was not decided on its merits (the issue was one of standing) and did not deal with specific treatment of patients, it showed that the court was called upon to decide a case concerning the provision of collective healthcare.

Education: 1989–1996

State Court Of the five cases decided by the state court of São Paulo (TJSP) between 1989 and 1996 regarding education, only three (60 per cent) made any reference to the Constitution. Of these three, two make reference to article 129, that is, the provision concerning the powers of the public prosecutor's office (or *Ministério Público*). The third case (RJTJSP 147/210) mentions article 5, XXXII, that is, consumer protection as a duty of the state. There is a meaningful absence of reference to article 6 of the Constitution (which lists social rights, including education) in all cases throughout all important phases of the suit: it has not been invoked by the plaintiff, by the defendant, or by the court. In short, in all cases, the issue was disposed of without any reference to constitutional social rights. It is noteworthy, too, that articles 205 and 214 are not mentioned. These are the constitutional provisions concerning education and educational policies. In short, class actions regarding education were decided without any interpretation of the social rights defined in the Constitution. None of the cases includes an argument in which the National Education Guidelines Act (*Lei de Diretrizes e Bases da Educação Nacional*, lei n. 4.024/61, lei n. 5.692/71, lei n. 9.131/95) is mentioned.

Of all five cases, only one was disposed of on the merits (20 per cent). Four were decided on (procedural) grounds, that is, in the majority of cases on questions of standing (80 per cent). In three of the cases (60 per cent) the Court acknowledged the standing of the public prosecutor.

Finally, all five cases have one common trait: they all deal with the payment of monthly or yearly school fees (in private schools). In this respect, they all concern the contractual relationship between the school and the students (their parents). In all cases the legal question was discussed in terms of consumer rights, with fee increases being discussed as an abusive unilateral rise in the price of a service.

Federal Court The only education rights case decided by the STJ between 1989 and 1996 was filed by a district attorney in Minas Gerais. The purpose of the suit was to prevent a private school from raising its fees in line with a wage increase given to its employees (teachers) (*Revista do STJ* 54/306). The claim rested on the *Consumer's Defense Code* (Lei n. 8.078/90) and on special legislation regarding school fees. The case was disposed of by the STJ on the basis that the district attorney lacked standing to sue as representative of the students or their parents. According to the court, public prosecutors have standing, both constitutionally and legally, to sue in cases of *diffuse* or *collective* interests (or rights). The Court found that the interests of a defined group of students (such as the students of a single private school) did not qualify as 'diffuse or collective'. It was rather a case of 'homogeneous individual interests', for which the public prosecutor had no standing to sue. The only constitutional reference made in the decision is to article 129, II of the Constitution, which gives the public prosecutor the power to 'watch over the effective protection of the rights granted in the Constitution, on the part of public power and the relevant public services, taking the necessary action for their guarantee'. There is a debate currently going on in Brazil as to the interpretation of the 'public relevance service' phrase in this and in other parts of the Constitution.[34]

Education: 1997–2003

State Court The TJSP published 16 decisions on class actions dealing with educational rights between 1997 and 2003. Four of these cases (25 per cent) had to do with private schools – price increases – and three of them were filed by the public prosecutor. In the three cases filed by the public prosecutor, the court had to decide the question of standing. In two of these cases, the court decided that the public prosecutor had no standing to sue private schools on matters of prices. All other cases (75 per cent) were filed by the public prosecutor and directly challenged the public school system, either questioning the number of places available for students of a certain neighbourhood, or questioning the whole state system (in terms of the reapportionment of school places). The court in general accepted_that the criteria applied by the State Education Secretary were reasonable, and within the administration's discretion.[35]

Federal Court The STJ did not publish any decision on class actions dealing with education rights in this period. This can be explained by the fact that after the 1994 monetary stabilisation plan (*Plano Real*) the cost of private schools was automatically curbed in line with inflation. This means that the most controversial issue between school owners and parents was satisfactorily settled with the considerable reduction of inflation rates. On the other hand, elementary and middle-level schooling are state, not federal matters and they will tend to be decided at the state level. Legislation dealing with price controls, however, including school prices, is federal, which is why the STJ had to decide cases during the hyper-inflationary period in the 1990s.

General Remarks on the Cases

The public interest cases canvassed above have at least four relevant features.

Constitutional Foundations of Social Rights In the last 30 cases decided by the São Paulo court, 17 (56 per cent) were decided on a *statutory* basis, and thirteen (44 per cent) were decided on a *constitutional* basis. Some constitutional discussion referred to the public prosecutor's standing, so only a minority of the decisions referred to the *constitutional merits*. One could argue that asserting one's claim directly on constitutional grounds could complicate bringing the cases in court, as it could be considered a strictly legal matter, reducing disclosure procedures (a constitutional matter would easily slip into 'exclusively *de iure* questions').

Another explanation for the scarcity of constitutional arguments in cases is that lawyers assume that constitutional social rights are sufficiently well known. It 'goes without saying' that education (and healthcare) are constitutionally protected interests or rights. This means it should be taken for granted that social rights are *accepted* as a matter of course. That assumption, however, leaves open one important technicality. Unless the claim raises a constitutional issue, the Supreme Court will refuse jurisdiction to rule on it at the 'extraordinary appeal' level.

A more plausible explanation is reached if we consider that school fees have been subject to specific statutory provisions in the last ten years, usually within the monetary stabilisation plans. In such cases, litigation would be initiated under specific statutes and reference to the Constitution would be unnecessary. At this level, it would be easier to use the class action as a consumer protection device. In that sense, the litigation we have found clearly shows *part* of the middle class (we have not investigated the social profile of the schools and parents involved) trying to assert their consumer rights instead of calling for the protection of welfare policies. This could mean that for these litigants social rights *qua* welfare programmes are *irrelevant* (either because there is a specific statute or because they do not recognise themselves as recipients of welfare benefits who may interfere in public policies).

It is noteworthy that in the last few years, as cases have been filed against the government, the discussion is increasingly being framed in constitutional terms.

The initial claims thus ordinarily refer to the constitutional provisions on education and healthcare as rights owed to 'all' by the state.

Consumer Protection The research showed that in the first decade of 'class action' litigation, the public prosecutor essentially served the interests of people or groups of people who had already left the public healthcare and education system. The cases were framed in terms of the protection of consumers of private services and have a middle-class profile (even if working middle class, that is, white-collar workers).

The main purpose of these cases was the defence of vested interests (contractual interests, with parents claiming the application of certain statutory rules and schools trying to justify the principles of free business and private property). Claimants did not, at this stage, ask for any change in public policies, or demand the active participation of the state.[36] The government's role was twofold: first, to enact legislation, and secondly, to provide the services of the public prosecutor.

Of course, calling for substantial reforms in the education system would considerably increase the cost of litigation, especially as it would have to accept medium or long-term results, which would not directly and immediately benefit litigating parents and their children.

The cases also reveal the gap between public and private services. In the absence of high quality public schools, parents have fled to private schools. No incentive was given to seek reforms in the public system. Private business (especially in the field of healthcare services) entered the space left by the public school system. In poorer areas of São Paulo, a 'welfare society'[37] was organised, mainly around neighbourhoods and parochial communities, to serve the needs of the working classes for nurseries and child day-care centres. These included a mixture of government funds, donations, and inexpensive labour provided by volunteer neighbourhood mothers. This, however, was not available at higher levels of the educational system, because it would have required greater investment and professionally skilled labour. This type of issue has not been judicialised.

There is a different and significant trend today. The numbers show that the public prosecutor has increasingly taken on the public health and education system. In the last seven years, 75 per cent of all class actions regarding education and 65 per cent of those regarding healthcare were filed against the administration in the state of São Paulo.

Standing of the Public Prosecutor and Political Representation The public prosecutor's office is not an organ of political representation according to the classic separation of powers doctrine. However, if it gains standing to file class actions whenever 'collective' or 'diffuse interests' are at stake, it may turn into a sort of judicial-political representative. With such standing, classic problems related to political representation may arise in litigation, which is exactly what most of the cases have been dealing with. It has been commonplace in the discourse of public prosecutors to define themselves as representatives of 'civil society'. Civil society, it is generally accepted, is not a group in itself. Aside from the different meanings of 'civil society', if the public prosecutor wishes to act in representation of civil society, they may be accused of defending private interests instead of the common good.

The trend was clear between the mid-1980s and 1990s. Instead of appealing to fundamental rights, public prosecutors have often claimed to be litigating on behalf of some 'collective' interest. This was evident from the number of class actions we were able to find in that first period; the largest number concerning private school fees. By defending the interest of parents who could afford to pay a moderate fee for their children's education, the public prosecutor was clearly acting on behalf of a limited sector of the population. If we further consider that litigation was divided into several actions filed against defendant schools accused of raising their fees in contravention of federal statutory rules, it is easy to understand the reluctance of certain courts to grant standing to the public prosecutor. In these cases, the public prosecutor has been accused of defending private interests and, in one court decision, was found to be taking the place of private lawyers. The court decided that the parents of the children should have hired a private lawyer, instead of using the services of the public prosecutor's office, which is constitutionally and legally prohibited from practising law, except for its defined institutional purpose.

The discussion of public prosecutors poses a political question. Can the public prosecutor 'represent' civil society, as their officials claim? If so, to what extent? Are public prosecutors representatives of a 'unanimous' or 'universal' point of view? Can they act as representatives of 'consumers' in general or of particular groups of consumers? These are important issues, as the question of 'political' representation before the courts has never been put like this before.

If public prosecutors count as defenders of *principles* or *fundamental rights*, it is understandable that they should not be subjected to the electoral process, as indeed they are not in Brazil. Thus, their 'representational' role would mean that they are in charge of sustaining the basic rules of democratic institutions, rather than majority rule. Once they start to litigate, the question of their standing naturally has to be judged from a political point of view. That is why, in the case of the right to education, the decision to file a suit against one particular private school becomes questionable. If what is at stake is the right of children to education, should the suit be developed in broader terms? Should education not be considered as an indivisible social right? Should the suit not be aimed at providing a larger number of children with public education instead? Who sets the directives for the litigation priorities of public prosecutors?

As things currently stand, each public prosecutor is an independent authority. Once a law school graduate has passed the relevant public exam (*concurso público*) she will be appointed to one of the several judicial districts (*comarcas*) in the state and start acting as a public prosecutor. There are no formal policy goals set by the institution as a whole. Considering that public prosecutors move frequently from smaller to larger districts – as they are in a career that encourages advancing towards larger cities – there is little chance that public scrutiny will act as a mechanism of accountability. Their personal priorities are not subject to public debate.

All of this is not viewed negatively, however. Some groups place a lot of confidence in the action of the public prosecutor. There is a tendency to believe that the authority and resources of a public prosecutor, who is professionally qualified and skilled, and is endowed with investigative powers, can help them. It probably saves them a great deal of resources, including attorney fees and efforts to mobilise and organise legally. If groups were left to themselves, they would face the free-rider effect and would have to spend money, both for lawyers' fees and to obtain evidence. The reverse effect is, of course, the de-mobilising and patronising effect on social movements.[38] The 1980s was a decade of social mobilisation in Brazil,[39] and the introduction of class actions in the legal system was partly thought to provide these groups with an effective remedy for some of their problems. The 1990s was a decade of de-mobilisation and institutionalisation. The public prosecutor's role can be seen as both a part and an example, however small, of this process. It is also a sign of the weakness of 'civil society', or the absence of a 'litigating culture'.

What is the Public Good? A final aspect of class action litigation led by the public prosecutor has to do with the definition of the 'public good'. The Brazilian Consumers' Defence Code (CDC) is frequently mentioned in class action cases, as it establishes a classification of interests as follows: (a) *diffuse* interests and rights are *indivisible* interests of *indeterminate subjects* held together by 'de facto' circumstances (a geographical neighbourhood, for instance); (b) *collective* rights and interests are *indivisible* interests of a *definite group* held together by one legal relation (for instance, members of a mutual credit group); (c) *homogeneous individual* rights are those with a common origin (the buyers of the same defective product). The right to clean air typically falls under (a), group health insurance or private pension plans under (b), and rights arising from defective products under (c). For anyone familiar with the development of political economy, political science, political philosophy or even some traditional legal reasoning, it is impossible to understand the very sophisticated classification of the Brazilian CDC unless stress is placed on the 'indivisible' character of the goods in groups (a) and (b). It is surprising then to find that this is never mentioned in any of the cases. There is a total silence in the already long discussion concerning public goods amongst economists and political scientists in relation to the welfare state.[40] None mention the indivisible character of the goods at stake and most frequently there is a tendency to identify *diffuse* and *collective* with *large numbers*. The easiest way to identify a 'diffuse' interest is to see that it may affect either *anyone* at random or *everyone*.

One noticeable example of the conceptual (and moral) confusion regarding the term 'public good' is the case decided by the 4th Federal Court of Appeals (in Porto Alegre). The public prosecutor had filed a class action against several beef importers, as well as the federal government (who had authorised the importation) on the grounds that some of the beef found on their premises had been contaminated by the Chernobyl nuclear accident. The public prosecutor petitioned for a prohibition of the public sale of that import. After the trial-level decision had been taken, the public prosecutor and the defendants filed an agreement: the charge was going to be dropped if the defendants sold the beef outside Brazil. The misunderstanding of the purposes of the class action by the public prosecutor is evident, as well as their understanding that their function is, after all, very much similar to that of a private practitioner.[41]

The Distributive Sting

Court decisions do not mention the greatest problem with the constitutional social rights clause, namely the issue of their universal character, that is, that 'everyone' (*todos*) is entitled to free education and healthcare. If that is the case, it is reasonable to assume that education and healthcare provided by the state should be universal, and that there will be sufficient funds to extend equal treatment to all citizens in the same position. A court decision on healthcare or education policy has to be designed so as to benefit all those in need of it. It has to count and calculate numbers.

Many of the class actions we found in our research totally ignore this problem. One striking characteristic of the recent series of class actions filed against the administration is that many of them benefit a specific person, even if the person may be treated as representative of a 'class', for instance, 'all children who suffer from epilepsy'. This is not what we have found, however. The class actions were filed and the injunction was sought (and sometimes given) to benefit that particular child or patient who had resorted to the public prosecutor's office.

The different panels in the TJSP have taken different decisions on these matters. Some panels have consistently granted the remedy (relief) to benefit single citizens based on the general provisions of the Constitution. The reasoning has been more or less as follows: if everyone is entitled to human dignity and if human dignity comprises getting a place in a public school, or special education, or a particular treatment with specific drugs, it is not for the courts to ponder costs. Their job is to grant that relief immediately.[42] In other cases, other panels have been less generous. In a case framed as a true class action, in which the public prosecutor claimed that the state government should hold a certain stock of medicine for hyper-thermic syndrome, the court dismissed the case by considering the statistical frequency of the disease and arguing that the chemical validity of the required stock would expire due to the rarity of the disease.[43] In another class action the public prosecutor requested that the state government immediately hire a certain number of healthcare professionals to make up for the number of retired or fired personnel. The court decided that this was an administrative decision that could only be made by elected officials.

When sued, the state government usually argues that court decisions will unduly interfere with the autonomy or discretionary power of the administration. The argument is generally rejected on the premise that the constitutional provision that entitles everyone to healthcare and education is of a higher 'nature'. In other words, it is a 'principle' and overrides all other 'rules' or 'political decisions'. What has not been argued in most cases is the universal provision of the healthcare or education service. No case has put the argument that if 'everyone' is entitled to that service, it should be designed to be provided for all who need it 'at the same time'. Let us suppose a certain treatment is extremely costly and has not been included in the general healthcare system because it would not be possible to extend it equally to everyone who needed it. Is there a good argument against a particular court providing it to a particular patient at the expense of the state budget?

Only one dissenting opinion mentioned this problem, even if indirectly.[44] Judge Hermes Pinotti argued precisely that if the court granted a specific treatment to the patient in the case before it, the court should prepare itself for a rush of similar cases, assuming the discretionary powers of decision traditionally given to the executive branch. The main point of his dissenting opinion was that the Constitution provides general and universal social rights to 'everyone', but does not provide criteria of precedence or priority. These have to be decided by the democratically elected political officers. He called the reasoning of his peers simplistic, on the basis that it is not possible to jump from the general and abstract terms of the Constitution to the right of a particular individual without going through a process of defining priorities and hierarchies in the education and healthcare systems. Only general policies included in budgets actually provide the general principles and are capable of granting rights simultaneously to all.

In fact, the 'universal' character of such rights needs to be considered from the perspective of the simultaneous provision of public services. Otherwise, courts would be creating a free-rider problem, or a 'rush' of cases, as argued by Judge Pinotti.

Class actions involving education emphasise the consumer protection aspect of their claim. It could be the result of a naïve belief in the possibilities of the judicial system to correct abuses. In this regard, it reflects the very structural and institutional limitations on the judicial branch itself. It cannot replace a policy-making organ, but it can correct specific 'wrongs'. To put it in classical terms, it cannot bring about distributive justice, but it can bring about corrective justice. If the claim in the class action involved a complete redesign of the education system, it would certainly fail. The only available remedy is to attempt a modest, piecemeal sort of correction – to correct one wrong at a time. What is disturbing about this option, but is common among all practising lawyers, public prosecutors and courts, is that it robs the case of its wider political implications and keeps legal reasoning away from matters of distributive justice.

Consumer protection is mentioned in several provisions of the Constitution. The two most important are article 5, XXXII ('the State shall provide for consumer protection, according to the law') and article 170, V ('the economic order, founded on the value of human labor and freedom of business, is aimed at assuring a decent life to everyone, in accordance with the rules of social justice and taking into account the following principles: (...) V- consumer protection'). From these provisions one might suspect that consumer protection is a political principle, after all. That part of the 'corrective' activity of courts is to allow for 'distributive principles' to be fairly weighed. It is not uncommon to find *obiter dicta* in the decisions considering these principles and these distributive purposes. But the overall remedies are mostly traditional. That is, the remedies sought and eventually granted are normally of a contractual nature. Of course, our investigation has been restricted to cases decided by courts. If a case does not reach the trial stage, that is, if procedures begin but the courtroom becomes a forum for mediation instead of adjudication, the agreement reached by the parties will not appear as a court decision. This is only natural as the result of a successful mediation is an agreement, in other words, a decision reached by the parties themselves rather than by the mediator. In any event, this will only confirm our suspicion (hypothesis) that courts have not been the institutional locus for distributive decisions. The question is here left open as to the non-confrontational character of Brazilian political culture.

Thus, the legal profession (courts, lawyers, and public prosecutors) tends to de-politicise the problem. From a political perspective of public policy, education becomes a private matter between private schools and parents who cannot afford their fees. Even consumer protection legislation is removed from its contextual setting in the Constitution. Framed as a suit in which a large number of parents confront one single school, the class action becomes a ground for 'collective' interest litigation, and very little attention is given to 'diffuse' interests. No discussion of the 'public good' is necessary, because it is limited to the good for a limited number of people, who have come together through factual (attendance at the same school) and legal (all have signed the same standard agreement with the same supplier of educational services) circumstances.

Social rights break with the uniform rules of corrective justice. By referring to social goods that must be enjoyed by large numbers at the same time, the rules of distributive justice and social rights do not have the exclusive zero-sum nature of individual rights, be they property or contractual rights. Distributive rights, as social rights, need a proportional rule, by which simultaneous access can be granted. In this respect, proportion means that those rights are to be distributed according to different rules.[45] Education, for instance, should be distributed according to a mix of need and talent (merit). Those who need the most and those who have more talent should be simultaneously considered. Social rights also depend on the visibility of differences. There are the needy, and they have a right just because they need it. Of course, social rights when left to the powers of the market, as has been the case in Brazil in recent years, will not be provided unless there are incentives to do so, since the most important incentive in a market system (price/profit) cannot be afforded by those who need the most. Social rights, therefore, imply differences, not equality. That is, they are rights of those who do not succeed in the competitive market by themselves, either for personal reasons (such as handicapped people), for social reasons (for instance, workers and immigrants), or for historical and social reasons (for instance, blacks, women, gays and Indians).

Concluding Remarks

The rise of social rights litigation puts stress on the judicial branch. Because of its public policy consequences, social rights litigation shows the irrationality of the whole appellate system. Entire social groups are divided between those who have the time to obtain a benefit while some court order is still valid, and those who do not obtain it. The absence of binding precedents and the federalised judicial structure create the image of the legal system as a lottery, as different courts in different places consider themselves to have jurisdiction and issue contradictory decisions. Using a class action to advance consumer rights is a far from ambiguous strategy. It may have a concentrating effect and leave a large number of non-consumers out of the court order. If not reined in by the judicial system it may be used to encourage the free-rider phenomenon in society, especially when, under the class action label, people claim private interests. The issue of a 'common good' may be absent in judicial decisions.

In considering the analytical challenge put by Gloppen's chapter in this volume one could say that the Brazilian legal system has been able to give the poor some *voice* in the courts. If it is the case that in the early 1990s class actions and the public prosecutor's office were captured by middle-class interests, by the late 1990s and early 2000s this trend has been partially reversed in the State of São Paulo. Class actions are trying to force changes in the public sector as the provider of health and education for the poor. Courts may be considered as an important channel to voice the needs and claims of the poorer parts of the population in certain areas of the country, at least.

The responsiveness and capability of courts should be analysed together. Courts have accepted many of the cases and have recognised that they have jurisdiction. This is especially true when a case has to do with health. A dying person usually gets a favourable decision, and courts usually say that human life is a priceless thing. But responsiveness is far more problematic in cases where the universal provision of a benefit is at stake. As I have tried to show, the lack of familiarity with equitable remedies and with negotiated solutions is an important obstacle to social rights adjudication. It is a legal and doctrinal – therefore cultural – difficulty, as law professionals do not always realise the difference between retributive and distributive disputes, and more often do not discuss the universality issue in their cases. In Gloppen's analytical framework, what counts as judges' capability would have to be extended to lawyers in general and has an immediate impact on the courts' responsiveness.

Finally, the survey I have conducted indicates (but does not demonstrate or prove) that compliance does happen in several cases. Final court decisions are usually implemented, but there are many different experiences. We need to construct typical cases to draw sharper differences. For instance, the difference between the reopening of the registration terms for children to enroll in class in the public school system, the provision of special educational facilities for handicapped children and the inclusion of handicapped children in the regular school system. The second case is naturally more complex.

A general impression that this survey gives is that Brazilian courts are receptive to social rights claims. And much in line with what has happened elsewhere, even when the case itself is not fully successful in court, the administration tends to be sensitive to the claim in the longer run and change its policies in later years. The cases brought to court have (although this was not the object of this research) had some impact on public opinion. Cases that voice some collective interest and that get some support in the arena of 'public opinion', even when the courts do not finally settle the issue, have had some impact on public policies in general.

Notes

1 I wish to thank Cesar Augusto Pisani, undergraduate student at the University of São Paulo Law School, for his help in researching the cases for the period after 1997.

2 Mauricio García Villegas, 'Derechos Sociales y Necesidades Políticas. La Eficacia Judicial de los Derechos Sociales en el Constitucionalismo Colombiano', in Boaventura de Sousa Santos and Mauricio García (eds), *El Caleidoscopio de las Justicias en Colombia* (2 vols, Bogotá: Uniandes, 2001), vol. 1, pp. 455–83.

3 T.H. Marshall, 'Citizenship and Social Class', in T.H. Marshall, *Sociology at the Crossroads and Other Essays* (London: Heineman, 1963).

4 Marcelo Neves, *A Constitucionalização Simbólica* (São Paulo: Acadêmcia, 1994), pp. 49–51.

5 Martin Shapiro, *Who Guards the Guardians?* (Athens, Ga.: University of Georgia Press, 1988), pp. 36–7.

6 Accessible at <www.stf.gov.br>.

7 Accessible at <www.stj.gov.br/webstj/processo/estatistica>. For the US Supreme Court numbers for 1994, and some comparative tables for the period 1990–94, see the *Harvard Law Review*, 109 (1996): 340–53. In 1994, the Court disposed of 200 cases on their merits with full opinions. Justice Rehnquist, Chief Justice, wrote the largest number of opinions (11), followed by Justice O'Connor (10) and Kennedy (10). The total number of cases disposed of by the Court in 1995 was 7,132. The Court assumed original jurisdiction in only two cases. 6,971 cases were disposed of by denial, dismissal or withdrawal of appeals or petitions for review. With such numbers, it is fairly easy to keep track of each justice's voting record and alignment, which allows a higher degree (as compared to Brazilian standards) of public scrutiny of their opinions and political inclination.

8 Court decisions, rulings or opinions in Brazilian reviews are published fully, including dissenting opinions. There is usually a very long time between the announcement of a

decision and its availability in full format. Decisions are taken in open court (there are no conferences). Appellate Courts sit in 'divisions' of three or more judges each. For each case lots are drawn to give one of the judges the role of 'reporter': this judge writes the summary report of the case, the facts, and the arguments of the parties and the judge, and then gives an opinion. The other judges in the panel may follow this opinion or dissent. They may also ask to view (*pedir vista*) the case to give it a fuller reading. If all opinions are given and the case is decided, the file is then handed to a clerical section of the court to record it and type the opinions (which in fact have already been handed in by the judges in typed form). The Official Gazette will publish the result of the ruling (affirmed, reversed, and so on) in a few days following the session. The 'typing' of the decision, however, may take several weeks or months to be completed. Only then does the Official Gazette publish the 'summary' of the ruling and only then are the parties summoned to file any further appeal or petition. The Court Review will publish the ruling several months later, sometimes a year or two later.

9 *Jurisprudência* is the general name given to court decisions in Brazil, as in some other civil-law countries. It approximates the term *precedent* in the English-speaking world, and connotes not just one single decision, but a group of cases decided in a similar vein. One must recall, however, that precedents are not binding in the civil-law tradition, but of course the role of precedents is increasing in Brazil as it is in all other civil-law countries.

10 All decisions are published in the Official Gazette (*Diário Official*) in an abridged form in order to be legally binding and to give notice to the parties (in fact, to their counsel and attorneys). Of course, this is merely legal publication, in the sense that the general public, including lawyers, do not actually read the Gazette.

11 Civil Procedure Code, article 541, *Regimento Interno do* STJ, article 255.

12 Civil class actions were introduced in Brazilian law in 1985 (Lei n. 7.347). Before that, from 1946, the Brazilian legal system included an *ação popular* (a sort of *qui tam action*), which was used to defend public property, and a few other examples of collective claims, such as those dealing with labour relations and liability suits against bankers in bankruptcy cases. Injunctions, *mandado de injunção*, first appeared in the 1988 Constitution. One can consider both *class actions* and *injunctions* as rather new and innovative remedies. It is clear that Brazil is going through a period of building precedents and doctrines around these two instruments. See Ada Pellegrini Grinover et al., *Código de Brasileiro de Defesa do Consumidor Comentado Pelos Autores do Anteprojeto* (Rio de Janeiro: Forense, 1992) and Rodofo de Camargo Mancuso, *Interesses Difusos: Conceito e Legitimação para Agir* (São Paulo: Revista dos Tribunais, 1991).

13 I have conducted another investigation on individual litigation dealing with private health insurance in the State of São Paulo, the results of which were published in José Reinaldo de Lima Lopes, 'Planos de Saúde e Consumidors – Relatório de Pesquisa do Brasilcon', *Revista de Direito do Consumidor* 28 (1998): 137–56 and José Reinaldo de Lima Lopes et al., *Saúde e Responsabilidade: Seguros e Planos de Assistência Privada à Saúde* (São Paulo: Revista dos Tribunais, 1999).

14 See the chapters by Joaquim de A. Falcão, José Eduardo Faria and José Reinaldo de Lima Lopes in José Eduardo Faria (ed.), *Direito e Justiça: A Função Social do Judiciário* (São Paulo: Ática, 1989).

15 Thomas Skidmore, *Brasil: de Catelo a Tancredo* (Rio de Janeiro: Paz e Terra, 1988), p.167; Gilmar Ferreira Mendes, *Jurisdição Constitucional* (São Paulo: Saraiva, 1996), p. 37.

16 In Roman Law, the *pacta* were compromises arrived at in the course of litigation concerning the division of common property (*communi dividundo*) among heirs or other similar situations. *Pacta* were not synonymous with *contractus* or *negottii* in general.

17 Pre-liberal contract doctrine was familiar with a division between *contractus separatorius* and *contractus communicatorius*: the first were one-shot affairs in which the parties had 'opposite' desires (that is, they were willing to exchange things as they wanted to have what the other party had and were willing to give up – exchange – what they had); the latter created co-operation, as the several parties all wanted the same thing and were willing to share what they had in view of a future gain – typically association, partnership, marriage.

18 Cass Sunstein, *The Partial Constitution* (Cambridge, MA: Harvard University Press, 1993), pp. 139–43.

19 J.J. Gomes Canotilho, *Direito Constitucional* (Coimbra: Almedina, 1991); José Afonso da Silva, *Curso de Direito Consitucional Positivo,* 9th edn (São Paulo: Malheiros, 1992); Robert Alexy, *Teoria de los Derechos Fundamentales* (Madrid: Centro de Estudios Constitucionales, 1993).

20 Robert Wood (ed.), *Remedial Law: When Courts Become Administrators* (Amherst: University of Massachusetts Press, 1990); Sunstein, *The Partial Constitution*; Owen M. Fiss, 'Foreword: The Forms of Justice', *Harvard Law Review*, 93 (1979): 1–58.

21 One such case is the collection of debt against a corporate debtor; other provisions are in the bankruptcy statute and in anti-trust legislation. They have had no significant impact in legal practice and are completely ignored by the majority of lawyers and judges.

22 This chapter is primarily concerned with the institutional problems involved in law and distributive justice. It seems clear, however, that social background, the selection of judges, political commitments, professional socialization, class structure and its influence on the profile of the legal profession all play decisive roles in this process, too. They all influence the judges' thinking, their self-image, the symbolism of the judicial function, and public debate on the matter.

23 It is tempting to recall here Kant's classification of rules: *moral rules* (applying to decisions/judgments of what is right or wrong, what is one's duty); *prudential rules* (applying to what is better or worse in one's own life to reach happiness); *technical rules* (guiding decisions on the means-ends relation). One might say that traditional law (or liberal, private-law reasoning) has been built on the moral-rules model, whereas the welfare state requires prudential rules (one can substitute *welfare* for *happiness* in this phraseology). From a contemporary point of view, within political science, reference may be made to the work of Giovanni Sartori, *A Teoria da Democracia Revisitada,* trans. Dinah de A. Azevedo (São Paulo: Ática, 1994), vol. 1, pp. 286–336 concerning decision-making processes.

24 Michael Walzer, *Spheres of Justice* (New York: Basic Books, 1983).

25 Richard Hare explains the processes of 'specification' of principles through singular decisions. It is only when we distinguish cases in which the principle obtains from cases where it does not that we fully understand it. In, short, it is only when we say that 'it is the case' that we make sense of a principle (Richard Hare, *A Linguagem da Moral* [orig. *The language of morals*] (São Paulo: Martins Fontes, 1996), p. 68).

26 Collective goods may include security, for instance, the provision of which is the most traditional task of nation-states. The fact that social rights provide collective goods is not in itself an obstacle to their justiciability, it is mostly a challenge to traditional legal thinking. But even this challenge is not an absolute thing, if we consider several distributive disputes legally defined in our own system, as is the case of bankruptcy and corporations. For a general theoretical approach and critique of the matter see Víctor Abramovich and Christian Courtis, *Los Derechos Socials como Derechos Exigibles* (Madrid: Trotta, 2002).

27 Charles Taylor, 'The Politics of Recognition', in Amy Gutman (ed.), *Multiculturalism* (Princeton, NJ: Princeton University Press, 1994).

28 José Luis Fiori, *Em Busca do Dissenso Perdido* (Rio de Janeiro: Insight Editorial, 1995).

29 Leda Boechat Rodrigues, *História do Supremo Tribunal Federal*, 2nd edn (Rio de Janeiro: Civilização Brasileira, 1991), vol. 3.

30 I have dealt with this history elsewhere. See José Reinaldo de Lima Lopes, *As Palavras e a Lei: Lei, Ordem e Justiça no Pensamento Jurídico Moderno* (São Paulo: Editora 34, 2004), passim.

31 Francisco José de Oliveira Vianna, *Problemas de Direito Corporativo* (Rio de Janeiro: José Olmpyo, 1938).

32 Gerald Rosenberg, *The Hollow Hope: Can Courts Bring about Social Change?* (Chicago: University of Chicago Press, 1991), Sunstein, *The Partial Constitution*; Abram Chayes, 'The Role of the Judge in Public Law Litigation', *Harvard Law Review*, 89 (1976): 1281–316; Fiss, 'Foreword: The Forms of Justice'; Lon L. Fuller, 'The Forms and Limits of Adjudication', *Harvard Law Review,* 92 (1978): 353–409.

33 We should note that procedural changes have recently been introduced in Brazil extending authority to courts to create specific remedies. This has been done in the name of the principle of greater activity of the state in the process, strongly opposing the adversarial model of litigation, which, after all, had not been so strong among us.

34 This decision of the STJ was later overruled (in February 1997) by the STF, granting standing to public prosecutors in such cases.

35 The issue was whether the students had a right to a certain school and to a certain school within a certain distance from their home. The state claimed that there were too many schools where the number of students attending them was not enough to justify their maintenance, and that they should be closed and their students sent to neighbouring schools.

36 Only 20 per cent of all children between 7 and 14 years of age study in private schools in the state of São Paulo. Eighty per cent of all children are enrolled either in city or state public (free) schools, according to data provided by the Fundação Instituto de Administração da Faculdade de Economia e Adminstração da USP (*Folha de São Paulo*, 17 March 1997, III, p. 10)

37 Michael Walzer, 'Socializing the Welfare State', in Amy Gutman (ed.), *Democracy and the Welfare State* (Princeton: Princeton University Press, 1988), p. 25.

38 Some Workers' Unions filed several class actions claiming differences between workers' compensation funds (FGTS). After some time, the *PM* filed its own class action, which, by judicial decision, encompassed all the others. It is curious that the most traditional criterion used for joining actions was time: the oldest claim would prevent the assumption of jurisdiction. Thus, the *PM* would have to join one existing suit; however, the decision was just the opposite. In other words, the *PM* ended up

'swallowing' the unions' initiative (18a. Vara Federal de S. Paulo, Proc. n. 93.0002350-0).

39 Wanderley Guilherme dos Santos, *Razões da Desordem* (Rio de Janeiro: Rocco, 1993); Evelina Dagnino, *Anos 90: Política e Sociedade no Brasil* (São Paulo: Brasiliense, 1994).

40 Kenneth Arrow, *The Limits of Organization* (New York: W.W. Norton & Co, 1974); John E. Roemer, *Theories of Distributive Justice* (Cambridge, MA: Harvard University Press, 1996); Shaun Hargreaves and Yanis Varoufakis, *Game Theory: A Critical Introduction* (London: Routledge, 1995). More traditional legal thinking was very familiar with the idea of public goods and indivisible goods. It is only with the development of modern, and more recently, liberal legal theory that indivisible and collective goods have practically vanished from the legal imagination. Until as late as 1625, Hugo Grotius had to develop legal reasoning based on the idea of a general good different from the sum of individual goods. He was perfectly familiar with that idea, as was Pufendorf, years later. Contemporary legal reasoning gave up any research on collective goods. One remarkable exception has been Tullio Ascarelli, who developed it mainly in his studies of corporations and partnership.

41 Cf José Reinaldo de Lima Lopes, 'A Definição do Interesse Público', in Carlos Alberto de Salles (ed.) *Processo Civil e Interesse Público* (São Paulo: Revista dos Tribunais, 2003).

42 Agr Instr 170.087-05, 11 October 2000; Agr Instr 78.38900, 8 November 2001.

43 Agr Instr 198.143-5, decided on 14 March 2001.

44 Apel Civ 68.359-0, 31 May 2001.

45 Walzer, *Spheres of Justice*, pp. 17–30.

Chapter 10

Courts Under Construction in Angola: What Can They Do for the Poor?

Elin Skaar and José Octávio Serra Van-Dúnem

Introduction

This chapter is about the role that may be envisioned for the courts in Angola with respect to the poor.[1] It analyses the factors that are necessary for getting social rights litigation successfully through the courts – and what kind of impediments exist.

To date, Angolan courts have not passed judgment in any single case that may be classified as a social litigation case, that is, a court case that tries to settle a dispute that has to do with a perceived violation of social or economic rights – as defined by the Angolan Constitution of 1991 and the International Covenant on Economic, Social and Cultural Rights of 1966 (which was ratified by the Angolan Government in 1991).

In spite of rather wide constitutional guarantees of a large number of social, economic and cultural rights, Angola is a highly unequal society where discrimination has been rampant in many spheres of social, political and economic life. Yet, the state has not been challenged to uphold these constitutional guarantees.[2] This chapter tries to identify some of the conditions necessary for such cases to be introduced into court and to be effectively ruled upon by judges. What obstacles would a poor litigant, whose rights had not been respected, be faced with? Would the case be likely to be brought to court – and if it were, would it be favourably received?

These are important questions to answer in a country where the vast majority of the population is poor and where the judiciary is in a phase of reconstruction – and hence in the process of gradually staking out a role for itself in cases that might help reduce the level of inequality. Given that the courts' capacity to deal with social litigation cases is at an infant stage in Angola, our chapter may serve as a baseline study for a later time-series analysis. It is also important to note at the outset that many of the points that we make in this chapter are of a general character, that is, they address access to justice problems more broadly – not only those relating to social and economic rights.

In the next part we map out the theoretical framework that structures the main analysis. To frame the empirical discussion, we proceed to give a brief historical overview of recent political developments and the extent of poverty in Angola. We then briefly analyse the formal legal framework in Angola. In the next part we identify factors that encourage or discourage the poor from raising their disputes regarding social and economic rights in the Angolan justice system, and from receiving a favourable response from the courts. In conclusion, we summarise our main findings.

Understanding Courts in Social Transformation

Some theories of democracy support a role for judges in social rights enforcement and others not.[3] According to Gargarella, the most common conclusion reached is that 'due respect for democracy requires judges *not* to enforce social rights' (emphasis ours).[4] Nevertheless, there is widespread agreement among proponents of social rights that these rights should not be treated differently from other rights, such as civil or political rights. We will not enter the theoretical/normative discussion on what role constitutions should ascribe to judges or what powers judges should arrogate to themselves. Rather, by choosing an empirical focus, we look at what judges actually do – and what factors determine their actions,[5] as well as the behaviour of the other central agent in social litigation: the litigant herself.

The Formal Legal Framework

We start with a brief comment on the formal legal framework. If the court system for several reasons cannot be *expected* to take on cases of social litigation, there is no reason to expect the poor to make the effort to bring such cases forward – even if they were able to do so. Factors that may determine whether courts may be expected to take on the cases in question are: (i) existing legislation; (ii) legal and political culture; (iii) the existence of alternative bodies for dispute resolution; and (iv) the traditional responsibility for solving problems pertaining to the violation of the poor's social and economic rights.

The nature of the legal system and the legal culture in a country are decisive for whether or not courts as institutions (or judges as individuals) have it in their mandate or perceive it as part of their function to pass judgments that may lead to social transformation. Following Gargarella, social transformation is here understood as 'the altering of structured inequalities and power relations in society in ways that reduce the weight of morally irrelevant circumstances, such as socio-economic status/class, gender, race, religion or sexual orientation'.[6] The main point here is the extent to which courts provide a channel for poor and marginalised groups to articulate rights-based claims that address these inequalities in substantive ways. Trying to reduce inequality and discrimination in a society has in most countries been the task of politicians and bureaucrats. For such matters to be relevant for the courts, they must usually operate in strict compliance with a constitutional framework.[7] Moreover, courts are bound by existing legislation.

Third, they must pay attention to the limits of their jurisdiction. And finally, judges must perceive it as their role to take on such cases.

Analysing the Role of Courts in Social Transformation

Siri Gloppen's theoretical framework serves as a useful point of departure for our analysis of poor people's access to justice in Angola.[8] The framework covers the entire process that a case has to go through, from the time it is presented to court until it is implemented. The process may conveniently be divided into four stages: (1) the willingness and ability of marginalised groups to bring social rights/transformation cases to court; (2) the courts' responsiveness to the case brought forward; (3) the capabilities of judges (which is closely linked to the responsiveness of the court); and, finally, (4) judges' authority and the possibility of enforcing the decision in practical terms. Each of these stages depends on a set of societal, cultural, institutional and judicial factors, as well as on the political context in the country.

We choose here to focus on the two first stages, for the following reason: Since there are no empirical examples to draw on in the Angolan case, it is hard to guess how judges are likely to have responded to such cases or to say anything about how these cases are likely to have been enforced. In our analysis we therefore limit ourselves to treating, as systematically as possible, the factors that would enhance – or hinder – the possibility of a social litigation case making its way through the Angolan justice system – from the presentation of the case to court to a potential hearing.

Recent Political Developments in Angola – A Brief Historical Overview

In order to assess whether Angolan courts can be expected to play a positive role in social transformation, one must take into account the recent turbulent history of Angola in general and the short history of the Angolan legal system in particular. Angola is in many ways a country in a state of deep transformation. There has only been peace, in the sense of absence of war, for less than three years. After two failures, the third peace agreement ended an almost 30-year-long civil war and was signed by the government party, the Movimento para a Libertacão de Angola (MPLA), and the opposition forces, União Nacional para a Indepêndencia Total de Angola (UNITA), in February 2002, upon the death of the UNITA leader Jonas Savimbi. This has opened up the possibility for political stability and, in turn, institutional development.[9] How this window of opportunity will be used is still an open question.

The sitting government, headed by Eduardo dos Santos, is facing multiple challenges. Close to 30 years of civil war have clearly taken their toll on people, institutions, and infrastructure. In spite of being one of the richest countries in Africa in terms of natural resources, Angola is considered one of the very poorest in economic terms. Angola is the second largest oil exporter on the continent (after Nigeria) and the third largest exporter of diamonds (after South Africa and Botswana). Enormous sums of money are pumped into state coffers every day.[10] Nevertheless, very few of these resources have benefited the majority of Angolans. Out of a population of roughly 13.2 million, about 2 million were recorded as internally displaced people after the war ended in 2002. Although most of these people have now been resettled, they are facing particular hardships.[11] The rest of the population is not much better off. Although exact figures on poverty are disputed, there is a widespread consensus that the vast majority of people in Angola may be defined as poor. According to the UN Human Development Report 2002, about 60 per cent of the population of Angola lives in 'extreme poverty'.[12] According to the government, 'only' 28 per cent live in 'extreme poverty' (under 0.76 USD per day) whereas 68 per cent live in poverty (under 1.70 USD per day).[13] Angola ranks as number 166 out of 177 countries on the Human Rights Index for 2003 (with Norway as number one and Sierra Leone as number 177).[14] Life expectancy at just over 40 years is the tenth lowest in the world. Infant mortality rates run at 154 per 1,000 live births – also among the most alarming in Africa. More than a quarter of all children born do not live beyond the age of five. There are no available statistics on literacy rates, but with a primary school enrolment rate of 30 per cent, one might expect these to be very low.[15] Due to the high levels of poverty, access to justice for the poor is a concern of significant magnitude. This problem is reinforced by the social and geographic structure of Angola: the elite is centred in the capital Luanda, where the functioning courts are also located, thus making the urban-rural divide very deep.

If Angola is to redistribute its oil wealth, and thus reduce poverty, serious changes must be made to the three branches of government. The country is currently in a phase where it is trying to build and strengthen its democratic institutions. Issues like constitutional reform, electoral reform and law reform have been on the present government's agenda since Savimbi's death, and have paved the way for the 'normalisation' of Angola's developmental concerns.

Although the current government has signalled its commitment to democratic development, there is reason for caution. There are still widespread human rights abuses and violation of basic freedoms, for which the government is responsible – especially in the north of the country.[16] Elections have been promised since Savimbi's death but have been repeatedly postponed. Although signals from parliamentary debates in 2005 suggested that elections might be held in 2006, this seems highly unlikely, if not virtually impossible.[17] Constitutional reform, initially expected to be completed in 2004, is still ongoing.[18] Economic redistribution is another sore point. The state economy is based on oil revenue rather than taxation, which means heavy state control of resources. The legacy of Marxism/one-party statism coupled with a concentration of economic and political power in the hands of a few, gives reasons to doubt the political will to ensure a more equal distribution of power and wealth. According to a recent report, more than four billion dollars in state oil revenue disappeared from Angolan government coffers from 1997–2002, roughly equal to the entire sum the government spent on all social programs in the same period.[19] The Angolan government has on repeated occasions been criticised internationally for non-transparency and lack of accountability. In the Transparency International Corruption Perceptions Index of 2002, Angola was ranked 98th in the world (together with Madagascar and Paraguay), and just before Nigeria and Bangladesh, who were ranked the second most and most corrupt respectively.[20] The Angolan government has also been criticised for attempting to influence judges. More specifically, the governing party, the MPLA, has been reported as having attempted to influence judges, especially in the provinces, in ways that have included financial inducements.[21] Experience from other countries indicates that reforming institutions and establishing democratic accountability is extremely difficult in settings with centralised power. The judiciary, which is often the weakest of the three state branches and therefore in urgent need of reform, is also the branch over which the executive frequently tries to wield control in order to ensure support for political decisions.[22]

In such a context, is it reasonable to expect the courts to be an institutional voice for the poor? As suggested above, Angola may be defined as a baseline case in the sense that no social rights case has yet successfully been presented to, or favourably dealt with by, the courts. We propose that the two most important obstacles in the way of access to justice for the poor (through the formal courts) are: (1) people's lack of formal legal strategies; and (2) the inability of courts to respond to claims – should they be presented. As the analysis below will demonstrate, both of these obstacles are historically conditioned.

Before venturing into an analysis of marginalised groups' chances of bringing cases to court, we give a brief presentation of the formal legal framework in Angola to map out the legal factors necessary (but not sufficient) for judges to rule in matters of social litigation.

Angola's Formal Legal Framework

There are two (general) conditions that must be in place for a case to be heard by a court. First, the citizen must be able to sue (here: the state). Secondly, there must be appropriate laws/legislation on which judges can act.

In principle, the case law of the Angolan Supreme Court appears to allow citizens to sue the state for violations of the law. In the *Laurinda Hoygaard* case, a woman successfully sued the Minister of Education for having wrongfully lost her position as a University rector to another person appointed by the Minister. In this administrative case, the Supreme Court (first in one of the specialised courts, and later in the Supreme Courts plenary) upheld Hoygaard's right to hold the position to which she had been duly elected, and also upheld her right to financial compensation for the harm suffered.[23] Hence, there is at least a potential for courts in Angola to hear cases brought against the state for the failure to guarantee social and economic rights.

As for existing legislation, constitutional guarantees of social and economic rights seem relatively comprehensive, whereas national legislation seems to be much less developed in these matters.

Formally, the 1991 Constitution of Angola (as amended in 1992) provides legal protection for many social and economic rights, such as:

- the right and duty to work; workers' right of fair remuneration, rest, holidays, protection and workplace hygiene and security; workers' right to freely choose their occupation (article 46);
- promotion by the state of the measures necessary to assure the exercise of the rights to healthcare, early childhood care, maternal health care, assistance for the disabled, the elderly and those incapable of working (article 47);
- promotion by the state of access by all to education, culture and sport (article 49); and
- duty of the state to create the political, economic and cultural conditions necessary for citizens to enjoy effectively their rights and fulfil their duties (article 50).[24]

Furthermore, article 21 recognises the 'integration into Angolan law of the rights embodied in the Universal Declaration of Human Rights, the African Charter on Human and Peoples' Rights and other international instruments to which Angola is a party'. The latter includes the International Covenant on Economic, Social and Cultural Rights of 1966 and several labour rights conventions.[25] Consequently, the Angolan government is constitutionally bound by international treaties guaranteeing a wide range of social and economic rights. More importantly, article 43 makes all the legally established rights justiciable by stating that citizens have the right 'to take judicial action against all acts that violate rights established in the Constitutional Law or other legislation'. This means that the government is not only bound by the Constitution and international legislation in social rights matters, but also by those rights that are stated in various national laws.

Legislation includes, for instance, the law on primary school education, which guarantees the right to free basic education. The responsibility of the courts in upholding these rights is stated in article 121: 'The courts shall guarantee and ensure compliance with the Constitutional Law, laws and other legal provisions in force, protection of the rights and legitimate interest of citizens and institutions, and shall decide on the legality of administrative acts.' Finally, article 36(2) of the Constitution states that citizens should not be prevented from obtaining legal redress because they lack financial means (an important point to which we shall return in more detail later). From this we may conclude that the Angolan Constitution itself offers quite wide protection for social and economic rights, and that it is within the competence of the judges to rule in such cases.

However, there is uncertainty about how much weight the Constitution of Angola carries, especially with respect to guarantees of social and economic rights. Judges will, in general, not refer to the Constitution directly in their judgments on specific rights – they will need these rights to be specified and detailed in national law. It is unclear how developed national legislation on social and economic rights is in Angola. It is our impression that much of the existing laws are inherited from the colonial period under the Portuguese. Legislation is changing very rapidly, and it is hard to get insight into laws and parliamentary debates on laws and proposed legislation.[26] What is clear, however, is that most legislation emanates from the executive, not from Parliament. According to a recent study, as much as 90 per cent of all legislation may originate in the executive's office, which means that Parliament plays a very marginal role in Angola.[27] Evidence further suggests that there has been a tendency in recent laws (such as the Land Law and the law regulating NGO activity) to restrict the rights of citizens, rather than to give them more rights.[28] For instance, the new Land Law rushed through Parliament out of session in 2004 has been criticised for not taking into account *usufructus* or traditional property. This is expected to cause extensive problems and conflict over land, especially for the thousands of internally displaced people, ex-combatants and refugees who are in the process of returning to their areas of origin. For indigenous pastoral groups in southern Angola, under constant threat of eviction, the issue is reported to be particularly urgent.[29] The tendency towards even tighter presidential control and the restriction of rights does not augur well for the judicial enforcement of social rights in Angola.

Likewise, the government's failure to fulfil the constitutional provision for the establishment of a judicial protectorate, which, according to article 142, 'shall be an independent public body, the purpose of which shall be to defend rights, freedoms and guarantees of citizens ensuring by informal means the justice and legality of the public administration', is worrisome. According to the Constitution, citizens have the right to present complaints to the judicial protectorate. Although this body, as of November 2004, had not yet been established, it is important to be aware of its potential existence.

In sum, the legal framework in Angola gives citizens a wide range of social and economic rights as well as constitutional guarantees for the right to seek redress should these rights be violated. Yet, as in many developing countries, there is a wide gap between the constitutional rights given to people and the actual enforcement of such rights. The fact that the vast majority of Angolans live in abject poverty without access to education, adequate health facilities, or job opportunities suggests that these rights are being systematically violated, by omission if not commission. In the next section, using Gloppen's theoretical framework, we systematically explore some of the factors that enhance – or, alternatively, hamper – access to justice for the poor, here defined as bringing social rights litigation to court. Note that although the focus is on a particular type of civil case, many of the arguments below pertain to the issue of access to justice more generally.

Why Courts in Angola Have Failed to Act as Vehicles for Social Transformation

Marginalised Groups' Voice

In Angola, the vast majority of people may be categorised as 'marginalised' in the sense that they are poor and thus lack adequate resources. For this reason alone, it is important to know what kind of resources the poor actually possess and what chance they have of approaching the formal judicial system for recourse when their social and economic rights are violated. Three groups of factors may help to explain why the poor bring social litigation cases to court (or why they do not): (i) societal and cultural factors; (ii) institutional and judicial factors; and (iii) the political context.

The first and most pressing problem in Angola is that there is no tradition of using the formal court system. Angolans are reported to be rather sceptical about using formal legal structures. Levels of trust in the formal legal system are generally low.[30] This may be partly due to a lack or negative experience of the formal legal system. Historically, the vast majority of disputes have been settled *outside* the formal court system. With respect to informal ways of solving disputes, there is a plethora of legal cultures and norms in Angola. At present no serious comparative research has been done on this, although a couple of studies are underway.[31] Clearly, most people prefer to settle disputes through local dispute resolution structures, especially at the village level. Elders and prominent men in the local environment are entrusted with finding solutions to disputes. Where these efforts fail, people are known to approach the formal courts as a second instance of appeal. This is particularly true for people in Luanda, who are the only ones who have access to courts in any meaningful sense of the word (see discussion below).

The reasons why people fail to use the formal legal system are complex, but may be summarised as a combination of the following: First, until 1975, during the period of colonial rule, the formal legal system was reserved mainly for Portuguese settlers and their descendants. Angolans had to find other ways of settling disputes and obtaining justice. The legacy from the colonial era discourages local people from using the formal legal system. Secondly, the protracted civil war involved a long period during which formal courts barely functioned at all. Thirdly, the present nature of the formal court system discourages the poor from using it (a point to which we shall return in more detail below). Fourthly, and linked to the previous point, the lack of particular kinds of resources has made it difficult for the poor to turn to the courts for redress (another point to which we shall return in more detail below). In short, there are a number of *access barriers*, such as lack of information, physical access to courts, financial costs and language barriers. Many of these problems are interlinked.

Since the majority of people (especially in rural areas) live far from a court, there is scarce *knowledge* about the formal court system. One may assume that the further the physical distance from a court, the less knowledge about the existence of the court and the procedures of bringing a case to court. There is also a problem regarding the general knowledge of what rights exist in the first place. Given the average low level of education and alarmingly high illiteracy rates, it is no surprise that people in general are not aware of the possibility of raising a court case over the violation of social or economic rights. A UN-sponsored study attempting to measure awareness of human rights among the poor in Luanda in 2000, covering around 1,500 respondents, concluded that about 15 per cent of the population had no knowledge or concept of rights at all. The remaining 85 per cent had only 'vague knowledge' of their rights, and did not know what to do in the event that their rights were violated.[32] Since this study was conducted, there have been some efforts at spreading information about human rights and the right to free legal aid through the radio and television. For instance, there are radio programmes that have sought to explain citizens' rights, where jurists are available to answer questions and explain the details of laws. These radio programmes are reported to have had a big impact in that they reach a broad segment of the population. By contrast, television is a less efficient way of transmitting knowledge on rights since very few among the poor in Angola have access to television.[33]

In addition to the social and cultural factors mentioned above, there are also important *institutional and judicial barriers* that the poor have to overcome. One major problem in Angola is *physical access* to courts. Out of 168 municipal courts countrywide, only 23 were working in 2003.[34] Outside Luanda, very few were operative, in the sense of being staffed by judges with lawyers to present a case. For all practical purposes this means that only the population in Luanda has physical access to formal courts at the lowest level. At present, roughly a third of the population lives in Luanda.[35] This, in consequence, reduces significantly the poor's chances of gaining access to court close to where they live. Travelling to the nearest court can be an impossible task for many since Angola is a huge country with vast distances and very poor infrastructure. Roads and bridges were largely destroyed during the war and rural areas are infested with land mines, which in turn makes travelling both difficult and risky.

If we for a moment assume that a poor person has physical access to court and knows how to go about presenting a case, the next concern is likely to be *financial costs*. In spite of constitutional guarantees of costs not being a barrier to justice, bringing a case to court in Angola is not free of cost. The first problem is hiring a lawyer. The large majority of Angola's roughly 600 lawyers work in Luanda. There are barely any in the rural areas, meaning that a person who wants to take a case to court has slim chances of doing so unless they live in the capital. The next problem is that of monetary cost. Substantial costs are involved at various stages of the litigation process. Legal fees vary widely. Up until 1996, the government set legal fees. Now lawyers may charge anything from US$100 to US$2,000–3,000 for the same service. Divorce cases cost up to US$5,000, making divorce unaffordable for most people.[36] According to a recent report, updates on the fee tables for the Notary's Office and other judicial services have been increased to a point where 'it is almost impossible for the common citizen to access them'. The report further notes that 'judicial cost fees are very high' and suggests that the Bar Association approve a minimum fee, so as to make costs more affordable and predictable for ordinary citizens.[37]

In the only known attempt to bring to court a complaint against the state regarding violations of social and economic rights in Angola, more specifically, the right to free education, the case failed due to the cost of bringing the case through court. In brief, an international non-governmental organisation (NGO), World Learning, has been providing a grant to an Angolan education coalition composed of ten Angolan NGOs. The education coalition hired a lawyer to discuss the possibility of taking the Ministry of Education to court over its failure to comply with the primary education law. This law states that all primary education up to grade six is free. However, according to World Learning, in practice, this law is not being implemented. In order for children to have access to primary education, parents have been forced to pay a bribe to school directors and teachers. All the lawyers contacted by the Angolan education coalition to do the preparatory work for the planned court case had been asking for over US$7,000, although the work was only estimated to take one month. This was beyond the coalition's financial capacity. The coalition next approached a number of donors to support this activity, but all requests were turned down. World Learning only had US$3,000 to offer the coalition for this activity, which was not enough. As a result, the project was dropped. Evidence suggests that there are no other cases against the Angolan state concerning social rights in the courts at the moment.[38]

The US$7,000 fee demanded by the lawyers approached by the educational coalition in Angola (supported by an international NGO) to prepare a case against the Ministry of Education is not uncommon. Ordinary Angolans, needless to say, are not likely to have the financial means necessary to hire a lawyer to take on a case. Even if they did, they may not have the financial means to ensure that the case was heard. Not only do lawyers demand high fees for their services. It is also costly to have the case taken through the court system. There is, further, widespread corruption in the Angolan justice system. This has, in part, to do with the fact that judges and functionaries are poorly paid.[39] Lawyers are often paid under the table. Court clerks and judges are paid to hear a case, and even more money is in turn required in order to have a case decided. There is also a practice of paying judicial tax. This applies to some cases, though not all (labour cases are exempted). For instance, in a divorce case the assets are divided, with ten per cent going to the judge. A particular rule applies to cases that are appealed to the Supreme Court in Angola. In such cases the person has to pay a judicial tax of ten per cent, which means that ten per cent of the monetary value of the issue in dispute goes to the court. If the person does not pay, the case stalls. Because many people are distrustful of decisions reached by judges in the municipal and provincial courts in general, a lot of cases are appealed to the Supreme Court. However, the ten per cent judicial tax is definitely a factor that restricts access to justice for the poor. In sum, substantial amounts of money are needed to bring a case to court, and even more to have the case acted upon.[40]

Although the state has a constitutional duty to provide *free legal aid* to those who do not have sufficient economic means (article 36(2)), there are several obstacles. First, as mentioned above, there are no lawyers in large areas of the country, which in practice means that legal aid is restricted to people living in the capital. Secondly, there is a chronic lack of educated lawyers, even in the capital. Thirdly, a person who wishes to take a case to court has to present a certificate proving that he or she earns less than a certain minimum amount. This in itself is a significant hurdle for people who may not know how to read or write, and not be familiar with bureaucratic structures. The Bar Association of Angola (OAA) has offered legal aid to a number of people – frequently for free.[41] The state is supposed to reimburse lawyers, but according to the head of OAA, the state is extremely slow in these matters.[42] It is often easier for a lawyer to do it for free than to try to get reimbursed through the bureaucracy. To compensate for the lack of qualified lawyers providing free legal aid through the state system, there are a couple of NGOs in Angola that offer free legal services to those who need it most, such as World Learning and Associacão Justica, Paz e Democracia (AJPD). In spite of these efforts, there is still a widespread lack of free legal aid.[43]

According to Gloppen's theoretical framework, language may constitute yet another potential obstacle to access to justice. Interestingly, this appears not to be a large problem in Angola, although one might have expected it to be since the formal courts in Angola operate in Portuguese. There are three large ethnic groups and a number of smaller groups, with clear linguistic distinctions.[44] Although it is unclear how many Angolans do not speak Portuguese, the figure is estimated at less than 20 per cent by a local NGO which works on access to justice issues. Importantly, almost everyone in Luanda – where the vast majority of courts are located – speaks Portuguese. Non-speakers of Portuguese who need translators in courts are reported to find them, and the courts operating outside Luanda seem to have enough translators. It also appears that judges in the countryside (read: provincial courts and a small number of municipal courts) speak at least one local native language.[45]

If we assume, for the sake of argument, that a poor person is aware of their rights, has decided to take a case to one of the Luanda courts, and has further managed to find and pay a lawyer to bring the case forward, what are the factors that will determine whether or not the court will actually take on the case and give it a favourable hearing?

Courts' Responsiveness

In Angola, the responsiveness of courts is not so much a function of the legal framework, the existence of legal strategies, or the existing legal culture as of the state of the justice system itself. Only parts of the formal justice system are actually functioning. The court system may, at best, be characterised as weak. The weak capacity of the Angolan courts is a problem that affects the treatment of all kinds of court cases, not only social rights litigation. Some of the following discussion is therefore of a general character.

The capacity of the courts is seriously limited by a lack of *human and technical resources*. This problem has historical roots. At independence in 1975, very few jurists (almost all of whom were educated in Portugal) stayed behind – there was only one judge, one prosecutor and about fifteen lawyers in the entire country.[46] The first law graduates from an Angolan university were only produced in 1984. Although there have been substantial improvements in the Angolan justice system in the last 20 years, there is still a great lack of qualified judges and lawyers. One or two judges often serve millions of people. An estimate in 2003 showed that Angola needed about 200 more judges.[47] Another problem is that the gender balance in the two professions is greatly skewed towards men.[48]

In spite of reforms in 1988, which restructured the entire justice system and guaranteed the judiciary formal independence (see Law No 18/88 (on the 'Unified system of justice')), much work remains before the judiciary becomes fully operational. In the three-tiered system (municipal courts, provincial courts, and the Supreme Court) administratively organised under the Ministry of Justice, the first level is barely functioning. As mentioned above, only 23 out of 168 municipal courts were reported to be operational in 2003. Two of those functioning were located in Luanda. The rest were concentrated in a few of the provinces. Consequently, people living in a majority of provinces in Angola do not have access to formal courts at the local/municipal level.[49] The government has expressed the hope that it will reopen two or three of its 145 closed municipal courthouses a year – a process that might take half a century, according to one estimate.[50] As such, the prospect for the poor to access courts at the primary level seems rather slim.

Access to courts at the provincial level is significantly better, however. There are 19 provincial courts in Angola – one in each of the 18 provinces plus two in the province of Benguela (Benguela city and Lobito). The provincial courts are composed of *salas* (specialised courts). The two *salas* likely to deal with social litigation cases are the *sala* for Cível e Administrativeo (civil and administrative) and the *sala* for labour relations. In practice, many cases are presented directly to the provincial courts rather than starting at the lowest level.

The Supreme Court is in operation, although only nine of its sixteen judges have been appointed so far. It is a particular concern that the Constitutional Court, provisions for which exist in the 1992 constitutional revision, has never been established. This means that the Supreme Court is the guardian of the Constitution and the final arbiter in constitutional matters – including the upholding of social and economic rights. This in itself is not a problem. What is problematic, however, is that the Supreme Court has been criticised for being too close to the government, and thus not fully independent. A prominent legal scholar concludes that the fact that the entire judicial pyramid is under the formal tutelage of the Ministry of Justice makes it 'seriously unconstitutional'.[51]

With respect to the possibility of seeking redress for violations of social and economic rights, it is a genuine concern that the Ombudsman's Office has not yet been established – in spite of constitutional provisions. There is, however, another dispute resolution body through which people may present complaints, namely the Human Rights Commission, established by the executive and located in the National Assembly. The Commission works broadly on human rights and civil rights, offering advice on a wide range of issues, such as land issues, housing rights, and violation of labour rights. It also offers free legal aid. The Commission handles around 200–300 cases per year, which is the overwhelming majority of the cases brought before it. Unresolved cases go to the Supreme Court.[52] The Parliamentary Commission on Human Rights is supposed to handle cases that would otherwise be brought before the Ombudsman's Office. Although the Commission seems to be working quite well, it is worrisome that it is located within government structures and hence not operating independently. This may seriously reduce the likelihood of people bringing forward their grievances against the state.

The fact that only some aspects of the Angolan justice system are working has to do partly with insufficient *financial resources* and partly with a lack of *human resources*. The judiciary has so far not been a priority item in the state budget. Before the Second Republic, which was constitutionally launched after the peace accords in 1991, less than one per cent of the state budget per annum was allocated to the judiciary.[53] This had historical reasons. According to the head of the Angolan Bar Association (Ordem dos Advogados de Angola), the meagre resources allocated to the judiciary has to do with the fact that, at independence, the state sectors in Angola were divided into 'productive' and 'non-productive'. The government channelled state resources into the more 'productive' parts, neglecting the 'non-productive' sectors, which besides the judiciary also included the health and education sectors. Since the judiciary was subordinated to the executive, it was not considered necessary to strengthen the judiciary. Although the judiciary was guaranteed constitutional independence with the Second Republic in 1992, it was not given financial autonomy. For all practical purposes, therefore, the resource situation did not change much.[54]

As a direct consequence of the lack of financial resources allocated to the judicial sector, human resources are also scarce. There are still judges who are not adequately trained, especially at the municipal level. Several of the provincial courts lack personnel, especially prosecutors. There is also a great need for more qualified lawyers, particularly outside the capital. Training of court lawyers and judges, however, has improved in recent years. There are now four law schools in the country: one public and three private. The first one, Agostinho Neto, was established in 1984, the last one in 2002. Eighty per cent of all law degrees in the country have been awarded by the Law Faculty at the Agostinho Neto University alone, but more diversity in education can be expected as the other, newer law schools start producing graduates. The number of law students has increased rapidly over the last few years. Hence, when these students start graduating, the staff component in the judicial system is likely to improve substantially.[55]

Jurisprudential resources are also relatively scarce. There is definitely a problem with infrastructure. The lack of computers, office furniture, and even pens and paper makes the everyday life of judges quite stressful – especially at the municipal and provincial levels. Another, more serious problem is the lack of written statements and judgments. Access to legal material is not easy, since it is not computerised. All Supreme Court judgments are written down and published in full text in legal magazines.[56] All these judgments are also collected in books. These books used to be published annually, but there seems to have been an interruption in that practice. The judgments are not automatically distributed to the provincial courts, only on request.[57] It is problematic that the judgments passed by the highest court in the country are not easily available to judges out in the provinces, and even less at the municipal level.

Tentative Conclusions

In a country like Angola, which has been ravaged by civil war for decades and where the population has been used to not expecting much from the state in any area of rights protection, it is perhaps not surprising that poor citizens have (so far) not taken the state to court over its failure to provide basic rights, such as health, education or housing.

In this explorative study we have tried to identify some of the structural conditions that must be in place for social rights litigation to be heard by courts along with a brief assessment of these factors. We have also tried to comment more generally on the barriers to access to justice for poor people in post-war Angola, since the hurdles that the poor face in bringing social litigation cases to court are most likely very similar to those they would face when bringing other types of cases to court. Gloppen's theoretical framework has proved useful in identifying factors that both capture the ability of marginalised groups to voice their claims in formal courts as well as the factors that explain the courts' responsiveness to such claims.

Our tentative conclusion is that the failure to implement social and economic rights in Angola is not primarily due to constitutional limitations, but rather due to a lack of resources among the poor as well as a lack of human and technical resources within the justice system itself.

Obviously, a lack of resources is a common problem in many developing countries. Yet, it is important to note that courts may be active even in weak states. What is peculiar to Angola is the existence of vast resources (which could potentially have been spent to reduce poverty and boost the justice sector) alongside abject and widespread poverty. The gap between constitutional guarantees of rights and the implementation of these rights is therefore particularly wide. In spite of the rather bleak picture presented in this chapter, there are some positive factors worth mentioning.

Our analysis has shown that several of the conditions necessary for judges to hear cases on social and economic rights in Angola are in fact present. First, citizens do have the de facto right to institute proceedings against the state. Secondly, the Angolan Constitution and the government's ratification of relevant human rights legislation provide (at least in theory) a favourable legal framework for judicial action in social transformation. This gives some reason for cautious optimism with respect to how the courts may act in the future.

Nevertheless, there are a series of obstacles to successful social rights litigation – and indeed, to access to justice more generally. Partly, this has to do with the national legal framework, where (to the extent that laws have given rights protection) there seems to be a tendency in national law revision towards less rather than more rights.[58] Importantly, the poor have, for a number of reasons, failed to take their grievances to court. The prime reason, perhaps, is that there has been no tradition of the poor using the formal courts.[59] In addition, lack of faith in the judicial system, lack of knowledge about rights, lack of physical access, and high costs have acted as barriers for people taking cases to court.

A second set of explanatory factors lies with the court system itself. To the extent that the poor have the *de facto* right to bring social rights cases to court, there are a number of structural features of the Angolan justice system that make it unlikely that these cases are actually heard by the courts. The court system is far from fully operational, especially at the municipal level. The urban elite/rural poor divide coupled with the extremely underdeveloped and understaffed structures of formal justice in rural areas has made access to (formal) courts outside the capital virtually non-existent. Lack of trained personnel and financial resources make the courts slow, inefficient, and corrupt – and, as a result, not much trusted.

The problems pertaining to Angolan courts are largely a product of the country's recent brutal history – the end of colonialism followed by prolonged civil war. In the ensuing short period of peace, there have been encouraging signs of improvement in the justice sector. Nevertheless, much work still needs to be done in the areas of improving infrastructure and equipment, increasing the salaries of judicial personnel (to attract good lawyers and judges, and also hopefully discourage corruption), improving the training of judges and functionaries, and carrying out other necessary reforms of the judiciary.[60] To ensure this, the government must prove that it is serious about strengthening the judiciary. Building well-functioning institutions along with educating people about their rights and removing some of the barriers to using the formal court system is urgently needed in order to improve access to justice for the poor in Angola, but it will take time. Before these improvements haven take place, we should not expect the courts to act as an institutional voice for the poor.

Notes

1 An earlier draft of this chapter was prepared for a workshop on 'Courts and Social Transformation in New Democracies: An Institutional Voice for the Poor?', Buenos Aires, 2–3 December 2004. We thank the workshop participants for constructive comments.
2 We have only looked at cases litigated against the state, not against individuals. We do not exclude the possibility that there have been cases regarding social and economic rights in provincial courts in Angola, though no such cases were brought to our attention by jurists interviewed in Luanda from March–April 2004.
3 See Gargarella's chapter in this volume.
4 Ibid., p. 13.
5 Note, however, that what judges actually do is conditioned by the role that is assigned to them, which is in turn a function of what the drafters of the constitution concerned think they ought to be doing. For example, a country may have a constitution that is based on a theory of democracy that suggests that judges ought to have a role in enforcing social rights, but may in practice not have vigorous social rights jurisprudence. One of the explanations for this might be that judges failed to accept the constitutional invitation to enforce social rights for various reasons, but it may also be that the constitution was based on an over-optimistic theoretical assessment of what judges can do, either in the abstract or in the context of the particular political and economic conditions pertaining in the country.
6 Cited in Gloppen's chapter in this volume, pp. 37–8.
7 One can imagine a country where the constitution is silent on the role of courts in social and economic transformation, but where courts nevertheless take on such a role. One can also imagine a kind of mid-level example, like India (see Sudarshan's chapter in this volume), where the courts have gone further than the constitution prescribes.
8 See Gloppen's chapter in this volume.
9 This is in contrast to the failed peace agreements of 1991 and 1994. See, for example, Economist Intelligence Unit, *Angola Country Report* (June 2004) pp. 2, 5. For an historical account of political development in Angola, see Neuma Grobbelaar, Greg Mills and Elizabeth Sidiropoulos, *Angola: Prospects for Peace and Prosperity* (Johannesburg: South African Institute of International Affairs, 2003); Inge Tvedten, *Angola: Struggle for Peace and Reconstruction*, in L.W. Bowman (ed.), *Nations of the Modern World* (Boulder: Westview Press, 2003).
10 For data on oil production and other economic indicators, see Economist Intelligence Unit, *Angola Country Report*.
11 The number of IDPs varies from source to source. A refugee expert reports 4.1 million IDPs living in camps or in urban areas throughout the country, and around 450,000 refugees living in neighbouring countries. See Andrea Lari, 'Returning home to a normal life? The plight of Angola's internally displaced', in Institute for Security Studies, *African Security Analysis Programme* (Institute for Security Studies, 2004). The number of IDPs estimated by a UK Foreign and Commonwealth country report on Angola is 4.5 million. Cited in International Bar Association Human Rights Institute, *Angola: Promoting Justice Post-Conflict* (London: International Bar Association, 2003) p. 15, fn. 10).
12 UNDP, *Human Development Report* (2002).

13 The estimates are based on 2001 figures (Angolan Government, *Poverty Reduction Strategy Paper* (2004)).

14 UNDP, *Human Development Report* (2003).

15 The facts and figures in this section are mostly from 2002, taken from the statistical section in UNDP, *Human Development Report* (2003).

16 See, for example, Jorge Casimiro Congo, Manuel da Costa, Fr. Raúl Tati, Agostinho Chicaia, and Francisco Luemba, *Cabinda 2003: A Year of Pain* (Luanda: Ad Hoc Commission for Human Rights in Cabinda, 2003); Human Rights Watch, *Some Transparency: No Accountability: The Use of Oil Revenue in Angola and Its Impact on Human Rights* (Human Rights Watch, 2004); US Department of State, *Angola: Country Reports on Human Rights Practices 2002* (Bureau of Democracy, Human Rights and Labor, 2002); US Department of State, *Angola: Country Reports on Human Rights Practices 2003* (Bureau of Democracy, Human Rights and Labor, 2003). A lack of respect for human rights has also been reported consistently in monthly reports from the United Nations Human Rights Office in Angola.

17 At the political level the discussion is reported to be on whether to hold the elections before or after the promulgation of a new constitution. According to a news report, after a heated argument between the majority and the opposition grouped around former UNITA rebels, an agreement was reached to hold elections before the revision of the Constitution. See Agencia Fidez <www.fides.org/eng/news/2005/0501/21_3952.html>, accessed 10 February 2005.

18 The Constitution of Angola dates back to the single party communist era. Although two rounds of constitutional amendments, in March and September 1991 respectively, formally changed Angola into a multiparty democracy with fundamental political rights and freedoms, the Constitution still contains remnants of single-party rule. A Constitutional Commission was established by the Parliament in 1998 to work out a new constitution aiming at further clarification of the separation of powers and the interdependence of the sovereign bodies of the state, as well as guaranteeing the principles of a democratic state based on the rule of law. For details, see Inge Amundsen, Cesaltina Abreu and Laurinda Hoygaard, 'Accountability on the Move: The Parliament of Angola', paper read at a workshop on *Institutional Development: The Case of the Angolan Parliament*, Luanda, 22 November 2004, p. 4. The Constitutional Commission had as of November 2004 not concluded its work.

19 Human Rights Watch, *Some Transparency*, p. 1.

20 Cited in Grobbelaar, *Angola*, p. 51. For a more detailed discussion of corruption in Angola and its impact on human rights, see Human Rights Watch, *Some Transparency*.

21 International Bar Association Human Rights Institute, *Angola*.

22 For a theoretical argument on this, and its implications for executive dominated Latin American countries, see Elin Skaar, *Judicial Independence: A Key to Justice. An Analysis of Latin America in the 1990s,* doctoral dissertation, Department of Political Science, University of California, Los Angeles, 2002, chaps 1 and 2.

23 The Supreme Court ruled in 2003 that Hoygaard was entitled to a financial compensation, but had as of November 2004 not set the sum for the compensation. Until that is done, the judgment in the case remains non-public (and not available).

24 From Constitutional Revision Law (Law 23/92 of 16 September 1992 (cited in UN Report: *Angola: The Post-War Challenges*, Common Country Assessment (2002)). The amendments to the Constitutional Law were introduced in March 1991 through Law No. 12/91, as part of the Angola Peace Accords, signed on 31 May 1991.

25 Labour rights conventions include Freedom of association and collective bargaining (Convention 87 and 98); Elimination of forced and compulsory labour (Convention 29 and 105); Elimination of discrimination in respect of employment and occupation (Convention 100 and 111) and Abolition of child labour (Convention 182). Cited in UNDP, *Human Development Report* (2003), Indicator 31.

26 In a UNDP-sponsored seminar on 'Justice and Law Reform in Angola' held in Luanda in May 2004, the quality of legislation, doctrine and national jurisprudence were mentioned as important areas for further study.

27 See Amundsen, 'Accountability on the Move'.

28 Information from authors' interview with Isabel Emerson, Luanda, 19 November 2004.

29 See United Nations Office for the High Commissioner of Human Rights, Project Document ANG/03/RB4 on Strengthening National Capacities for Human Rights, Democracy and the Rule of Law in Angola to Consolidate Peace (Luanda: UNHCR, 2003) p. 8.

30 Grobbelaar, *Angola*, p. 50. See Humanos/TROCAIRE and Procuradoria Geral da Repúblicana na Província de Luanda, Inquérito ao Conhecimento, Exercício e Defesa dos Direitos Humanos (Luanda: Angola Instituto de Pequisa Económica e Social, 2000/2001).

31 One of the conclusions from a UNDP-sponsored seminar on 'Justice and Law Reform in Angola' held in Luanda in May 2004, was that there is a need to recognise the existence of customary law and to establish criteria to define and integrate customary law into the formal judicial system. See Universidade Agostinho Neto, Faculdade de Direito, 'Mesa Redonda Sobre Direito Costumeiro' (August 2003).

32 Alfonso Barragues and Mario Alberto Adauta de Sousa, 'Towards the Development of Indicators to Measure the Levels of Awareness on Knowledge, Exercise and Defense of Human Righs in Angola' (Montreaux: Human Rights Division, United Office in Angola and Instituto de Pesquia Económica e Social, 2000), p. 11. To the best of our knowledge, this is the only rights-based study carried out in Angola.

33 See Humanos/TROCAIRE and Procuradoria Geral da Repúblicana na Província de Luanda.

34 International Bar Association Human Rights Institute, *Angola*, p. 4.

35 Though data on population statistics is not readily available, the current (formal and informal) urban population of Luanda is estimated at 4 million people. This number is estimated to possibly increase to 5.1 million by 2010. See Angola Press Agency, *Luanda may have 5.4 million inhabitants by 2010* (Luanda, 2005). Available at <http://allafrica.com/stories/200502150620.html>, accessed 15 February 2005.

36 Information taken from International Bar Association Human Rights Institute, *Angola*, p. 32.

37 Cited in Manuel Goncalves and José Octávio Serra Van-Dúnem, 'Final Report', paper read at the UNDP-sponsored 'Seminário a Reforma da Justicia e do Direito', Luanda, 28–30 May 2004, p. 24. The same report recommends the creation of a citizen's public defence service by the Angolan Bar Association, more specifically a Judiciary Assistance Institute (ibid., p. 27).

38 The information was provided by Fern Toledo and Anecleta Pereira in an interview with the authors in Luanda, 2 April 2004, followed up by email communication with Fern Toledo, 4 November 2004.

39 Corruption is a serious problem in all state sectors, mainly owing to the poor salaries paid to low-level officials. That there exists widespread corruption in the justice sector

in Angola was confirmed by a number of informants interviewed in Luanda in March-April 2004. For a more thorough discussion, see Raul C. Araújo, 'Os Custos com o Accesso á Justica e o Exercísio do Directo ao Patrocinio Judiciário' paper read at the 'Seminário a Reforma da Justicia e do Direito', Luanda, 28–30 May 2004, p. 5.

40 The information on judicial taxes and fees was provided by lawyer Paulette Lopes in an interview with the authors in Luanda, 6 April 2004.

41 The laws regulating legal aid and the number of cases in which the lawyers pertaining to the Bar Association (OAA) have assisted are detailed in Araújo, 'Os Custos com o Accesso á Justica'. Although Law 15/95 of 10 November states that salaries are to be paid annually to lawyers offering legal aid, this is not done in practice.

42 Information from Raúl Araujo, OAA, in interview with authors in Luanda, 30 March 2004.

43 For a discussion on free legal aid, see Araújo, 'Os custos com o accesso á justica'.

44 The last census in Angola distinguishing ethnic affiliation was carried out in 1960. The largest ethnic group, the Ovimbundu then made up 37 per cent of the population, followed by the Mbundu (25 per cent), and the Bakongo (15 per cent). Other major ethno-linguistic groups are the Lunda-Chokwe (8 per cent) and Nanguela (7 per cent). There are also several smaller southern groups, such as Nyaneka, Owambo, and Herero. For more detailed information, see Tvedten, *Angola: Struggle for Peace and Reconstruction* , pp. 106–109.

45 The information on access for non-speakers of Portuguese to the formal court system is reported in International Bar Association Human Rights Institute, *Angola*, pp. 61–2.

46 Armando Marques Guedes, Carlosa Feijó et al., *Pluralismo e Legitimação – A Edificação Juridica Pós-colonial de Angola* (Lisbon: Editora Almedina, 2003). Supplemented with interview material.

47 International Bar Association Human Rights Institute, Angola, p. 38.

48 This is likely to change in the future as women now represent about half of the students at the country's four law faculties.

49 This has been confirmed by several studies. See for instance European Union, *Estudio de Identificação e Viabilidade para um Apoio á Reforma da Administração da Juticia na República de Angola (Relatorio Preliminar)* (Luanda: European Union, 2003); Marques Guedes, *Pluralismo e Legitimação*; United Nations, *Angola: The Post-war Challenges* (Luanda: United Nations, 2002).

50 International Bar Association Human Rights Institute, *Angola*, p. 42.

51 Marques Guedes, *Pluralismo e Legitimação.*

52 Information on the Human Rights Commission was given in an interview with Dr. Milton da Silva, President of the Human Rights Commission, in Luanda, 6 April 2004.

53 Figure based on report from European Union, cited in Araújo, 'Os Custos com o Accesso á Justica', p. 3.

54 Ibid., pp. 3–4.

55 Note, however, that having more law schools does not necessarily solve the problem of poor or inadequate training. See Goncalves, 'Final Report', pp. 45–6.

56 Information given in an interview with Fern Teodoro, World Learning, in Luanda, 2 April 2004. The most recent annual publication we came across during our fieldwork was from 1994.

57 Information given in an interview with Vice President of the Supreme Court, Dr. Caetano de Sousa, in Luanda, 6 April 2004.

58 Gloppen's theoretical framework mentions the nature of the legal system as a factor influencing when and how the voice of the poor is heard. It might have been useful to further stress the importance of national legislation detailing constitutional guarantees of various rights in order for these rights to have legal bearing in a society.

59 A more systematic exploration of the connections between civil law and customary law would be useful. This is a concern raised by practitioners of law as well as academics in Angola. See, for example Goncalves, 'Final Report'.

60 The urgent need to reform the Angolan justice sector has been pointed out by various actors and been the topic for a number of conferences and seminars over the last couple of years. For recommendations as to what is needed in terms of reform, see, for instance, European Union, *Estudio de Identificação*; Goncalves, 'Final Report'; International Bar Association Human Rights Institute, *Angola*.

Chapter 11

Weak Courts, Rights and Legal Mobilisation in Bolivia

Pilar Domingo

Introduction

This chapter examines the process by which rights-based development and citizenship has become a feature of sub-altern political discourses in Bolivia, the degree to which this has prompted recourse to legal mobilisation strategies by disadvantaged groups, and the response by a court system which has been the object of important reforms in the last decade. The chapter is developed within a volume which seeks to explore the capacity for social transformation through legal mobilisation and judicial activism. Here we take Gargarella's definition of *social transformation* as the 'altering of structured inequalities and power relations in society in ways that reduce the weight of morally irrelevant circumstances, such as socio-economic status/class, gender, race, religion or sexual orientation' (see Gloppen in this volume).

In contrast to other cases in this volume, Bolivia is an example of weak rule of law and poor quality justice administration. Moreover, recourse to legal mobilisation as a route to social transformation is limited. Nonetheless in recent years there has been a growing presence of rights-based discourses as part of sub-altern forms of appropriating law and legal forms to achieve social change. Given the current context of political instability, and judicial underdevelopment in Bolivia, the chapter takes a broad view of the emancipatory potential of the law and legal channels and the degree to which, and the different ways in which, this is manifesting itself. Thus the analysis will look beyond social and economic rights litigation to consider also other aspects and forms of legal mobilisation and appropriation of rights discourses in the pursuit of transformative processes. Here the question is about understanding how, despite weak rule of law, there are changes taking place in Bolivian society which speak of shifts in the larger normative picture regarding contemporary understandings of rights, citizenship and law. To some extent this process has been supported by recent institutional reform, but it also coincides with an emerging global trend of socially inclusive and culturally diverse notions of rights, as necessary components of active and capable citizenship.[1]

The Bolivian case is interesting for its combination of recent innovative institutional reform, but also a changing normative context towards a rights-based political discourse appropriated by diverse political actors, and rooted in a grass-roots politics of mobilisation. Judicial reform may be contributing in incipient ways to changing patterns in litigation and how rights issues are being framed, but courts are not pioneering pro-poor judicial activism in Bolivia. At best they are reacting, in some cases through progressive rulings (for instance within the Constitutional Tribunal) to deeper changes in other institutions and social actors; at worst they continue to reproduce traditional vices of responding to political and economic interests (for instance, the land courts). Nor can we speak of important changes in litigious activity or levels. Nonetheless, there is, first, a new Constitutional Tribunal in place which marks a timid break with past attitudes within the justice system, and a new point of legal interface regarding rights issues. Secondly, there are changes and innovations taking place in terms of how legal *voice* is being articulated. To the extent that this is channelled through formal means, this is in large part a consequence of how the new human rights Ombudsman (*Defensor del Pueblo*) has developed from its first days, by encouraging and pioneering novel forms of 'societal accountability' through rights.[2] Both the Constitutional Tribunal and the Ombudsman were created through a constitutional reform in 1994.

These institutional changes have taken place in tandem with new forms of social and political struggle. These include – among other political strategies – new expressions of rights-centred discourses of change emerging as bottom-up claims, and which reflect normative and ideological shifts both in the political strategies of new social and political actors, but also in how state-society relations are being conceived. These new claims have a legal translation of sorts in the way in which rights and entitlements are being imagined, but do not necessarily correspond to neat categories – or sequences – of civil, political or social and economic rights claims within either classical liberal or social democratic frameworks. These are of course highly relevant, and indeed are present in the Bolivian Constitution, but the component of cultural and ethnic diversity in a society such as the Bolivian, which moreover now has *political* voice, creates a more complex picture of how entitlements are being imagined and constructed. The chapter thus also examines how a language of rights is being incorporated into the political struggle for social transformation in a context of institutional (and legal) change which has facilitated new opportunities for political and legal mobilisation, and new forms of identity politics around claims for the recognition of indigenous rights and legal pluralism. Finally, the political left in some respects is re-inventing itself (following the trends outlined in Couso's chapter) either by being absorbed into the new social movements (most of which to varying degrees are also rooted in identity politics of indigenous claims), or by adopting human rights discourse as the route to social transformation.

In some ways, then, Bolivia raises issues regarding the dangers of trusting weak courts with the guardianship of certain social and economic rights in societies where judicial institutions are still particularly vulnerable to manipulation and capture by powerful economic (and political) interests. (This is especially so for the land courts, but not, as we will see, for the Constitutional Tribunal.) At the same time, though, judicial reform and legal innovation have opened up new channels for citizens and underprivileged groups to acquire a greater awareness of rights generally, albeit in uneven and unsatisfactory ways. And this is taking place at a time of political renovation and broader institutional change, firstly through state reform, but now also with the prospect of a new constituent process, with all the uncertainties this entails.

The chapter firstly provides a brief overview of Bolivia's post-transition experience, and the nature of political and ethnic cleavages that have emerged in as far as these impact on voice and the articulation of rights claims and legal mobilisation. The second (and main) part of the chapter will examine recent developments in the justice sector which have constituted important aspects of top-down endeavours of rule-of-law construction. It will examine their impact on legal voice, effectiveness in pro-poor legal mobilisation and adjudication. The reforms have been potentially far-reaching. For the purposes of this chapter the focus will be on the new Constitutional Tribunal and the human rights Ombudsman. Brief reference will also be made to changes regarding recent constitutional and other reforms which acknowledge legal pluralism in a multi-ethnic society. Overall, while there has been some impact on voice, and the Constitutional Tribunal has modestly, but significantly ruled on a number of rights issues, we cannot speak of a significant shift towards pro-poor judicial activism.

The chapter concludes by remarking on the growing (although still modest and uneven) process of bottom-up appropriation of rights discourse, which forms one of many fronts by which social transformation is sought. Although legal mobilisation by no means constitutes a principal strategy for change, the appropriation of rights-based discourse and the discovery of the law by sub-altern groups is nonetheless a novel feature of the political and social landscape.

Political Context and Social Transformation

Bolivia is one of the poorest countries in Latin America. It features high levels of inequality, poverty and social exclusion.[3] While some human development indicators (literacy, infant mortality and life expectancy) have improved in the last 30 years, poverty reduction has been meagre, the total number of people under the poverty line has increased, and income inequality has deteriorated in the last 15 years.[4] Poverty is higher in rural areas, and higher still amongst the indigenous population.[5]

Against this chronic picture of socio-economic and racial exclusion, Bolivia's political history prior to 1982 was characterised by cyclical patterns of radical social mobilisation, political experiments in inclusive social reform, and subsequent cycles of repressive backlashes. Early reform pressures and initiatives in the first half of the twentieth century culminated in the 1952 National Revolution, an essentially bourgeois revolution by most classifications, which nonetheless instituted redistributive land reform, nationalisation of tin mines, and universal suffrage.[6] Soon the nationalist revolutionary experiment spiralled into rapid economic crisis, increasing political polarisation as the alliances that made up the revolutionary family fell apart, and military rule set in in the 1970s. Democratisation began in 1977 on a stop-and-go course, and it was only from 1982 onwards that there has been uninterrupted civilian rule (although, since 2000, with escalating levels of political and social unrest).

Specifically from 1985 onwards, and following a crisis of extreme economic instability under conditions of hyperinflation of 23,000 per cent, *representative electoral democracy* and *neo-liberal economic rule* have been the core features of Bolivia's political and developmental model. Early apparent stability and political and social consensus around the model was fuelled by initial societal relief at the effectiveness with which drastic austerity measures had brought an end to hyper-inflation. There was also considerable initial enthusiasm with the promises of electoral democracy.

Key characteristics of the political and economic model since 1985 have been, first, government through multiparty majority coalitions in Congress, which until 2003 secured relatively stable democratic rule, but deteriorated into a climate of self-complacency, and high and chronic levels of corruption among the parties that shared the spoils of coalition government – albeit with alternating parties in power. This 'traditional political class' (which includes the nationalist revolutionary party of 1952, the MNR – Movimiento Nacionalista Revolucionario) is perceived as preserving the interests of the *criollo* or 'white' elites, and has become increasingly discredited, leading to a crisis of regime legitimacy that has seriously destabilised the fragile democratic polity, and culminating in the early resignation of the MNR president in October 2003, Gonzalo Sanchez de Lozada, an architect of Bolivia's neo-liberal economic model.[7] Since then, Bolivia has been struggling to find political peace, and the political crisis claimed another presidential casualty in May 2005.

A second 'failing' feature is the economic model premised on economic liberalisation and privatisation policies throughout the 1980s and 1990s. Its failure to deliver not only on poverty reduction, but also on long-term sustainability (in part given Bolivia's particular characteristic as a weak, highly dependent economy with extreme vulnerability to external shocks) has led to its growing discredit. The recent discovery of rich gas resources within a legal framework perceived as benefiting international oil companies has only served to fuel social unrest and political polarisation. The escalating social unrest of the last five years is an expression of an accumulating rejection of an economic model that is perceived as exclusionary and socially unjust.[8] Moreover, successive democratic government administrations have had to resort to repressive states of emergency to ensure the passage and implementation of economic reforms aimed at furthering the process of liberalisation and privatisation of state enterprises.

Thirdly, throughout the 1990s, a number of institutional and constitutional reforms were undertaken under the umbrella of state reform, in part following the trends set by the international donor community's good governance agenda, with a view to strengthening democratic institutions and enabling market-led growth. These have combined, paradoxically, the creation of new opportunity structures for the political inclusion of new social movements, such as the 1994 Law of Political Participation (a law of municipal decentralisation), and changes in the electoral system, with a deepening of the neo-liberal economic model. State reform has also included other institutional changes, such as a sweeping range of reforms in the justice sector that will be reviewed in this chapter for their impact on social and economic rights claims.

A fourth feature has been the emergence of new socio-political groupings that have displaced (or absorbed) the old Marxist left, and now advance new political discourses that offer variations on different combinations of indigenous claims, demands for social justice, and a redistributive economic model (only very vaguely articulated) – and most with reference to rights as empowering entitlements. (Some are explicitly indigenous, others are the new faces of old left-wing groups.) Two new organisations stand out: first, the MAS movement (Movement to Socialism), led by an indigenous leader whose original social base lies with the coca-producers, but who has broader appeal with a disenchanted left-wing constituency, and increasing presence in other rural sectors. Significantly, the MAS leader, Evo Morales, came second in the 2002 presidential election, much to the alarm of urban elites. A second actor is the MIP (Movimineto Indigena Pachakutic), a smaller, but socially volatile *aymara* indigenist movement which has spearheaded some of the more radical social protests in recent times.

Of relevance for this chapter is the novel fact that these so called 'anti-system' movements combine electoral strategies with social protest tactics, but more significantly embrace a rights-based political discourse as a route to social change – albeit with differing notions of citizenship, community and entitlements. Changes in the language of rights, and in the advance of certain forms of legal mobilisation in society must also be read against a backdrop of a rapidly polarising political situation, where nonetheless even the more radical voices articulate rights-based political claims. Thus Bolivia's fragile democracy is experiencing a particularly rocky moment as it lurches towards the uncharted and heady waters of an impending constituent assembly seen as a promising opportunity for these new political forces. But this is taking place in a context of growing political polarisation and escalating social unrest.[9]

Despite the weak democratic tradition or respect for constitutional forms in Bolivia, it has a constitutional history rich in socially progressive fundamental charters. As far back as the 1930s Bolivia was espousing modern social and economic rights, on paper at least. The gains of the 1952 Revolution were reflected in the 1967 constitutional text (later amended in 1994 in important ways). The current *magna carta*, then, has an inclusive set of rights (civil, political, social and economic, and since 1994 cultural rights). However this has been poorly reflected in social structures and power relations that are unequal, exclusionary and increasingly fraught with latent (but rarely explicit) racial tension as indigenous political leaders gain electoral ground. Moreover, the courts, prior to the reforms of the 1990s, have by no means been a forum for progressive judicial activism.

In this context of institutional fragility – but also institutional innovation – and political polarisation, changes are nonetheless taking place regarding how rights, and expectations of social transformation through rights discourse are being constructed – if perhaps not much as rights claims channelled through the courts, and generally expressed in very uneven and unclear ways.

Constitutional and Institutional Reform

The Judiciary

Traditionally, the judicial system in Bolivia has been subordinated to political and economic interests, institutionally weakened by political instability and meagre resources, and very poorly embedded in society. The judiciary has a bad public image, which has not hugely improved with the reforms of the 1990s, and is largely inaccessible for most Bolivians.[10] This section will first examine the obstacles to adequate legal voice through problems of access to justice and weak judicial independence; secondly, the reforms undertaken during the 1990s, some specifically to address these issues; and, thirdly, the degree to which the establishment of the Constitutional Tribunal has made a difference to legal culture, with reference also to social and economic rights litigation and changing receptiveness to pro-poor litigation.

While Bolivia does not exhibit the scale of institutional fragility that we find in Angola (see the chapter by Skaar and van-Dúnem in this volume), nonetheless, rule of law is traditionally weak. Reliable data is hard to come by, and only recently have there been efforts to build databases.[11] One of the more reliable sources since 1998 is the information generated by the human rights Ombudsman (and to some extent by the Constitutional Tribunal), and its findings are relevant for assessing changing patterns in legal mobilisation – perhaps more reliably than can be drawn from the judiciary.

Access and Voice Legal voice in Bolivia is limited for reasons that have to do both with the internal workings of the judiciary and the extent of its physical presence across the national territory, and also with contextual societal factors that range from the impact on access of severe socio-economic inequality and exclusion in one of the poorest countries in Latin America, to questions of ethnic diversity that accentuate the cultural distance between indigenous groups and formal legal institutions. (Assessments of access to justice are tentative – and somewhat intuitive – given the scarcity of reliable empirical data.)

One of the principal problems of access in Bolivia lies in the geographic distance for large sectors of the rural population from courthouses. In 2001, there was one court of first instance per 12,400 inhabitants (one of the lowest in the Andean region).[12] Although first-instance courts have increased in number, largely due to the reforms of the 1990s and an increase in budgetary resources, it is still the case that 60 per cent of the municipalities in the country do not have a first-instance tribunal.[13] A second factor has to do with the scarcity of resources for legal aid. The state's obligation to provide public defence for criminal cases was only institutionalised in 1993 with the creation of the Ministry of Justice. Since then matters have improved somewhat, largely as a consequence of recent judicial reforms and access to justice projects funded by the international donor community.[14]

Additional barriers have to do with the cost of litigation, and the excessive formalism and bureaucratic complexity of legal proceedings. The Bolivian judicial system is particularly characterised by Byzantine, inaccessible and almost ritualistic legal formalisms. For most legal action, claimants require the presence of lawyers, and the proceedings are inaccessible for the non-specialist.[15] This includes the individual constitutional review claims. These obstacles act as a powerful deterrent to legal mobilisation. Notably, recent reform projects have sought to address some of these issues. These include, for instance, the abolition of officially sealed paper as a formal requirement for presenting legal claims[16] (although the practice of requesting this formality has not completely disappeared, and claimants are still expected to meet certain requirements such as the use of a particular type of Bond paper, with strict observance of margins, spacing and ink colouring). Under the auspices of an Inter-American Development Bank (IADB) project on civil society and access to justice, resources have been directed towards funding legal advice centres, and programmes directed at training and increasing awareness of rights among the more vulnerable sectors of society, encouraging alternative mechanisms of conflict resolution.[17] The array of reform efforts funded and directed by the international donor community is impressive, although the impact of many of the measures is still subject to assessment.

Problems of access in part account for Bolivia's relatively low and unchanging levels of litigious activity, mostly concentrated in urban centres. The more vulnerable groups will tend to avoid contact with formal legal proceedings, which are viewed with distrust and apprehension.

Many of the above issues are typical obstacles of access to justice that work to inhibit legal voice in most democracies – and variations are more a matter of degree. In pluri-cultural and multi-ethnic societies such as Bolivia, however, legal voice is further complicated by linguistic and cultural barriers. We will discuss in more detail the implications of legal pluralism for social transformation below. Here what is important to note is that low levels of litigation reflect not only poor access, but also the fact that parallel conflict resolution mechanisms exist in the form of community justice. This also affects the likelihood of resorting to legal mobilisation for rights claims outside the community.

Although there is no data which adequately assesses access to justice by ethnic groups, figures from the human rights Ombudsman provide interesting information regarding the ethnic make-up of sectors most likely to take complaints to this office. Using linguistic groups (where the first language is not Spanish) as an indication of ethnic identity, Ombudsman statistics show that in 2002 almost 60 per cent (relatively consistent over time since the establishment of this office in 1999) of complaints brought to the Ombudsman are brought by *aymara* speakers (38 per cent) and *quechua* speakers (21 per cent) – in both cases mostly urban-based.[18] While clearly this cannot be correlated to corresponding patterns in litigation, not least because the human rights Ombudsman is perceived as a 'friendly' institution by vulnerable groups, in contrast to the formal justice system, it nonetheless suggests that there is a growing awareness of rights entitlements among certain disadvantaged groups.[19] It is also interesting to note that, of the complaints on violated rights, the number of cases regarding social, economic and cultural rights brought to the Ombudsman had risen to 24.4 per cent in 2002.[20] While this tells us little about how these rights have been handled by the courts, the human rights Ombudsman is perceived as a friendly 'processor' of complaints or queries on these issues, with an impact of sorts on voice.

Political Independence of Judges A factor which inhibits voice, but also receptiveness of the judiciary to pro-poor claims, is the longstanding tradition of subservience of the judiciary to political and powerful economic interests at the national and local level.[21] It is assumed that judges have clear political loyalties. Even with the reforms of the 1990s, which to a considerable extent have sought to reduce political dependence, the public perception remains that judges at all levels continue to rule through political rather than judicial logic.

At the top level of the judicial system prior to the reforms of the 1990s, the Bolivian judiciary was stuck in a mire of corruption and political scandals. Moreover, the return to democracy in 1982, instead of strengthening judicial independence, led to political parties going to great lengths to ensure political loyalties in the higher courts. Indeed, the Supreme Court has been party to a number of political conflicts resulting in various attempts by conflicting political parties in Congress to impeach some of its members. More than reflecting real conflicts between powers, these scandals mirrored political battles in which Supreme Court magistrates were involved by virtue of their political loyalties rather than as a matter of legal or constitutional principle. The solution to these inter-branch crises has generally been sought through accommodation between the political parties, and not through the appropriate legal channels.[22] The problems of weak judicial independence at the top were replicated at lower-level courts due to a pyramidal appointment structure concentrated in the Supreme Court. Things have changed in principle with the creation of a judicial council in a 1994 constitutional reform. The success with which more merit-based appointments of judges at all levels, now managed through the judicial council, are impacting on the judiciary remains to be seen. The constitutional reform of 1994 also changed the appointment mechanism for members of the Supreme Court, to a system of two-thirds vote in Congress, in principle rendering its members less susceptible to political pressures.

The problem of weak judicial autonomy has replicated itself in the new land tribunals created in a 1996 land reform law, to the disadvantage of more vulnerable rural groups in land disputes. By contrast, the new Constitutional Tribunal has fared much better. The issue of judicial independence in principle has been tackled in the various reforms of the 1990s in changing appointment mechanisms and enhanced budgetary autonomy of the courts.

Judicial Reforms in the 1990s The reforms of the 1990s have signified a major revamping of the justice sector. Prompted by the international donor community, Bolivia over two government administrations (Gonzalo Sánchez de Lozada from 1993–97 and Hugo Banzer between 1997–2002) engaged in a number of reforms, the effects of which still need to develop fully, but which touch most areas of the justice system. The Bill of Rights has not changed other than with regard to the new reference to indigenous justice (this appears as a separate article, article 171).

First, in 1993, a new law on the organisation of the judiciary was passed which included the creation of the Ministry of Justice. This laid the groundwork for the constitutional reforms of 1994. Importantly, these created a number of new institutions, which would fundamentally reorganise the judiciary. The new institutions include: a Constitutional Tribunal, a Judicial Council, the office of the public prosecutor, independent from the judiciary, and a human rights Ombudsman (*Defensor del Pueblo*). Most only came into effect after 1998. For the purposes of the chapter we will focus on the Constitutional Tribunal and the human rights Ombudsman (although clearly the Judicial Council's development is of relevance regarding the quality of justice administration and levels of independence of lower-level courts).

Other reforms which affect the justice system and issues of access include a new criminal procedure code,[23] which, importantly, introduces orality into the criminal justice system, recognises legal pluralism in some areas of criminal justice (still not fully legislated), and establishes the right to translation of court procedures into the relevant indigenous language. Finally, there is also an assortment of reforms that have to do with: creating mechanisms for merit-based appointments, increasing judicial salaries, increasing the number of courts in the country, improving court administration and case management, improving access and promoting alternative dispute resolution mechanisms, much of this funded by the international donor community.[24]

How have these reforms affected the social transformation potential of courts, or patterns of legal mobilisation? It is important to stress that the reforms are relatively recent, in many cases they have been resisted by judicial 'operators', and in some cases have inevitably created inter-institutional rivalries. Notably, the Supreme Court has viewed with considerable distrust and jealousy the creation of a Constitutional Tribunal that has stripped it of many of its review powers.

The Constitutional Tribunal The Constitutional Tribunal (CT) is one of the more important innovations in the judicial system. Following the 1994 constitutional reforms, and the 1998 Regulatory Law (Law no.1836), the CT came into being in June 1999. It is made up of five members appointed for ten-year terms (renewable) with two-thirds vote in Congress.[25]

The CT concentrates constitutional review functions, and acts as supreme guarantor of the Bill of Rights. Its main functions in terms of rights protection and constitutional review include: abstract or constitutional review of laws, decrees and non-judicial resolutions at the request of the president, any member of Congress, the attorney-general or the human rights Ombudsman; constitutional review of tax issues; and attending individual constitutional review claims and *habeas corpus* suits.

The individual constitutional review claim (*recurso de amparo constitucional*) is the closest to the Colombian *tutela* (see Uprimny's chapter in this volume), but by no means amounts to the same degree of protection or accessibility. Only in the case of *habeas corpus* does the claimant not require the presence of a lawyer, and all other claims need to follow strict formalistic procedures, and to have exhausted prior administrative or judicial remedies. Moreover, despite important cases on some rights issues, the Bolivian CT has by no means consciously developed the type of pro-poor judicial activism we find in the Indian, Colombian or South African cases. To some extent, to the degree that it has had to engage with potentially controversial social and economic rights issues, this somewhat reflects the 'judicial activism' pushed by the human rights Ombudsman.

In this regard, the fact that the human rights Ombudsman can file direct or abstract actions to test the constitutionality of laws and other acts of power in its own right, as well as on behalf of individual claimants as regards individual constitutional review claims and *habeas corpus*, has been of considerable importance.[26] Given the early forceful drive of the Ombudsman's office towards encouraging both legal mobilisation strategies by citizens and pro-poor judicial activism in the CT, its role in this regard has been highly significant. At the same time, the Ombudsman's office claims to have deliberately chosen *not* to resort to frequent active participation in presenting constitutional suits on behalf of individual claimants, taking the line that this should not be its main role, and that citizens need to be instructed through legal advice and information as to how to mobilise themselves legally and present their own claims to court.[27] Up to and including 2003, the Ombudsman's office had presented 30 cases of constitutional review, selected somewhat on the basis of their public interest value in promoting public debate and awareness of certain rights, and in pushing constitutional jurisprudence to its limit on these. The Ombudsman has reported that in 18 of these cases the CT ruled in favour of the claimants presented by the Ombudsman's office; in three cases, partially in favour; in seven cases, against; and, at the time of the report, two cases were pending.[28] While the report does not enter into details, advances were made in respect of the following rights: maintaining due process during states of emergency;[29] the right to life and to health (on haemodialysis and HIV treatment); civil liberties and political rights; and freedom of speech.[30]

If we look at the CT, it appears on the whole not of its own will to have promoted progressive or pro-poor judicial activism. On the other hand, its rulings represent a timid but important break with the past in terms of a visibly greater commitment to rights protection through constitutional review. Secondly, its jurisprudence marks important *garantiste* and in some cases pro-poor decisions on a number of rights issues.[31]

First, the CT has been most active on civil liberties and due process, especially regarding practices in criminal justice. To name a few significant examples: early on it developed jurisprudence to correct a long-standing tradition of illegal detentions by the police.[32] Also, the court has ruled to dismiss a criminal justice case in its entirety in which the defendant had not had access to a public defence lawyer.[33] More recently, following the political violence in February 2003, in a confrontation between the military and members of the police force who were demonstrating over a controversial tax issue, which resulted in a number of casualties, the CT ruled that in matters of human rights violations the military were subject to civilian, and not military jurisdiction.[34] Given Bolivia's appalling record on civil rights and due process, and a tradition of judicial 'negligence' in this regard in the past, these rulings are no small achievement, especially in recent times as democratic governments have increasingly resorted to repressive measures in their endeavours to face down growing social unrest.

On social and economic rights, there is no consensus on how 'active' the CT has been of its own will. Nonetheless, a number of rulings have established progressive jurisprudence on some social rights, notably regarding labour and health, but significantly not regarding pensions, following the privatisation of the public pension scheme in the 1990s, which left a sector of society unprotected. Regarding the right to health, the most important cases (ten in total) have to do with haemodialysis treatment. Here the CT has not only ruled in favour of the claimants, but has done so in recognition of the right to health, in its connection to the right to life.[35] It is important to stress the role of the Ombudsman in raising the public profile of these cases, which may have acted to push the CT in the direction of progressive rulings. On labour rights, the CT has also ruled progressively with regard to public sector employees subjected to being moved to lower-paid positions as a result of changing political conditions. In Bolivia, typically with each new political appointment at any level of the public sector, there tends to follow the hiring of the politically loyal, and the firing of employees taken on by the previous occupant. The CT has ruled that moving an employee to another position is acceptable, but not at the cost of a diminished salary.[36]

These cases are important and should not be underrated. But some caveats need to be noted. First, where the limits of the constitutional jurisprudence are felt is both in its scope and, it seems, in the effectiveness of ensuring compliance.[37] Here, returning to Gloppen's framework, the effect of judicial action is also limited by broader questions of compliance, and state capacity (and/or political will) to enforce legal decisions. Secondly, the CT has not of its own accord pushed for socially progressive judicial activism. Notably, it recently rejected a claim of unconstitutionality regarding the privatisation laws of the 1990s put forward by the MAS (left-wing party) in what was considered as an important blow to and attempt to challenge through legal means the neo-liberal economic model that has been in place since 1985.[38] It appears that the CT is not married to a pro-poor agenda as a guiding principle. This may, however, reflect legal caution rather than political preference. Thirdly, given procedural difficulties in resorting to judicial review, claimants whose cases reach the CT are unlikely to come from the poorest or more vulnerable groups in society. Here we come back to the problem of access mentioned above. Fourthly, although this is a broader issue to do with how to manage the role of judges generally in taking decisions that affect public policy and resource allocation, it is worth noting the extremely precarious nature and small size of Bolivia's public finances, so that a handful of rulings on expensive health treatments can result in what could arguably seem a disproportionate claim on an already under-funded health budget to the detriment of perhaps a larger number of equally or more vulnerable individuals. (This issue is discussed at a theoretical level elsewhere in this volume.)

In any event, it should be noted that the CT is still a very recent creation, and, to date, has established for itself a relatively unblemished reputation of autonomy and juridical integrity – in contrast to past practices at other levels of the judiciary.[39] Moreover, while the political left views it with suspicion, it is not irrelevant that resorting to the occasional constitutional claim also features now as one of the political strategies of the main left-wing and indigenous party, the MAS. This suggests a degree of credibility regarding the CT, which is in stark contrast to the traditional image of the Supreme Court and other branches of the judiciary, and signifies no small feat in the process of rule-of-law construction. And finally, its rulings on some rights issues indeed mark a step towards promoting a culture of rights and due process that has clearly been lacking in Bolivian political history.

We now turn to the human rights Ombudsman.

The Defensoría del Pueblo *– Human Rights Ombudsman*

The human rights Ombudsman's office was created with the 1994 constitutional reform, its regulatory law passed in 1997, and the first *Defensora* was appointed in 1998. There is no doubt that the Ombudsman has been the most effective of the reforms in terms of advancing a rights culture and promoting active citizenship.

The Ombudsman is appointed by a two-thirds majority in Congress for a period of five years, renewable for one additional term. The role of the Ombudsman is to protect and promote human rights in a number of ways. It can investigate and denounce violations of human rights at the hands of public or state authorities, and make corresponding recommendations. It acts as an oversight agency to ensure that the public sector carries out its functions regarding respect for citizens' rights and delivery of services. The Ombudsman can take cases of unconstitutionality to the

CT in its own right, but can also act in the name of third parties before the courts in individual constitutional review claims. The Ombudsman can propose changes to laws, decrees and non-judicial resolutions regarding human rights issues. It can promote the adoption of international norms regarding human rights and oversee their corresponding implementation. It can also monitor whether the state meets its commitments regarding recognition of and respect for legal pluralism. Finally, the human rights Ombudsman's office informs the public about rights issues, and provides advice and guidance on legal and administrative processes.[40] The Ombudsman presents annual reports of its activity to Congress. These to date, in contrast to reports submitted by other public agencies, reflect a commitment to transparency in how it operates, and an endeavour to report and collect data on the work and findings of the Ombudsman's office.

The Ombudsman in Bolivia has been especially pro-active, and to some extent has exceeded its original mandate. Within a very short space of time it established itself as a forceful, independent oversight agency, with a progressive pro-poor agenda structured around an inclusive and culturally sensitive rights-based notion of citizenship. In large measure this relative 'success' is linked to the personality of the first Ombudsman, Ana Maria Romero Campero, an independent, experienced and respected journalist. In the fulfilment of its oversight functions, the ombudsman's office has become a novel channel for articulating rights-based claims at the individual but also broader social level. Moreover, it has devoted its energies not only to denouncing wrongdoing, but also to actively encouraging public debate on rights issues.

Some specific achievements include: first, that the Ombudsman's office has taken an active role in articulating *and* facilitating voice on rights-based grievances across all the different groups of rights. Secondly, it has endeavoured to activate and publicise the different complaints services it offers for the public. Between 1998 and 2002, the Ombudsman dealt with 27,448 cases.[41] Although its recommendations are not binding, nonetheless they give backing to complaints that would otherwise go unheeded. Here it is interesting to note that compliance regarding its recommendations on behalf of the public authorities at issue has not been negligible, averaging according to the Ombudsman's office's calculation around 65–70 per cent[42] Thirdly, it has been active in the promotion of a rights culture, through a wide range of imaginative and resourceful publicity and awareness campaigns and training programs, and by providing information on rights. It has actively sought to make itself accessible to vulnerable sectors of society on specific rights issues. It has sought to establish an enabling network of activities and support for a range of themes and organisations, such as women's rights movements, the National Plan on the Prevention and Eradication of Domestic Violence, protecting prostitutes from harassment by the police, encouraging the development of a political programme on indigenous rights, providing support to landless *campesinos* (rural workers), and actively monitoring children's rights, with special regard for street children.[43]

In addition, the Ombudsman's office under the direction of Ana Maria Romero (although this has subsided under the second Ombudsman in office since 2003) undertook the role of mediator and conciliator in times of escalating political and social unrest between different political and social groups prior to the October 2003 events which resulted in the president's early resignation.

Finally, it carries out its own unprompted investigations on particular areas of abuse or where certain rights are problematic. A striking example of this is its report on the deficiencies of the land courts, a new judicial body created in a Land Reform law of 1996, and which are part of a broader land reform measure to 'tidy up' rural land titling.[44] The Ombudsman report is a damning indictment of the entire land reform structure including the new land court system, in terms of its detrimental impact on land rights for the poorer sectors of the rural population.[45] The importance of this kind of investigation cannot be overstated, given the central place of land rights and holdings for a rural population which combines extreme conditions of poverty and marginality.[46]

The Ombudsman's office, therefore, has become not only a formidable oversight agency that other public authorities cannot lightly dismiss, such as had not existed in the past in Bolivia, but has contributed actively towards providing a dynamic and pro-poor channel for legal voice on *all* rights issues. In no small way has it contributed, then, to a broader process of discursive and political transformation in which rights and the law are being appropriated by grass-roots social movements and individual citizens. Through its promotion of a rights culture, and legal mobilisation, it has also pushed a number of rights issues onto the public agenda as a matter of public interest. Thus the Bolivian experience shows that pro-poor judicial processes can be enabled outside the courts through such agencies as the human rights Ombudsman.

This, in turn, has been possible because the creation of the Ombudsman coincided with that of the Constitutional Tribunal, which came into being a year later. It may be that the CT, as suggested above, was pushed in directions it may have preferred to avoid by the Ombudsman. At the same time, the CT provided a useful legal 'structure of opportunity' for the Ombudsman to flex its muscles. Secondly, the Ombudsman was well-received by a population already well on its way to embracing a culture of rights, in part also articulated, albeit in complex ways, by new social-cum-political movements vying for a place in the political power structures, and espousing a radical and socially transformative political agenda based on rights.

The political setting has paradoxically allowed for the creation of these new legal and quasi-legal institutions through the 1994 constitutional reforms, which in turn have become powerful limiting bodies on political action. This raises the complex question as to what prompts political bodies voluntarily to strengthen control mechanisms that constrain their power.[47] In the Bolivian case, 'self-restraining' state reforms carried out during the 1990s were the consequence of a combination of political calculations and pressures. These ranged from the need to boost political legitimacy and electoral appeal by the ruling coalitions, to responding to pressures (and tempting funding offers) by the international donor community; to probably also underestimating and miscalculating the impact of the institutions that were being created (not always mistakenly).

In this case, once activated, the Ombudsman has generated considerable discomfort in the traditional ruling political parties, to the extent that they have tried to rein in the institution. This reached grotesque proportions in 2003, when the Ombudsman's office was up for renewal, alternatively, a new appointment. The executive, under President Gonzalo Sanchez de Lozada (ironically the office had been created during his first presidential administration), went to great lengths to secure a two-thirds majority in Congress to ensure that Romero Campero's mandate would not be renewed, and to appoint a politically compliant new Ombudsman, even in the face of public opposition. The new appointment, Ivan Zegada, remained in office for only a few days, and was one more contributing factor to the social protests in October of that year that forced Sanchez de Lozada to leave office just over one year into his presidency. A less controversial candidate was then found, and achieved the consensus of most political parties.

Overall, the Ombudsman has contributed to changing social attitudes regarding rights, and has opened up new channels for the articulation of grievances regarding rights and other areas of wrongdoing in public office. It has made a point of making itself accessible to the public, and has through its actions touched sensitive nerves in the power structures of Bolivia, both through its denunciations of civil rights violations, but also in its active promotion of pro-poor rights litigation which, in some cases (land rights issues, for instance, in the eastern lowlands, where there has been a growing process of reconcentration of land holdings in the hands of the local elite) have prompted angry political backlash. At the same time, the Ombudsman's office has been deliberately careful to defend its political autonomy, not only from parties in power, but also from opposition groupings.

Multiculturalism and Legal Pluralism

Finally, the chapter turns to the question of multi-culturalism and the pluri-ethnic nature of Bolivian society, and its impact on discourses of rights-based social transformation. Any process of social change through rights must pass through an understanding of the cultural and ethnical diversity of this population, in which legal pluralism has featured *de facto* since colonial times. Assessments of how rights have progressed, therefore, cannot be remitted to classical liberal conceptions of rights sequencing (for instance, following Marshall's classic study on citizenship[48]). In Bolivia, where 60 per cent of the population has an indigenous identity, notions of citizenship are textured by indigenous community structures of power, authority and conflict resolution, and also by intercultural dynamics of identity, and relations of domination between different ethnic groups.

In these conditions, especially where social exclusion coincides closely with ethnic cleavages, there are culturally diverse understandings of social transformation which need to be taken into account. The Amazonic indigenous communities in the eastern lowlands have a different conception of, for instance, land rights and territory, and will pursue protective strategies, say against encroachment on community territory by cattle ranchers. This is very different from the perspective on citizenship and social transformation of a highland *aymara* small land-holder (with community ties to notions of property, but property nonetheless) on the Andean highplain. And again this will contrast with the coca producer of *quechua* origin in the central valleys, ideologically connected to the Marxist roots of the miners' union radical tradition (many unemployed tin miners have turned to coca production), but now organised also around the identity politics of indigenous rights, as well as *campesino* (rural worker) land claims. There is a blossoming literature on the politics of legal pluralism, citizenship and indigenous rights.[49] This chapter will not engage with the complexity of these issues, but merely stress the point that concepts of citizenship *and* social transformation are also culturally determined.

This needs to be located within three parallel but inter-related processes of political mobilisation, and the emergence of a rights-based discourse of social transformation. First, since the late 1970s Bolivia has seen the emergence of identity politics as an important strand of political mobilisation among Andean rural workers, moving away from assimilationist models of social transformation through class struggle, towards a culturally informed political discourse of rural workers' demands increasingly centred around identity and also land. The Amazonic indigenous communities, with different demands about territory and land, began to organise during the 1990s. Under different and successive political and rural worker union formations, indigenous movements have mobilised politically, and during the 1990s have achieved important electoral gains resulting, for instance, in the MAS becoming the second political force in the election of 2002. Electoral politics are combined with street protest mobilisation strategies. Indigenous claims are therefore now a prominent feature of the political landscape.

Secondly, these new movements have both benefited from, and prompted, the various institutional and constitutional reforms during the 1990s which formally acknowledge multi-culturalism as a feature of Bolivian society, and have become incorporated into the institutional structures of power and definition of rights – at least on paper. This, in turn, has provided further opportunity structures for indigenous political formations to flourish. The four main reforms that have absorbed the principles of cultural and ethnic diversity are: the 1994 Law of Popular Participation, a measure of municipal decentralisation; the 1994 constitutional reform, which acknowledges the 'multi-ethnic and pluri-cultural' nature of Bolivian society (article 1), and establishes the basis for a later legislative formalisation of legal pluralism and recognition of indigenous rights (article 171); the new criminal justice code, which recognises indigenous forms of criminal justice resolution; and the controversial 1996 Land Reform Law which nonetheless acknowledges culturally diverse forms of land holding. These are important legal and constitutional innovations which give room for potentially far-reaching processes of social transformation within the context of culturally diverse understandings of justice and rights. For now the impact of these changes is unclear, and to a large extent is also dependent on how the forthcoming Constituent Assembly develops.

The third related process has to do with the international 'rights revolution' regarding cultural rights in the context of the global drive towards rights-based democratisation. Following the ILO 169 Convention in 1989, changes in the international discourse and legal instruments regarding indigenous rights provide a supportive and enabling transnational environment for the claims of identity politics to flourish in the form of demands for indigenous rights and recognition of cultural diversity in how power relations are structured. Indigenous rights-discourses from below demand that contemporary democratic processes be sensitive to cultural diversity.[50] And in large measure this is at the root of much of the recent political conflict in Bolivia, as dominant power structures from above are resistant to change. It is clear that the courts, given the levels of political and social polarisation reached, will not be able to clear the conflict at hand. It is also evident that social transformation as articulated in sub-altern discourses in Bolivia now includes multi-cultural understandings of citizenship and rights

Conclusion

If we return to Gloppen's framework, what do these features of constitutional change and social mobilisation in Bolivia tell us about the direction of social and economic rights litigation and the capacity of the justice system to enable social transformation? First, as has been noted elsewhere in this volume, we need to be modest in our expectations about what courts can achieve in terms of substantive change in power structures in any society. The impression is that progressive litigation can have a piecemeal and cumulative effect in contributing towards transformative processes, and this may even be far-reaching. But in general terms its impact needs to be assessed in most cases against the broader context of shifting normative values in any society, changing political structures and forms of political conflict, and new opportunities for innovative social change – all the complex processes that social theory in its diverse variants has sought to come to terms with. Having said this, experiences in democracies in the last fifty years indicate that litigation and legal mobilisation can be a contributing factor to social change not least because it also forms part of the complex web of power structures and regulating institutions that order societies. Moreover, its weight will also reflect changing societal perceptions regarding what the role of different state institutions should be, and which ones should be prominent in allocating values and resources. In the current context of democratic 'deficits' everywhere, where representative institutions are discredited (parliaments, parties, and so on), hopes and aspirations for social change seem increasingly to be turned towards rights and law, and therefore also, rights-protecting institutions – namely, the courts – for now.

Turning to Bolivia, overall, social transformation is not being pioneered by the courts. Nonetheless, there are important changes taking place at almost all the stages that Gloppen identifies in her framework. And this coincides with a dramatic moment of regime crisis.

Regarding voice, there continue to be problems of access and distrust with legal proceedings. Interestingly, though, voice is increasingly channelled through the Ombudsman's office, which is playing an important role in facilitating the development of a rights-based political culture. Moreover, it actively promotes an inclusive notion of rights that accommodates social and economic rights, as well as indigenous rights at the same level as civil and political rights. And this has found resonance in a bottom-up appropriation of an emanicipatory discourse of rights by new social movements (including, but not only, indigenous movements). Increasing social and economic rights litigation is not a specific outcome of this, but the emancipatory potential of rights and the law is now a feature of sub-altern notions of social transformation, at least at an aspirational level. And the maximum expression of this lies – rightly or wrongly – in the expectations surrounding the forthcoming constituent assembly which will draft a foundational charter. This is in contrast to a traditional distrust of the law by the left in the past (as Couso rightly reminds us in his chapter).

Regarding receptiveness by courts, there is no doubt that the judicial reforms of the 1990s have had an impact on how rights cases are processed, especially in the new Constitutional Tribunal. Overall, though, courts have not pioneered progressive judicial activism, and their approach has been that of passive 'receiver' of claims. Nonetheless some important rulings have established novel jurisprudence on social and economic rights in some areas. There is also the continuing perception (in some cases with supporting evidence) that lower-level courts and the land courts have been captured by political and economic interests.

The capacity of the system to process demands has improved with reforms (to do with access and court administration, but also significant increases in resources). Finally, compliance with court rulings is not evidently straightforward. Judicial sentences in Sucre (which houses the main judicial bodies – the Supreme Court and the Constitutional Tribunal) are unlikely to carry much weight in the Beni backwaters of cattle farming land, where strongman tactics of intimidation by far outweigh the state's capacity (and in some cases, will) for law enforcement.

Several factors form the backdrop to these processes. First, over the last 20 years, Bolivia has undergone important institutional and constitutional changes, including reforms in the judicial sector and recognition of legal pluralism, albeit with limited results. Secondly, these have not sufficed to reform habits of impunity in office, which, together with the failings of the economic model, have led to a growing crisis of regime legitimacy. Thirdly, and in part linked to the experience of both democratic opening but also the subsequent legitimacy crisis, changing structures of political mobilisation through new social movements have led to new modes of political discourse with more explicit allusion than in previous democratic endeavours in Bolivia to rights entitlements as the basis for social transformation. This signals a newfound confidence in the transformatory potential of legal forms, and the law.

Notes

1 Boaventura de Sousa Santos, *Toward a New Legal Common Sense* (London: Butterworth LexisNexis Group, 2002), Guillermo O'Donnell, 'Notas sobre la Democracia en America Latina', in *El Debate Conceptual sobre la Democracia* (PNUD, 2004).

2 See Catalina Smulovitz and Enrique Peruzzotti, 'Societal and Horizontal Control: Two Cases of a Fruitful Relationship', in Scott Mainwaring and Christopher Welna, *Democratic Accountability in Latin America* (Oxford, Oxford University Press, 2003), pp. 309–32 for a discussion of societal accountability.

3 UNDP, 'Informe de Desarrollo Humano en Bolivia' (2002) reports Bolivia's human development index in 1999 at 0.648 in contrast to the average for Latin America with 0.760.

4 UNDP, 'Informe de Desarrollo Humano en Bolivia' (2002).

5 Poverty is higher among the indigenous population both in rural and urban areas. In 2002 rural and urban poverty were higher among the indigenous population: 86 per cent in indigenous population against 74 per cent non-indigenous, in the rural areas, and 59 per cent compared to 47 per cent in urban areas. Moreover, extreme poverty has increased among the indigenous population between 1997 and 2002. See World Bank, 'Bolivia: Datos Destacados. Pueblos Indígenas, Pobreza y Desarrollo Humano en América Latina 1994-2004' (Washington: World Bank, 2005).

6 See essays in Merilee Grindle and Pilar Domingo (eds), *Proclaiming Revolution: Bolivia in Comparative Perspective* (Cambridge, MA: ILAS/Harvard University Press, 2003).

7 His presidency ended after a month of protest and repressive measures resulting in 60 deaths. The protests were sparked off by the intention to export nature gas to the US and Mexico through Chile, in the context of a gas law which has been perceived as favourable only for the gas companies. See Willem Assies, 'Bolivia: A Gasified Democracy'; *Revista Europea de Estudios Latinoamericanos y del Caribe,* 76 (2004): 25–43.

8 Assies, 'Bolivia: A Gasified Democracy'.

9 See Willem Assies and Ton Salman, *Crisis in Bolivia: The Elections of 2002 and their Aftermath* (London: ILAS, 2003).

10 Germán Burgos, 'Hacia un Estado de Derecho? Relato de un Viaje Inconcluso', in Joan Prats (ed.), *El Desarrollo Posible, las Instituciones Necesarias* (Barcelona: IIG, 2003), pp. 225–308; Eduardo Gamarra, *The System of Justice in Bolivia: An Institutional Análisis* (Miami: Centre for the Administration of Justice, 1991); Eduardo Rodriguez 'Legal Security in Bolivia', in John Crabtree and Laurence Whitehead (eds), *Towards Democratic Viability: The Bolivian Experience* (Houndmills: Palgrave, 2001).

11 Carlos A. Pelaez, 'Incorporación de Tecnología Informática a la Gestión Jusridiccional y Administrativa en el Poder Judicial Boliviano', manuscript (2002).

12 Burgos, 'Hacia un Estado de Derecho?'. Overall, this is one of the most complete recent works on the Bolivian judiciary. Scholarly research on judicial politics in Bolivia is

scarce, and until recently data was lacking, and where it existed unreliable. Recent reforms have amongst other things sought to improve data management through new technology. See Pelaez, 'Incorporación de Tecnología Informática; Defensor del Pueblo *V Informe Annual al H. Congreso Nacional* (La Paz, 2003) calculates that since 1990 the number of courts has increased by 60 per cent.

13 Burgos, 'Hacia un Estado de Derecho?' and Mikel Barreda and Joan Prats, *Perfil de Gobernabilidad de Bolivia* (Barcelona: IIG, 2004).

14 CAJPE. In 2001 the Ministry of Justice claimed that 160 public defence officers had provided assistance to 54 per cent of criminal justice defendants, marking an important improvement from the past, see PNUD Informe de Desarrollo Humano en Bolivia, p.122.

15 Burgos, 'Hacia un Estado de Derecho?'

16 Ibid.

17 CAJPE (Comisión Andina de Justicia Penal) *La Reforma Judicial en la Región Andina,* (2000), and Burgos, 'Hacia un Estado de Derecho?'.

18 Defensor del Pueblo, *V Informe Annual al H. Congreso Nacional* (La Paz, 2003).

19 It is interesting to note that later annual reports from the ombudsman's office do not register ethnicity indicators.

20 Defensor del Pueblo, *V Informe Annual.*

21 See Rodriguez, 'Legal Security in Bolivia'. The perception of a 'captured' judicial power, moreover, is likely to outlive the reality. In the light of recent reforms it is expected that some positive impact will have produced itself, but perceptions are likely to change at a slower rate.

22 Rodriguez, 'Legal Security in Bolivia'.

23 Law 1970, 1999.

24 See <www.cajpe.org.pe/RIJ/BASES/REFORMA/bol.htm>, and CAJPE generally, and Burgos, 'Hacia un Estado de Derecho?' and PNUD, 'Informe de Desarrollo Humano en Bolivia', p. 122.

25 The requirements are the same as those for a member of the Supreme Court, namely: 35 years of age, no criminal record, to hold a law degree and have practised the profession for at least ten years. The appointments mechanism to the Supreme Court has also changed from a system requiring an absolute majority of votes in the lower chamber from a list of nominations drawn up by the Senate to a necessary two-thirds vote in Congress.

26 See Law 1836 of 1998 on the CT and Law 1818 of 1997 on the Ombudsman.

27 See the Defensor del Pueblo, *V Informe Annual,* pp. 42–4.

28 Defensor del Pueblo, *V Informe Annual.*

29 This is relevant given the frequency with which, since 1985 and the implementation of economic liberalisation, escalating social protest has been put down through states of emergency, with growing incidences of violence ultimately resulting in the resignation of the President Sanchez de Lozada in 2003, in this case following excessive use of force.

30 It is also important to point to earlier annual reports by the Ombudsman where the view was that the CT was not responding favourably overall on social and economic rights claims.

31 See José Antonio Rivera Santibáñez, 'La Doctrina Constitucional en la Jurisprudencia del Tribunal Constitucional' (Tribunal Constitucional de Bolivia, 2003); Uggla, 'The

Ombudsman in Latin America', www.cajpe.org.pe/rij/bases/juris-nac/esquemabo.HTM; Defensor del Pueblo, *V Informe Annual*.

32 CT sentences 313/99-R, 421/99-R, 431/99-R and 092/00-R.

33 CT sentence 0305/2003

34 CT sentence 663/2004-R.

35 CT sentence 411/2000-R and 687/2000-R.

36 CT sentence 310/2000-R.

37 On rulings regarding haemodialysis treatment, there is a least one case (from the author's interviews with jurists) where the corresponding authority did not comply with the continuation of the treatment. According to one jurist this was also a reflection of the fact that the constitutional resolution did not specifically provide details on measures to be taken – in contrast to later rulings on the same issue. (CT Sentence 411/2000-R.) By contrast, the official line is that all CT jurisprudence is binding and must result in the corresponding corrective action being taken by the relevant public authority. See Willman R. Duran Ribera, 'La Fuerza Vinculante de las Resoluciones del Tribunal Constitucional' (Tribunal Constitucional de Bolivia, 2003).

38 See <www.tribunalconstitucional.gov.bo/article207.html>. Also on the privatisation of the pension scheme the CR has not ruled progressively. By contrast, in the first quarter of 2005 (a particularly convulsive period in great measure due to the social protests in favour of renationalising Bolivia's gas production), the CT declared that existing contracts with the transnational gas companies may not have been fully validated by the required congressional approval, thus weakening their claims to bring the Bolivian state before an international arbitration panel. See *La Prensa*, 9 May 2005.

39 Author's interviews with jurists and political analysts attest to this in no small measure. If anything, a growing concern is that the CT tribunal does not sufficiently bear in mind political and economic conditions.

40 Law 1818, which regulates the Ombudsman. See also Burgos, 'Hacia un Estado de Derecho?', and the PNUD, *Informe de Desarrollo Humano: Bolivia 2002*; Mark Ungar, 'Human rights in the Andes: The Defensoría del Pueblo', in Jo-Marie Burt and Philip Mauceri (eds), *Politics in the Andes: Identity, Conflict, Reform* (Pittsburgh: Pittsburgh University Press, 2004), pp. 164–86; and Fredrik Uggla, 'The Ombudsman in Latin America', *Journal of Latin American Studies*, 36 (2004): 423–50.

41 Defensor del Pueblo, *V Informe Annual*.

42 Uggla, 'The Ombudsman in Latin America'. Also in the Defensor del Pueblo, *IV Informe Annual* provides information on compliance by the different authorities. It is interesting to note that later reports do not provide this data.

43 Defensor del Pueblo, *V Informe Annual* (2003); Defensor del Pueblo, *IV Informe Annual* (2002); and Defensor del Pueblo, *III Informe Annual* (2001)

44 Defensor del Pueblo, *Informe Especial: Los Derechos a la Propiedad y la Tenencia de la Tierra y el Proceso de Saneamiento* (La Paz, 2003).

45 This chapter does not dwell on the land courts, but mention needs to be made of the recent land reform because of the importance of land rights for social transformation purposes, given that the rural population is still as high as 40 per cent, but concentrates the worst indices of poverty and marginality. The 1996 Land Reform Law (Ley INRA), was an attempt to revamp the remains of the 1953 land reform. The new agrarian structure in principle is designed to resolve the titling mess of the past, and within a framework which acknowledges culturally distinctive forms of land holdings (communal lands, and recognition of indigenous territorial claims, notably), and pre-

empts on paper – but not in reality – reconcentration of large land-holdings. It carries out its tasks through a number of institutions, principally the Instituto de Reforma Agraria (one of whose main tasks is to clean up land titles for rural property), and a judicial framework of land courts organised under the National Land Tribunal. In reality both the Institute and the land courts are perceived as ineffective and especially vulnerable to corruption and cooptation by powerful interests of large landholders. In terms of social transformation, not only have land rights not progressed for poorer rural sectors, but in some respects they have been further weakened by the deficient and vitiated development of the INRA and the land courts. The consensus on this is widespread. At the same time, though, data is extremely unreliable regarding rural land issues, and the impact of the land courts on social transformation remains understudied. See Defensor del Pueblo, *Informe Especial* and also Oscar del Álamo, 'Bolivia Indígena y Campesina: Un Panorama de Conflictos e Identidades', in Prats, *El Desarrollo Posible*, pp. 539–98.

46 PNUD and Oscar del Álamo, 'Bolivia Indígena y Campesina'.

47 See, for insightful discussions on this, Stephen Holmes, 'Lineages of the Rule of Law', in Jose Maria Maravall and Adam Przeworski (eds), *Democracy and the Rule of Law*, (Cambridge: Cambridge University Press, 2003), pp. 19–61, and the chapters in Andreas Schedler, Larry Diamond and Mark Plattner (eds), *The Self-restraining State* (Boulder: Lynne Reiner, 1999).

48 T.H. Marshall and Tom Bottomore, *Citizenship and Social Class* (London: Pluto Press, 1991).

49 See, for insightful discussions on the issues, Xavier Albo, 'Como Manejar la Interculturalidad Juridica en un Pais Intercultural?', in Instituto de la Judicatura de Bolivia (ed.), *Justicia Comunitaria en los Pueblos Originarios de Bolivia* (Sucre: IJB, 2003), pp. 85–115 and Rene Orellana Halkyer, 'Practicas Judiciales en Comunidades Indígenas Quechuas', in Instituto de la Judicatura de Bolivia (ed.), *Justicia Comunitaria*, pp. 11–41; Willem Assies, 'El Constitucionalismo Multi-étnico en América Latina: El Caso de Bolivia', XII Congreso Internacional 'Derechos Consuetudinario y Pluralismo Legal: Desafíos en el Tercer Milenio' (Chile, 2000); and Donna Lee van Cott, 'A Political Analysis of Legal Pluralism in Bolivia and Colombia', *Journal of Latin American Studies*, 32 (2000): 207–34.

50 See essays in Rachel Sieder (ed.), *Multiculturalism in Latin America* (London: Palgrave, 2002) and in Willem Assies, Gemma van der Haar and André Hoekma (eds), *The Challenge of Diversity: Indigenous Peoples and Reform of the State in Latin America* (Amsterdam: Thela Thesis, 2000).

Courts, Rights and Social Transformation: Concluding Reflections

Roberto Gargarella, Pilar Domingo and Theunis Roux

The Rise of Judicially Enforced Social Rights

The case studies in this volume are drawn from four very different parts of the world – Latin America, Eastern Europe, Africa and Asia – and yet they indicate that the last fifteen years have seen a significant turn towards judicially enforced social rights. This phenomenon is all the more remarkable when one considers that, in 1990, the debate about the judicial enforcement of social rights was mostly hypothetical. Today, that debate has moved on to the point where the wisdom of giving judges the power to enforce social rights is no longer seriously questioned, at least in the four regions studied. Instead, sociologists, political scientists and lawyers alike are grappling with a common set of questions about the practical effect of justiciable social rights, and the potential of such rights to deliver on the promise of social transformation through law.

Two of the chapters in this book, in particular, throw some light on the reasons behind this development. Couso's chapter, for one, paints a convincing picture of the trajectory followed by social rights in Latin America, from their initial rejection by the left to the point today where they are beginning to be taken seriously. Confronted by the stark reality of failed socialist states and the traumatic experience of military rule, the Latin American left in Couso's view became more reformist, looking to examples of rights-based strategies elsewhere in the world for a model of how to use the law to drive social change. At the same time, ideology in Latin America, far from dying, became the preserve of neo-classical economists, resulting in the curious contest Couso describes between, on the one hand, progressive groups using social rights as legally encoded economic precepts, and, on the other, technocrats convinced of the rightness of their presently ascendant economic theory.

In what is almost a mirror image of these developments, Sajó's chapter shows how social rights were retained in the Hungarian Constitution because of the political impossibility of abandoning the communist welfare state. In Central and Eastern Europe, of course, social rights had been around for a long time. In the absence of an independent judiciary, however, their potential was just that: a latent energy waiting to be released. When it eventually occurred, the judicial enforcement of social rights in Eastern Europe had unexpected results. Far from acting as agents of social transformation, social rights in Hungary and other post-communist countries have been used to defend key aspects of the old welfare system against market reforms.

In South Africa, although not raised in Dugard and Roux's chapter, a corresponding story may be told. As late as February 1990, the African National Congress (ANC) was still advocating nationalisation of the means of production,[1] a view that made the enforcement of individual rights by an independent judiciary seem almost unthinkable. Today, in a remarkable turnaround, the 1996 South African Constitution contains a comprehensive set of social rights that is regarded as among the most far-reaching in the world. The reasons behind this development are complex and still disputed. However, the conventional wisdom now seems to be that, as soon as it became clear that a constitution on the liberal model was the inevitable cost of transition, the ANC insisted on the inclusion of social rights as a counter to civil and political rights.[2] As was the case in Latin America, therefore, the rise of social rights in South Africa seems to be attributable to the peculiar balance of power between left and right at the beginning of the 1990s. In this period, the uncertainty created by the collapse of communism persuaded many on the left that the cause of human emancipation would be best pursued in the language of humans rights, albeit suitably modified to reflect the left's traditional concerns with market failure and the public provision of basic goods.[3]

Whether one agrees with this explanation or not, it cannot completely account for the rise of judicially enforced social rights over the last fifteen years since social rights have not only been enforced, but have also thus far defied predictions that their enforcement would prove politically disastrous for the courts concerned. That these predictions have turned out to be wrong is all the more interesting in view of the fact that social rights have been enforced most readily in new or fragile democracies, where the judicial branch has typically not had the time to build the legitimacy required to survive political conflict, and where the resources needed to implement social rights are typically fewer than elsewhere. How has this come about, and why is social rights litigation in practice, if not exactly flourishing, at least now a subject worthy of serious study? The answer, the contributions to this book suggest, lies partly in various theoretical weaknesses in the sceptics' case, and partly in the legal, political and global context in which the judicial enforcement of social rights is being pursued.[4]

The next section of this chapter begins by rehearsing the main theoretical arguments that were made against justiciable social rights before 1990, and then attempts to illustrate how the practice of judicial social rights enforcement over the last fifteen years has shown up certain weaknesses in these arguments. The third section goes on to dissect 'the anatomy of social rights litigation', using Gloppen's chapter as a framework for assessing what our case studies tell us about the capacity of the poor to use social rights as a vehicle for social transformation. The next section reflects on what we now know about the specific legal procedures that have in practice contributed to successful social rights litigation. In addition to these procedures, judges themselves have invented various devices, on the one hand to overcome their assumed lack of institutional means, and on the other to avoid potential conflict with the political branches. This is the subject of the fifth section. The sixth section changes tack somewhat to reflect more broadly on the politics of social rights litigation, trying to find an answer, beyond mere legal innovations, as to why it is that social rights, like other previously contested rights, are gradually becoming an accepted feature of democratic politics in the countries studied. Finally, the last section, in a deliberate echo of the language used by social rights sceptics, spells out some of the remaining limits on the judicial enforcement of such rights. The important point made in this section is that our understanding of what those limits are has changed considerably over the last fifteen years, from a position where the factors limiting the justiciability of social rights were adduced as reasons for not giving judges the power to enforce these rights, to the position today, where these factors contribute to a realistic, experience-based assessment of what the left can expect to get out of social rights.

Theoretical Problems

In the early theoretical debates three main arguments against the judicial enforcement of social rights were made. First, it was said that social rights were qualitatively different from civil and political rights, and therefore that they were not amenable to judicial enforcement. Secondly, it was contended that the judicial enforcement of social rights was incompatible with the separation of powers. Thirdly, in what really amounted to an elaboration of the second objection, the judicial enforcement of social rights was said to be anti-democratic.

The fact that social rights have been actively enforced in different regions of the world over the last fifteen years, and that the courts in these countries have thus far survived the repercussions of their decisions, suggests that these objections were not well founded. The remainder of this section highlights the contribution that the case studies in this book make to our developing understanding of this issue.

The Claim that Social Rights are Different in Kind to Civil and Political Rights

To the extent that it depended on the idea that social rights are especially costly to enforce, the view that social rights are different in kind to civil and political rights has now been thoroughly discredited. As Holmes and Sunstein have pointed out, 'all rights depend on taxes',[5] and the judicial enforcement of a civil or political right may be just as costly as the enforcement of a social right.[6] The difference is rather that, in many countries, civil and political rights are routinely enforced, so that the cost of enforcing these rights is hidden by the ordinariness of the process by which it occurs. It is only when civil and political rights are taken away (as for example in those countries that deny prisoners the right to vote),[7] or where the infrastructure for the enforcement of civil and political rights does not exist, that the cost of enforcing civil and political rights is revealed.

This point is best illustrated in this book by the chapter by Skaar and Van-Dúnem, who describe a kind of state-of-nature situation in Angola, at least in the provinces, where all rights are equally unenforceable because of a chronic shortage of lawyers and the absence of a functioning court system. In situations like this, to object to the judicial enforcement of social rights because it involves judges in allocating resources seems misplaced. Given the scarcity of resources, almost any judicial order against the state would have this effect.

The alleged difference between the two main categories of rights depends on a further distinction, of course, between 'negative' and 'positive' rights, that is, rights that require the state to refrain from acting, and rights that require the state to act positively in order to fulfil its obligations. It is one thing, this argument goes, to expect judges to prohibit certain types of state conduct, quite another for them to instruct the state to act in particular ways. What if the state refuses to act? How are judges expected to enforce their decisions?

This argument, too, does not survive the simplest of thought experiments. Take the right to freedom of religion, which is a traditional civil right. Is it enough for the state merely to refrain from acting in order to ensure that this right is respected? What if the adherents of a particular religion have historically been subject to discrimination? Does the right to religious freedom in this case not require the state to take positive measures to ensure that the religion's adherents are able to practise their religion without interference? The same questions could be asked about property rights, which require an elaborate system for their maintenance and protection. In truth, most rights are partly negative and partly positive. The attribution of one or the other of these terms to whole categories of rights is really just a function of a priori assumptions about the proper role of the state.

Sajó's chapter is particularly interesting in this regard. As he points out, in Hungary, the Communist Party built an entire system around the protection of social rights, only for those rights to be threatened by post-transition 'austerity' measures. In ruling that some of these measures were unconstitutional, the Hungarian Constitutional Court enforced 'positive' social rights in the same way in which civil and political rights have always been enforced – by ordering the state to refrain from acting. The fact that, to arrive at this order, the Court found it necessary to analogise social rights to civil and political rights (in this case property rights) probably stemmed from the Court's greater familiarity with the negative enforcement of the latter category of rights. There was no reason in principle, however, why social rights should not have been enforced negatively in their own right – a point that has long been recognised in international law.[8]

The Hungarian example, like the Angolan one, illustrates that the nature of the obligations imposed by social rights cannot be determined by resort to the supposedly inherent characteristics of this category of rights. Rather, whether social rights are costly to enforce, and whether they give rise to positive or negative obligations, depends on the type of state action at issue and the extent to which the right has already been fulfilled.

The Claim that the Judicial Enforcement of Social Rights Violates the Separation of Powers Doctrine

According to this claim, when enforcing social rights judges necessarily become involved in allocating resources, and thereby exceed the limits of their role in a constitutional system based on the separation of powers. The first difficulty with this claim has already been canvassed, that is, that the judicial enforcement of civil and political rights also entails the allocation of resources. If this is a problem at all, therefore, it is not a problem unique to social rights.

Acceptance of this point leaves two possibilities: either the separation of powers objection must be raised against supreme-law bills of rights *per se*, or it must be broadened from judicial involvement in the allocation of resources to other instances of alleged judicial overreach. The first possible reformulation of the objection is not addressed in this book since the question we are interested in is not the wisdom and democratic legitimacy of adopting supreme-law bills of rights, but the specific issues raised by the judicial enforcement of social rights.

The second possible way of reformulating the separation of powers objection depends first on an argument about what the proper function of the three branches of government is, and then on the notion that, in enforcing social rights, judges somehow intrude 'too far' into domains of power reserved for the other branches. To sustain their argument, objectors pursuing this second line of attack must first describe the domains of power they claim are reserved for the political branches, and then justify why the judicial branch should not intrude into these domains. To make out a completely convincing case, the objectors need finally to demonstrate why the judicial enforcement of social rights raises particular problems that are not raised by the judicial enforcement of civil and political rights.

The clearest statement of the appropriate limits of the judicial role is contained in Lon L. Fuller's essay, 'The Forms and Limits of Adjudication'.[9] In this essay Fuller posits two main limitations on the judiciary: the fact that judges are generally not democratically elected, and the fact that they lack the institutional means to decide 'polycentric' issues. Both these limits may be rephrased as positive statements of the domains of power typically reserved for the other two branches of government. Because it is chosen directly by the people, the legislative branch is said to have the power to take fundamental decisions (in the form of generally applicable legislation) affecting the way the people are governed, and in particular the sacrifices that individuals are expected to make in favour of the public good. Similarly, the executive branch is said to be especially suited to deciding polycentric issues, tasked as it is with co-ordinating the administration's efforts to implement the ruling party's electoral mandate.

One might raise various quibbles at this stage about whether parliamentarians typically *are* adequately equipped (professionally speaking) to give effect to the people's will in the form of legislation, but no one would seriously object to this broad delineation of the contours of their domain. The weakness in the objectors' case really comes in at the next stage of the argument, when they are required to make out a case for why the judicial branch must not intrude into the political branches' domains of power, or at least why the judicial enforcement of social rights necessarily involves judges in intruding *too far* into those domains. The obvious problem with the first notion is that it depends on a 'pure' or 'strict' conception of the separation of powers doctrine that rarely applies in practice and is seldom defended in theory. In all the examples canvassed in this book, for instance, the countries concerned have adopted constitutional models premised on a system of 'checks and balances' (as opposed to pure separation of powers). This system in fact *requires* the different branches to intrude into each other's domains so as to ensure that the special powers given to each branch are not abused.

Far from being some real-world modification of an ideal theory, the system of checks and balances is best understood as being integral to the very notion of separation of powers, such that the one cannot be said to exist without the other. Thus, in its Madisonian formulation, the primary purpose of 'partition[ing]' power among the three 'departments' of state is to prevent the concentration of power in a single department.[10] The best way of achieving this goal, in turn, is said to be to give 'those who administer each department the necessary constitutional means and personal motives to resist encroachments of the others'.[11] Importantly (because this statement on its own could be understood to favour the objectors' argument), resistance to encroachment in Madison's view does not occur at the margins of each branch's domain of power, but rather through an elaborate system of mutual interference in each other's domains. On this approach, the best way of maintaining a constitutional system based on the separation of powers is to blur those powers so that they are not wholly attributed to one branch or the other.[12] There is no contradiction in this since the instrumental reason behind the separation of powers doctrine, according to Madison, is not to keep the various powers separate, but to prevent one branch of government from dominating the others.

It follows that the mere fact that the judicial enforcement of social rights may and does result in judges interfering in the political branches' domains of power does not constitute a violation of the separation of powers doctrine. On the contrary, for a constitutional system based on this principle to work, judges *must* 'interfere' in the affairs of the other branches – reproaching them for abusing their power, signalling their mistakes, and generally suggesting better alternatives to chosen courses of conduct.

The separation of powers objection to the judicial enforcement of social rights (as distinct from civil and political rights) must therefore rest on the only remaining alternative, viz. the argument that *in practice* the assumption by judges of this power necessarily involves them in violating the separation of powers doctrine. This is an empirical claim that fifteen years' ago might have had some credibility. Today, however, this claim is no longer credible because of the increasing number of instances of judicial social rights enforcement that have not had the predicted result. It is to this growing body of evidence that the case studies in this book hope to contribute.

The Claim that the Judicial Enforcement of Social Rights is Anti-democratic

Judges themselves typically justify their resistance to the enforcement of social rights by resort to arguments from democratic theory. They say that they do not have the mandate required to make certain decisions, or that they do not want to interfere with decisions that the people have already made. However, as Gargarella notes in his contribution, these claims are in many cases based on contradictory or incomplete notions of democracy.[13] In some instances, judges justify their hostility to social rights by pointing to the more traditional (or austere) aspects of the constitution they are enforcing, which they consider incorporate the 'sedate', reflexive, or real will of the people. Arguably, this is the case in Chile, where most judges seem to assume that the intention of the constitutional delegates was to create a constitution that had, as its overriding goal, the protection of property rights. In other cases, judges justify their hostility to social rights by referring to the 'inactivity' of the legislature with regard to these rights. This seems to be the case in Argentina, where judges claim that they cannot substitute their will for that of the legislature in a situation where the latter is not willing to implement social rights.

Amongst other things, these claims call for clarification regarding the 'locus' of the sovereign will. As Gargarella points out, judges who rely on such claims need to be more open about their chosen theory of interpretation (and their justification for choosing it), and what their understanding of democracy is. Judges who claim that their main duty is to ensure strict compliance with the demands of an austere constitution should not write their opinions as if this commitment implied only one possible reading of the constitution. Likewise, those judges who (more or less explicitly) claim that it is their duty to respect the current will of the people should be prepared to justify a conception of democracy that does not seem to fit in with the idea of having a constitution at all. In addition, they should explain in what cases they would defer to the current will of the people, and in what cases they would not, and for what reasons.[14]

Trying to avoid some of the problems that he associates with these theories, Gargarella suggests adopting an alternative one, based on the deliberative-democratic ideal. In his opinion, this conception of democracy is more defensible than alternative ones, at least in relation to the judicial enforcement of social rights, since it requires judges to adopt a dialogic (rather than a deferential or intrusive) attitude towards the other branches.[15] And indeed, the performance of some of the more successful social-rights-enforcing courts described in this book, such as the Colombian, South African and Indian courts, can be described in these terms.[16]

At the same time as our theoretical understanding of the judicial enforcement of social rights has developed in this way, changes have been taking place in the actual practice of courts with regard to social rights. This changing practice is of course the product of a complex mix of social, institutional, juridical, cultural and political factors. It is to these factors that we now turn in an endeavour to dissect the different stages and components of social rights litigation.

The Anatomy of Social Rights Litigation

A mistake that needs to be avoided when studying processes of social rights litigation is that of exclusively focusing on judicial decisions – their quantity, the arguments made, and the orders handed down. These decisions represent only one part – and probably not even the most important part – of the process. Above all, one must remember that the adjudication of social rights claims is mainly a reactive activity, meaning that judges need to receive claims before they can think about how to respond. If people do not want to bring, or are not capable of bringing, their cases to court, it would make no sense to complain about the absence of judicial decisions enforcing social rights. By the same token, it would make no sense to talk about a successful social rights litigation process if well-reasoned and progressive judicial decisions have no impact in the real world.

The case studies in this book accordingly try to identify and define the main factors that characterise a successful (or failed) process. Following the model outlined in Gloppen's chapter, four main stages are distinguished: the ability of groups whose rights are violated to articulate their claims and *voice* them in the legal system; the *responsiveness* of courts at various levels to social rights claims once voiced; the *capability* of judges to respond to claims – that is, their ability to find adequate means to give effect to social rights; and whether the social rights judgments that are handed down are authoritative, in the sense that they are accepted, *complied* with and implemented through legislation and executive action. In dissecting these stages, the case studies assume that the outcome of each stage also depends on a complex interaction between different factors. The findings under each heading are summarised below.

Voice

Voice is in large measure constrained by the problem of access. In order to be able to voice their claims, claimants must first be aware of the rights they have, and recognise when their rights are violated and what they can do in order to seek redress from the courts. To overcome these difficulties, people need to be educated about their rights, and the environment (including the media and the public sphere generally) needs to be supportive of the process of legal education. In addition to basic knowledge about rights, litigation requires specialised technical knowledge, which is often monopolised by lawyers and legal experts. Prospective social rights claimants therefore also need to have access to legal expertise, either through state legal aid or organisations providing free legal assistance. If they do not, they may not even be able to put the machinery of the law into motion.

The examples discussed in this book include both cases where social rights litigation has been prevented because of obstacles of this kind, and cases where social rights litigation has exploded because of the legal system's openness to hearing claims. A tragic example of the first situation is Angola where, according to Skaar and Van-Dúnem, the legal system seems to be failing dramatically in all the areas referred to, making access to justice almost impossible. And in Bolivia, legal awareness and 'voice' have been constructed less within the courtroom and more through recourse to the human rights ombudsman, and through demands for the recognition of legal pluralism. By contrast, in Colombia, Hungary, South Africa and India, the judiciary has been favourably disposed to hearing social rights claims, albeit with different effects.[17] Brazil, as the chapter by Lopes shows, is an intermediate case of novel forms of legal mobilisation, but not necessarily structured around social and economic rights, or motivated by a pro-poor agenda. The key explanatory factors in these more successful experiences relate to the existing level of legal formalisation and the criteria for *locus standi*, including the possibility of bringing class actions (to which we will return later).[18]

Once the machinery for adjudicating social rights claims has been set into motion, many other factors need to be present in order for these claims to be successfully processed. For example, a lawsuit may be discouraged or directly stopped by the certainty or suspicion that the process is vitiated by corruption, endless delays, class bias, and so on. In addition, the daily (even if minor) costs involved in litigation (telephone calls, photocopies, transport), the geographical distance to court, or the bureaucracy that has to be confronted, may also push litigants out of the legal process. In some African and Latin American countries these latter factors seem to have played a crucial role in the low levels of litigation on behalf of disadvantaged groups.

Finally, voice is also affected by cultural readings of both rights and justice and the validity of legal mobilisation strategies. This is particularly evident in multicultural and pluri-ethnic contexts (notably Latin America and Africa) where it is not only a matter of limited resources, lack of information and widespread distrust of formal legal channels, but also in some cases of disputed conceptions of social transformation. Legal pluralism, especially as it becomes increasingly formalised through constitutional recognition, adds further complexity to notions of social transformation through law. Nonetheless, legal mobilisation strategies have become one of several protective measures undertaken by indigenous communities in these regions (for example, the U'wa community in Colombia).

Responsiveness

The responsiveness of the legal system depends in part on the first stage of the process, namely, on the ways in which claims are articulated, the litigation strategies used, and the specific legal abilities of the litigants. However, there are many other factors that help to shape the final judicial outcome. First, it is important to consider the legal traditions of the country concerned, and particularly the legal and doctrinal status of social rights.[19] Are social rights expressly included in the constitution or not? Are they deemed to be non-enforceable rights or mere directive principles? What obligations has the country assumed with regard to international treaties, and does it comply with those obligations? In addition, we need to know how judges approach constitutional issues, and particularly what types of interpretative theories judges use, and in what way. Finally, it is important to acknowledge that the process so far described – how legal norms and demands are received, interpreted, and processed – may depend to a significant degree on attitudinal factors. These factors relate to the social composition of the bench (that is, the professional and social background of judges, and the diversity of the tribunal in terms of ideology, gender, race and class).[20] We know, for example, that the personal characteristics of judges have made a significant difference to the ideological orientation of the courts in Argentina, Colombia, and India.[21] Our case studies also demonstrate how much these factors have affected the content of the courts' decisions and their legitimacy. Justice Pius Langa of the South African Constitutional Court has referred to the importance of one of the above-mentioned factors – race – in relation to the performance of the apartheid courts: 'One of the controversies surrounding the administration of justice in general, and the judiciary in particular, has been its grossly unrepresentative nature in terms of race and gender [that] impacted directly on the credibility and legitimacy of the courts. The judiciary was severely compromised.'[22] In other words, it is not enough for judges to have a proper legal education or political independence in order to transform the courts into respectable public bodies, capable of deciding cases in an impartial way. They must also be prepared to enforce rights that may run against their own class, race and gender interests.

Judicial Capability

The operation of the judicial process is also obviously linked to the means that judges have at their disposal. The word 'means' here refers to a diversity of judicial tools that are required at different levels of this process. First, do judges have access to appropriate legal materials? Do they have the time and opportunity to do research? Do they have access to comparative materials (jurisprudential and doctrinal)? Do they have sufficient financial resources?[23] Secondly, are judges able to find adequate legal remedies to repair violations of the law? What is the existing practice and what are the prevalent assumptions regarding the remedies that judges have at their disposal in order to ensure that their decisions are implemented? Finally, how much do judges economically depend on the other branches of government? How much independence do lower courts have from higher courts? And how much independence do they enjoy from the political branches?

Many of the courts we examined have been affected by a long history of dependence on the political branches. This factor, which is evident in many African and Latin American countries, has an obvious but variable impact on social rights litigation, with courts becoming more or less 'active' depending on the particular needs of the government. Equally, there is no direct causal relationship between greater judicial independence and better prospects for pro-poor court rulings, as evidenced by the examples of Mexico since 1994 and Chile.

Compliance

The final stage of the legal process concerns the events that follow the judicial decision. Whether the relevant public authorities comply with a particular decision depends, in part, on the abilities, independence and legitimacy of the court. However, the fact that a specific ruling is implemented also depends in part on factors that are external to the courts. Thus, we need to pay attention to the existing balance of forces between parties and social groups. We also need to know whether the ruling government has the political will, the administrative capacity and the economic resources required for the implementation of the decision. Where court rulings are 'ideologically' aligned with the policy preferences of government, compliance is more likely, as illustrated by the South African case. By contrast, the Colombian Constitutional Court is facing increasing hostility from the other branches to the point where constitutional reforms to limit its mandate have become a serious political consideration.[24] Where court rulings are at odds with broader political and economic trends, the need for compliance inevitably creates political tensions that can lead to inter-branch conflict. The issue is all the more relevant, as Couso suggests, given that the broader political agenda is still dominated by a pro-market economic model that undermines the assumptions behind social rights. We have already discussed how the dialogue between branches can develop in a constructive manner to allow for levels of judicial activism that need not undermine the principles of deliberative democracy. However, when courts rule in ways that interfere either with broader policy directives or specific interests, sustained compliance becomes problematic. The political context, then, is a crucial determinant of the prospects for social rights litigation. We return to this point below

Finally, it goes without saying that other significant and quite unpredictable events can have a profound impact on this entire process (for example, climate changes, violence and unrest, economic depression, and unemployment). In addition, we must emphasise the peculiar and interrelated nature of all the factors listed here. Thus, a negative or positive outcome in one of these stages may not only undermine or bolster the specific process at play, but also deeply influence the way in which this type of litigation is developed in the future.

Procedures that Contribute to Successful Social Rights Litigation

The case studies indicate that the availability or absence of certain legal procedures may influence the results of social rights litigation. Although several examples may be mentioned in this respect, the following appear to be particularly important:

rules of standing, legal formalities, class actions, judicial appointment procedures, and courts' control of their docket. We consider each of these factors in turn.

Rules of Standing

The prevailing rules of standing seem to play a crucial role in explaining the vigour of social rights litigation. Arguably, India represents the most advanced example in this respect. Justice Bhagwati of the Supreme Court explicitly recognised in the existing rules of standing the most important factor in preventing the poor from using the courts. In his words: 'The Supreme Court of India found that the main obstacle which deprived the poor and the disadvantaged of effective access to justice was the traditional rule of standing, which insists that only a person who has suffered a specific legal injury by reason of actual or threatened violation of his legal rights or legally protected interests can bring an action for judicial redress'.[25] The Indian Supreme Court accordingly began to develop creative ways of dealing with this issue, challenging the traditional approach to the rules on standing to sue. In 1976, for example, it held that, '[w]here a wrong against community interest is done, "no *locus standi*" will not always be a plea to non-suit [in relation to] an interested public body chasing the wrong doer in court'.[26]

We found a similarly liberal, open attitude in the Hungarian Constitutional Court. According to Sajó, '[a]ny Hungarian citizen may address the Court if he or she believes that any legal rule, decree, or Act of Parliament is unconstitutional. No *locus standi* rule applies'.[27] Moreover, citizens may complain about public officers' decisions on the ground that the person in question decided the case according to a norm that was unconstitutional. Courts have the power to annul the law in question, declare it retroactively invalid, and make decisions even in the absence of a case or controversy.[28]

Legal Formalities

In connection with the previous point, it is important to stress the impact that a reduction in legal formalities may have in favouring social rights litigation. It seems clear, for example, that the creation by the Indian Supreme Court of the so-called 'epistolary jurisdiction' (which allows every person or group to 'activate' the Court, by simply writing a letter on behalf of the poor), gave enormous impetus to litigation on behalf of disadvantaged groups. As Justice Bhagwati explained, the Court 'felt that when any member of a public or social organisation espouses the cause of the poor, he should be able to move the Court by just writing a letter, because it would not be right or fair to expect a person acting *pro bono publico* to incur expenses from his own pocket in order to go to a lawyer and prepare a regular petition to be filed in Court for endorsement of the fundamental rights of the poor'.[29] The *tutela* action in Colombia is also characterised by a lack of legal formalism and openness, as is the *amparo* writ used in Costa Rica's Constitutional Court.[30]

Class Actions

Also closely related to the previous factors, the significance of allowing individuals to act in concert when they confront common grievances needs to be highlighted. The possibility of organising the judicial system so as to allow these collective demands seems to be more reasonable and more efficient than the alternative of requiring each individual to initiate a separate case, which entails a waste of social energy and a weakening in the strength of the claim.[31] The growing development of class actions in several of the countries studied, particularly in Latin America, promises a significant improvement in the pursuit of social justice through the use of courts.

Changes in Appointment Procedures for Judges

Our case studies also suggest that the enforcement of social rights is significantly enhanced by the appointment of judges who are particularly sensitive to the suffering of disadvantaged groups. So far, however, these changes in the composition of the bench have not been the product of formal changes in the appointment procedures of judges, but rather a consequence of the 'good will' of a few, powerful political actors. The exception is Argentina, where President Néstor Kirchner, in his Decree 222, committed himself to a more transparent procedure for selecting Supreme Court justices, including the direct participation of NGOs and social activists, and to ensuring a more socially diverse bench, particularly in terms of gender and the geographical origin of the judges.[32]

Judicial appointment procedures in much of Latin America have also been changed to promote greater judicial independence from the executive – in some cases to relatively good effect (for example, in Mexico). But the impact of these measures on social rights litigation has not as yet become evident.

Courts' Control over their Docket

Another element that may significantly affect the quality of judicial decisions in the area of social rights relates to courts' control over their docket. Where a court is not allowed to choose the cases in which it wants to concentrate its attention (given, for example, the influence, significance, or urgency of the cases) its ability to implement a pro-poor political agenda may be negatively affected. Social rights cases may also simply get lost amidst the sheer number of other cases decided. Argentina's Supreme Court, for example, decides approximately 15,000 cases per year, while in the US (which is seven times more populous than Argentina) the Supreme Court – on which the Argentinean Court has been modelled – decides between 70 and 90 cases annually (less than one per cent of the number of cases that the Argentinean Court decides). Similarly, the Indian Supreme Court decides more than 30,000 cases annually, which 'may enhance the Court's legitimacy [but only at the cost of its] ability to focus sustained attention on particular issues'.[33]

In South Africa, the Constitutional Court has made a virtue out of the reverse situation. Faced by jurisdictional provisions that make the development of a political question doctrine difficult, and a comparatively low caseload that means that it almost impossible for the Court to avoid taking on controversial cases, the Court has used the time at its disposal to write carefully constructed opinions that serve to sweeten the pill of constitutional reprimand that sometimes follows.[34]

Judges and Institutional Means

In our analysis of contemporary judicial decisions on social rights we have frequently found justifications for judicial restraint based on a lack of institutional means. This lack of means appeared at different levels (see the section on 'the anatomy of social rights litigation' above). On some occasions it affected judges' capacity to have access to socially significant cases. On other occasions it undermined their chances of finding the evidence necessary for adjudicating a case. And finally, it prevented them from ensuring respect for their decisions, given their inability to monitor their prescribed solutions.

As Courtis argues in this volume, 'the absence of adequate procedural mechanisms does not mean that it is impossible to overcome the framework of bilateral/property-oriented suits by devising new procedural mechanisms. The argument concerning procedural mechanisms merely highlights a certain state of affairs, which in fact *prima facie* violates the state's obligation to provide procedural guarantees when recognising a constitutional right, including socio-economic rights.' In this respect, many of the cases studied allow us to conclude that judges who are willing to take an active role regarding social rights can manage to create new instruments or find ad hoc solutions, even though they have to act in the midst of serious difficulties (such as extreme poverty, inequality, and social tension).

The case of India is undoubtedly exemplary in this respect.[35] As we know, when judges encountered difficulties in assuming jurisdiction over – what they believed were – socially relevant cases, they invented the *epistolary jurisdiction*, which allowed virtually everyone to have access to court. When they encountered problems in finding the evidence they needed, they created *special commissions of inquiry*.[36] When they did not find adequate *remedies* in the traditional legal repertoire, they created new ones.[37] And when they feared that their orders would not be properly enforced over time, they created *monitoring agencies* in charge of enforcing their orders.

The courts' development of new procedural mechanisms and legal remedies has been perhaps less spectacular but equally important in other parts of the world. The *Grootboom* case in South Africa stands as a telling example of how a creative court can decide social rights claims within the limits of its powers, and the material constraints that it normally faces. As we know, in this case, the Constitutional Court declared that the 1996 South African Constitution required the state to 'devise a comprehensive and co-ordinated program progressively to realise the right of access to housing'.[38]

We also found interesting examples in this respect from Latin America. We know, for instance, that some courts in Argentina took advantage of section 43 of the 1994 Constitution to directly modify the traditionally narrow approach to *locus standi* (Courtis). Colombia also provides examples of the creativity of the Constitutional Court in finding new legal remedies to be applied in social rights cases.

An additional device used by the courts has been to analogise social rights to traditional civil rights. In the Hungarian case, for instance, social rights were analogised to property rights, and in South Africa, at first tacitly but later explicitly,[39] to equality rights. On reflection, this development is not surprising. In the face of the argument that judges are not institutionally equipped to decide complex policy issues, it is far easier for a court to reframe the question put to it as one that concerns the enforcement of existing rights or equal treatment.

A final crucial device available to judges is the discretion they enjoy in framing their orders. Judges can thus improve the odds on compliance and acceptance of their rulings through creative use of the legal instruments at hand, but also through a politically sensitive framing and presentation of cases that will allow for better inter-branch relations, especially when cases are decided against government interests. We turn now to this broader political dimension of social rights litigation.

The Politics of Social Rights Litigation

Thus far, we have focused mostly on a court-centred analysis of social rights litigation in order to explore how the courts and legal mobilisation strategies can be socially progressive or can generate pro-poor outcomes, and the merits of this as a suitable path to social transformation. Our case studies, however, also point to a broader sense of the emancipatory potential of the law and the appropriation of a language of rights from several developmental, political and social perspectives. In some respects, courtrooms are becoming an arena for the staging of political battles framed in the language of rights and constitutional entitlements – with greater or lesser levels of confrontation.[40] Even in those cases, such as Bolivia, where the courts have been reluctant to take on these battles, social mobilisation strategies, through the appropriation of an emancipatory discourse of rights, include channelling cases and complaints to other more supportive quasi-judicial agencies (for instance, a human rights ombudsman). But most significantly there appears to be an emerging pattern of a growing normative acceptance of the justiciability of social and economic rights, and the merits of promoting pro-poor state action through the courts.

These trends in social rights litigation and progressive court activism tell us of three related phenomena, which work as both cause and effect. First, there is a growing presence of the notion of rights-based development as the normative basis for both political projects of democracy, and also socially just models of economic growth. Secondly, it also suggests a sort of 'discovery' of the law and legal channels from below by citizens that are more aware and demanding of their rights, and with changing expectations regarding what can be achieved through strategies of legal mobilisation. Thirdly, a redefinition of the role of courts in modern democratic polities may be emerging, loosely manifested in different forms of 'judicialisation' of political and social conflict. Some of the cases in this volume demonstrate the practical validity of social rights litigation in support, moreover, of theoretical justifications of social rights. We have also tracked the different and inter-related factors that shape the prospects for pro-poor court activism through the anatomy of social rights litigation. But we need also to situate these changing patterns in court action in the context of broader debates regarding contemporary political development and economic growth.

In both cases there is a growing rights-based approach towards promoting democracy and development. A first relevant contextual element, then, is the relatively recent '(re)discovery' of the transformative potential of social and economic rights. This in part is linked to Amartya Sen's work, which embraces the view that long-term sustainable development requires an autonomous, active and participatory democratic citizenship, endowed with minimum levels of social and economic welfare best articulated in the form of rights.[41] Significantly, much of this has been translated into the normative basis for the UNDP Human Development reports, and is gradually being accepted by a range of international and domestic actors.[42] More recently, from a political science study of democratic processes, this has been picked up in the discussion regarding the 'quality' of democracy, reflecting an analytical shift away from more top-down institutional understandings of political processes towards a more rights-based and citizen-centred evaluation of the democratic model.[43] Couso rightly points to the continued dominance of the neo-liberal model, even as the premises of the 'Washington consensus' have by now been largely discredited. Nonetheless, the parallel emergence of more effective social and economic rights litigation alongside a more forceful language of socially progressive rights-based development in the economic and political debate is not coincidental. From a more radical perspective, the emancipatory potential of law can be realised in the form of 'counter-hegemonic' legal strategies aimed at challenging the injustices of unequal power relations through legal means.[44]

The second, related phenomenon that adds further body to the transformative impact of legal processes is the 'judicialisation' of political and social conflict, through a greater prominence of courts in democratic states in general.[45] If this is a wider trend of modern democratic polities, then it should not surprise us that courts are also taking on social and economic issues, precisely because these are increasingly presented as justiciable, in keeping with the above 'rights revolution'. At the same time, though, the greater presence of courts in resolving political and social conflict need not translate into pro-poor court activism. Here, our anatomy of the litigation process based on Gloppen's framework allows us to identify the range of institutional, procedural, structural, cultural, access-determined and attitudinal factors – and their complex interaction – that guide us towards a better understanding of the (changing) role of courts. And this in turn is shaped by developments in the broader political and social context. Structural changes, for instance in the configuration of social and political forces (like the transition to democracy in South Africa), in some cases combined with constituent processes or reforms which redefine judicial independence, judicial review powers, or the bill of rights (Colombia), can translate into pro-poor court activism.

Finally, and inextricably linked to the above two processes, we have increasing manifestations of the 'discovery' of the law and the adoption of different forms of legal mobilisation strategies from below. The change of heart on the part of the 'left' regarding the usefulness of legal strategies for social transformation is a novel feature of the political landscape in Latin America, as Couso indicates. But also the locus of social struggle has shifted to new forms of social movements in which sub-altern discourses are framed in terms of rights, contributing to at least exploring the usefulness of legal channels for the promotion and protection of these conquests – with hugely varying levels of success.[46] The global human rights revolution and the specific experiences of transitional justice (especially where positive results were obtained) has been instrumental in contributing to a process of socialisation of a rights culture supported by a growing network of domestic and transnational human rights NGOs.[47] Judicial reforms, in turn, aimed at improving access are also a contributory factor. A range of disadvantaged groups is proving to be particularly innovative in the use of law (in different ways) as a means of either winning political battles or consolidating hard-won rights. Although our cases have not focused on this issue, the transformative discourse of women's movements and indigenous movements provides ready examples of a resourceful use of legal mobilisation by disadvantaged groups in combination with other forms of social mobilisation and struggle.

If we look briefly at indigenous movements in Latin America, for instance, political (and transformative) struggles are framed in terms of rights, ultimately to be tested in the courts. Legal channels become a means of empowerment on at least three levels: first, through growing (and increasingly successful) demands for substantive recognition of legal pluralism and community justice; secondly, through reforms designed to improve access, say through the introduction of official translation of court proceedings into the appropriate indigenous language; and, finally, through increasing resort to legal strategies, both to protect the community (for instance from encroachment on indigenous lands or territory by oil companies, as in Colombia) but also in the pursuit of social and economic rights, or redistributive land entitlements. Clearly, this discovery of the law by indigenous communities has throughout Latin America been manifested in very different ways, and with very different results. Notably, in Colombia, the Constitutional Court has ruled in favour of what is considered a radical recognition of indigenous community justice. In Bolivia, indigenous struggles fought in the land tribunals have been less effective.

In any event, rights litigation, when it involves an innovative probing of either the justiciability or the validity of what are perceived as 'new' rights in any given social order, is about testing different views on the distribution of political, social or economic power. (Here the Hungarian example is in fact about protecting 'old' rights from a newer economic order that threatens to redefine economic power structures.) Rights battles have a redistributive effect on resource and power allocation and, whether they are fought out in court or elsewhere, are unlikely to be politically or economically neutral. Once a right has been consolidated and has acquired wide acceptance in the public imagination (women's voting rights, or the right to free public education across gender and race), the initial controversy or polemic abates, but normally as a result of a societal and political adjustment to its incorporation in the social order. This in turn can prove to be a long-drawn out, conflictive, and even reversible process. The consequences of pro-poor court action are deeply political, and when successful inevitably involve trade-offs which signify alterations, however minor, in power structures. These alterations may be the subject of greater or lesser controversy and confrontation. This depends on the nature of the trade-offs, who the perceived losers are and what interests are at stake.

Equally, when court activism (pro-poor or otherwise) is in line with the ideological bent or policy preferences of the other branches, as in the case of South Africa, relations between powers are less subject to strain, and compliance or implementation of court decisions is less problematic. Sustained conflict between court rulings and the policy interests of the other branches is clearly more problematic and could evolve into inter-branch conflict. While this has not been the case in India, as mentioned before, it is not an impossible scenario in Colombia. Here, though, the scale of political violence and human rights violations has reached such proportions that, in any case, the Constitutional Court appears as truly exceptional in terms of the legitimacy and social acceptance that it has built up in such a short space of time, in contrast to the rest of the judicial branch, and state institutions in general. Possibly in consequence of this, the executive has already expressed its desire to curtail the Court's powers.

The courtroom context of rights litigation has the effect of 'depoliticising' the issues at stake, and in some ways minimising the confrontational aspect of the struggle at hand. Courtroom battles are often perceived to be less threatening to the broader political and social order than other forms of social mobilisation or struggle. This may also explain why in most of the cases studied here where social and economic rights litigation has been successful it has tended to be less politically controversial. This is particularly the case if the courts enjoy political legitimacy and societal acceptance.

The Limits of Social Rights Litigation

We end our discussion by considering the limitations of social rights litigation as an agent of social transformation. This volume has studied novel levels of judicial activism in social rights litigation in fragile democratic settings, and has identified the factors that need to be considered in our assessment of changing court practices, and societal attitudes towards legal mobilisation strategies. Where the cases in this volume are less conclusive, and more research is required, is in pinpointing exactly which social groups are most likely to benefit from increased pro-poor judicial activism, and how much social transformation can actually be achieved through courts. Nonetheless, our studies make clear that there is a significant difference between successful social rights litigation and social transformation. Even where pro-poor judicial decisions are taking place in innovative and rather exceptional ways, it is also clear that there are limitations on how this translates into social transformation.

There are numerous things to evaluate in this respect, but first a previous clarification is in order. Here we are not assuming that the interests of the disadvantaged can only be advanced through successful litigation – by winning a case. It may well happen that certain groups choose to litigate even when they know that the courts are likely to dismiss their claim and deny their rights. Undoubtedly, to lose a case in court may have very negative consequences for the disadvantaged: it may discourage the litigants; it may make them think that they were actually wrong in making their claim (especially when there may have been initial doubts about it); it may create a bad legal precedent; and it may also be a waste of time and energy. However, none of these factors indicates that there may not also be some good reasons for this type of litigation. Following Jules Lobel, we could mention at least three reasons for litigating when one has few chances of winning the case.[48] First, one may choose to go to court in order to instigate political action and influence over public debate. Secondly, one may litigate in order to 'keep alive an oppressed community's vision of the law'.[49] Thirdly, one may initiate a case to foster a 'culture of legal struggle' that 'continually informs and inspires future generations to challenge oppressive practices'.[50]

Having said this, we need to go back to our initial point about the limits of social rights litigation. In this respect, we share the conclusions of a flourishing literature that challenges a 'juricentric approach' to legal issues.[51] By 'juricentric approach' is meant approaches that take 'the judiciary as the exclusive guardian of the Constitution',[52] and neglect the influence that other groups and institutions have in the entire legal process. The groups we are thinking about are different, as is the way in which they exercise their influence.

First, we consider that the capacity of courts alone to produce social change is limited (see Gloppen in this volume).[53] Along with a growing community of scholars, we would argue that courts need the cooperation of both the legislature and the executive in order to ensure respect for their decisions.[54] Empirically, the meaning of the constitution in many countries seems to be defined through 'ordinary politics', namely 'outside the courts'.[55] Normatively, we would agree with this trend, since questions of fundamental justice *ought to* be defined through a process where the political branches play a central role.[56]

Secondly, we would also defend various descriptive and normative claims regarding the role of extra-institutional groups and social movements. These groups, we maintain, should and do in fact play a role in defining society's main constitutional commitments, their shape and contents. The ways in which these groups influence the legal process are numerous. Sometimes, they *initiate* a litigation process in order to guarantee their basic rights (frequently, but not exclusively, with the help of NGOs and public-interest litigants), as we have repeatedly seen in the cases of Argentina, Bolivia, Mexico, India and South Africa. In addition, these groups influence judicial outcomes by exerting pressure on public authorities (for example, by organising demonstrations, making *amicus curiae* applications, and generally garnering the support of civil society). Of course, there are no formal institutional means capable of guaranteeing that the claims of disadvantaged groups have any impact, that is to say, courts can still decide according to their own preferences, even in spite of massive social protests and mobilisation. However, it is undeniable that in many cases the decisions of courts have been greatly influenced by the persistent demands of certain groups.[57] Finally, social movements also enter into the legal process by the way in which they receive and integrate the decisions of courts. As Marc Galanter has argued, '[the] messages disseminated by courts do not … produce effects except as they are received, interpreted and used by [potential] actors'.[58] Similarly, Michael McCann has demonstrated that 'citizens routinely reconstruct legal norms into resources for purposes quite unintended by judicial officials … the judicially articulated legal norms take a life of their own as they are deployed in practical social action'.[59]

Concluding Remarks

This volume has been about the possibilities of social rights litigation as a path to social transformation. In pursuing this question, we have deliberately – but not exclusively – selected countries that illustrate new practices in court action on social rights. In that sense, our studies do not claim to be a representative sample of trends in modern democracies generally. Rather, they are weighted towards cases in which social rights litigation has been creative and pro-poor, and moreover in fragile or weak democratic settings. In this context we have found that, despite the structural constraints of scarcity, dramatic socio-economic inequalities and widespread poverty, pro-poor court action is possible, and is perceived as legitimate, thus defying theoretical assumptions about the proper place of social rights litigation in these democracies. Our studies also included countries where social rights litigation is not prominent, but where the transformative potential of law and a rights-based approach to development forms part of the normative landscape of both top-down institution-building projects and bottom-up political struggles.

In the course of this work we have developed a theoretical framework that has led us to a better understanding of what makes courts more or less receptive to engaging in pro-poor action. We hope that this volume has also opened up new questions for further research on what are still uncharted waters regarding the conceptual and empirically testable links between the law, judicial institutions and processes of social transformation.

Notes

1 See Patrick Bond, *Elite Transition: From Apartheid to Neoliberalism in South Africa* (London: Pluto Press, 2000), pp. 15–16.

2 See Dennis Davis, 'Deconstructing and Reconstructing the Argument for a Bill of Rights Within the Context of South African Nationalism', in Penelope Andrews and Stephen Ellmann (eds), *The Post-Apartheid Constitutions: Perspectives on South Africa's Basic Law* (Johannesburg: Witwatersrand University Press, 2001), p. 202. Of course, since this time, the ANC has moved considerably rightwards, adopting a macro-economic policy that many have described as amounting to a self-imposed structural adjustment programme. The ANC's shift to the right explains the curious situation currently pertaining in South Africa where social movements and other organs of civil society are attempting to use social rights to force interstitial changes in government policy, without seriously threatening the liberation movement's stranglehold on political power.

3 The counter-example that bucks this trend, of course, is India, where the Supreme Court began enforcing social rights in the late 1970s. See, for example, *Maneke Gandhi v. Union of India* 1978 1 SCC 248; *State of Himachal Pradesh v. Umed Ram Sharma* (1986) AIR SC 847 (poor people's access to roads enforced via article 21 – right to life) and *Olga Tellis v. Bombay Municipal Corporation* [1987] LRC (Const) 351 (pavement dwellers' protected from arbitrary eviction through right to livelihood, an aspect of the right to life). The first thing to note about the Indian case, however, is that the text of that country's constitution could not be clearer in distinguishing civil and political rights from social rights, with the latter category of rights mostly relegated to a separate, non-justiciable chapter on Directive Principles of State Policy. That social rights have been enforced at all in India is therefore the result of the extraordinarily activist stance on the part of some of the judges on the Supreme Court, which is in turn a function of the unusual popular legitimacy that the Court enjoys. The special nature of the Indian caste system also makes ordinary left-right analyses difficult to apply to that country. It is therefore not surprising that the fate of the East European command economies should have had less of an impact on the trajectory followed by social rights in India.

4 Court-centred social rights litigation has been the main focus of this volume. But recourse to rights-based discourse – which may be tested in courts – as a mode of social transformation is also manifested in other ways. The chapters on Bolivia and Angola, although peripheral in many respects to the debate on the justiciability and viability of social rights litigation, nonetheless point to contexts where law and legal strategies are

being used in social and political struggles aimed at social transformation and promotion of rights-based citizenship.

5 Stephen Holmes and Cass R. Sunstein, *The Cost of Rights* (New York: W.W. Norton, 1999). See further Craig Scott and Patrick Macklem, 'Constitutional Ropes of Sand or Justiciable Guarantees? Social Rights in a New South African Constitution', *University of Pennsylvania Law Review*, 141 (1992): 1–48; Cass R. Sunstein, 'State Action is Always Present', *Chicago Journal of International Law*, 3 (2002): 465–545, 467; Cass R. Sunstein, *The Second Bill of Rights: The Last Great Speech of Franklin Delano Roosevelt and America's Unfinished Pursuit of Freedom* (New York: Basic Books, 2004).

6 This point was recognised by the South African Constitutional Court in its so-called *First Certification* decision: *Ex parte Chairperson of the Constitutional Assembly: in re Certification of the Republic of South Africa Constitution 1996* 1996 (4) SA 744 (CC) paras 77–8.

7 See *August v. Electoral Commission* 1999 (3) SA 1 (CC) (holding that the failure of the South African government to make proper arrangements to enable prisoners to register and vote violated those prisoners' right to vote).

8 See UN Committee on Economic, Social and Cultural Rights General Comment 3 para. 9 (suggesting that social rights may be violated by 'deliberately retrogressive measures'). See further the *First Certification* judgment, para 78: 'At the very minimum, socio-economic rights can be negatively protected from improper invasion.'

9 *Harvard Law Review*, 92 (1978), 394–404.

10 James Madison, 'The Federalist No. 51', in Alexander Hamilton, James Madison and John Jay, *The Federalist, Or, The New Constitution* (London: J.M. Dent Ltd, 1992), p. 265.

11 Ibid., p. 266.

12 'On the slightest view of the British Constitution', Madison wrote, 'we must perceive that the legislative, executive, and judiciary departments are by no means totally separate and distinct from each other. The executive magistrate forms an integral part of the legislative authority… One branch of the legislative department forms also a great constitutional council to the executive chief, as on another hand, it is the sole depositary of judicial power in cases of impeachment, and is invested with the supreme appellate jurisdiction in all other cases. The judges again, are so far connected with the legislative department as often to attend and participate in its deliberations, though not admitted to a legislative vote.' (James Madison, 'The Federalist No. 47', in Hamilton, Madison and Jay, *The Federalist*, pp. 247–8.)

13 For example, writing about the United States, Post and Siegel refer to the extraordinary change in the views of many conservative judges and academics regarding federalism, democracy and judicial review, from the 1960s to the 1990s (R. Post and R. Siegel, 'Equal Protection by Law: Federal Antidiscrimination Legislation after Morrison and Kimel', *Yale Law Journal*, 110 (2000): 441–77).

14 In addition, Gargarella suggests that a commitment to such a view of democracy may require judges to be more attentive to the social and economic conditions which that view presupposes. See also F. Michelman, 'Law's Republic', *Yale Law Journal*, 87 (1988): 1493–537 (proposing that courts should preserve the conditions necessary for supporting self-government).

15 See Sunstein, *The Second Bill of Rights*.

16 Craig Scott and Patrick Macklem, for example, have argued that the Indian Supreme Court 'has emphasized a co-operative dialogue between the judiciary and the executive and legislative branches, as opposed to the standard separation of powers conception based on watertight jurisdictional functions' (Scott and Macklem, 'Constitutional Ropes of Sand', p. 122).

17 In India, the Supreme Court's openness to hearing social rights claims seems to be undermined by a weak institutional framework for legal mobilisation, underfunded legal aid and an insufficiently resourced network of rights-based organisations (Charles R. Epp, *The Rights Revolution: Lawyers, Activists and Supreme Courts in Comparative Perspective* (Chicago: University of Chicago Press, 1998), pp. 108–10).

18 In this respect, it is interesting to compare the case of India with that of South Africa. As Dugard and Roux argue in this volume, although the South African Constitutional Court was 'premised on an inclusive public interest ideal', it has interpreted its direct access rules in an exceedingly restrictive way.

19 The case studies in this book demonstrate the importance of legal traditions in Latin America and Eastern Europe in explaining the courts' contrasting behaviour towards social rights (their 'passivity' in most of the Latin American cases, and their 'activism' in the case of Hungary or Poland). Of course, legal traditions do not preclude changes in the attitude of courts regarding social rights. An extreme example in this respect is that of India, where the colonial constitution became the point of departure for intense judicial activism during the 1980s. As Judge Bhagwati put it, in spite of 'a legal architecture designed for a colonial administration and a jurisprudence structured around a free-market economy', the Indian Courts managed to introduce substantive innovations regarding social rights. In his view, 'social activism has opened up a new dimension of the judicial process, and this new dimension is a direct emanation from the basic objectives and values underlying the Indian Constitution', quoted in P. Hunt, *Reclaiming Social Rights* (Sydney: Dartmouth, 1996), p. 154.

20 In the conclusion of their first report on 'Ideological Voting on Federal Courts of Appeals', Cass Sunstein, David Schkade and Lisa Ellman affirmed: 'We have found striking evidence of a relationship between the political party of the appointing president and judicial voting patterns. We have also found that much of the time, judicial votes are affected by panel composition' C. Sunstein, D. Schkade, and L. Ellman, 'Ideological Voting on Federal Courts of Appeals', unpublished working paper (Joint Center for Regulatory Studies, University of Chicago, 2003). See also, in general, on the so-called 'attitudinal model', J. Segal and H. Spaeth, *The Supreme Court and the Attitudinal Model* (Cambridge: Cambridge University Press, 1993); J. Segal and H. Spaeth, *The Supreme Court and the Attitudinal Model Revisited* (Cambridge: Cambridge University Press, 2002).

21 In Argentina, changes in the composition of the Supreme Court contributed to a change from a liberal jurisprudence (1983–91) to a highly conservative one (1991–2003), and now seemingly back again. In Colombia, the remarkable progressivism of some of the members of the Constitutional Court undoubtedly influenced that Court's recent pro-poor jurisprudence, which is a novelty in the very long legal history of Colombia. In India, the activist and 'pro-poor' Supreme Court of the 1970s based its decisions on the same document that had persistently been interpreted in a quite different, conservative way. On the other hand, the force of legal culture may sometimes inhibit progressive judges' capacity to contribute to pro-poor social transformation. See Theunis Roux,

'Pro-poor Court, Anti-poor Outcomes: Explaining the Performance of the South African Land Claims Court', *South African Journal on Human Rights*, 20 (2004): 511–43.

22 P. Langa, 'The Role of the Constitutional Court in the Enforcement and Protection of Human Rights in South Africa', *St. Louis University Law Journal*, 41 (1997): 1259, 1261. As Nelson Mandela asked in his speech from the dock: 'Why is it that in the courtroom I face a white magistrate, am confronted by a white prosecutor, and escorted into the dock by a white orderly? Can anyone honestly and seriously suggest that in this type of atmosphere the scales of justice are evenly balanced? I feel oppressed by the atmosphere of white domination that lurks all around in this courtroom. Somehow this atmosphere calls to mind the inhuman injustices caused to my people outside this courtroom by this same white domination. It reminds me that I am voteless because … the white minority has taken a lion's share of my country and forced me to occupy poverty-stricken Reserves, over-populated and over-stocked. We are ravaged by starvation and disease' (quoted in L. Berat, 'Courting Justice: A Call for Judicial Activism in a Transformed South Africa', *St. Louis University Law Journal*, 37 (1993): 849, 849–50).

23 It has been frequently said that these problems are particularly relevant to social rights litigation, which does not merely involve the adjudication of vested interests, but also often an attempt to change social structures, Gerlad Rosenberg, *The Hollow Hope: Can Courts Bring About Social Change?* (Chicago: University of Chicago Press, 1991). However, as José Reinaldo de Lima Lopes demonstrates in his chapter in this book, there are ways of minimising at least some of these difficulties. In the case of Brazil, he maintains, decisions in social rights cases did not require 'any large reform action' because 'traditional principles of litigation [in this case, those created under consumer protection law] have generally served [the courts] well enough', p. 196.

24 Comision Colombiana de Juristas, 'Informe alterno al quinto informe periódico del Esado Colombiano ante el Comité de Derechos Humanos de Naciones Unidas' (July 2003).

25 P. Bhagwati, 'Judicial Activism and Public Interest Litigation', *Columbia Journal of Transnational Law*, 23 (1985): 561–77, 570–71.

26 *S P Gupta v. Union of India* 2 SCR (1982) 365, 520 (quoted in Hunt, *Reclaiming Social Rights*, p. 164).

27 A. Sajó, 'Reading the Invisible Constitution: Judicial Review in Hungary', *Oxford Journal of Legal Studies*, 15 (1995): 253–67, 255.

28 Ibid.

29 Bhagwati, 'Judicial Activism', p. 571.

30 See Bruce Wilson, Juan Carlos Rodriguez Cordero and Roger Handberg, 'The Best Laid Schemes … Gang Aft A-gley: Judicial Reform in Latin America – Evidence from Costa Rica', *Journal of Latin American Studies*, 36 (2004): 507–31. Costa Rica's version of a constitutional court has also shown itself to be innovative in social rights litigation.

31 Scott and Macklem, 'Constitutional Ropes of Sand', p. 141.

32 The Argentinean Supreme Court has traditionally being staffed by male lawyers from Buenos Aires.

33 Epp, *The Rights Revolution*, p. 109.

34 See Theunis Roux, 'Legitimating Transformation: Political Resource Allocation in the South African Constitutional Court', in Siri Gloppen, Roberto Gargarella and Elin Skaar (eds), *Democratization and the Judiciary: The Accountability Function of Courts in New Democracies* (London: Frank Cass, 2004), p. 92.

35 Hunt, *Reclaiming Social Rights*, chap. 4.
36 In the *Agra Protective Home* case, the Court commissioned the District Judge to visit the protective home and report to the Court on the living conditions there. In the *Bandhua Mukti Marcha* case, the Court institutionalised the 'practice of appointing socio-legal commissions of inquiry for the purpose of gathering relevant material in public interest litigation' (Bhagwati, 'Judicial Activism', p. 575).
37 See, for example, *Bandhua Mukti Morcha v. Union of India* 3 SCC (1984) 161.
38 *Government of the Republic of South Africa v. Grootboom* 2001 (1) SA 46 (CC) para. 99.
39 See *Khosa v. Minister of Social Development* 2004 (6) BCLR 569 (CC).
40 See Elsa van Huyssteen, 'The Constitutional Court and the Redistribution of Power in South Africa: Towards Transformative Constitutionalism', *African Studies,* 59 (2000): 245–65.
41 See Amartya Sen, *Development as Freedom* (New York: Anchor Books, 2000). This, of course, is rooted, as Couso tells us in his chapter in this volume, in the social democratic tradition of the post-war years.
42 The literature on human development is acquiring greater prominence precisely as a counterpoint to the neo-liberal model.
43 Guillermo O'Donnell, 'Notas sobre la Democracia en America Latina', in Programa de las Naciones Unidas para el Desarrollo, *El Debate Conceptual sobre la Democracia* (New York: PNUD, 2004), pp. 7–82. Given the reluctance in mainstream political science to engage with more normative notions of political development, this constitutes no minor analytical shift in the literature on transitions to and consolidation of democracy.
44 Boaventura de Sousa Santos, *Toward a New Legal Common Sense* (London: Butterworth LexisNexis Group, 2002).
45 See C. Neal Tate and Torbjörn Vallinder, 'Judicializaction and the Future of Politics and Policy', in C. Neal Tate and Torbjörn Vallinder (eds), *The Global Expansion of Judicial Power* (New York: New York University Press, 1995), pp. 515–29.
46 See the various essays in Susan Eva Eckstein and Timothy P. Wickham Crowley (eds), *What Justice? Whose Justice? Fighting for Fairness in Latin America* (Berkeley: University of California Press, 2003); and Susan Eva Eckstein and Timothy P. Wickham Crowley, *Struggles for Social Rights in Latin America* (New York: Routledge, 2003).
47 There is a rapidly growing literature in this regard: Thomas Risse, Stephen C. Ropp and Kathryn Sikkink (eds), *The Power of Human Rights: International Norms and Domestic Change* (Cambridge: Cambridge University Press, 1999); Margaret Keck and Kathryn Sikkink, *Activists Beyond Borders* (Ithaca: Cornell University Press, 1998).
48 See J. Lobel, 'Losers, Fools & Prophets' ,*Cornell Law Review*, 80 (1995): 1331–425. See also R. Cover, 'The Supreme Court, 1982 Term – Foreword: Nomos and Narrative', *Harvard Law Review*, 97 (1983): 4–68.
49 Lobel, 'Losers', p. 1347.
50 Ibid., p. 1353.
51 See, for example J.M. Balkin, 'Populism and Progressivism as Constitutional Categories', *Yale Law Journal*, 104 (1995): 1935–1990; J.M. Balkin, 'Idolatry and Faith: The Jurisprudence of Sanford Levinson', *Tulsa Law Review*, 38 (2003): 553–794; J.M. Balkin, and S. Levinson, 'Understanding the Constitutional Revolution', *Virginia Law Review*, 87 (2001): 1045–109; Cover, 'The Supreme Court'; P. Erick and S. Silbey, *The Common Place of Law* (Chicago: Chicago University Press, 1998); S. Griffin,

American Constitutionalism (Princeton: Princeton University Press, 1996); Larry D. Kramer, 'Foreword: We the Court', *Harvard Law Review*, 115 (2001): 4–169, 130–58; Larry D. Kramer, *The People Themselves: Popular Constitutionalism and Judicial Review* (Oxford: Oxford University Press, 2004); Larry D. Kramer, 'Popular Constitutionalism, Circa 2004', *California Law Review,* 92 (2004): 959–1012; S. Levinson, *Constitutional Faith* (Princeton: Princeton University Press, 1988); S. Levinson, 'Constitutional Populism: Is It Time for "We the People" to Demand an Article Five Convention?', *Widener Law Symposium Journal*, 4 (1999): 211; M. McCann, 'Reform Litigation on Trial', *Law & Social Inquiry*, 17 (1992): 715–43; M. McCann 'Causal vs. Constitutive Explanations', *Law & Social Inquiry*, 21 (1996): 457–82; Martha Minow, 'Interpreting Rights: An Essay for Robert Cover', *Yale Law Journal*, 96 (1987): 1860–915; W. Moore, *Constitutional Rights and Powers of the People* (Princeton: Princeton University Press, 1996); R. Parker, 'Here, the People Rule, A Constitutional Populist Manifesto', *Valparaiso University Law Review*, 27 (1993): 531–48; Post and Siegel, 'Equal Protection by Law'; R. Post and R. Siegel, 'Protecting the Constitution from the People: Juricentric Restrictions on Section Five Power', *Indiana Law Journal*, 78 (2003): 1–46; R. Post and R. Siegel, 'Popular Constitutionalism, Departmentalism, and Judicial Supremacy', *California Law Review*, 92 (2004): 1027–44; D. Reed, 'Popular Constitutionalism: Toward a Theory of State Constitutional Meaning', *Rutgers Law Review*, 30 (1999): 871–932; Lawrence G. Sager, 'Justice in Plain Clothes: Reflections on the Thinness of Constitutional Law', *Northwestern University Law Review*, 88 (1993): 410–35; R. Siegel, 'Text in Context: Gender and the Constitution from a Social Movement Perspective', *University of Pennsylvania Law Review*, 150 (2001): 297–352.

52 See Post and Siegel, 'Protecting the Constitution from the People', 2; and also Post and Siegel, 'Equal Protection by Law' and Post and Segal, 'Popular Constitutionalism'.

53 In this sense, we do not fully subscribe to the conclusions of Rosenberg, *The Hollow Hope*, who refers to an inherent incapacity on the part of courts for promoting social change, as a consequence of three main constraints, namely: 'the binding limitations of legal precedents and rights traditions'; the 'lack of judicial independence from other government branches and public opinion'; and the 'restrictive judiciary's capacity for developing and implementing effective social policies'. See McCann, 'Reform Litigation on Trial', 717.

54 J. Fleming, 'Book Review: Taking the Constitution Away From the Courts, by Mark Tushnet', *Cornell University Press,* 86 (2000): 215–49; S. Levinson, *Constitutional Faith* (Princeton: Princeton University Press, 1988); W. Moore, *Constitutional Rights and Powers of the People* (Princeton: Princeton University Press, 1996); K. Whittington, 'Extrajudicial Constitutional Interpretation: Three Objections and Responses', *North Carolina Law Review*, 80 (2002): 773–851; C. Sunstein, *The Partial Constitution* (Cambridge: Harvard University Press, 1993); L. Sager 'Justice in Plain Clothes'.

55 S. Griffin, *American Constitutionalism* (Princeton: Princeton University Press, 1996), p. 45.

56 Sunstein, *The Partial Constitution*; Mark Tushnet, *Taking the Constitution Away from the Courts* (Princeton: Princeton University Press, 1999); Jeremy Waldron, *Law and Disagreement*, (Oxford: Oxford University Press, 1999).

57 It must be noted, however, that, as some of the studies included in this volume suggest, this seems to be particularly the case when the victims at stake are representative of middle-class groups (see Lopes and Sajó in this volume, and also C. Smulovitz and E.

Peruzzotti, 'Social Accountability in Latin America', *Journal of Democracy*, 1 (2000): 147–58).

58 M. Galanter, 'The Radiating Effects of Courts', in K. Boyum and L. Mather (eds), *Empirical Theories about Courts* (New York: Longmans, 1983), pp. 117–42.

59 McCann, 'Reform Litigation on Trial', 733.

Bibliography

Abramovich, V., Añón, M. J., and Courtis, C., *Derechos Sociales: Instrucciones de Uso* (México: Fontamara, 2003).

Abramovich, Víctor and Courtis, Christian, *Los Derechos Sociales como Derechos Exigibles* (Madrid: Trotta, 2002).

———, *Los Derechos Sociales en el Debate Democrático* (Buenos Aires: Colección Claves para Todos, 2005).

Ackerman, Bruce, 'The Rise of World Constitutionalism', *Virginia Law Review*, 83 (1997): 771–99.

———, *We the People: Volume 2: Transformations* (Cambridge, MA: Harvard University Press, 1998).

Alberdi, J.B., *Obras Completas* (Buenos Aires: La Tribuna Nacional, 1886).

Álamo, Oscar del, 'Bolivia Indígena y Campesina: un Panorama de Conflictos e Identidades' in Prats, Joan (ed.), *El Desarrollo Posible, las Instituciones Necesarias* (Barcelona: IIG, 2003), pp. 539–98.

Albo, Xavier, '¿Cómo Manejar la Interculturalidad Jurídica en un País Intercultural?', in Instituto de la Judicatura de Bolivia (ed), *Justicia Comunitaria en los Pueblos Originarios de Bolivia* (Sucre: IJB, 2003), pp. 85–115.

Alexy, Robert, *Teoría de los Derechos Fundamentales* (Madrid: Centro de Estudios Constitucionales, 1993).

Amundsen, Inge, Abreu, Cesaltina and Hoygaard, Laurinda, 'Accountability on the Move: The Parliament of Angola', paper presented at a workshop on *Institutional Development: The Case of the Angolan Parliament*, Luanda, 22 November 2004.

Andreis, Massimo,'La Tutela Giurisdizionale del Diritto alla Salute' in Gallo, C.E. and Pezzini, B. (eds) *Profili Attuali* (Milan: Giuffre, 1998).

Angolan Government, *Poverty Reduction Strategy Paper* (2004).

Arango, Rodolfo, 'Los Derechos Sociales Fundamentales como Derechos Subjetivos', *Pensamiento Jurídico* 8 (1991): 63-72.

Araújo, Raul C., 'Os Custos com o Accesso á Justica e o Exercísio do Directo ao Patrocinio Judiciário' paper presented at the *Seminário a Reforma da Justicia e do Direito*, (Angola, 2004).

Ariza, Libardo, 'La Prisión Ideal: Intervención Judicial y Reforma del Sistema Penitenciario en Colombia', unpublished paper, Universidad de los Andes (2004).

Arrow, Kenneth, *The Limits of Organization* (New York: W.W. Norton & Co, 1974).

Assies, W., 'Bolivia: A Gasified Democracy', *Revista Europea de Estudios Latinoamericanos y del Caribe* 76 (2004): 25–43.

———, 'El Constitucionalismo Multi-Étnico en América Latina: el Caso de Bolivia', XII Congreso Internacional 'Derecho Consuetudinario y Pluralismo Legal: Desafíos en el Tercer Milenio' (Chile, 2000).

Assies, Willem, van der Haar, Gemma and Hoekma, André (eds), *The Challenge of Diversity: Indigenous Peoples and Reform of the State in Latin America*, (Amsterdam: Thela Thesis, 2000).

Assies, Willem and Salman, Ton *Crisis in Bolivia: The Elections of 2002 and Their Aftermath* (London: ILAS, 2003).

Balkin, J., 'Idolatry and Faith: The Jurisprudence of Sanford Levinson', *Tulsa Law Review* 38 (2003): 553–79.

———, 'Populism and Progressivism as Constitutional Categories' *Yale Law Journal* 104 (1995): 1935–90.

Balkin, J. and Levinson, S., 'Understanding the Constitutional Revolution', *Virginia Law Review* 87 (2001): 1045–1109.

Barragues, Alfonso and Sousa, Mario Alberto Adauta de, 'Towards the Development of Indicators to Measure the Levels of Awareness on Knowledge, Exercise and Defense of Human Rights in Angola', (Montreaux: Human Rights Division, United Office in Angola and Instituto de Pesquisa Económica e Social, 2000).

Barreda, Mikel and Andrea Costafreda, 'Crisis Política y Oportunidad democrática' in Prats, Joan (ed.) *El Desarrollo Posible, las Instituciones Necesarias* (Barcelona: IIG, 2003), p.149-217.

Bhagwati, P.N., 'Judicial Activism and Public Interest Litigation', *Columbia Journal of Transnational Law* 23 (1985): 566–79.

Bhagwati, P.N., Iyer, V.R. Krishna, *Report on National Juridicare: Equal Justice-Social Justice* (Ministry of Law, Justice & Company Affairs, 1976).

Berat, L., 'Courting Justice: A Call for Judicial Activism in a Transformed South Africa', *St. Louis University Law Journal* 37 (1993): 849–50.

Berensztein, Sergio, Spector, Horacio, 'Business, Government and Law', in G. della Paolera and A. Taylor *A New Economic History of Argentina* (Cambridge: Cambridge University Press, 2003), pp. 324–69.

Berlin, I., 'Two Concepts of liberty' in I. Berlin, *Four Essays on Liberty* (Oxford: Oxford University Press, 1969), pp. 118–72.

Bernal Pulido, C., *El Principio de Proporcionalidad y los Derechos Fundamentales* (Madrid: Centro de Estudios Políticos y Constitucionales, 2003).

Beverley, John and Oviedo, José, 'Introduction' in John Beverley, José Oviedo, and Michael Aronna (eds), *The Postmodernism Debate in Latin America* (Durham: Duke University Press, 1995), pp. 1–18.

Bickel, Alexander, *The Least Dangerous Branch: The Supreme Court at the Bar of Politics* (New Haven: Yale University Press, 1986).

Bilchitz, David, 'Giving Socio-Economic Rights Teeth: The Minimum Core and Its Importance', *South African Law Journal* 119 (2002): 484–501.

———, 'Towards a Reasonable Approach to the Minimum Core: Laying the Foundations for Future Socio-Economic Rights Jurisprudence', *South African Journal on Human Rights* 19 (2003): 1–26.

Boechat Rodrigues, Leda, *História do Supremo Tribunal Federal*, 2edn. (4 vols., Rio de Janeiro: Civilização Brasileira, 1991).

Bollyky, T., 'R if C > P + B: A Paradigm for Judicial Remedies in Socio-Economic Rights Violations', *South African Journal on Human Rights* 18 (2002): 161–200.

Bond, Patrick, *Elite Transition: From Apartheid to Neoliberalism in South Africa* (London: Pluto Press, 2000).

Bonham, J. and Rehg, W., *Deliberative Democracy* (Cambridge, MA: The MIT Press, 1997).

Bork, R., 'The Impossibility of Finding Welfare Rights in the Constitution' in *Washington University Law Quarterly* (1979) 695–702.

———, *The Tempting of America: The Political Seduction of the Law* (New York: The Free Press, 1989).

Botana, N., 'La Transformación del Credo Constitucional', *Estudios Sociales*, Universidad Nacional del Litoral (1996), pp. 23–48.

Brand, Danie, 'The Proceduralisation of South African Socio-Economic Rights Jurisprudence, or "What Are Socio-economic Rights for?"' in Henk Botha, André van der Walt and Johan van der Walt (eds), *Rights and Democracy in a Transformative Constitution* (Stellenbosch: Sun Press, 2003), pp. 33–56.

Brix, Maja K., 'The Impact of Judicial Activism in India', unpublished Masters thesis, University of Bergen (2004).

Budlender, Geoff, 'Access to Courts', *South African Law Journal* 121 (2004): 339–58.

Buenahora, Jaime, *El Proceso Constituyente* (Bogotá: Tercer Mundo, 1992).

Bujosa Vadell, L., *La Protección Jurisdiccional de los Intereses de Grupo* (Barcelona: J.M. Bosch, 1995).

Burgos, Germán, '¿Hacia un Estado de Derecho? Relato de un Viaje Inconcluso' in Joan Prats (ed.) *El Desarrollo Posible, las Instituciones Necesarias* (Barcelona: IIG, 2003), pp. 225–308.

Barreda, Mikel, 'Perfil de Gobernabilidad de Bolivia' in Joan Prats (ed.) *El Desarrollo Posible, las Instituciones Necesarias* (Barcelona: IIG, 2003).

CAJPE (Comisión Andina de Justicia Penal), *La reforma judicial en la región andina* (2000).

Camargo Mancuso, Rodofo de, *Interesses Difusos: Conceito e Legitimação para Agir* (São Paulo: Revista dos Tribunais, 1991).

Cappeletti, Mauro, 'Necesidad y Legitimidad de la Justicia Constitucional', in *Tribunales Constitucionales Europeos y Derechos Fundamentales* (Madrid: Centro de Estudios Constitucionales, 1984), pp. 599–649.

Carrió, G., *Notas sobre Derecho y Lenguaje* (Buenos Aires: Abeledo-Perrot, 1964).

Cassels, J., 'Judicial Activism and Public Interest Litigation in India: Attempting the Impossible?', *The American Journal of Comparative Law* 37 (1989): 508–21.

Castañeda, Jorge, *Utopia Unarmed: The Latin American Left After the Cold War* (New York: Alfred Knopf, 1993).

Cepeda, M.J., 'Democracy, State and Society in the 1991 Constitution: The Role of the Constitutional Court', in Eduardo Posada Carbó (ed.), *Colombia: The Politics of Reforming the State* (London: Macmillan Press, 1998), pp. 76–91.

———, 'La Defensa Judicial de la Constitución', in Fernando Cepeda (ed.), *Las fortalezas de Colombia* (Bogotá: Ariel, BID, 2004), pp. 145–87.

Chayes, Abraham, 'The Role of the Judge in Public Law Litigation', *Harvard Law Review* 89 (1976): 1281–1317.

Chemerinsky, Erwin, 'Can Courts Make a Difference?', in Neal Devins & Davidson Douglas (eds), *Redefining Equality* (New York: Oxford University Press, 1998), pp. 191–204.

Chinchilla, Tulio Elí, *¿Qué Son y Cuáles Son los Derechos Fundamentales?* (Bogotá: Temis, 1999).

Cifuentes, Eduardo, 'El Constitucionalismo de la Pobreza,' *Lecturas Constitucionales Andinas* 3 (1994).

Cohen, J., 'The Economic Basis of a Deliberative Democracy,' *Social Philosophy and Policy* 6 (1989): 25–50.

Collier, David and Collier, Ruth, *Shaping the Political Arena: Critical Junctures, the Labor Movement, and Regimes Dynamics in Latin America* (Princeton: Princeton University Press, 1991).

Comisión Colombiana de Juristas, 'Informe alterno al quinto informe periódico del Estado Colombiano ante el Comité de Derechos Humanos de Naciones Unidas' (July 2003).

Congo, Jorge Casimiro, Costa, Manuel da, Tati, Fr.Raúl, Chicaia, Agostinho, and Luemba, Francisco, *Cabinda 2003: A Year of Pain* (Luanda: Ad Hoc Commisison for Human Rights in Cabinda, 2003).

Constitutional Tribunal, *A Selection of the Polish Constitutional Tribunal's Jurisprudence from 1986 to 1999* (Warszawa: Trybuna Konstytucyjny 1999).

Cooley, T., *A Treatise on the Constitutional Limitations Which Rest Upon the Legislative Power of the States of the American Union* (Boston: Little, Brown, and Co., 1868).

Corte Constitucional & Consejo Superior de la Judicatura, *Estadísticas sobre la Tutela* (Bogotá: Autores, 1999).

Cossío, J.R., 'Los Derechos Sociales como Normas Programáticas y la Comprensión Política de la Constitución' in E.O. Rabasa, (ed.), *Ochenta Años de Vida Constitucional en México* (México: Cámara de Diputados-UNAM, 1998), pp. 295–328.

Cover, R. 'The Supreme Court, 1982 Term – Foreword: Nomos and Narrative', *Harvard Law Review* 97 (1983): 4–62.

Craven, Matthew, *The International Covenant on Economic, Social and Cultural Rights: A Perspective on Its Development* (Oxford: Clarendon Press, 1995).

Cruz Parcero, J.A., 'Los Derechos Sociales como Técnica de Protección Jurídica' in M. Carbonell, J.A. Cruz Parcero, and R. Vázquez (eds), *Derechos Sociales y Derechos de las Minorías* 2ed. (México: UNAM-Porrúa, 2001), pp. 89–112.

Currie, Iain, 'Judicious Avoidance', *South African Journal on Human Rights* 15 (1999): 138–55.

Dagnino, Evelina, *Anos 90: Política e Sociedade no Brasil* (São Paulo: Brasiliense, 1994).

Dahl, Robert, *A Preface to Democratic Theory* (Chicago: University Of Chicago Press, 1963).

Dakolias, Maria, *Court Performance Around the World: A Comparative Perspective*, World Bank Technical Paper 430 (Washington, DC: The World Bank, 1999).

Dasgupta, M., 'Social Action for Women? Public Interest Litigation in India's Supreme Court', *Law, Social Justice & Global Development Journal* 1 (2002).

Davis, Dennis 'Deconstructing and Reconstructing the Argument for a Bill of Rights Within the Context of South African Nationalism' in Penelope Andrews and Stephen Ellmann (eds), *The Post-Apartheid Constitutions: Perspectives on South Africa's Basic Law* (Johannesburg: Witwatersrand University Press, 2001), pp. 194–223.

Defensor del Pueblo, *Informe Especial: Los Derechos a la Propiedad y la Tenencia de la Tierra y el Proceso de Saneamiento* (La Paz, 2003).

Defensor del Pueblo, *III Informe Anual al H. Congreso Nacional* (La Paz, 2001).

Defensor del Pueblo, *IV Informe Anual al H. Congreso Nacional* (La Paz, 2002).

Defensor del Pueblo, *V Informe Anual al H. Congreso Nacional* (La Paz, 2003).

Demophilus, *The Genuine Principles of the Ancient Anglo Saxon* (Philadelphia, 1776).

Dezalay, Yves and Garth, Bryant, *The Internationalization of Palace Wars: Lawyers, Economists, and the Contest to Transform Latin American States* (Chicago: University of Chicago Press, 2002).

Dhavan, R., Sudarshan, R. and Khurshid, S., *Judges and the Judicial Power* (London: Sweet & Maxwell, 1985).

Doepp, Peter von, 'Comparing the Political Role of the Courts in Zambia and Malawi', paper presented at the ASA annual meeting in New Orleans (11–14 November 2004).

Domingo, Pilar and Sieder, Rachel (eds), *Rule of Law in Latin America: The International Promotion of Judicial Reform* (London: Institute for Latin American Studies, 2001).

Domínguez Jorge I. (ed.), *Technopols: Freeing Politics and Markets in Latin America in the 1990s* (University Park Penn.: Pennsylvania State University Press, 1997).

Dumont, Louis, *Homo Hierarchicus* 2edn (Chicago: University of Chicago Press).

Durán Ribera, Willman R., 'La Fuerza Vinculante de las Resoluciones del Tribunal Constitucional' (Tribunal Constitucional de Bolivia, 2003).

Dworkin, Ronald, *Taking Rights Seriously (*Cambridge, MA: Harvard University Press, 1977).

———, *Law's Empire* (Cambridge, MA: Harvard University Press, 1986).

———, *Freedom's Law: The Moral Reading of the American Constitution* (Oxford: Oxford University Press, 1996).

Easterbrook, Frank, 'Abstraction and Authority', *University of Chicago Law Review*, 59 (1992): 349–82.

Echeverría, E., *Dogma Socialista de la Asociación de Mayo, Precedido de una Ojeada Retrospectiva sobre el Movimiento Intelectual en el Plata desde el Año 37* (Buenos Aires: Librería La Facultad, 1915).

Eckstein, Susan Eva and Wickham Crowley, Timothy P., *Struggles for Social Rights in Latin America* (New York: Routledge, 2003).

———, (eds), *What Justice? Whose Justice? Fighting for Fairness in Latin America* (Berkeley: University of California Press, 2003).

Economist Intelligence Unit, *Angola Country Report* (June 2004).

Edelman, P., 'The Next Century of Our Constitution: Rethinking Our Duty to the Poor', *Hastings Law Journal* 39 (1987–88): 1–63.

Edwards, Michael, 'NGO Performance-What Breeds Success? New Evidence from South Asia', *World Development* 27 (1999): 361–74.

Eide, A., Krause, C., Rosas, A. (eds), *Economic, Social and Cultural: A Textbook* (The Netherlands: Kluwer, 1994).

Ellmann, Stephen, 'Weighing and Implementing the Right to Counsel', *South African Law Journal* 121 (2004): 318–38.

Elster, J., (ed.), *Deliberative Democracy* (Cambridge: Cambridge University Press, 1998).

Elster, Jon, & Slagstad, Rune (eds), *Constitutionalism and Democracy* (Cambridge: Cambridge University Press, 1988).

Ely, John Hart, *Democracy and Distrust: A Theory of Judicial Review* (Cambridge, MA: Harvard University Press, 1980).

———, *Democracia y Desconfianza* (Bogotá: Universidad de Los Andes, 1996).

Epp, Charles R., *The Rights Revolution: Lawyers, Activists and Supreme Courts in Comparative Perspective* (Chicago: University of Chicago Press, 1998).

Epstein, Lee, Shvetsova, Olga and Knight, Jack, 'The Role of Constitutional Courts in the Establishment and Maintenance of Democratic Systems of Government', *Law & Society Review* 35 (2001): 117–63.

Erick, P. and Silbey, S., *The Common Place of Law* (Chicago: Chicago University Press, 1998).

European Union, *Estudio de Identificação e Viabilidade para um Apoio á Reforma da Administração da Juticia na República de Angola (Relatorio Preliminar)* (Luanda: European Union, 2003).

Fabre, C., *Social Rights under the Constitution* (Oxford: Clarendon Press, 2000).

Falcão, Joaquim de A., 'Democratização e Serviços Legais' in J.E. Faria (ed.), *Direito e Justiça: A Função Social do Judiciário* (São Paulo: Ática, 1989).

Falk Moore, Sally, *Law as Process: An Anthropological Approach* (Oxford: Oxford University Press for the International African Institute, 1978).

Faria, José Eduardo, 'Ordem Legal x Mudança Social: a Crise do Judiciário e a Formação do Magistrado' in J.E. Faria (ed.), *Direito e Justiça*, pp. 95-110.

Ferrajoli, L., 'El Derecho como Sistema de Garantías', in *Derechos y Garantías. La Ley del más Débil* (Madrid: Trotta, 1999), pp. 28-31.

Ferreira Mendes, Gilmar, *Jurisdição Constitucional* (São Paulo: Saraiva, 1996).

Ferrer MacGregor, E., *Juicio de Amparo e Interés Legítimo: la Tutela de los Derechos Difusos y Colectivos* (México: Porrúa, 2003).

Fiori, José Luis, *Em Busca do Dissenso Perdido* (Rio de Janeiro: Insight Editorial, 1995).

Fiss, Owen, 'The Forms of Justice', *Harvard Law Review* 93 (1979): 58–151.

Fleming, J., 'Book Review: The Constitution Outside the Courts', *Cornell Law Review* 86 (2000): 215–49.

Fraser, Nancy, 'Social Justice and the Age of Identity Politics: Redistribution, Recognition, and Participation', in Grethe Paterson (ed.), *The Tanner Lectures On Human Values* (Utah: University of Utah Press, 1998), pp. 3–67.

Ffrench-Davis, Ricardo, *Economic Reforms in Chile: From Dictatorship to Democracy* (Ann Arbor: University of Michigan Press, 2002).

Fuller, Lon L., 'The Forms and Limits of Adjudication', *Harvard Law Review* 92 (1978): 353–410.

———, *The Principles of Social Order* (Durham, N.C.: Duke University Press, 1981).

Galanter, M., 'The Radiating Effects of Courts' in K. Boyum and L. Mather (eds), *Empirical Theories about Courts* (New York: Longmans, 1983), pp. 117–42.

Gamarra, Eduardo, *The System of Justice in Bolivia: An Institutional Analysis*, (Miami: Centre for the Administration of Justice, 1991).

García de Enterría, Eduardo, *La Constitución como Norma y el Tribunal Constitucional* (Madrid: Civitas, 1985).

García, Mauricio & Uprimny, Rodrigo, 'Tribunal Constitucional e Emancipaçã Social na Colombia', in Boaventura de Sousa Santos (ed.), *Democratizar a Democracia. Os Caminhos da Democracia Participativa* (Rio de Janeiro: Editora Civilizaçao Brasileira, 2002), pp. 298–339.

García Villegas, Mauricio, 'Derechos Sociales y Necesidades Políticas. La Eficacia Judicial de los Derechos Sociales en el Constitucionalismo Colombiano', in Boaventura de Sousa Santos & Mauricio García (eds), *El Caleidoscopio de las Justicias en Colombia* (2 vols., Bogotá: Uniandes, 2001), vol. 1, pp. 455–83.

Gardner, David, 'Weighed Down by an Old Economy', *Financial Times* 17 October 2000, p. 21.

Gardner, John, *Legal Imperialism: American Lawyers and Foreign Aid in Latin America* (Madison: University of Wisconsin Press, 1980).

Gargarella, Roberto, '"Too Far Removed from the People": Access to Justice for the Poor: the Case of Latin America', UNDP Issue Paper (Bergen: Chr. Michelsen Institute, 2002).

———, *La justicia frente al gobierno* (Barcelona: Ariel, 1996).

Garretón, Manuel Antonio, 'Human Rights in Democratization Processes' in Elizabeth Jelin and Eric Hershberg (eds), *Constructing Democracy: Human Rights, Citizenship, and Society in Latin America* (Boulder: Westview Press, 1996), pp. 39–59.

Giddens, Anthony, *The Constitution of Society* (Berkeley: University of California Press, 1984).

Gidi, A. and Ferrer MacGregor, E. (eds), *La Tutela de los Derechos Difusos, Colectivos e Individuales Homogéneos. Hacia un Código Modelo para Iberoamérica* (Bogotá: Porrúa-Instituto Iberoamericano de Derecho Procesal, 2003).

———, *Procesos Colectivos. La Tutela de los Derechos Difusos, Colectivos e Individuales en una Perspectiva Comparada* (México: Porrúa, 2003).

Gomes Canotilho, J.J., *Direito Constitucional* (Coimbra: Almedina, 1991).

Goncalves, Manuel and Dúnem, José Octávio Serra Van-, 'Final Report', unpublished paper presented at the UNDP-sponsored 'Seminário a reforma da Justicia e do Direito' (Luanda, 28-30 May, 2004).

Góngora Mera, E., *El Derecho a la Educación en la Constitución, en la Jurisprudencia y en los Instrumentos Internacionales* (Bogotá: Defensoría del Pueblo, 2003).

Goodin, R., *Reflective Democracy* (Oxford: Oxford University Press, 2003).

Gordon, R.W., 'Nuevos Desarrollos de la Teoría Jurídica', in C. Courtis, *Desde otra mirada. Textos de Teoría Crítica del Derecho* (Buenos Aires: EUDEBA, 2000) pp.333-46.

Griffin, S., *American Constitutionalism* (Princeton: Princeton University Press, 1996).

Grindle, Merilee, and Domingo, Pilar, (eds) *Proclaiming Revolution: Bolivia in Comparative Perspective* (Cambridge, MA: ILAS/Harvard University Press, 2003).

Grobbelaar, Neuma, Mills, Greg and Sidiropoulos, Elizabeth, *Angola: Prospects for Peace and Prosperity* (Johannesburg: South African Institute of International Affairs, 2003).

Habermas, Jürgen, *Between Facts and Norms* trans. William Rehg (Cambridge: Polity Press, 1996).

Hale, C., *Mexican Liberalism in the Age of Mora, 1821–1853* (New Haven: Yale University Press, 1968).

Hamilton Alexander, Madison, James, and Jay, John, *The Federalist, Or The New Constitution* (London: J.M Dent Ltd, 1992).
Hammergren, Linn, *The Politics of Justice and Justice Reform in Latin America* (Boulder, Colorado: Westview Press, 1998).
Hampton, Jean, *Political Philosophy* (Colorado: Westview Press, 1997).
Hare, Richard, *A Linguagem da Moral* [orig. *The language of morals*] (São Paulo: Martins Fontes, 1996).
Hargreaves, Shaun and Varoufakis, Yanis, *Game Theory: A Critical Introduction* (London: Routledge, 1995).
Harris, Olivia (ed.), *Inside and Outside the Law: Anthropological Studies of Authority and Ambiguity* (London: Routledge & Kegan Paul, 1996).
Hart, H.L.A., 'The Concept of Law', in G. Carrió, *Notas sobre Derecho y Lenguaje* (Buenos Aires: Abeledo-Perrot, 1964), pp. 45–60.
Hayek, Friedrich Von, *Law, Legislation and Liberty* (London: Routledge and Paul Kegan, 1973).
———, *The Road to Serfdom* (London: Routledge, 1944).
Held, D., *Models of Democracy* (Stanford University Press, 1997).
Heller, Thomas C. and Jensen, Erik G., (eds), *Beyond Common Knowledge: Empirical Approaches to the Rule of Law* (Stanford: Stanford University Press, 2003).
Helmke, Gretchen, *Courts Under Constraints: Judges, Generals, and Presidents in Argentina* (Cambridge: Cambridge University Press, 2005).
Hite, Katherine, *When the Romance Ended: Leaders of the Chilean left, 1968–1998* (New York: Columbia University Press, 2000).
Holmes, Stephen and Sunstein, Cass R. *The Cost of Rights* (New York: W.W. Norton, 1999).
Holmes, Stephen, 'Lineages of the Rule of Law' in José María Maravall and Adam Przeworski (eds), *Democracy and the Rule of Law* (Cambridge: Cambridge University Press, 2003), pp. 19–61.
———, *Passions and Constraint. On the Theory of Liberal Democracy*, (University of Chicago Press, 1995).
Humanos/TROCAIRE and Procuradoria Geral da Repúblicana na Província de Luanda, Inquérito ao Conhecimento, Exercício e Defesa dos Direitos Humanos (Luanda: Angola Instituto de Pequisa Económica e Social, 2000/2001).
Human Rights Watch, *Some Transparency: No Accountability: The Use of Oil Revenue in Angola and Its Impact on Human Rights* (Human Rights Watch, 2004).
Hunt, P., *Reclaiming Social Rights* (Sidney: Dartmouth, 1996).
Huyssteen, Elsa van, 'The Constitutional Court and the Redistribution of Power in South Africa: Towards Transformative Constitutionalism' in *African Studies*, 59 (2000): 245–65.
'Informe Anual sobre los Derechos Humanos en Chile 2003. Hechos de 2002', (Santiago: Facultad de Derecho, Universidad Diego Portales, 2003).

International Bar Association Human Rights Institute, *Angola: Promoting Justice Post-Conflict* (London: International Bar Association, 2003).

Iyer, V.R. Krishna, 'Essays in Honour of Justice' in Rajeev Dhavan, Khurshid, Sudarshan, (eds), *Judicial Power* (London: Sweet and Maxwell, 1981).

Iyer, V.R. Krishna, 'Judiciary: A Reform Agenda I & II', *The Hindu,* 14–15 August 2002.

Jacob, Herbert, Erhard Blankkenburg, Herbert Kritzer, Doris Marie Provine, Joseph Sanders, (eds), *Courts, Law, and Politics in Comparative Perspective* (New Haven: Yale University Press, 1996).

Jaramillo Uribe, J., *El Pensamiento Colombiano en el Siglo XIX*, (Bogotá: Temis, 1964).

Jelin, Elizabeth, 'Citizenship Revisited: Solidarity, Responsibility, and Rights' in Elizabeth Jelin and Eric Hershberg (eds), *Constructing Democracy: Human Rights, Citizenship, and Society in Latin America* (Boulder: Westview Press, 1996).

Jones, Peris and Stokke, Kristian (eds), *Democratising Development: The Politics of Socio-Economic Rights in South Africa* (Leiden: Martinus Nijhoff, 2005).

Kalmanovitz, Salomón, 'Las Consecuencias Económicas de los Fallos de la Corte Constitucional', *Economía Colombiana,* 276, (1999).

Keck, Margaret and Sikkink, Kathryn, *Activists Beyond Borders* (Ithaca: Cornell University Press, 1998).

Kirpal, B.N., Desai, Ashok H., Subramanium, Gopal, Dhavan, Rajeev and Ramachandran, Raju, (eds), *Supreme But Not Infallible: Essays in Honour of the Supreme Court of India* (Delhi: Oxford University Press, 2000).

Kramer, Larry D., 'Popular Constitutionalism, circa 2004', *California Law Review* 92 (2004) 959–1011.

———, *The People Themselves: Popular Constitutionalism and Judicial Review* (Oxford: Oxford Press, 2004).

———, 'The Supreme Court, 2000 Term – Foreword: We the Court', *Harvard Law Review* 115 (2001): 5–170.

Langa, Pius N., 'The Role of the Constitutional Court in the Enforcement and Protection of Human Rights in South Africa', *St. Louis University Law Journal* 41 (1997): 1259–77.

Lari, Andrea, 'Returning Home to a Normal Life? The Plight of Angola's Internally Displaced' in *African Security Analysis Programme* (Institute for Security Studies, 2004).

Leal, M.F.M., *Açoes Coletivas: História, Teoria e Prática* (Porto Alegre: Sergio Fabris, 1998), pp. 187–200.

Lee van Cott, Donna, 'A Político Analysis of Legal Pluralism in Bolivia and Colombia', *Journal of Latin American Studies* 32 (2000): 207–34.

Levinson, Sanford, *Constitutional Faith* (Princeton: Princeton University Press, 1988).

———, 'Constitutional Populism: Is It Time for "We the People" to Demand an Article Five Convention?', *Widener Law Symposium Journal* 4 (1999): 211–18.

Lewin, B., *Rousseau en la Independencia de Latinoamérica* (Buenos Aires: Depalma, 1980).

Liebenberg, Sandra, 'Socio-economic Rights', in S. Woolman et al. *Constitutional Law of South Africa,* 2edn (Cape Town: Juta, 2004), chap. 33.

Lobel, J., 'Losers, Fools & Prophets', *Cornell Law Review* 80 (1995): 1331–1422.

Lopes, José Reinaldo de Lima, 'A Definição do Interesse Público' in Carlos Alberto de Salles (ed.), *Processo Civil e Interesse Público* (São Paulo: Revista dos Tribunais, 2003), pp.91-99.

———, 'A Função Política do Poder Judiciário' in J.E. Faria (ed.), *Direito e Justiça*, pp.123-143.

———, *As Palavras e a Lei: Lei, Ordem e Justiça no Pensamento Jurídico Moderno* (São Paulo: Editora 34, 2004), passim.

———, 'Direito Subjetivo e Direitos Sociais: o Dilema do Judiciário no Estado Social de Direito", in J.E. Faria (ed.), *Directos Humanos, Directos Sociais e Justiça* (San Pablo: Malheiros, 1994), pp. 114–38.

———, 'Planos de Saúde e Consumidor – Relatório de Pesquisa do Brasilcon', *Revista de Direito do Consumidor* 28 (1998): 137–56.

———, *Saúde e Responsabilidade: Seguros e Planos de Assistência Privada à Saúde* (São Paulo: Revista dos Tribunais, 1999).

Lorenzetti, R.L., *Las normas fundamentales del derecho privado* (Santa Fe: Rubinzal-Culzoni, 1995).

Loveman, Briank, *The Constitution of Tyranny: Regimes of Exception in Spanish America* (Pittsburgh: University of Pittsburgh Press, 1993).

Madison, James, 'The Federalist No. 47' in Alexander Hamilton, James Madison and John Jay, *The Federalist, Or, The New Constitution* (London: J.M. Dent Ltd, 1992), pp. 246–53.

———, 'The Federalist No. 51' in Alexander Hamilton, James Madison and John Jay, *The Federalist, Or, The New Constitution* (London: J.M. Dent Ltd, 1992), pp. 265–69.

Mancuso, R.de C., *Açao Civil Pública* (San Pablo: Revista dos Tribunais, 1999).

Manin, B., 'On Legitimacy and Political Deliberation', *Political Theory* 15 (1987): 338–68.

Marques Guedes, Armando, Feijó, Carlosa, et. al., *Pluralismo e Legitimação – a Edificação Juridica Pós-colonial de Angola* (Lisbon: Almedina, 2003).

Marshall, T.H., 'Citizenship and Social Class' in *Sociology at the Crossroads and Other Essays* (London: Heineman, 1963).

Marshall, T.H. and Bottomore, Tom, *Citizenship and Social Class* (London: Pluto Press, 1991).

McCann, Michael W., 'Reform Litigation on Trial', *Law & Social Inquiry* 17 (1992): 715–43.

———, 'Causal versus Constitutive Explanations (or, On the Difficulty of Being so Positive…)', *Law & Social Inquiry* 21 (1996): 457–82.

McClymont, Mary and Golub, Stephen (eds), *Many Roads to Justice: The Law-Related Work of Found Foundation Grantees Around the World* (New York: Ford Foundation, 2000).

Mattewal, H.S., *Judiciary and the Government in the Making of Modern India*, (Delhi: Eastern Book Company, 2002) 1 SCC (Jour).

Méndez, Juan E., O'Donnell, Guillermo and Pinheiro, Paulo Sérgio (eds), *The (Un)Rule of Law & the Underprivileged in Latin America* (Notre Dame: University of Notre Dame Press, 1999).

Michelman, F., 'Law's Republic' *Yale Law Journal* 87 (1988): 1493–1531.

———, 'Possession vs. Distribution in the Constitutional Idea of Property', *Iowa Law Review* 72 (1987): 1319–51.

———, 'The Constitution, Social Rights and Reason: A Tribute to Etienne Mureinik'', *South African Journal on Human Rights* 14 (1998): 499–508.

Mill, John Stuart, *On Liberty and Other Essays* (Oxford: Oxford University Press, 1991).

Minow, M., 'Interpreting Rights: An Essay for Robert Cover', *Yale Law Journal* 96 (1987): 1860–1916.

Montecinos, Verónica, *Economists, Politics and the State: Chile 1958–1994* (Amsterdam: CEDLA, 1998).

Moon, Penderel, *Strangers in India* (London: Faber and Faber).

Moore, W., *Constitutional Rights and Powers of the People* (Princeton: Princeton University Press, 1996).

Mutua, Makau wa, 'The Ideology of Human Rights', *Virginia Journal of International Law* 36 (1995–1996): 589–659.

Nader, Laura, 'Certainties Undone: Fifty Turbulent Years of Legal Anthropology, 1949–1999', *Journal of the Royal Anthropological Institute* 7 (2001): 95–116.

———, *No Access to Law: Alternatives to the American Judicial System* (New York: Academic Press, 1980).

Neves, Marcelo, *A Constitucionalização Simbólica* (São Paulo: Acadêmcia, 1994).

Ngcukaitobi, Tembeka, 'The Evolution of Standing Rules in South Africa and Their Significance in Promoting Social Justice', *South African Journal on Human Rights* 18 (2002): 590–613.

Nino, C. S., *The Ethics of Human Rights* (Oxford: Oxford University Press, 1991).

———, *The Constitution of Deliberative Democracy* (New Haven: Yale University Press, 1996).

Novoa Monreal, Eduardo, *El Derecho como Obstáculo al Cambio Social* (México: Siglo Veintiuno, 1975).

Ocampo, José Antonio, 'Reforma del Estado y Desarrollo Económico y Social', *Análisis Político* 17 (1992), pp. 5-40

O'Donnell, Guillermo, 'Notas sobre la Democracia en América Latina' in *El Debate Conceptual sobre la Democracia* (New Cork: PNUD, 2004).

Oliveira Vianna, Francisco José de, *Problemas de Direito Corporativo* (Rio de Janeiro: José Olmpyo, 1938).

Oraá, Jaime, 'La Declaración Universal de Derechos Humanos' in Felipe Gómez Isa and José Manuel Puerza (eds), *La Protección Internacional de los Derechos Humanos en los Albores del Siglo XXI* (Bilbao, Spain: Universidad de Deusto, 2003), pp. 142–63.

Orellana Halkyer, Rene, 'Prácticas Judiciales en Comunidades Indígenas Quechuas' in Instituto de la Judicatura de Bolivia (ed.), *Justicia Comunitaria en los Pueblos Originarios de Bolivia* (Sucre: IJB, 2003), pp. 11–41.

Osiatynski, Wiktor, 'Social and Economic Rights in a New Constitution for Poland' in András Sajó (ed.), *Western Rights? Post-communist Application* (The Hague: Kluwer, 1996), pp. 233–69.

Parker, R., 'Here, the People Rule, A Constitutional Populist Manifesto' *Valparaiso University Law Review* 27 (1993): 531–85.

Parra Vera, O., *El Derecho a la Salud en la Constitución, la Jurisprudencia y los Instrumentos Internacionales* (Bogotá: Defensoría del Pueblo, 2003).

Parry, J.H., *The Spanish Seaborne Empire* (Berkeley: University of California Press, 1990).

Pelaez, Carlos A., 'Incorporación de Tecnología Informática a la Gestión Jusridiccional y Administrativa en el Poder Judicial Boliviano', manuscript, (2002).

Pellegrini Grinover, Ada, et al., *Código de Brasileiro de Defesa do Consumidor Comentado Pelos Autores do Anteprojeto* (Rio de Janeiro: Forense, 1992).

Pérez Guilhou, D., *El Pensamiento Conservador de Alberdi y la Constitución de 1853* (Buenos Aires: Depalma, 1984).

Pezzini, Barbara, 'Principi Costituzionali e Politica della Sanità: il Contributo della Giurisprudenza Costituzionale alla Definizione del Diritto Sociale alla Salute' in C.E. Gallo and B. Pezzini, (eds), *Profili Attuali del Diritto alla Salute* (Giuffrè: Milan, 1998).

Pillay, K., 'Addressing Poverty Through the Courts: How Have We Fared in the First Decade of Democracy?', unpublished paper presented at University of KwaZulu-Natal Conference on 'Celebrating a Decade of Democracy', Durban, 23–25 January 2004.

Pisarello, G., *Vivienda para Todos. Un Derecho en (De)Construcción* (Barcelona: Observatori DESC-Icaria, 2003).

Post, Robert and Siegel, Reva, 'Equal Protection by Law: Federal Antidiscrimination Legislation after Morrison and Kimel', *Yale Law Journal* 110 (2000): 441–527.

———, 'Popular Constitutionalism, Departmentalism, and Judicial Supremacy' *California Law Review* 92 (2004): 1027–43.

———, 'Protecting the Constitution from the People: Juricentric Restrictions on Section Five Power', *Indiana Law Journal* 78 (2003): 1–47.

Preuss, Ulrich K., 'The Conceptual Difficulties of Welfare Rights', in András Sajó (ed.) *Western Rights? Post-Communist Application* (The Hague: Kluwer, 1996), pp. 211–16.

Puymbroeck, Rudolf Van, *Comprehensive Legal and Judicial Development: Toward an Agenda for a Just and Equitable Society in the 21st Century* (Washington, D.C.: World Bank, 2001).

Ramachandran, Raju, 'The Supreme Court and the Basic Structure Doctrine', in B.N. Kirpal, Ashok H.Desai, Gopal Subramanium, Rajeev Dhavan and Raju Ramachandran, (eds) *Supreme But Not Infallible: Essays in Honour of the Supreme Court of India* (Delhi: Oxford University Press, 2000), pp. 107–33.

Rawls, John, 'The Idea of Public Reason' in James Bohman and Willam Regh (eds), *Deliberative Democracy: Essays on Reason and Politics* (Cambridge, MA: MIT Press, 1997), pp. 93–141.

Reed, D., 'Popular Constitutionalism: Toward a Theory of State Constitutional Meaning', *Rutgers Law Review* 30 (1999): 871–933.

Reich, Norbert, 'Judge-made "Europe à la Carte": Some Remarks on Recent Conflicts between European and German Constitutional Law Provoked by the Banana Litigation', *European Journal of International Law* 7 (1996): 103–111.

Risse, Thomas, Ropp, Stephen C. and Sikkink, Kathryn, (eds), *The Power of Human Rights: International Norms and Domestic Change* (Cambridge: Cambridge University Press, 1999).

Rivera Santibáñez, José Antonio, 'La Doctrina Constitucional en la Jurisprudencia del Tribunal Constitucional', (Tribunal Constitucional de Bolivia, 2003).

Rodriguez, Eduardo, 'Legal Security in Bolivia' in John Crabtree and Laurence Whitehead (eds), *Towards Democratic Viability: The Bolivian Experience*, (Houndmills: Palgrave, 2001).

Roemer, John E., *Theories of Distributive Justice* (Cambridge, MA.: Harvard University Press, 1996).

Romero, J.L., *Las Ideas Políticas en la Argentina* (México: Fondo de Cultura Económica, 1969).

Rosenberg, G.N., *The Hollow Hope: Can Courts Bring About Social Change?* (Chicago: University of Chicago Press, 1991).

Rousseau, J.J., *The Social Contract* (London: Penguin Books, 1968).

Roux, Theunis, 'Legitimating Transformation: Political Resource Allocation in the South African Constitutional Court', in Siri Gloppen, Roberto Gargarella and Elin Skaar (eds), *Democratization and the Judiciary: The Accountability Function of Courts in New Democracies* (London: Frank Cass, 2004), pp. 92–111.

———, 'Pro-poor Court, Anti-poor Outcomes: Explaining the Performance of the South African Land Claims Court', *South African Journal on Human Rights* 20 (2004): 511–43.

———, 'Understanding *Grootboom* – A Response to Cass R Sunstein', *Constitutional Forum* 12 (2002): 41–51.

Sager, L., 'Justice in Plain Clothes: Reflections on the Thinness of Constitutional Law', *Northwestern University Law Review* 88 (1993): 410–36.

Sajó, András, 'How the Rule of Law Killed Hungarian Welfare Reform', *East European Constitutional Review* 5 (1996): 31–41.

———, 'Reading the Invisible Constitution: Judicial Review in Hungary', *Oxford Journal of Legal Studies* 15 (1995): 253–67.
———, 'Socio-Economic Rights and the International Economic Order', *New York University Journal of International Law and Politics* 35 (2002): 221–61.
Samper, J.M., *Historia de una Alma. Memorias Íntimas y de Historia Contemporánea* (Bogotá: Imprenta de Zalamea hnos., 1881).
Sandel, M., *Democracy's Discontent. America in Search of a Public Philosophy* (Cambridge: Harvard University Press, 1996).
Santos, Boaventura de Sousa, *De la Mano de Alicia; lo Social y lo Político en la Post-modernidad* (Bogotá: Siglo del Hombre, 1998).
———, *Toward a New Legal Common Sense* (London: Butterworth LexisNexis Group, 2002).
Santos, Boaventura de Sousa Santos, 'Justiça Popular, dualidade de poderes e estratégia socialista' in J.E. Faria (ed.) *Direito e Justiça*, pp.185-204.
Santos, Wanderley Guilherme dos, *Razões da Desordem* (Rio de Janeiro: Rocco, 1993).
Sarfatti, Magali, *Spanish Bureaucratic-Patrimonialism in America* (Berkeley: Institute of International Studies of the University of California at Berkeley, 1966).
Sartori, Giovanni, *A Teoria da Democracia Revisitada*, trans. Dinah de A. Azevedo (¿? vols., São Paulo: Ática, 1994), vol. 1, pp. 286–336.
Sastre Ibarreche, R., *El Derecho al Trabajo* (Madrid: Trotta, 1996).
Sathe, S.P., 'Judicial Activism: The Indian Experience', *Washington University Journal of Law and Policy* 6 (2001): 29–107.
Schedler, Andreas, Diamond, Larry and Plattner, Mark (eds), *The Self-restraining State"* (Lynne Reiner: Boulder, 1999).
Schumpeter, J., *Capitalism, Socialism and Democracy* (London: George Allen, 1943).
Scott, Craig and Macklem, Patrick, 'Constitutional Ropes of Sand or Justiciable Guarantees? Social Rights in a New South African Constitution', *University of Pennsylvania Law Review* 141 (1992): 1–148.
Segal, J. and Spaeth, H., *The Supreme Court and the Attitudinal Model* (Cambridge: Cambridge University Press, 1993).
———, *The Supreme Court and the Attitudinal Model Revisited* (Cambridge: Cambridge University Press, 2002).
Sen, Amartya, *Development as Freedom* (New York: Anchor Books, 2000).
Shapiro, Martin and Stone Sweet, A., *On Law, Politics, and Judicialization* (Oxford: Oxford University Press, 2002).
———, *Who Guards the Guardians?* (Athens, Ga.: University of Georgia Press, 1988).
Sherman, M., *A More Perfect Union: Vermont Becomes a State* (Vermont: Vermont Historical Society, 1991).
Sieder, Rachel, (ed.), *Multiculturalism in Latin America*, (London: Palgrave, 2002).

Siegel, Reva B., 'Text in Contest: Gender and the Constitution from a Social Movement Perspective', *University of Pennsylvania Law Review* 150 (2001): 297–351.

Sikkink, Kathryn, 'The Emergence, Evolution, and Effectiveness of the Latin American Human Rights Network' in Elizabeth Jelin and Eric Hershberg (eds), *Constructing Democracy*, pp.67-78.

Silva, José Afonso da, *Curso de Direito Constitucional Positivo*, 9ed. (São Paulo: Malheiros, 1992).

Skaar, Elin, *Judicial Independence: A Key to Justice. An Analysis of Latin America in the 1990s,* doctoral dissertation, Department of Political Science, University of California, Los Angeles, 2002).

Skidmore, Thomas and Smith, Peter, *Modern Latin America*, 3edn. (New York: Oxford UP, 1992).

Skidmore, Thomas, *Brasil: de Catelo a Tancredo* (Rio de Janeiro: Paz e Terra, 1988).

Sloth-Nielsen, Julia, 'Extending Access to Social Assistance to Permanent Residents', *ESR Review* 5/3 (2004).

Smulovitz, Catalina, and Peruzzotti, Enrique, 'Social Accountability in Latin America', *Journal of Democracy* 11/4 (2000): 147–58.

———, 'Societal and Horizontal Control: Two Cases of a Fruitful Relationship', in Scott Mainwaring and Christopher Welna (eds), *Democratic Accountability in Latin America* (Oxford: Oxford University Press, 2003), pp. 309–32.

Sotelo, Luis Carlos, 'Los Derechos Constitucionales de Prestación y sus Implicaciones Económico-Políticas', *Archivos de Macroeconomía* Paper no. 133 (2000).

Soto, Hernando de, *The Mystery of Capital: Why Capitalism Triumphs in the West and Fails Everywhere Else* (New York: Basic Books, 2000).

Steiner, Henry and Alston, Philip, *International Human Rights in Context* (Oxford: Clarendon Press, 1996).

Storing, H., *The Complete anti-Federalist* (Chicago: The University of Chicago Press, 1981).

Stotzky, Irwin (ed.), *Transition to Democracy in Latin America: The Role of the Judiciary* (Boulder: Westview Press, 1993).

Sunstein, C.R., *The Partial Constitution* (Cambridge, MA: Harvard University Press, 1993).

———, *Legal Reasoning and Political Conflict* (New York: Oxford University Press, 1996).

———, *Designing Democracy: What Constitutions Do* (New York: Oxford University Press, 2001).

———, 'State Action is Always Present', *Chicago Journal of International Law* 3 (2002): 465–69.

———, *The Second Bill of Rights: The Last Great Speech of Franklin Delano Roosevelt and America's Unfinished Pursuit of Freedom* (New York: Basic Books, 2004).

Sunstein, C., Schkade, D., and Ellman, L., 'Ideological Voting on Federal Courts of Appeals', unpublished working paper (Joint Center for Regulatory Studies, University of Chicago, 2003).

Tate, C. Neal and Vallinder, Torbjörn, 'Judicializaction and the Future of Politics and Policy', in C. Neal Tate and Torbjörn Vallinder (eds), *The Global Expansion of Judicial Power* (New York: New York University Press, 1995), pp. 515–29.

Taylor, Charles, 'The Politics of Recognition' in Amy Gutmann (ed.), *Multiculturalism* (Princeton, N.J.: Princeton University Press, 1994), pp.25-73.

———, 'What's Wrong with Negative Liberty,' in *Philosophy and the Human Sciences, Philosophical Papers* (Cambridge: Cambridge University Press, 1986), vol. 2, pp. 211–29.

Tejeda, J., *Libertad de la industria* (Lima: Hora del Hombre, 1947).

Teitel, Ruti, 'Transitional Jurisprudence: The Role of Law in Political Transformation', *Yale Law Journal* 106 (1997): 2009–80.

Touraine, Alain, *The Self Production of Society* (Chicago: University of Chicago Press, 1977).

Tribe, L., *American Constitutional Law* 2edn. (Mineola: Foundation Press, 1988).

Trujillo Pérez, I., 'La Questione dei Diritti Sociali', *Ragion Pratica* 14 (2000) 43-63.

Tushnet, Mark, 'An Essay on Rights', *Texas Law Review* 62 (1984): 1363–1403.

———, *Taking the Constitution Away from the Courts* (Princeton: Princeton University Press, 1999).

Tvedten, Inge, 'Angola: Struggle for Peace and Reconstruction' in L.W. Bowman (ed.), *Nations of the Modern World* (Boulder: Westview Press, 2003), pp. 106–9.

Uggla, Fredrik, 'The Ombudsman in Latin America', in *Journal of Latin American Studies* 36 (2004): 423–50.

UNDP, *Human Development Report* (2002).

UNDP, *Human Development Report* (2003).

UNDP, Informe de Desarrollo Humano en Bolivia (2002).

Ungar, Mark, 'Human Rights in the Andes: The Defensoría del Pueblo' in Jo-Marie Burt and Philip Mauceri (eds), *Politics in the Andes: Identity, Conflict, Reform* (Pittsburgh: Pittsburgh University Press, 2004), pp. 164–86.

UN Office for the High Commissioner of Human Rights, Project Document ANG/03/RB4 on Strengthening National Capacities for Human Rights, Democracy and the Rule of Law in Angola to Consolidate Peace (Luanda: UNHCR, 2003).

UN Report: *Angola: The Post-War Challenges,* Common Country Assessment, (Luanda: United Nations, 2002).

Uprimny Yepes, Rodrigo, 'El Derecho a la Salud en la Jurisprudencia Constitucional Colombiana', in *La Salud Pública Hoy* (Bogotá: Universidad Nacional de Colombia, 2003).

———, 'Legitimidad y Conveniencia del Control Constitucional de la Economía', *Revista de Derecho Público* 13 (2001).

———, 'The Constitutional Court and Control of Presidential Extraordinary Powers in Colombia', *Democratization* 10 (2003): 47–69.

US Department of State, *Angola: Country Reports on Human Rights Practices 2002* (Bureau of Democracy, Human Rights and Labor, 2002).

US Department of State, *Angola: Country Reports on Human Rights Practices 2003* (Bureau of Democracy, Human Rights and Labor, 2003).

Valenzuela, Samuel, 'The Chilean Labor Movement: The Institutionalization of Conflict' in Arturo Valenzuela and Samuel Valenzuela (eds), *Chile: Politics and Society* (New Brunswick, N.J.: Transaction Books, 1976), pp. 135-171.

———, *Democratización Vía Reforma: La Expansión del Sufragio en Chile* (Buenos Aires: Ediciones del IDES, 1985).

Verma, Ajay, 'The Experience in India', in Roger Blanpain (ed.), *Law in Motion* (The Hague: Kluwer Law International, 1997).

Vile, M.J.C., *Constitutionalism and the Separation of Powers* (Oxford: Oxford University Press, 1967).

Waal, Johan de, Currie, Iain and Erasmus, Gerhard, *Bill of Rights Handbook*, 4edn (Cape Town: Juta, 2001).

Waldron, J., *Law and Disagreement* (Oxford: Oxford University Press, 1999).

Walzer, Michael, 'Philosophy and Democracy', *Political Theory* 9 (1981): 379–99.

———, 'Socializing the Welfare State' in Amy Gutmann (ed.), *Democracy and the Welfare State* (Princeton: Princeton University Press, 1988), pp. 13-26.

———, *Spheres of Justice* (New York: Basic Books, 1983).

Wayne, William, 'The Two Faces of Judicial Activism', in David O' Brien (ed.), *Judges on Judging: Views from the Bench* (New Jersey: Chatham House Publishers, 1997).

Wesson, M., '*Grootboom* and Beyond: Reassessing the Socio-economic Jurisprudence of the South African Constitutional Court', *South African Journal on Human Rights* 20 (2004): 284–308.

Whittington, K., 'Extrajudicial Constitutional Interpretation: Three Objections and Responses', *North Carolina Law Review* 80 (2002): 773–853.

Wilson, Bruce, Rodriguez Cordero, Juan Carlos and Handberg, Roger, 'The Best Laid Schemes ... Gang Aft A-gley: Judicial Reform in Latin America – Evidence from Costa Rica', *Journal of Latin American Studies* 36 (2004): 507-531.

Wood, G., *The Creation of the American Republic* (New York: W.W. Norton & Company, 1969).

Wood, Robert (ed.), *Remedial Law: When Courts Become Administrators* (Amherst: University of Massachusetts Press, 1990).

World Bank, 'Bolivia: Datos Destacados. Pueblos Indígenas, Pobreza y Desarrollo Humano en América Latina 1994–2004' (Washington: World Bank, 2005).

Zaldívar Lelo de Larrea, A., *Hacia una Nueva Ley de Amparo* (México: UNAM, 2002).

Index